Outsmarting the Terrorists

OUTSMARTING THE TERRORISTS

RONALD V. CLARKE
GRAEME R. NEWMAN

Global Crime and Justice

PRAEGER SECURITY INTERNATIONAL
Westport, Connecticut • London

Library of Congress Cataloging-in-Publication Data

Clarke, R. V. G.
  Outsmarting the terrorists / Ronald V. Clarke and Graeme R. Newman.
    p. cm. — (Global crime and justice, ISSN 1931-7239)
  Includes bibliographical references and index.
  ISBN 0-275-99230-6 (alk. paper)
1. Terrorism—Prevention. 2. Terrorism—United States—Prevention. 3.
Terrorism—Government policy—United States. 4. National security—
United States. 5. War on Terrorism, 2001– 6. Security, International. I.
Newman, Graeme R. II. Title.
  HV6431.C475 2006
  363.325′160973—dc22   2006021060

British Library Cataloguing in Publication Data is available.

Library of Congress Catalog Card Number: 2006021060
ISBN: 0-275-99230-6
ISSN: 1931-7239

First published in 2006

Praeger Security International, 88 Post Road West, Westport, CT 06881
An imprint of Greenwood Publishing Group, Inc.
www.praeger.com

Printed in the United States of America

The paper used in this book complies with the
Permanent Paper Standard issued by the National
Information Standards Organization (Z39.48–1984).

10 9 8 7 6 5 4 3 2 1

Contents

Preface

WE DID NOT originally set out to write what this book has become. It arose out of our work for the Center for Problem-Oriented Policing when we were commissioned by the U.S. Office of Community Oriented Policing Services (the COPS Office) to write a guide for police on terrorism. We quickly identified a large gap in the literature concerned with reducing opportunities for attack that we should try to fill. To do so, we used our experience of situational crime prevention, that is, the science of reducing opportunities for crime.

Terrorism is a form of crime in all essential respects. The fact that it is differently motivated from other crimes matters not a bit. Rape is differently motivated from burglary, but both are the result of situational opportunity and both can be prevented by reducing such opportunities. In fact, we see it as an important strength of our approach that we do not get bogged down in the source of motivations. We are much more interested in learning about *how* terrorism is committed than *why*. Understanding how it is done helps us better know how to intervene.

We argue in this book that terrorism can be reduced by identifying and removing the opportunities for it to occur. We can do this by systematically analyzing the opportunities that terrorists exploit when committing acts of terrorism, and then finding economical and acceptable means to block these opportunities. Each time we succeed in doing this, we can expect that, before long, those bent on violence will adapt to the changed circumstances and find new ways to act. We must try to anticipate what they will do, and when this fails, act quickly to close the new opportunities they have discovered. This is what "outsmarting terrorists" means.

At first sight, these ideas might seem uncontroversial, even obvious, but we know from our work in crime prevention that they will not be readily accepted. Few experts think that opportunity plays a part in such extreme behavior as terrorism and few would accept that it can be prevented by reducing opportunities. Even if the most vulnerable targets were protected, they think the terrorists would simply redirect their attacks to ones that had not been protected. Even though bank robbery, homicide and other serious forms of crime have been successfully reduced using our approach, they believe that the analogy with terrorism is flawed, because deep political and religious motivation sets terrorism apart from crime.

Those who would make such arguments believe that, for terrorists to commit such evil acts, they must be driven by hatred and other twisted motives. It is these extreme dispositions that should be the focus of prevention and remediation. This "dispositional bias" is so strong that it pervades much academic analysis of social problems, especially in criminology and criminal justice. The first thought is always to change the deviant individual, not the features of the physical and social environment that make the behavior of terrorists possible.

Our argument will also meet resistance because it diminishes the roles of most counterterrorism experts and officials. Most academic experts are political scientists, media specialists, or psychiatrists and psychologists, who generally think that the kind of situational controls we discuss in this book are of minor importance in fighting terrorism. They are more likely to advocate measures to address the deep cultural and ideological gulf between the terrorists and Western democracies, or the exclusionary effects of global capitalism on the less developed world. Such measures would appeal to politicians and diplomats and would match the agendas of international agencies. As for counterterrorism officials, they are likely to favor identifying and apprehending suspected terrorists as the main preventive strategy because this is the role of the police and intelligence agencies under their control.

A third reason for resisting our prescriptions is that these measures seem difficult and expensive. Protecting all vulnerable targets and controlling all the tools and weapons that terrorists might use seems an impossible task. And when the threat of terrorism recedes, might we not be left with a collection of outmoded defenses, like the nuclear shelters of the Cold War? Indeed, the task would be impossible if it all had to be done at once and, yes, it would result in a massive waste of resources if terrorism were suddenly to disappear. But it will never disappear, just as crime will never disappear, and even if it might diminish, the world must nevertheless deal with the terrorism that it currently faces. The massive costs can and must be shared between the private and public sector. Governments must work closely with businesses and industries that, in Western democracies at least, own many of the vulnerable targets and manufacture the tools and weapons that terrorists employ. In fact, the private sector can probably do more than governments to reduce society's vulnerabilities to attack and, whatever the policies pursued by governments, businesses and industries are increasingly likely to take protective measures. They will do this for self-preservation and because the measures they take will have the dual benefit of protecting them from crime.

Would this not also result in severe restrictions on personal liberties, which might destroy our way of life? The approach we advocate in this book encroaches little on the civil liberties of ordinary people. It does not seek to identify individual terrorists through such means as "profiling" and, built into its methodology is a systematic consideration of the social costs of any proposed interventions. It offers many ways to protect ordinary people from terrorist attack. These carry costs, but our experience is that ordinary people are willing to bear such costs if they can see clearly how it benefits their increased personal security.

We would like to thank the COPS Office and the director of the Center for Problem-Oriented Policing, Michael Scott, for their patience as we have worked our way through this challenge. We are also grateful to our respective institutions, Rutgers University and the University at Albany, for their support. We received detailed and helpful comments on the first draft from John Eck, Brian Jenkins, Nick Ross, Norman Samuels and Alex Schmid. In some cases, they suggested extensive rephrasing that we shamelessly adopted. We are most grateful that they made the time to help us improve the book. Phyllis Schultze, director of the Don M. Gottfredson Criminal Justice Library at Rutgers-Newark, provided an enormous service in obtaining books and articles for us, often at very short notice and in helping with many bibliographical details. Mangai Natarajan advised us on network analysis, and, finally, we thank our research assistants Sara Berg, Miriam Callen, and Henda Hsu for collecting and analyzing data as we needed it.

The Gap in Our Defenses

In This Chapter

> ➤ To protect ourselves from terrorism, we must identify and remove the opportunities that terrorists exploit to mount their attacks.
> ➤ Governments have little experience to guide them in undertaking this task and have neglected it in favor of "taking out the terrorists."
> ➤ Situational crime prevention provides a set of principles to assist with this task. These principles must be applied separately for each specific kind of terrorism.
> ➤ The first step is to uncover the opportunities—the target vulnerabilities, the tools and weapons employed by the terrorists, and the facilitating conditions of everyday life—that make these acts possible. These are the four pillars of terrorist opportunity.
> ➤ Situational prevention provides a wide repertoire of measures to close these opportunities as well as guidance in choosing among them.
> ➤ The likely terrorists' adaptations to closing these opportunities must be anticipated and prevented.
> ➤ The measures must be implemented through partnerships among a wide range of public and private agencies.

IMMEDIATELY AFTER THE 9/11 attacks, the Bush administration declared "war" on terrorism, specifically on Al Qaeda, the source of the attacks. It embarked on a vast program to strengthen national and international resolve to deal with the organization, to identify, detain or kill its operatives and, through military action, to eradicate its support in Afghanistan and Iraq. At the same time as it acted against Al Qaeda, the government put in place a raft of controls designed to ensure that terrorists could never again take over an airliner and crash it into a building such as the Pentagon or the World Trade Center. It hired many more sky marshals, permitted pilots to carry guns, reinforced cockpit doors, required passengers to remain seated within 20 minutes of take-off and landing and began to screen applicants for flight school. It created the Transport Security Administration, which took over the screening of passengers and baggage from the airlines. It required passengers to produce an official photo ID, to remove shoes and jackets when being screened and to undergo searches and random inspections. It improved screening equipment and it continues to refine procedures to make these more efficient and less irksome to passengers. These measures should make it much harder, if not impossible, to repeat the 9/11 attack. Even if terrorists did succeed in taking over an airliner, it is unlikely, knowing what was in store, that the crew and passengers would comply with their demands or that the government would hesitate to shoot down the plane.

It is controls of this kind, designed to prevent a specific form of terrorism, rather than action directed at the terrorists themselves, that is the focus of this book. We seek a higher profile for this approach in government policy and we describe a method of making it more rigorous and effective. In fact, many public and private entities are now taking stock of their particular vulnerabilities and introducing security measures to reduce them. This activity encompasses a vast range of ports, transport systems, chemical plants, reservoirs, bridges and tunnels, schools, hospitals, malls and many other facilities. In its *National Strategy for the Physical Protection of Critical Infrastructure and Key Assets*, issued in February 2003, the U.S. government identified areas where security should urgently be improved and has begun to think about ways to do this. However, there has been little public discussion of the assumptions underlying this strengthened security and the questions it raises. Although there are some well-documented examples of its effectiveness—the antihijacking measures of the 1970s (discussed in Chapter 4), the program to prevent embassy takeovers (Chapter 12) and the "ring of steel" to prevent IRA bombings in Belfast (Chapter 13)—many people still question the wisdom of this "target hardening." They doubt that it will deter terrorists and they worry about its enormous costs and its effects on civil society. Doubters think it makes little difference to the terrorists as to which targets they attack and, because we cannot protect them all, terrorists will always have many from which to choose. They think that increased security means having to endure irksome inconvenience and intrusive surveillance at every turn. They worry that their lives will change forever.

To date, there has been no coherent reply to these concerns, but in this book we shall argue that the concerns are exaggerated and that the benefits of improved security are considerable—indeed, that we should be investing more, not less in security. We offer a program, based on situational crime prevention, that provides a structured approach to assessing the likely costs and benefits of any proposed measures, many of which are little different from those already used widely to prevent crime. Situational prevention also provides a sound scientific basis for thinking about some of the most difficult questions about security. How likely is it that the terrorists will switch their attacks to some other targets if we successfully protect their preferred ones? Why do they prefer certain kinds of targets? How many of these must we protect if we are to discourage them from further attack? How long will it take them to adapt to our measures and come up with new forms of attack? To what extent is terrorism fuelled and encouraged by easy opportunities to commit the attacks?

We say a little more about situational prevention later in this chapter, but first we should clarify our position about the need for society to make a greater investment in security. We are not arguing that improved security can replace the need for the many other approaches taken to guard ourselves against terrorism. Indeed, this could never be the sole approach. Western democracies must try to protect themselves from terrorism in many other ways, including (1) winning the hearts and minds of those who might be encouraged to support terrorism by political, social and economic policies; (2) removing the support for terrorists provided by particular countries and regimes through diplomatic means; (3) developing detailed plans for minimizing harm when attacks are made; (4) winning the confidence of home populations so that society is less easily frightened and disrupted by terrorist attacks; (5) strengthening laws and improving legal and judicial procedures to bring terrorists to justice; and (6) where compatible with a hearts and minds campaign and with international law, "taking out" individual terrorists and terrorist leaders. As a last resort, of course, this may involve conventional war.

While we may not support all these objectives equally, our purpose in this book is not to undertake a comprehensive critique of terrorism policy. Thus, we know that the diplomatic service and the military have centuries of experience in pursuing foreign policy objectives either by persuasion or by force, even if there have been some foreign policy and military disasters. We believe that local police, ambulance and emergency services know in principle how to respond to disasters, even if they must learn how to adapt these procedures to the new kinds of attacks that terrorists might unleash. We also accept that intelligence agencies know in principle how to identify, capture or kill foreign terrorists, or how to exclude them from the country, even though these actions are difficult in practice. Our main criticism of these policy objectives is that they have diverted government attention from the essential task of reducing opportunities for terrorism. This is particularly true of the take-them-out mindset that pervades law enforcement and military thinking, with its attractive but specious logic that "if there weren't any terrorists out there we wouldn't have to waste money on hardening the targets." The reality, of course, demonstrated by years of experience in Northern Ireland and the Middle East is that there is no possibility of being able to eliminate all terrorists (although one might eliminate a particular group) or even a sufficient number of them to eliminate the threat of terrorism.

REMOVING OPPORTUNITIES FOR TERRORISTS

The take-them-out mindset is one important reason why reducing opportunities for terrorism has been neglected by governments, but another is that the task seems so overwhelmingly difficult. How can we possibly protect every vulnerable target or person? How can we control the everyday tools that terrorists must use in carrying out their attacks? How can we control their weapons when we cannot even keep guns out the hands of ordinary criminals? In this book, we show that these tasks are indeed manageable. We specify an effective methodology and provide a body of relevant experience to help close this yawning gap in our defenses. To do so, we must identify vulnerable targets, prioritize them for protection, analyze their specific weaknesses and provide them with protection appropriate to their risks. We must identify the tools and weapons needed for each form of attack, we must curtail the terrorists' access to them and, where possible, we must modify them so that they are less readily used for terrorism. Finally, because we are faced with determined adversaries, we must anticipate how they will try to defeat our actions. We must put in place further measures to prevent this and we must be prepared to act quickly if they do succeed. This is what we mean by "outsmarting the terrorists"—undertaking the same analysis of vulnerabilities and opportunities that terrorists themselves undertake in planning their operations.

As we have said, the methodology for outsmarting the terrorists and the body of relevant practice offered in this book are drawn from the field of situational crime prevention, a branch of criminology that the authors have helped to develop over the past 30 years.[1] Essentially, situational crime prevention is the science of reducing opportunities for crime. While other methods rely on trying to change people, situational crime prevention focuses on changing the circumstances in which people find themselves. It consists of analyzing the situational and environmental factors that make possible specific forms of crime, and removing or altering those factors that are most amenable to change. Situational crime prevention is supported by a strong body of theory concerning the relationship between the motivational and situational determinants of crime. It has developed a classification of 25 ways to reduce opportunities for crime and improve security and it has assembled more than 100 successful case studies applying these techniques to a wide range of different crimes.

Indeed, every society beset by terrorism has already adopted situational approaches, often very effectively as we shall see. This book aims to give this approach its rightful priority and provide a more systematic basis for implementation.

FROM CRIME TO TERRORISM

Some might criticize our approach on the ground that there are so many differences between crime and terrorism that the experience of preventing one will have little relevance on the experience of preventing the other. These differences include the following: (1) the motivations for crime and terrorism are vastly different—the former being committed for self-gratification, the latter for a higher cause; (2) terrorists are so much more determined than criminals; (3) terrorism requires much more planning and is much less opportunistic than most crime; (4) terrorism depends on external funding; (5) terrorism usually involves much larger-scale acts; and (6) terrorism can only be committed by organized groups, whereas crime is more often a solitary undertaking.

In reality, these supposed differences between crime and terrorism are not really so marked. Here are some illustrations of what we mean:

Different motivations. There is often a high degree of overlap between the motives of "ordinary" criminals and terrorists: peer pressure, a sense of belonging and excitement. In any case, not all terrorists are working for a higher cause; indeed, for many of them, especially those lower in the organization, the principal rewards might include status, excitement, employment and group support—which is little different than for many kinds of crime. Indeed, if accounts of Islamic terrorism are to be believed, the motives can also include sex, because the martyrs are promised sex in the afterlife with 72 virgins.

Greater determination. While suicide bombers plan to lose their lives,[2] and we must plan for that accordingly, this is not the case for every terrorist. Many terrorists are careful with their lives and take great pains to avoid being apprehended or killed—just like many serial murderers or career robbers.

Planning and opportunity. As for planning, committing a car bombing, for example, is no more complicated than, say, a bank robbery. Furthermore, both kinds of acts are strongly assisted by opportunity factors—in the former case by carelessly designed and poorly policed parking arrangements and in the latter by inadequate bank security.

Funding crime. To fund their activities, terrorists frequently indulge in conventional crime and sometimes almost entirely rely on it. Furthermore, many terrorists, having been inducted into conspiracy, theft, smuggling and violence, indulge in conventional crime as an adjunct to their terrorist activities, or after leaving the terrorist organization. In Northern Ireland, for example, a great deal of crime that has occurred since the IRA and Loyalists ceasefires has been generated by former paramilitary members. External funding, therefore, is not essential, though it can be a significant facilitator in sustaining routine terrorism (see Chapters 11 and 12).

Large-scale events. Acts of terrorism can be large events, with much greater impact than crime, but a great deal of terrorism involves the kidnapping or murder of single individuals, just as occurs in crime. Furthermore, crime can also be committed on a large scale. For example, dacoits in India have been known to hold up trains and rob hundreds of passengers in a single incident; some frauds involve hundreds or even thousands of victims; several Internet scams have targeted millions.

Organized acts. Although it is the case that terrorism is mostly a group act, so is much crime—organized crime and drug dealing being prime examples.

In fact, there are as many differences among the different kinds of terrorism and crime as there are between these two broad categories. Thus, crime is composed of a vast range of prohibited acts—such as graffiti, shoplifting, fraud, assaults, bank robbery, rape and murder—committed for a wide variety of motives by a heterogeneous group of offenders. There may be fewer varieties of terrorism and fewer groups of people involved, but considerable variation is subsumed under this term. Terrorist acts include hostage takings, kidnappings, assassinations, suicide bombings, car bombings and hijackings of planes, trains and boats. There are religious terrorists (including Christian, Sikh, Hindu, Jewish, Islamic and others); nationalists (such as Palestinians, Irish, Kurds, Tamils, Chechens and so on); left-wing terrorists (such as Shining Path in Peru) and right-wing terrorists along with neo-Nazis, racists and white supremacists; anti-Communists; cults such as the Aum Shinrikyo of Japan; and single-issue terrorists such as animal rights or environmentalist extremists (Chapter 11). These terrorist groups range from highly complex organizations and networks, such as Al Qaeda, to groups of relatives or friends (Timothy McVeigh and Terrence Morris) or loners such as Eric Rudolf, the antiabortionist who bombed the Olympic Games in Atlanta. Some terrorists operate in inhospitable rural outlands, some in cities; some use paramilitary forces, others are civilians.

The supposed differences between crime and terrorism therefore rarely stand close scrutiny and from the perspective of situational prevention are of marginal importance. Indeed, it is no exaggeration to say that "terrorism is crime with a political motive."[3] The central fact is that both crime and terrorism depend on the conjunction of motivation (of whatever nature and whatever source) with opportunity (whether defined in terms of the risks, efforts or rewards of the act). Situational crime prevention is accustomed to dealing with any form of crime on this basis—in every case, it focuses on reducing opportunities—and the same will be true of its application to the different forms of terrorism. It matters no more that political or religious motives drive terrorism than sexual motives drive rape. In both cases, these motives are difficult to change. The main reason for understanding them is that this can assist our understanding of how opportunities for committing the acts are sought and exploited. In turn, this understanding helps us to find ways of changing the opportunity structure to make the acts more risky, more difficult, less rewarding and less excusable. This is the key to the situational prevention of terrorism, as we shall explain in subsequent chapters.

So, when outsmarting the terrorists, we must not be overwhelmed by speculations about their deeper motivations. We should have some basic understanding of these motivations, but we should recognize that the terrorist is principally committed to the successful completion of the task at hand. That is the immediate motive, and it is no different from that of the burglar.[4] Many insights for situational prevention follow from this simple observation. For example, suicide bombers do not have to plan an escape route, which means a wider variety of targets can be considered, as we will see in Chapter 5. It is extremely important to the bombers, however, that they reach their targets, so those that are easy to access will figure high on the list of likely targets, and simultaneous attacks will be preferred to increase the chances of reaching an identified target. As we will see, many other significant guides to preventive action are revealed when we look at the variety of terrorist acts through a situational prism.

THE OPPORTUNITY STRUCTURE FOR TERRORISM

We have distilled 20 principles from the situational crime prevention literature for outsmarting the terrorists, which we list at the end of this chapter and which we discuss throughout the book. In a nutshell, they require us to identify the opportunity structure of particular kinds of terrorist attacks, describe the steps that terrorists take from the beginning to the end and aftermath of their terrorist attacks and, finally, identify points at which we may intervene in order to interrupt the terrorist's journey to destruction. Because these are general principles, we do not systematically apply them to protecting particular targets of terrorism (such as ports or transport systems) or to controlling particular tools and weapons (such as nuclear material or explosives). To do this requires detailed work by security practitioners, who in many cases have developed guides and manuals describing the procedures involved.[5] These publications, however rarely touch on the broader policy questions facing governments that we address in this book. We offer a way of thinking about a country's vulnerabilities to attack that is intended to assist the development of a sound and rational preventive policy. Our approach begins with an analysis of what we call the opportunity structure for terrorism, by which we mean the arrangements of everyday life that create the opportunities that terrorists exploit.

We diagram the concept in Figure 1.1, which is premised on the assumption that all human action is the outcome of an interaction between motivation and opportunity. We discuss this premise in more detail in Chapter 3; here we make but a few points to assist our argument:

Sources of conflict. It is widely recognized that many sources of conflict—historic, ethnic, religious, political, economic and ideological (boxes 1–3 in Figure 1.1)—breed hatred and extremism, the motivations to attack. Depending on the historic period, the structures of physical environment, technology, governmental systems and private systems (boxes 4–7) create the framework within which terrorist groups operate. For example, in the current age, globalization serves to increase nationalism and at the same time direct hatred toward foreign countries; communications and transportation systems increase the ability to establish international networks. Hatred against occupying forces,[6] resentment and extremist ideologies feed the justifications for terrorism and help develop the social networks (box 7) that are exploited by terrorist groups (box 12).

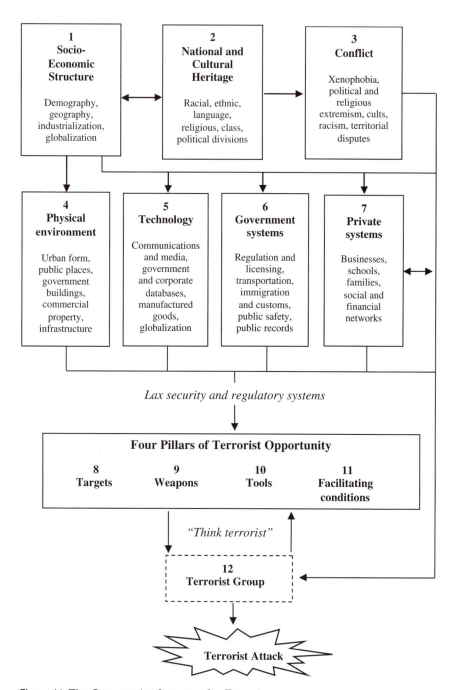

Figure 1.1 The Opportunity Structure for Terrorism

Motivation to attack. The motivation to attack depends on actual and perceived opportunities for attack. Those who live close to mountains, and see them every day, think more often about climbing them than those who do not. And because the thought is father to the deed, more of those who think about climbing mountains make plans to do so. Terrorists are no different. They respond to opportunities they perceive for making attacks, as much as they seek these out and create them. The physical environment, technologies and social systems (boxes 4–7) make up the landscape that terrorists survey for opportunities to exploit.

The four pillars of opportunity. The opportunities afforded terrorists fall into four basic categories: targets, weapons, tools and facilitating conditions (boxes 8–11 in Figure 1.1). We call these the "four pillars of terrorist opportunity." They are the result of technology, the physical environment of society and the systems and services that help it to function (boxes 4–7) These, in turn, are collectively the product of the socioeconomic structure of society (box 1). No attack can be planned, let alone carried out successfully, without careful consideration of how to take advantage of these different opportunities. We say a little more about the four pillars of opportunity in Table 1.1 below and, because they are central to understanding the terrorist enterprise, we have devoted one chapter to each.

Table 1.1 The Four Pillars of Terrorist Opportunity

1. Targets	In theory, there are an unlimited number of targets for terrorist attack (subway systems, buses, trains, airliners, power plants, reservoirs, embassies, public buildings, prominent individuals, etc.), but they do not all offer the same opportunity. Terrorists must choose among the various distinguishing characteristics of targets (see Chapter 7).
2. Weapons	Not all weapons (explosives, guns, missiles, toxic substances, nuclear materials) are equally appropriate for every task or target. Weapons also have several basic distinguishing characteristics from which the terrorist must choose (see Chapter 8).
3. Tools	Without the tools of everyday life (cars, trucks, identity papers, etc.), it is much harder for a terrorist to reach a target or use a weapon. When choosing weapons or targets, the tools that will help make maximum use of those choices must be available (see Chapter 9).
4. Facilitating conditions	Specific societal conditions such as the enormous availability of small arms and the proliferation of nuclear technology and materials enhance opportunity. The utility of the terrorist's tools is often enhanced by weaknesses or loopholes in the services and systems that support them, such as banking practices that help money laundering (see Chapter 10).

Specific opportunities. Terrorists gain their advantage by recognizing opportunities that other people might not. For example, what ordinary person would have thought that a jetliner filled with aviation fuel could be turned into a missile of destruction ("think terrorist" in Figure 1.1; also see Chapter 2) or would have taken that possibility seriously until the events of 9/11?[7] It was the terrorists' willingness to accept the inevitability of dying in the attack that turned a theoretical opportunity into a practical and dreadful reality. Once Al Qaeda used airliners in this way, this opened up the possibility of their being used again by other terrorist groups, who might never have thought of this themselves. We must therefore recognize that when specific opportunities for attack are closed to the terrorists, they will try to think up new forms of attack. We must not assume, however, that that they will always succeed in this or that they can do it immediately (see Chapters 3 and 4).

Organized groups. Terrorists form groups (box 12) to maximize their opportunities. The 9/11 attack could not have been achieved by a lone terrorist, because the opportunities available could only be exploited by a coordinated group (planning, pilot training, false documentation and so on).

OUR AUDIENCE

Situational prevention uncovers opportunities for terrorism that lie hidden in the ordinary details of everyday life: the buying and selling of goods and services (using fertilizer as an explosive), the communications systems we take for granted (using cell phones to detonate bombs), the public and private means of transportation that we use every day (bombing of trains and buses) and the infrastructure on which we all depend (poisoning of reservoirs and bringing down the Internet). Those who can influence and change the routine ways we do things are therefore the real audience for this book. We think of this world as populated by problem solvers and designers. The problem solvers must work on the "frontlines" so to speak, trying to figure out how to respond to a specific, pressing problem. They would include local government officials, city managers, police chiefs, engineers, architects and the managers of large public and private facilities. The "designers" are those who, learning from these efforts, are in the position to implement changes that may have far-reaching preventive effects. They include legislators, high-level federal and state officials and leading corporate executives. Each of these groups must confront the issue of which responses are likely to produce the most effective protection for citizens.

What courses of action will best prevent terrorist attacks and reduce the harm that could result? The methodology, or rather the way of thinking, we provide in this book offers policymakers at all levels a way to answer this difficult question. A simple beginning along this path would be for policymakers and managers to reorient their staff to recognize the four pillars of terrorist opportunities. We call this a simple beginning; however, because of the pre-dominance of the take-them-out mindset, to introduce the training that staff require to take on the responsibilities of identifying specific vulnerabilities of targets, weapons, tools and facilitating conditions, assessing their priorities for protection and designing appropriate interventions will demand nothing short of a massive reorientation of the many law enforcement agencies now charged with fighting terrorism and protecting us from terrorist attacks. Extensive training and re-education of agency staff will be necessary. In the United States, this responsibility should be taken up by the Department of Homeland Security and, in the United Kingdom, by the Home Office.

If the power of our argument does not convince policymakers to reorient their approach to preventing terrorism, there is one persuasive reason for them to listen to us: the threat of calamitous law suits. On October 27, 2005 a jury found the New York Port Authority 68 percent liable for the first World Trade Center bombing.[8] The primary reason given for the judgment was that the own-ers of the Twin Towers had failed to heed security experts' advice to block off public access to the parking garage beneath the Twin Towers. This simple method of "hardening targets" is a standard part of the situational prevention array of intervention techniques (see Chapter 15). Furthermore, the Twin Towers were owned by the private sector, which means that the business community has a heavy stake in how government approaches the protection of targets from terrorist attack. It is clear that any successful attempt to implement our approach will require partnerships among a wide range of public and private agencies.

OUTSMARTING THE TERRORISTS—20 PRINCIPLES

Following are the 20 principles we have interpreted from the situational crime prevention literature for outsmarting the terrorists.

1. We must not rely on changing the hearts and minds of terrorists. The motivation for terrorism results from long-term social, cultural and psycholog-ical pressures, which are difficult to alter. But motivation is only part of the formula for terrorism. The other is the opportunity for attack that derives from the social, technical and physical features of society that facilitate acts of ter-rorism. Opportunity is easier to reduce than the terrorists' motivation and op-portunity reduction brings more immediate protection. In any case, easy opportunities encourage terrorists to attack.

2. We must not depend on "taking out" the terrorists. We must protect ourselves by this means, but we must recognize that individual terrorists are in most cases easily replaced. In addition, an overly aggressive policy of iden-tifying and taking out terrorists can inflame anger and create more terrorists.

3. We must develop solutions for each distinct form of terrorism. When thinking about preventing terrorism, it is vital to focus on specific forms of terrorism rather than on terrorism in general. This is because the opportunity structures for different forms of terrorism—aircraft hijacking, car bombing, suicide bombing, assassination, hostage taking, chemical attacks—are different from the other forms and the preventive interventions will also be different. Even the same form of attack—for example, suicide bombings—will demand different preventive action in different contexts.

4. We must accept that terrorists are rational. Sometimes terrorist outrages seem so callous that they are described as "mindless" and those who commit them are called mad, subhuman or quite "unlike us." But terrorists are rational. Their acts might vary greatly in sophistication and the degree of planning and organization required, but in all cases the terrorists are seeking to maximize their benefits, while reducing the effort required and the risks of failure. Generally speaking, the benefits constitute harm to the society attacked—in terms of loss of life, destruction, disruption of commerce and heightened fear.

5. We must learn how terrorists accomplish their tasks. In describing the opportunity structure for each form of terrorism we must analyze step by step how the acts are committed and how terrorists take advantage of opportunities available to them. Without this understanding, we cannot formulate effective preventive actions.

6. We must control the tools and weapons of terrorism. Without cars, credit cards, guns, explosives and cell phones it would be much more difficult for terrorists to mount successful attacks. Without the ability to establish credit or to access funds, it would also be difficult for them to act. Situational prevention has much experience to offer in modifying these objects and systems to make them less readily used in crime.

7. We must concentrate preventive resources on the most vulnerable targets. Although considerable benefit may be obtained by raising the minimal level of security for all targets, it is impossible to protect every conceivable target of terrorism to the same degree. Not all targets are of equal value to the terrorists and thus they do not all require the same level of protection. Some are also much more difficult to reach. Securely protecting the most attractive targets for terrorism will not necessarily result in less attractive targets being selected instead, and it might even discourage the terrorists from all such attacks. And if less attractive targets are selected, the harm to society and the benefits for the terrorists will be correspondingly lower.

8. We must formulate separate preventive policies for terrorism at home and overseas. Attacks on the homeland generate greater public fear, but foreign terrorists find it easier to attack us overseas. We must therefore devote equal attention to preventing overseas attacks and attacks at home.

9. We must accept that the threat of terrorism will never disappear. We can reduce the risks and harms of specific forms of terrorism and we can be successful in eliminating particular terrorist groups. This will produce tangible benefits for society, but we must not be lulled into a false sense of security. In time, other terrorist groups will arise and new forms of attack will be developed. Each of these new forms will need to be tackled in turn.

10. We must always be one step ahead. Assuming that the motivation for terrorism will persist, new forms or methods of attack will be developed. In some cases, this will be the result of technological or social changes that produce new opportunities for terrorism. We must therefore continuously analyze target vulnerabilities and enhance security where needed. In those cases in which the motivation for terrorism diminishes, obtrusive and inconvenient measures can be dismantled.

11. We must learn from the past and anticipate the future. Improving security takes two equally important forms: (1) anticipating and designing out new target vulnerabilities and (2) retrofitting security in existing facilities and systems.

12. We must match the rationality of terrorists in devising solutions. There are four basic approaches to reducing opportunities for terrorism: (1) increase the effort involved, (2) increase the risks of failure, (3) reduce the rewards of terrorism and (4) remove temptations, provocations and excuses.

13. We must beware of the magic bullet. There is rarely one "best" solution to a specific kind of terrorism. Rather, there are a variety of solutions, which may be equally effective, but which may vary considerably in their social and economic costs and, therefore, in their acceptability. In most cases, it is necessary to develop a package of solutions rather than to rely on a single measure that may prove easy to defeat.

14. We must make security decisions within the context of predetermined budgets. Working within a predetermined annual budget will force the federal government, states, cities and municipalities (and businesses and corporations) to make hard decisions about what most urgently needs protection.

15. We must ensure that federal antiterrorism budgets are disbursed according to risk. Population counts alone are not an adequate basis for disbursing funds and priority must be given to developing procedures for estimating differential risks for states and cities.

16. We must not depend on government to do it all. Because commercial and private interests own or manage the majority of terrorism targets, government must partner with businesses, industries and other nongovernmental agencies in reducing opportunities for terrorism.

17. We must develop dual benefit solutions. In persuading nongovernmental partners to improve security in their spheres of influence, it is important to identify solutions that are not unduly costly and that also benefit their normal operations.

18. We must not take public goodwill for granted. The public has been willing to surrender some freedoms and endure some inconvenience in the interests of reducing opportunities for terrorism. But public support must not be squandered by imposition of unduly restrictive and intrusive measures. Conversely, we should not assume that far-reaching interventions that affect the everyday lives of the public are necessarily intrusive or restrictive.

19. We must not let secrecy be a cloak for incompetence. Reducing opportunities for terrorism not only requires a continuing commitment to research and evaluation, but it must also be open to—indeed must seek—input from business and industry as well as from government and academia. New ways of forging research partnerships among these different entities must be found that safeguard each of their essential interests.

20. We must not be daunted by the enormous task before us. The task of reducing opportunities for terrorism is so great that some will dismiss it as impossible. It would indeed be impossible if we tried to do everything at once. Viewed as a long-term, probably permanent commitment, it becomes less daunting and more manageable. The alternative is to leave ourselves open to further catastrophic attacks.

BOOK OUTLINE

As we have noted, we offer a different way of thinking in his book—one that views terrorism through the lens of opportunity reduction. Thus, our analysis in the first three parts provides many insights into how we might anticipate terrorist attacks and how we might prevent them. In Part IV, we translate the insights gained from this view of terrorism into a coherent prescription for prevention, training and research. Throughout the book we refer to many different terrorist groups to illustrate our points or to provide background for our argument. Unavoidably, we rely more heavily on some terrorist groups, such as the Irish Republican Army (IRA), Al Qaeda and the terror groups in the occupied territories of Israel, because they are the groups that have been most studied and about which there is more written information. Most of the information available about these groups is descriptive, although some statistical data are available for the IRA in Northern Ireland and for the numbers and rates of attacks in Israel. We also make use of the Rand Memorial Institute for the Prevention of Terrorism (MIPT) database of terrorism to illustrate our points[9] and in some places have collected our own data, particularly regarding suicide bombing in Israel.

The book generally follows the sequence of the 20 principles. In Part I we describe how we must analyze our vulnerabilities, beginning in Chapter 2 with the need to think like a terrorist to identify our vulnerabilities (and theirs). Chapter 3 discusses the relationship between opportunity and action in more detail, and Chapter 4 uses the example of airliner hijackings to examine the question of whether reducing opportunities would simply displace terrorist attacks. Chapter 5 discusses the need to understand precisely how attacks are mounted using the example of suicide bombings and, because few terrorist attacks are carried out by a lone individual, Chapter 6 examines terrorist group decision making, with the intention of finding points of intervention.

In Part II we examine more closely the four pillars of terrorist opportunity—targets, tools, weapons and facilitating conditions—looking again for effective ways to intervene. We ask what is it about particular targets that make them more attractive to terrorists than others? Why do terrorists choose particular weapons from the many that are available? What tools do they find most appropriate for what kinds of missions? This analysis inserts us into the decision-making process of the terrorists and allows us to point the way to establishing priorities for protection. For example, we develop the EVIL DONE model of attractive targets; these targets must be some combination of the following: Exposed, Vital, Iconic, Legitimate, Destructible, Occupied, Near and Easy.

Part III applies the well-known principle of situational crime prevention that location is (almost) everything. The three chapters consider in detail the different challenges of preventing attacks at home and overseas, or near and far, warning that, while we may learn much from analyzing attacks that occur abroad, we must be careful in transferring assumptions about the operations of such attacks to dealing with "homegrown" terrorism. We examine the greater difficulty for terrorists to mount regular attacks on targets that are distant from their base of operations and the adjustments they must make to their planning in order to be successful.

In Part IV we lay out a set of more detailed requirements drawn directly from our situational prevention approach for closing the gap in our defenses and outsmarting the terrorists. We outline a framework for thinking about prevention and discuss the respective roles of government and business and the necessity for partnerships between the two. We argue that, while we must be constantly aware of the dangers of infringing on privacy of citizens in our zeal to prevent terrorist attacks, it does not follow that even far-reaching interventions that affect the daily lives of all people necessarily infringe on those rights. In addition, some interventions that may have some privacy costs may be outweighed by other benefits beyond those of security. We argue that the kinds of interventions and data collection necessitated by a situational approach to prevention are less likely to infringe on civil liberties than those collected by the intelligence-led approach that necessitates collection of extensive information of individuals, leading unavoidably to profiling of one kind or another to identify "potential" terrorists. We end by identifying the great deal of work—and creative thinking—that needs to be done in training, research and the development of collaborations among the many sectors of government and business that must play a part in protecting us all from terrorist attacks.

PART I

Analyzing Our Vulnerabilities

2

Think Terrorist

In This Chapter

➤ If we are to thwart terrorist attacks, we must understand the choices that they make at each step of the way—preparation, target selection, commission of the act, escape and aftermath.

➤ To do this, we must "think terrorist," that is, adopt their point of view and see the task from their perspective.

➤ Doing so allows us to better understand how to increase the costs of mounting the attack and reducing the benefits for them.

➤ We must do this separately for each different kind of attack, because these differ so much in terms of the decisions required and the variables that must be considered.

➤ We must not imagine that terrorists are all ruthless fanatics who cannot be stopped. Nor are they all supremely intelligent individuals who meticulously plan every detail. Rather, they improvise, they make less than optimal decisions and they can be defeated by increasing the difficulty of attacks, increasing the risks and reducing the rewards.

IT HAS BEEN proven essential in situational crime prevention to see the world from the offender's perspective. In trying to prevent specific kinds of crime from occurring, one must always try to understand the offenders' purposes in committing these crimes and determine how they set about the task of accomplishing them. While the theme of this chapter focuses on the need to understand that these very same processes are at work for terrorists, we should first explain how adopting the offender's perspective has helped crime prevention.

The first principle of this approach is to regard the offender as being engaged in a decision-making process that is little different from that of everyday life. All of us are constantly faced with decisions, small and large, in which we are trying to maximize our benefits. This is true of choosing a meal in a restaurant and of deciding which course to take at college. While we always try to get the best results for ourselves, we don't have unlimited time to make these decisions. Nor do we always have good information on which to base them. We may be falsely optimistic in our judgments and we may be swayed by other opinions or passing emotions. Finally, chance plays a part in the outcome. This means, of course, that our decisions do not always turn out for the best. This decision-making process has been described as "bounded rationality" by economic theorists[1] and it has proven to be a powerful tool in analyzing offenders' behavior and finding ways to prevent them from meeting their goals.[2] In the crime prevention literature, the tool is encapsulated by the phrase "think thief!" It means that one must try to enter the minds of the offenders to understand what they are hoping to gain from the crimes in question, and to trace the sequence of decisions they must make, at each stage of the crime, in accomplishing their goals.[3]

This process does not involve attempting to psychoanalyze the offenders to expose the deep roots of their delinquency. The focus is not on these distant causes of criminality, but on the here and now. What specifically do the offenders think they will gain by committing this act? What costs do they weigh in embarking on the act? How do they plan to solve the problems involved in the successful completion of the act? How do they obtain the necessary tools and enlist any necessary accomplices? How do they overcome any security and subdue victims? How do they escape? How do they reduce the chances of subsequent detection? How do they dispose of the goods? If we know the answers to these questions, we are in a better position to think about ways of frustrating offenders by making it more difficult and risky to commit the crime and by reducing its rewards.

THINK TERRORIST, THINK THIEF

Before discussing how to "think terrorist" it may be helpful to explain how we can draw on the extensive theoretical and practical experience gained in tackling conventional crime. After all, "thinking thief" has become a highly successful approach, and it arms us with an understanding that we can adapt directly into the counterterrorist role.

In trying to think thief, the guiding assumption is that a general understanding of human nature will usually suffice. If one is to enter the minds of the offenders, it is important to think not only about the crimes they are planning, but also about their everyday lives and the opportunities the crimes provide them to meet normal human needs for such things as companionship, admiration, status and love. If we do so, we might more clearly see why ghetto youths find sanctuary in gangs and are willing to shoot a rival for showing disrespect. We might also better understand why deprived teenage girls become single mothers and why some of them form alliances with drug dealers and pimps. This is not to make excuses for the offenders, because they have chosen to behave the way they do, but merely to gain greater insight into their motives. As soon as we resort to labeling the crimes as mindless or senseless, we have failed in our attempt to think thief and we will probably fail in our goal of prevention.

One should only try to think thief for closely defined categories of crime. This is because the decision-making processes and the variables considered by offenders vary greatly from crime to crime. For a start, crimes differ greatly in the benefits they confer and thus in the offenders' motives. A rape is committed for quite different reasons from a house burglary, even if habitual offenders sometimes commit both kinds of crime. Preventing rape is therefore a very different problem from preventing burglary—that is, if one is not merely content to arrest habitual offenders and imprison them for long periods.[4]

In fact, it is not sufficient to distinguish merely between broad categories of crime such a rape or house burglary when thinking about the decision-making process. These broad labels cover many distinct kinds of crimes that, again, must be analyzed and understood separately if realistic means are to be found of preventing them. Thus, from a preventive perspective, acquaintance rape is a quite different problem from stranger rape, and the variables that must be manipulated to reduce the likelihood of either are also quite different. For example, increased patrolling by the police of city streets might conceivably help prevent stranger rapes, but this could not be expected to reduce acquaintance rape, which often occurs in private settings. Furthermore, acquaintance rape in a college dorm-room setting is a different problem, with potentially different solutions, from acquaintance rape resulting from late-night barroom pickups. This general point is true of every broad category of crime. It is of very limited utility to analyze the decision-making processes of broad categories of offenders because this yields only general guidance about prevention, not clear practical suggestions.

Box 2.1 provides a further illustration of this point using a careful study of house burglary in a British city. This study revealed that the problem of house burglary in the newer suburbs of the city was quite different, and required different solutions, from burglary in the inner core of the city. The former was committed by offenders with cars and the latter was committed mostly by offenders on foot. As explained, this led to different implications for prevention.

HOW TO "THINK TERRORIST"

While we are not suggesting that the particular methods used in crime or the measures used to prevent it are the same as for terrorism, the choices that criminals and terrorists make in pursuing their diverse ends are conditioned in exactly the same way by the opportunities open to them. The particular objectives and opportunities are different in both cases, but the determinants of choice are largely the same. Both groups must match their skills and resources to the tasks needed to succeed in the environments open to them, and perception and evaluation of these opportunities are conditioned by the knowledge

Box 2.1 The Decisions of Burglars

All crimes are the result of decisions made by the offender who must match his or her actions to the opportunities available. Barry Poyner and Barry Webb have shown this process at work in their study of residential burglaries in one British city. They found that there were two distinct forms of burglary in the city. In the older, inner-city core, burglars targeted cash and jewelry, whereas in the newer suburbs they targeted electronic items such as TVs and VCRs. This was the result of the different burglary opportunities provided in these two different environments. In the inner-city core, it was difficult for burglars to operate in cars as there were no spaces to park them in the busy streets. Furthermore, because most of the houses in the inner city were row houses, burglars could only get into them through the front door or windows. This meant that they had to be very quick getting in and out of the house or they might be seen by passers-by or someone living in the opposite row. Even if they could have parked their cars nearby, it would be too risky to make several trips carrying bulky electronic goods. So they stole only small items like cash and jewelry that they put in their pockets and that would not prevent them from running away, if challenged. Burglars in the suburbs, on the other hand, had no such constraints. Most of the houses were empty in the day because people were out at work. The layout of the housing permitted burglars to park their cars, without attracting the attention of neighbors, near the backs of the houses. They had many more choices of entry points to each house, which generally consisted of single-family homes. They could go back and forth from the house to the car, loading it with valuable goods. In fact, the two groups of burglars were probably quite separate. In the inner-city core, it is likely that the burglars were young, opportunistic thieves with few resources beyond their daring. Those in the suburbs were probably better set up with vehicles to transport the goods they had stolen, places to hide them temporarily and customers who would purchase them. However, both groups were responding to the opportunities available to them and matching their burglary techniques to the particular pattern of opportunities in each setting.

Poyner and Webb's suggestions to prevent the inner-city burglaries focused on improving security of front doors and windows and trimming any bushes that blocked the view of the front door and ground-floor windows from the road. Their suggestions for preventing the suburban burglaries were more comprehensive, involving reduced access to rear yards, improving the security of all doors and windows, fitting burglar alarms, targeting known fences of electronic goods and so forth.

Sources: Poyner (2005); Poyner and Webb (1991).

of their own capacities and limitations. The task of preventing each group from meeting their objectives and completing their acts is also essentially similar. We must understand how they go about their work, step by step, and we must think about ways we can intervene at every stage to make their tasks more difficult, more risky and less rewarding. This involves us in the same process of seeing the world from the perspective of each group.

In fact, it is even more important to think terrorist than to think thief because terrorism is much less common than crime and it is also much harder for researchers to gain access to terrorists. Consequently, it is often impossible to conduct analyses of large samples of the kinds of events we are trying to prevent and hard to interview the individuals involved, which are techniques widely used in crime prevention.[5] We must therefore rely more heavily on our own imaginative construction of the events in trying to understand the decisions that the terrorists must make so that we can find effective ways of intervening. That this is possible is shown by the Tylenol incident described in Chapter 15 (Box 15.1). Rather few of the incidents of tampering with Tylenol packages occurred, but it was not difficult to imagine how they were committed, nor was it difficult to see how to prevent it from happening again by using tamper-proof packaging. Following are five principles for undertaking these tasks and learning how to think terrorist.

1. *Resist demonizing terrorists.* It is natural that we react with horror and disgust when terrorists kill and injure innocent people, and that we condemn them as bestial and inhuman. While this can serve a useful purpose in countering propaganda about the justice of their cause, in other ways it is unhelpful for prevention.[6] It inflames calls for revenge and leads to an unproductive, although understandable preoccupation with punishment rather than prevention. Counter to the argument of this chapter, it suggests that terrorists are a race apart, that their motives and behavior fall outside the scope of ordinary analysis and that they can only be understood by trained psychologists. It also lumps all terrorists together and obscures the fact that they vary as much as any other large group of individuals in their backgrounds, in their skills and capacities, and in their aspirations and goals. Not all of them are ruthless bigots or even fanatically dedicated to their cause. Most of them are ordinary people who might believe in the cause, but who have joined the group principally because of the particular benefits membership brings them. For some, these are anticipated rewards after death; for others, they are the more mundane rewards of employment, status, adventure and camaraderie.

2. *Focus on specific forms of terrorism.* Each manifestation of terrorism is different from another—in the rewards it confers, in its risks and in its difficulties. Note from Table 2.1[7] that many of the objectives can be self-serving (there may be a need to test or "blood" new recruits, for example) and that different terrorists groups may pick and mix different items from the menu of objectives. This means that while terrorists might share the same broad range of objectives, the different forms of terrorism do not serve these ends equally. This fact is highlighted in Table 2.2, in which the respective benefits of the 9/11 attack and the attack on the USS *Cole* are compared, but it is also true for the same form of terrorism—for example, suicide bombings—when undertaken in different settings such as Jerusalem or London. In each case, the costs and benefits are different. Palestinian bombers are revered as martyrs by a wide swathe of their home communities, whereas the London

Table 2.1 The Terrorists' Goals

1 Cause as much destruction and death as possible

2 Create a climate of fear

3 Create media sensation

4 Disrupt everyday life

5 Disrupt a specific activity (e.g., recruiting police cadets)

6 Disrupt commerce and industry

7 Demoralize security forces

8 Extort concessions (e.g., release of prisoners, remove troops, change policies)

9 Eliminate an opponent or an offensive icon

10 Humiliate officials and governments

11 Force or tempt government to overreact

12 Exaggerate the perception of the terrorist threat so that a relatively small terrorist group can exert great leverage

13 Create the impression of an all pervasive force: "the enemy within"

14 Show off to supporters and thereby consolidate followers or members of the terrorist group

15 Intimidate rival political or terrorist factions

16 Maintain discipline within the group

17 Test or "blood" new recruits or train followers

18 Intimidate the population in the terrorists' bases of operations

19 Exploit "weaknesses" in democracies (e.g., rule of law, free speech, laws against torture or pretrial detention)

20 Break the enemy's will

suicide bombers in July 2005 were angrily rejected by most British Muslims. Although it might have been easier for the London bombers to reach their targets—they simply had to board a train with their deadly backpacks—it was harder for their associates to evade arrest. This was because the police could freely enter the neighborhoods where these associates lived and expect to receive assistance from residents.

Terrorists cannot meet all of these objectives on every occasion; they must do what is achievable given the opportunities and resources available to them at a particular time and in a particular place. They must constantly weigh the balance between obtaining one or more of their objectives against the opportunities and resources available. Criminals must do exactly this in meeting their goals. Of course, like criminals, terrorists can take advantage of opportunities presented to them by various technologies and systems, and in later chapters we will see how this happens. They must, however, also make

Table 2.2 Terrorist Benefits from Attacking the World Trade Center and the USS *Cole*

Objective	World Trade Center Attack (New York City, September 11, 2001)		USS *Cole* Attack (Port of Aden, Yemen, October 12, 2000)	
	Score	Considerations	Score	Considerations
Destroy and kill	10	Target completely destroyed. 3,000 people killed.	3	Ship substantially damaged, but did not sink; 12 servicemen killed.
Fear	9	Fear has declined with time.	3	American people not directly affected because act occurred at distant location.
Create media sensation	10	Needs little comment.	4	Received considerable media coverage because of lives lost and innovative method of attack.
Disrupt everyday life	9	Immediate disruption in New York, but security precautions have now merged into everyday life.	1	Disruption confined to USS *Cole*, the U.S. Navy and diplomatic and government personnel.
Disrupt commerce	9	Drastic impact with some longer-term effects.	1	Event confined to naval/military operations.
Force government compliance with demands	1	No explicit demands were made, but Al Qaeda had consistently demanded U.S. withdrawal from holy lands.	1	Security was improved; the United States has not withdrawn from the harbor.
Force government to overreact	9	Government adopted the doctrine of preemptive war and condoned the use of torture.	1	There was no powerful government reaction that could have given succor to the terrorists.
Exploit "weaknesses" of democracy	9	The Iraq invasion led to fierce political discord at home and among allies.	1	People galvanized to support families and military because of servicemen's lives lost.
All pervasive force	9	Constant concern about "sleeper cells" in the United States.	4	Event confined to military target in foreign waters, although "sleeper cells" were involved.
Humiliation	10	U.S. government exposed as vulnerable to a handful of foreign operatives.	3	Although lives were lost, naval personnel were seen to have acted courageously.

Note: 10 = highest score; 1 = lowest score.

their own opportunities by developing skills and by training their personnel to overcome barriers—some natural, given the sheer magnitude of the tasks they may set themselves, and others that we must try to place in their way in our fight against terrorism. In deciding what kind of terrorist attack to mount, the terrorist must take account of three principal considerations. They must decide, first, on the scope of the mission. Which of their various objectives will the mission seek to meet? How complicated will the mission be? Will it be so complicated that it will require a lot of training of personnel and so on? Second, they must decide on the type of target, such as specific individuals or buildings that people inhabit, and how these target features relate to the overall objectives of the attack. Having decided on the nature of the target, they must then decide which specific target to hit. Third, they must identify weapons, technology or other facilitators available to carry out the attack. The purported manuals of Al Qaeda found by occupying forces in Afghanistan clearly delineate these elements of preparation and planning.[8] We deal later in this chapter with the scope of terrorist attacks, their complexity and the resources needed (we have also devoted separate chapters in the book to targets, tools, weapons and facilitating conditions).

3. Do not waste time on the roots of terrorist ideology. However useful this might be in framing other responses to terrorism, it is unproductive when planning situational interventions to spend a great deal of time trying to understand the political and cultural roots of the terrorists' ideology. This rarely produces any concrete or practical suggestions for prevention. It is true that if we could change ideology we might reduce the chances of attack, but any successful efforts of this kind could only be mounted over a considerable span of time. This would bring no immediate relief from terrorism and might be overtaken by events quite outside the planning of governments. For example, who would have thought that the IRA would have its support in the United States so rapidly swept away by the 9/11 attacks and that this would lead them to renounce violence?

4. Analyze how the act is accomplished. It is vital for prevention to think carefully about the steps the terrorists must take, and the decisions they must make, to accomplish their acts. This must be done, in detail, for every stage of the attack from initial planning through target selection and the launch of the attack to escape. (See Chapter 5 on the stages of suicide bombing.) It can also be important to analyze how the terrorists attempt to manipulate the media treatment of the attack by issuing communiqués and releasing videos. At every juncture, the terrorists are confronted with a wide array of choices, and if we can work out which ones they are likely to make, we can find ways to make them less advantageous. We must try to work out what influences the choice of target, how terrorists acquire the tools and weapons to mount the attack and how they take advantage of the everyday arrangements of social and economic life to accomplish their acts. In doing so, we should not fall prey to the myth of the supremely intelligent, meticulous planner who

arranges every last detail of the attack. In many cases, terrorists will improvise the attack and will sometimes make hasty and poor decisions. Their
bombs may explode prematurely, killing only themselves. They may
assassinate the wrong person or be outwitted by those they have kidnapped.
In other words, they are normal fallible human beings doing the best they can
under conditions of stress, uncertainty and extreme risk. If we understand this,
we can make their chances of failure even greater.

   5. *Do not doubt that terrorists can be stopped.* Even when terrorist acts
cannot be stopped, their effects can be hugely mitigated. For example, the
adoption of blast-absorbing net curtains in the United Kingdom saved many
civil servants from injuries caused by flying glass resulting from IRA bombs.
Similarly, placing vehicle barriers around U.S. embassies has forced terrorists
to abandon car bomb attacks against them.

   Some argue that there is little point in protecting highly vulnerable targets, because the terrorist will simply move on to attack the next most vulnerable one, which has been left unprotected, and nothing will have been gained.
Even if that is true, however, it is not without value. For example, if terrorists
are thwarted from bombing U.S. embassies they will be obliged to go further
down their list of preferred targets with less impressive results.

   In any case, the risk of "displacement," as this is known in crime prevention (see Chapters 3 and 4), has been shown to be overstated. Most research
studies find little evidence of displacement when high-risk targets or places
are given protection.[9] These places and targets are high risk for a reason: they
provide a particularly attractive combination of benefits at low cost. Indeed,
this combination might be so attractive that it induces crime—that is, people
are tempted to commit crimes they might not otherwise have considered while
habitual criminals step up their normal rate of offending—rather than simply
being the preferred choice of offenders. Once these opportunities are removed,
crime declines. There are many examples of specific crimes being almost
wiped out by the introduction of situational prevention. One might imagine
that this will not hold true for terrorism because we assume that terrorists are
fanatics and therefore not as rational as ordinary criminals. This is a mistake.
As we shall see in Chapter 4, situational prevention can achieve the same
results for terrorism: there is strong evidence that hijacking of airliners was
largely eliminated in the 1970s and 1980s by a range of security measures
introduced by the government and the airline industry. It is true that, eventually, loopholes in the measures were discovered by the 9/11 attackers (see
Box 2.2), but until then we were mercifully free from hijackings.[10]

THE COMPLEXITY OF A TERRORIST ACT

The scope of a terrorist act will dictate the level of complexity needed to pull
it off. Thus, the ambitious scope of the 9/11 attack, which achieved nearly

---

Box 2.2 9/11 Again

It is worth pausing to consider just how many barriers the planners of the 9/11 attack had to overcome. Their overriding goals were obviously to achieve every one of those listed above. The target, if it could be destroyed, promised to deliver on all objectives. However, there were no available weapons to bring about the destruction of the towers, as was discovered from the first failed attempt to bring them down. The idea of using commercial airplanes as missiles was certainly an innovative solution, but it required years of preparation to do this. Personnel who were willing to lose their lives had to be selected and groomed. They had to undergo training that was costly and risky, because it took a long time and exposed "sleeper" operatives to risks, such as taking flying lessons and using false identities to obtain driver's licenses. Finally, ways had to be devised to gain control of aircraft without traditional weapons, which were, in principle at least, subject to search by airline security. The use of box cutters as weapons along with hand-to-hand combat training was another innovative solution.

---

every one of the objectives of terrorism that we identified in Table 2.1, necessarily demanded that extraordinary steps be made to overcome the many barriers in the way of meeting that goal (see Box 2.2). Principal factors that determine the complexity of a terrorist act are as follows:

Availability of motivated personnel. Sometimes there is a ready supply of terrorist recruits. For example, the Madrassas (privately funded Islamic schools) in Saudi Arabia and Pakistan and the refugee camps of Palestine have produced many willing suicide bombers.[11] Often specific events swell the ranks of volunteers (undoubtedly IRA recruitment benefited hugely from internment in Northern Ireland in 1971);[12] occasionally quite sophisticated indoctrination is required (as with Al Qaeda recruitment among European students, some of whom were not previously religious or politically motivated); and sometimes followers are recruited through cults or even in rare circumstances through kidnap (such as the notorious case of Patty Hearst and her recruitment to the Symbionese Liberation Army in 1974).

The level of skill needed to successfully complete the tasks required of the mission. The IRA bomb that nearly killed Margaret Thatcher at a Brighton hotel in England in 1984 took considerable planning and reasonably sophisticated bomb-making using long-term timers. On the other hand, Timothy McVeigh learned from friends and a handbook how to mix common fertilizers to create his bomb in Oklahoma.

The required training. Some of the 9/11 hijackers had limited training; others had spent years preparing for the event, including learning to fly commercial airliners. Even single suicide bombers must be trained and coached about their mission, how to reach their target without being detected, how to detonate the bomb, and so on. At the other end of the scale, Timothy McVeigh did his own training by practicing mixing and detonating explosives that he would later use in his attack.

The organizational infrastructure needed. The bombing in Oklahoma City did not take much organization, because essentially only two people were involved. There were some attempts to link these individuals to a wider organization known to have an interest in confronting the U.S. government, but the use of a sophisticated or even simple organization was clearly unnecessary to carry out this attack. We examine this issue in Chapter 11.

The amount of planning required. The planning for the 9/11 attack was clearly extensive (see Box 2.2). However, the planning for a suicide bombing also requires much planning. The target must be selected and a path to it chosen. These must be matched to the selection of the suicide bomber. The amount of explosive to be detonated and alternative targets to be selected in case of interception must also be determined.

Availability of weaponry. In Iraq during the American-led occupation, the availability of weaponry does not seem to have been a problem. In the United States, obtaining grenade launchers and heavy explosives takes much more effort, while in the United Kingdom it is difficult to obtain even a handgun.

The amount of money needed to finance the enterprise. Al Qaeda is reported to be funded by billions of dollars received from its various supporters (see Chapter 6). The 9/11 report estimated that the actual cost of blowing up the World Trade Center was around $500,000.

The complexity of planning also affects how often a particular kind of attack can be made. There are some types of attack that have been used regularly, such as suicide bombings in Israel and bombings by the IRA in London and Northern Ireland. Given the challenges of planning we have outlined, we can infer that once these attacks are planned and practiced, they can be made routine, as long as the necessary supportive and facilitative conditions remain in place. Clearly, to mount a constant series of suicide bombing attacks, one needs a steady stream of bombers and a plentiful supply of explosives and bomb jackets. The design of paths to targets and the selection of targets therefore become crucial to the routinization of a terrorist act. Furthermore, the terrorists must devise a method of selecting targets and paths that will not become predictable. This is why Israel has built various barriers and walls (which was also done in Northern Ireland) to make it more difficult for the terrorist to select targets that were reachable, and more difficult to plan the path to the target. As we will see in subsequent chapters, the accessibility of targets is a major factor in their selection.

CONCLUSION

In this chapter, we have tried to explain how we must try to get inside the mind of the terrorist and learn how to "think terrorist." This does not mean trying to psychoanalyze terrorists to understand the deep sources of their motivation. It means, instead, that we must try to see the world from their perspective and understand how they go about their tasks of planning and carrying out attacks. By uncovering the decision-making processes and identifying the factors that influence their decisions, we can find points of weakness—ways in which we can interfere with the decisions they make. We know that they may be too strongly committed to their cause to allow us to change their mind. But we can use the information we get from their actions (which reveal their choices) to devise preventive strategies and, perhaps, weaken their resolve if we can cause them to repeatedly fail (see Chapter 6). In doing so, we need to understand what leads them to select a particular kind of terrorist action over another. Is this choice dictated by their overall objectives, their access to particular tools and weapons, or by the vulnerability or strategic importance of particular targets? Answers to these questions will help us to take preventive actions of our own. We should always "think terrorist" when trying to answer these kinds of questions. In doing so, we would meet the need identified by the 9/11 Commission "to find a way of routinizing, even bureaucratizing, the exercise of imagination" in dealing with the terrorism threat.[13]

3

The Key Role of Opportunity

In This Chapter

- ➤ Research demonstrates that opportunity plays a large part in such deeply motivated acts as suicide and homicide.
- ➤ Opportunity also plays a key role in terrorism because of the large number of suitable targets for attack and the easy access to tools and weapons.
- ➤ We need not protect every target, only those that offer the most rewarding opportunities for the terrorists.
- ➤ Protecting these targets will not simply result in terrorists choosing other targets (displacement) because these alternative targets are not as easy or as rewarding.
- ➤ Reducing successful attacks will result in fewer copycat attacks by other terrorist groups.

THIS CHAPTER IS about theory. We deal with practical issues in later chapters. Academic theorizing might seem to be a low priority when faced with the deadly, practical task of defeating terrorism, but theory is important because, without its underpinnings, policymakers are likely to reject situational answers because of incorrect presumptions.

There are two main intuitive objections to protecting targets from terrorist attack rather than applying our energies elsewhere: (1) we cannot possibly protect every potential target; and (2) if we cannot protect them all, the terrorists will simply switch their attention from protected to unprotected targets.

These objections lead automatically to the view that our responses to terrorism must be limited to killing or capturing them, to defeating their aims or ideals so they have no more recruits, and to cleaning up as effectively as possible after they have struck.

Much the same objections are raised when dealing with other social problems—that it is people, not circumstances, stupid—and we should mention one example in particular: road accidents. When serious attention was first devoted to reducing accidents, everyone "knew" that the most urgent need was to improve driving skills; after all, it is drivers that cause highway accidents, not highways or vehicles on their own. In fact, this supposition proved to be quite wrong. Dramatic reductions were achieved in accidents and deaths (see Box 3.1) and almost all of them were won through improving cars and roads (i.e., through situational means). Of course, it might be much easier to help people avoid accidents than to stop them from engaging in acts of crime or terrorism, which they are determined to commit. But whether a terrible thing happens through carelessness, recklessness or cunning, people's disposition is only part of the equation that makes up the event.

In this chapter, we will explain why it is possible to deny terrorists opportunities for achieving their preferred attacks and how we can prevent their success or at least diminish it. We will explain more about why displacement is less inevitable than people assume and point out that even a displaced terrorist activity is at least likely to delay the terrorists and diminish their success. First, however, we need to explain why a terrorist's *motivation* is not necessarily the overriding factor in calculating how best to defeat him or her.

OPPORTUNITY AND TERRORISM

It is natural for people to see opportunity as subsidiary to motivation. After all, we are conscious every day of trying to fulfill our various goals and objectives, and we are aware of all the choices we make, big and small. We therefore tend to see ourselves as in control of our destinies. This is especially the case in the United States where everyone is encouraged to believe they can become rich or be elected president. However, we generally are not aware, on a daily basis, of the determining effects of the opportunities that structure the choices we make. For example, at the cafeteria at work we might take pleasure in choosing a meal that is enjoyable and healthy, but we might not notice the limited choices available to us in terms of all possible meals. We know that we would not find filet mignon or lobster mayonnaise, but we tend not to consciously think about that fact. We therefore might have made a good choice—something that we like to eat and that is good for us—but only among the limited opportunities provided by the menu.

This might be true of small decisions about meals, but what about the much larger choices we are concerned with in this book, decisions to mount an ambush or a suicide attack? Surely, we might think, choices with such momentous consequences are not governed by opportunity? Is not the primary driving force behind such acts the hatred felt by the terrorists? Should we not therefore be focusing our efforts on ways to reduce this hatred of our country and way of life? This might seem a compelling argument, but the truth is that any behavior is the outcome of an interaction between organism and environment. This means that the causes of crime, suicide, alcohol abuse and any other form of deviance, including terrorism, lie in a complex interaction between motivation and opportunity. Indeed, terrorism is committed in part because it is possible and, when terrorists succeed, they make the possibility

Box 3.1 Reducing Road Accidents by Reengineering Cars and Roads

The benefits of seeking to reduce opportunities rather than dispositions are vividly illustrated by an analysis of traffic safety policy in the United States. Six times as many people drive today in the United States as in the 1920s, and the number of motor vehicles in the country has increased more than tenfold to well over 200 million. The number of miles driven is also 10 times higher than in the mid-1920s. Despite this steep increase in travel, the annual death rate has declined from 18 per 100 million vehicle miles traveled in 1925 to less than 2 per 100 million 70 years later.

This remarkable achievement, mirrored in other parts of the developed world, was primarily the result of measures to improve the safety of cars and highways. Systematic motor-vehicle safety efforts began in 1966 with laws that authorized the federal government to set standards for motor vehicles and highways. Many changes in vehicle and highway design quickly followed. Vehicles were built with new safety features, which included head rests, energy-absorbing steering wheels, shatter-resistant windshields and safety belts. Roads were improved by better delineation of curves (edge and center-line stripes and reflectors), use of breakaway sign and utility poles, improved illumination, addition of barriers separating oncoming traffic lanes and guardrails. Graded speed limits were also introduced suitable to road conditions.

The results were rapid. By 1970, motor-vehicle-related death rates were already decreasing rapidly, and this decrease continued until the end of the century. While these changes were reinforced by laws requiring the use of safety belts, child safety seats and motorcycle helmets—and were accompanied by the enforcement of laws against drunk driving, speeding and underage drinking—the improvements to cars and highways were the key factors in driving down death rates. If road accident policy had focused exclusively on driver education or enforcement of traffic rules, and had not reengineered cars and roads to make them safe, the dramatic reduction in road deaths would never have been achieved.

These changes in design of cars and roads required a considerable change of mindset—perhaps equivalent to the change we are seeking in ways to prevent terrorism. The mindset among law enforcement, the car manufacturers and the general public was "bad drivers, not cars, cause accidents." In 1965 a General Motors vice president told the *New York Times*, "If the drivers do everything they should, there wouldn't be any accidents, would there?" The discovery by William Haddon that a large portion of deaths in road accidents was caused by a "second crash"—that is, by the impact of the driver or passenger hitting some part of the interior of the car—led eventually to the compulsory fitting of seat belts in all cars, which has contributed to saving countless lives. If you reside in the United States, there is a better than 70 percent chance that you wear your seat belt when you drive. If you live in Australia, there is a better than 95 percent chance that you will buckle up. Seat belt legislation was passed in the face of vocal opposition from car manufacturers (would cost too much) and the public who complained about infringement on civil liberties.

Source: Centers for Disease Control (1999).

more obvious to others who are tempted to try their hand. We would go further and argue that if we make terrorism less rewarding by protecting the targets that produce the greatest rewards for any given effort, the terrorists will not switch wholesale to attacking other much less rewarding targets. Some of the more determined terrorists will persist in their attacks, but these will result in less harm for society. Many others will be discouraged from the cause and divert their energies toward more personally rewarding activities.

We cannot demonstrate these points through research because the relevant studies of terrorism have not been undertaken, but they rest on a sound foundation of theory and research in situational crime prevention. Throughout the remainder of the book we will turn to this body of work to support our arguments. In this section, we will review evidence showing that opportunity is an important cause of suicide and homicide—two behaviors with considerable relevance for terrorism.

SUICIDE AND HOMICIDE

Both suicide and homicide are commonly regarded as deeply motivated acts, committed only by determined or desperate individuals. Suicide, in particular, is thought to be an act so extreme that it can only be the result of a deep drive for self-destruction. However, many people become suicidal as a result of a recent misfortune, such as bereavement, disappointment in love or failure at work. They may be preoccupied by thoughts of suicide for a while, but in time such depression usually lifts and they get on with their lives. Conversely, if an acceptable means of suicide is available, they might kill themselves before their despair lifts.

Many studies have shown that reductions or increases in suicide result from changes in everyday life. Thus, the most common form of suicide in the United States used to be poisoning, but now, as a result of the increased ownership of handguns, it is shooting. The introduction of emission controls, which removed deadly carbon monoxide from car exhaust gases, led to a reduction in suicides by this method. In fact, it is now almost impossible to commit suicide by using the exhausts of modern cars.[1] A more recent example is that suicides have fallen in Britain as result of a government requirement that painkillers cannot be supplied in packets of more than thirty-two. This requirement was intended to reduce the likelihood of impulsive suicides, and it appears to have worked.[2]

It might be thought that the reduction or removal of the means to commit suicide, such as car exhaust gas, would simply result in suicide victims choosing some other way to kill themselves. This assumes that all methods of death are equally available or equally acceptable to people considering suicide— but this is not the case, as shown dramatically by the results of detoxifying the gas supplied to homes in Britain between 1958 and 1977.[3] In 1958, "putting one's head in the oven," to use the common expression, was the most frequent method of suicide in Britain with almost half of the 5,298 people who killed themselves in that year using this method. Changes in the manufacturing process for gas during the 1960s substantially reduced the amount of carbon monoxide in domestic gas. This was followed in the 1970s by the replacement of manufactured gas by natural gas from the North Sea, which completely removed carbon monoxide from the gas supply. Overall, suicides were 25 percent lower in 1977 than in 1958 and only 0.2 percent of the 3,944 suicides in 1977 made use of domestic gas. This means that, while there was some displacement to other means of suicide following the changes to the gas supply, many people who otherwise would have killed themselves did not do so. The reasons lie in the unique combination of advantages of using domestic gas as a method of suicide. It was readily available in everyone's home. It required little preparation, older people could readily make use of it and it involved no pain, blood or disfigurement, which are all features that made it an attractive method of suicide.

It is also the case that homicides are not always deeply motivated, carefully planned acts. Many are committed spontaneously when someone, who may be intoxicated, explodes with rage as a result of a dispute. If a weapon is at hand, such as a handgun, it is likely that it will be used. In fact, it has been shown in many studies that homicide rates are higher when guns are readily available. Perhaps the clearest evidence comes from a comparison of the homicide rates between England and Wales and the United States. It is well known that the homicide rate is higher in the United States and widely believed that the much greater availability of guns there (a situational variable) provides the explanation. However, it is the details of the comparison that make a compelling causal argument. A study of the two countries conducted in the 1980s showed that the overall rate of homicides in the United States was 8.5 times higher, the gun homicide rate was 63 times higher and the handgun homicide rate was 175 times higher than in England and Wales. Most telling of all is that the average number of handgun murders for the United States in the mid-1980s was a little over 9,300; that for England and Wales was just under 12.

For those who wanted to deny the causal role of handguns in homicide, it was possible to argue in the 1980s that the United States was a much more crime-ridden and violent society than England and Wales. This argument, however, is no longer credible. Steady declines in crime in the United States have resulted in crime rates for most common offences now being lower, sometimes markedly so, than those of England and Wales. More notable, comparative victimization surveys, not available in the 1980s, show that the rates of assault in England and Wales are higher than in the United States.[4] While rates of homicide have declined in the United States, they are still six times higher than in England and Wales and greater handgun availability still provides the explanation. This does not mean that the availability of a weapon is the sole determinant for homicide, but it clearly establishes that opportunity is a powerful cause of homicide. If this is true of homicide, it must also be true of the remainder of crime, and terrorism as well.

Findings such as these lead us to conclude that opportunity plays a vital role in eliciting criminal behavior. We do not deny that dispositional factors make the offender more prepared to break the law, but we insist that the perception of crime opportunities (temptation) also motivates the offender to commit crime. There are two main ways that opportunity elicits criminal behavior (and thus, terrorist behavior):

1. Criminally disposed individuals will commit a greater numbers of crimes if they encounter more criminal opportunities. Regularly encountering such opportunities could lead these individuals to seek even more opportunities.
2. Individuals without preexisting dispositions can be drawn into criminal behavior by a proliferation of criminal opportunities and temptations and the perception that these can yield rewards.

It seems likely that these propositions hold true for terrorism. Terrorism is learned behavior that is made possible by the vulnerabilities of our society to terrorist attack. This is why our antiterrorism policy must pay as much attention to reducing opportunities for terrorism (through protecting vulnerable targets and controlling the tools and weapons of terror) as it now pays to taking out individual terrorists and dismantling terrorist organizations. Terrorists do respond to opportunities, they are encouraged by their own successes and those of other terrorists, and ordinary individuals become terrorists because they are attracted to the rewards.

PROTECTING THE TARGETS OF TERROR

Criticisms of our approach are most apparent in relation to targets, so we will concentrate in this chapter on targets rather than on tools and weapons. Even if it is accepted that opportunity, in the form of vulnerable targets, plays an important role in terrorist attacks, the difficulties of protecting these targets might seem insuperable. The initiative rests entirely with the terrorists, which means they can strike where and when they want. How can we possibly protect every school, train station, shopping mall, town center, bridge and reservoir in the country?

The answer is that we do not have to—or, rather, that we do not have to protect every target to the same level. We know this to be true of crime, because thieves are only attracted to a small proportion of manufactured goods—in general, those that are CRAVED: concealable, removable, available, valuable, enjoyable and disposable (see Chapter 7). This means that shoplifters do not prey on furniture stores, but they do steal from stores that sell cigarettes, cassettes, condoms and fashion jewelry.

It seems likely that the same general point holds true for terrorism. Although the evidence is not yet as clear as for theft (the research has not yet been done), not all targets are of equal value to the terrorists. Terrorists have limited freedom of maneuver, limited resources and limited capabilities. They want to make the best use of what they have by inflicting the greatest possible damage each time they act. This is why they would prefer to plant a bomb in a shopping mall in Washington, DC, than in a general store in Iowa or Arkansas. A bombing in the nation's capital would suggest that terrorists could strike when and where they wanted. Attacking Washington would also receive wider media coverage simply because of the concentration of media resources in the capital city. Similarly, if the terrorists wanted to crash an airliner into a large building (as they did on 9/11), they would prefer to attack one in a busy city with many people than one in an isolated spot occupied by few people, such as a power station or a trash incinerator. This is true because killing people results in much greater levels of fear than merely destroying structures. If terrorists wanted to take out an electricity generating station, they would prefer to attack a nuclear-powered one than one fired by coal, once again because this would cause much more fear. In Chapter 7, we develop these arguments and identify the parameters that guide the terrorist's choice of targets, which enables us to prioritize potential targets for protection. But what if we protect only some targets or protect them differentially? Will not the terrorists simply strike elsewhere?

THE RISK OF DISPLACING THE ATTACKS

One of the main reasons that situational prevention continues to meet with resistance from academics, police and policymakers is the crime displacement hypothesis. This hypothesis states that, faced with reduced opportunities, criminals will simply displace their attention to some other time, place or target; will change their methods; or might even begin to commit some other form of crime. This has always been an overblown argument, based on the assumption of predisposition that "bad will out." This argument ignores the fact that much crime is highly opportunistic and, that which is not, depends heavily on opportunity factors. Certain crimes emerge as a serious problem because offenders discover they are rewarding and easy. Their successful commission encourages more people to try their hand at committing the crimes. When the authorities act to reduce the opportunities for the crimes, the increased risk or effort needed to commit them elsewhere, or in some other way, might not be judged worthwhile. When crime is made less rewarding or more difficult and risky, there is no necessary reason for people to commit or continue committing crime.

It is also becoming increasingly clear from experience that it is possible to entirely eliminate categories of crime without displacement. For example, gradual improvements in technology have now made safe-cracking an extinct art.[5] And guards, bullet proof screens, cameras and cash reduction policies have, with rare exceptions, rendered obsolete bank robberies committed by organized gangs. The most usual form of bank robbery nowadays is committed by a lone offender, often a drug addict, who waits in line and hands the teller a note that demands money and says he has a gun or bomb. The cash haul is usually small, limited to what the teller has in his or her draw, perhaps as little as $50 or $100. Carefully designed research studies have shown that little displacement results from the successful implementation of situational prevention measures. These measures have reduced many different forms of crime, including robbery, burglary, fraud, car thefts and drive-by shootings with few displacement costs. (See Chapter 17 for a more complete list of these crime prevention successes.) In the most recently published review of displacement research, it was concluded that no displacement had occurred in 22 of the 55 studies examined after the introduction of opportunity-reducing measures, and that only limited displacement was found in the remainder.[6] In fact, it has been found that opportunity-reducing measures can have wider benefits than expected because criminals often believe that more targets or a greater area have been protected than is the case.[7]

It could be claimed that this research has questionable relevance to terrorism because most crime is much more opportunistic and less well-planned than terrorist attacks. However, improved security has largely eliminated the bank heists and safe breakings that were committed by organized criminals. We have also seen that when the gas supply was detoxified in Britain there was only limited displacement to other methods of suicide. The fact is that every form of crime and terrorism depends on the opportunities presented by everyday arrangements of society. These arrangements are appraised and acted on by terrorists and organized criminals, just as much as they are by ordinary burglars and robbers. When we reduce these opportunities, terrorists have to reconsider their positions. They can try to find ways around the new barriers and might persist with these attempts even if they fail more often. This may be the case with suicide bombing in Israel, where there is evidence that more attacks have been launched despite a higher failure rate (see Box 3.2). But, it

---

Box 3.2 Successful and Unsuccessful Suicide Bombings in Israel

The Israeli Defense Force chart displays the number of successful suicide bombings in Israel contrasted to "thwarted" suicide bombings. The latter are defined as those thwarted by Israeli authorities and incomplete bombings, such as detonation too early or other "accidental" detonations. Thwarted attacks include targeted killings by Israeli forces of operatives involved in the preparation of the attacks and raids on terrorist hideouts to seize explosives and avert anticipated bombings. This means that the increase in "thwarted attacks" could reflect an increase in proactive measures being taken by the Israelis between October 2000 and April 2004 and that "thwarted attacks" is not a pure measure of the terrorists' motivation. This important caveat aside, this chart holds some useful lessons:

1. Operation Defensive Shield began in March 2002 when the number of successful bombings was at its highest. It consisted of the erection of fences, walls and barriers; the placing of guards at entrances of potentially targeted locations; and the use of intelligence to identify handlers of bombers. Following its introduction, the number of successful bombings declined rapidly from the high of 17 between January and April 2002 to an average rate of roughly 2 per month in 2004. This suggests that the defensive shield was very successful in thwarting the suicide bombings.
2. The shield seems not to have been successful at deterring the bombers from *attempting* to carry out their attacks—while the number of successful attempts declined, the number of thwarted attacks considerably increased (once again this assumes that "thwarted attacks" is not just a measure of a more proactive Israeli policy).

If the number of attempts did in fact increase, the reasons are unclear. It could be that the more the bombers were thwarted, the stronger their commitment became to try even harder. That is, the interventions might have made the bombers even more determined. Or they might have been forced into using more risky approaches that were more vulnerable to being thwarted. Or, those controlling the bombers might have decided that the rewards obtained from the successes (although these were fewer) were great enough to justify the effort of mounting more attacks. In other words, it could be that sending in more bombers imposed relatively few costs on the organizations established to mount the attacks routinely.

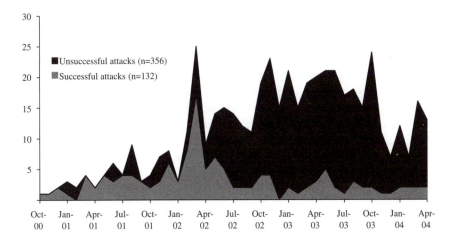

Source: Adapted from Israel Defense Forces (2006).

is not beyond our capacity to make some acts so difficult as to prevent most terrorists from trying to repeat them. As we shall show in the next chapter, this was the case for airliner hijackings, which were almost eliminated from America during the last 15 years of the twentieth century.

Lest this sounds complacent, we should recognize that even if we can successfully introduce opportunity-reducing measures that curb terrorist attacks with little resulting displacement, other terrorists will in time find ways to defeat the initially successful measures (as was tragically demonstrated by the 9/11 airliner hijackings). In the crime prevention literature, this phenomenon is called "adaptation." It differs from displacement, which is the term reserved for the short-term reaction of the offenders whose crimes resulted in the introduction of the preventive measures and who then have to solve the problem of "What do we do now?" Adaptation refers to a longer-term process whereby the offender population, constantly on the lookout for new crime opportunities, subsequently discovers weaknesses in the defensive measures or is presented with some new technology that could defeat the measures, and is then able to begin committing the crimes again. The process of adaptation has been likened to arms races in which rival states continually have to improve their offensive and defensive weapons to match their enemy's developments. If only in this one respect, the metaphor of the war on terrorism is an apt one.[8]

CONCLUSION

In this chapter, we have shown that substantial research in the fields of public health and criminology support our theoretical premise that opportunity plays a major role in terrorism. In the following chapters, we begin to address the practical demands of uncovering the opportunities available for each type of terrorist act and to think through each step of these acts from initial planning to their cataclysmic ends. We show that it is possible to identify and protect the most vulnerable targets. And we show it is possible to cut off the terrorists' access to the tools and weapons that make their task easier.

These are very difficult tasks, however, requiring considerable resources and determination to see them through. We know also that we can never eliminate terrorism entirely. Our enemies are too cunning and determined. Even if we exhaust the energies of one particular group or organization, others will try to defeat our defenses and impose their political demands upon us. However, we can and we must make their attacks more difficult. In doing so, we can reduce their frequency and deadliness and discourage others from copying the attacks.

4

Airliner Hijackings: The Lessons of Reducing Opportunity

In This Chapter

> Passenger and baggage screening introduced in U.S. airports in 1973, together with an agreement reached in the same year between the United States and Cuba to deal harshly with hijackers, sharply reduced hijackings of U.S. airliners.

> Hijackers did not displace their attacks to airliners in other countries—the growth in airline hijackings elsewhere is mainly the result of new conflicts.

> The antihijacking measures did not cause terrorists to switch to sabotage bombing of airliners.

> The 9/11 hijackers exploited loopholes in passenger and baggage screening and in the antihijacking training given to airliner crews.

> These findings suggest relatively little short-term displacement in terrorist attacks, but some longer-term adaptation in the face of defensive measures.

> The possibility of displacement should not deter us from putting defensive measures in place, but we must try to anticipate the forms of longer-term adaptation.

IN CHAPTER 3, WE began to examine the "displacement hypothesis," the idea that in the face of increased protective measures terrorists will simply displace their attacks to different targets or will adopt different approaches. We argued that this hypothesis ignores the powerful role of opportunity in facilitating and encouraging terrorist attacks, and it also ignores the effect of successful attacks in encouraging their repetition. In this chapter, we develop and expand these arguments by examining the effect of preventive measures to reduce airline hijackings. We begin by looking at hijackings since World War II and at the effectiveness of the preventive measures that have been introduced. We conclude that these measures have been highly successful in reducing hijackings and that the changes that have occurred in the pattern of airline hijackings are not the result of displacement, but rather are the result of changes in the pattern of conflicts giving rise to terrorist action. We then examine whether terrorists have switched to sabotage bombings of airliners in the face of the increased difficulties of hijacking and whether they are likely to make more use of surface-to-air missiles. We conclude that the former does not appear to have happened and that the latter is unlikely to occur on a large scale. As shown by the events of 9/11, this does not mean that we can be complacent about airline security. In fact, the authorities have been forced to rethink the premises of airline security now that hijackers have shown they will commit suicide to ensure the success of their attacks.

Before proceeding, we repeat some points about the displacement hypothesis covered in Chapter 3, starting with the fact that research has generally found much less displacement than predicted by the critics of opportunity reduction. We mentioned that the most recently published review of displacement findings concluded that no displacement had occurred in 22 of the 55 studies examined after the introduction of opportunity-reducing measures, and that only limited displacement was found in the remainder. In fact, opportunity-reducing measures can have wider benefits than expected, because criminals often believe that more targets or a greater area have been protected than is the case. At the very least, when displacement does occur, it obliges the terrorist to abandon the sought-after target and go for one that is less favored.

The fact is that every form of crime and terrorism depends on the opportunities presented by the everyday arrangements of society. These are appraised and acted on by terrorists and organized criminals, just as much as they are by ordinary burglars and robbers. When we reduce these opportunities, terrorists have to reappraise their position. They can try to find ways around the new barriers and might persist with these attempts even if they fail more often. This may be the case with suicide bombing in Israel, where there is evidence that more attacks have been launched despite a higher failure rate (see Chapter 3, Box 3.2). But, as we shall show, it is not beyond our capacity to make some acts so difficult as to prevent most terrorists from even trying to repeat them, at least for awhile. This can provide very valuable respite from attacks even if some new terrorist group might in time adapt to and defeat the initially successful measures.[1]

AIRLINER HIJACKINGS

Airliner hijackings placed terrorism on the world stage in the late 1960s, long before the advent of the suicide bomber or the car bomb. Although many hijackings have been committed by the mentally deranged or by criminals for escape or extortion, the first-ever recorded airline hijacking was politically motivated. This occurred in Chile in 1930 when Peruvian revolutionaries seized a Pan American mail plane and directed the pilot to drop propaganda leaflets over Lima. No further hijackings were recorded until the late 1940s/early 1950s when a spate of hijackings occurred from Eastern Europe to the West. Since then, more than 1,000 airline hijackings have been recorded.

It was not until the late 1960s, however, that the epidemic of political hijacking was unleashed, when large numbers of U.S. airliners were hijacked to Cuba (about 70 between 1968 and 1970). Starting at about the same time, but lasting much longer, successive groups of Palestinian and Islamic terrorists hijacked dozens of airliners in several high-profile incidents. These hijackings sometimes stretched over days, if not weeks, and involved events of high drama, such as when a hijacked Air France airliner was successfully stormed by Israeli commandoes at Entebbe in 1973. Since the 1990s, dissidents and terrorist groups in the former Soviet block and in the developing world have regularly hijacked airliners to further their causes, but the overall numbers of hijackings have not approached those of the 1970s. The following list provides a rough chronology of hijackings, showing the main groups involved:[2]

- 1947–52: Eastern European asylum seekers hijack airliners to the West.
- 1958–61: Cubans loyal to the Batista regime divert Cuban airliners to the United States.
- 1968–70: Cubans dissatisfied with life in the United States hijack airliners back to Cuba.
- 1968–72: Criminal hijackings in the United States for escape/extortion.
- 1968–78: Wave of hijackings by the Palestinians and their allies following the Arab defeat in the Six-Day War.
- 1979–82: Shiite Moslem hijackings, mostly of Middle Eastern Airlines planes out of Beirut.
- 1980–83: Reverse flow of Cubans from the United States in the aftermath of mass exodus by Cuban "boat people" in 1980.
- 1983–88: Islamic fundamentalist hijackings of U.S/European airliners.
- 1990–2005: Hijackings in former Soviet-block countries and in the developing world.

It is easy to understand why hijacking has so frequently been employed by terrorists. First and foremost, a hijacking attracts enormous publicity for reasons that have been vividly explained:[3]

> Of the available forms of theatre, few are as captivating as a skyjacking. The very fact that 200–300 potential hostages are packed into the metal shell of a jet airliner hundreds of times a day and sent hurtling through the skies provides terrorists not only with a target whose cosmopolitan innocence imbues it with a "there but for the grace of God" emotionalism, but one that is packed with a supermarket flair, ideal for selling through millions of television sets.

Add to this the fact that many people are terrified of flying, and it is easy to see how a hijacking is a gift to the media and a publicity boost for the terrorists.

A second advantage of hijackings for the terrorists is that airlines symbolically represent the countries to which they belong—Air France, British

Air, Pan American—and attacking an airliner is to strike a blow at the hated country. Furthermore, most of the passengers of a national airline are passengers from that country. In effect, therefore, airliners solve one of the terrorist's conundrums—how to get close enough to strike the enemy, because they bring the enemy to them. (We discuss the importance of this in more detail in Chapters 11 through 14.)

A third advantage for the terrorists relates to the international dimensions of a hijacking. The airliner might belong to one country, be hijacked from a second and be taken to a third—perhaps to a fourth or a fifth. This makes it easy for hijackers to gain concessions by exploiting differences among countries in policies for dealing with hijackers. Some governments try to pursue a "no deals" policy, while others put a premium on saving the lives of their citizens.[4] Exploiting these differences not only helps terrorists get what they want, but also makes it appear that governments have completely lost control of the situation.

Finally, an airliner has many advantages for the physical act of hostage taking, including the following:

- It contains large numbers of hostages who can be released one-by-one, or in small groups, in return for significant concessions. Because many hostages remain, this can be done without diminishing the terrorists' bargaining power.
- It can be parked at an open spot on the airport where it cannot easily be "rushed" by police or the military.
- It offers a means of escape from any airport where the authorities are uncooperative or threatening.
- It considerably simplifies the problem of control because passengers are confined in seats. It is difficult for passengers to rush the hijackers in a group and dangerous to do so because bullets fired by the terrorists or explosives discharged could bring the plane down with the loss of everyone's lives.
- It provides no hiding places for passengers or ways of escape.
- Cabin staff will help in calming distressed passengers and look after those who become ill.
- Because most of its passengers are strangers to one another, it is less likely that they could successfully plot to escape or overwhelm the hijackers.

U.S. EFFORTS TO PREVENT HIJACKINGS

The early political hijackings emanated from Eastern Europe and Cuba and were welcomed by the United States, which treated the hijackers as heroes who had risked their lives to escape from repressive regimes. This very quickly changed, however, at the end of the 1960s with the increase of hijackings from the United States to Cuba. Some of these were committed by criminals escaping from the United States, but most were committed by Cubans who had fled the Castro regime and then became disillusioned with life in America. At first, these returning exiles were treated as political refugees and were welcomed by Cuba, which no doubt fueled the increase, but quite quickly the Cuban authorities realized that few of the hijackers they were receiving were in fact politically motivated, notwithstanding their claims. The Cuban authorities announced that they were no longer willing to receive hijacked airliners, and a period of long, cautious negotiation between the United States and Cuba ensued, which resulted in the signing of a five-year agreement on February 15, 1973. This agreement stipulated that each government would no longer offer safe haven to hijackers and would prosecute them in their courts. In situational prevention terms, this agreement removed the rewards of hijacking airliners between the two countries.

At about the same time as these events were unfolding in the Americas, a more dangerous series of hijackings led by Palestinian terrorist organizations was occurring in the Middle East and elsewhere, some of which involved U.S. airliners. The U.S. authorities were galvanized into action to deal with this broader threat and a raft of new security measures was introduced, including the profiling of suspect passengers, the introduction in 1970 of 1,500 armed sky marshals on domestic and international flights (the program was terminated in 1972, reintroduced in 1980 and substantially strengthened in 2001), the upgrading of airport perimeter security and the training of flight crews in resisting the demands of hijackers. Most important, screening of all embarking passengers and their luggage was introduced on January 5, 1973, by the Federal Aviation Administration (FAA). In situational prevention terms, the screening of all passengers and their luggage greatly increased the difficulties of undertaking a successful hijacking by detecting concealed weapons.

Each year, this screening results in the confiscation of hundreds of weapons and explosives. For example, from 1973 to 1988, more than 38,000 firearms were detected and some 19,000 related arrests were made. The FAA estimated that 118 airline hijackings and related crimes might have been prevented. It is certainly the case that the implementation of these security measures, together with the Cuban-U.S. agreement, was immediately followed by substantial reductions in the hijackings of U.S. airliners. In the five years before the introduction of the measures, 1968 to 1972, there were 135 hijackings of U.S. airliners; in the five years after the measures were introduced, from 1973 to 1977, there were 28 hijackings of U.S airliners, a reduction of nearly 80 percent (See Table 4.1). Of the 135 airliners hijacked in the five years before the measures, 92 were destined to reach Cuba; in the five years after the measures, only 3 of the 28 hijackings were destined for Cuba.

The data in Table 4.1 do not allow us to say which of the two groups of measures—those relating to the U.S.-Cuban pact or those relating to tightened

Table 4.1 Airliner Hijackings and Sabotage Bombings (Attempts and Completed), 1961–2003

Period	Number of Years	Mean Hijackings per Year		Mean Sabotage Bombings per Year Worldwide
		U.S.	Foreign	
1961–67	7	1.6	3.0	1.0
1968	1	20.0	15.0	1.0
1969–70	2	30.5	58.0	4.5
1971–72	2	27.0	33.0	4.5
1973–85	13	9.4	22.7	2.2
1986–89	4	2.8	9.0	2.0
1990–2000	11	0.3	18.5	0.3
2001–3	3	1.3	5.7	0.0
1961–2003	43	6.7	17.9	1.6

Sources: Hijackings: Dugan, LaFree and Piquero (2005). We are indebted to the authors for supplying the data used in their article.
Sabotage bombings: U.S. President's Commission on Aviation Security and Terrorism (1990); U.S. Federal Aviation Administration (1994–96); U.S. Federal Aviation Administration (1996–99); U.S. Department of State (2005).

security at U.S airports—had the greater effect.[5] Because some of the U.S. airliners hijacked after 1973 were boarded overseas, where security was not always as tight as in the United States, the figures in Table 4.1 might even understate the value of the measures taken in 1973. Even so, it is clear that these have been very successful and that they have brought about a large and sustained reduction in hijackings, which has lasted for more than 30 years despite very large increases in the numbers of U.S. airline flights during that time.[6]

DID THE U.S. MEASURES RESULT IN DISPLACEMENT?

Next, we examine whether any displacement occurred following the successful introduction of measures to curb the hijacking of U.S. airliners. First, is there any evidence that that the hijackings were displaced to some other part of the world? According to Table 4.1, the answer is no, because there was no immediate increase in the number of hijackings in the rest of the world—in fact, the reverse is the case: There was a decline worldwide in hijackings after 1973, which may have resulted from the fact that other countries adopted many of the same security measures as those in the United States. Over the long term, the blips in this general pattern reflect mostly the waxing and waning of new terrorist groups, not any switching of targets in response to increased security.

Table 4.1 also allows us to examine the validity of another claim—that the success of the antihijacking measures has resulted in terrorists resorting instead to sabotage bombings of airliners.[7] Again, it is clear that this did not happen. Sabotage bombings of airliners have rarely been undertaken by terrorists and were no more used after the introduction of the 1973 antihijacking measure than before. This is not surprising because hijackings and bombings serve quite different purposes—the former is used to gain sympathy for the terrorists' cause and to extract concessions from the enemy, the latter is used principally to murder and destroy. Sabotage bombings are much more likely than hijackings to produce revulsion and a loss of support for the terrorists, which may help to explain why responsibility for a sabotage bombing has only rarely been claimed by a terrorist group.[8]

Some more detailed analyses of the hijacking data summarized in Table 4.1 have been undertaken using econometric and other statistical techniques. Unsurprisingly, these analyses generally have concluded that the antihijacking measures were effective.[9] However, they have also explored some other questions that seem misconceived or cannot be answered by the analytic methods employed, and the sometimes conflicting answers have served to obscure the achievements of the antihijacking measures. Following are the misconceived or unanswerable questions that have been explored:

- Did the successful antihijacking measures result in terrorists switching their attention from the airlines to some other kinds of targets, somewhere else in the world, that require different forms of attack?
- Which of the panoply of antihijacking measures that have been employed (metal detectors, baggage screening, Cuban-U.S. treaty, sky marshals, profiling, enactment of severe penalties for terrorism, United Nations (UN) resolutions, military retaliatory strikes, and so on) were responsible for the greatest effects? How many hijackings did each of the measures prevent?
- Did the antihijacking measures have a greater effect on "criminal" hijackings than on more deeply motivated "terrorist" hijackings?

None of the researchers exploring the first question seem to have been familiar with the research on displacement (see Chapter 3). Knowledge of this literature would have helped them to avoid the doubtful assumptions that terrorists see targets and methods of attack as interchangeable. In fact, the nature of the attack and the target chosen cannot be separated from the terrorists' objectives (to extort concessions, to draw attention to their cause, to destroy the enemy, and so on) and, depending on their objectives, some forms of attack could be quite counterproductive for the terrorists (we have already given the example of sabotage bombings of airliners). Furthermore, it cannot be assumed that terrorist groups are equally competent or knowledgeable about all forms of attack or that they have ready access to the tools or weapons needed for the different acts. For example, it is not as easy as it sounds to switch from hijacking airliners to taking over embassies. Embassies are often protected by soldiers and other armed professionals and, unlike airliners, they cannot be whisked away to another country when the authorities refuse to cooperate.

A further questionable assumption is that terrorist groups are somehow closely connected worldwide (in the ways that the Mafia is said to be)—that they are watching each other's successes and failures and that they are learning from each other. There are likely to be some copycat attacks and, in the long run, terrorists probably do learn from each other's experience (e.g., the suicide tactics invented by the Tamil Tigers have spread to other parts of the world). What mostly determines their actions, however, is not what other groups are doing or not doing—it is what they themselves can do and want to do, here and now. For example, the fact that the opportunities for airliner hijackings were eliminated for Middle Eastern terrorists probably had little impact on the activities of the IRA in Belfast, which had never tried to hijack a plane and who continued unabated with their bombings and shootings.

Apart from its misconceptions, we doubt that the first question could be satisfactorily answered with the data available. The recording of airliner hijackings may be reliable over time because they are such highly visible events, but this is not the case for the many other kinds of terrorist attack, including bombings and shootings (especially those in developing countries), which are recorded with far less consistency and regularity. The problem is complicated by the relatively small numbers of hijackings compared with the much larger number of other terrorist events. This makes it very difficult to detect resultant increases in other kinds of terrorism when airliner hijackings were reduced. A further problem is that the statistical methods employed are all based on correlation. Inferring a causal connection on the basis of a correlation between a decline in one kind of attack and the rise of another kind somewhere else in the world is hazardous, because the latter might have increased for some quite unrelated reason, such as the forming of a new terrorist group. The only exception to this is when the correlations are extremely strong (which they were not in any of the studies we are considering) and a clear and direct link can be established between cause and effect. As we have argued, the displacement hypothesis does not meet this criterion, because it is disputed on theoretical grounds and has been given only weak support in empirical studies.

The second question assumes that the various antihijacking measures are of potentially equal value, but there are strong theoretical grounds for doubting this assumption. The idea that they would be deterred by UN resolutions seems particularly unrealistic, but the more credible idea that offenders (and terrorists) would respond to increases in mandated punishments is given little support by decades of criminological research. On the other hand, as documented throughout this book, offenders do pay careful attention to increased risks of being caught and can be put off crime when it is made more difficult to commit (which passenger and baggage screening accomplishes). Furthermore, we doubt that the data would allow the effect of any particular measure to be isolated. The measures were introduced at more or less the same time, and the hijacking incidents are too few in number and too clustered in time to permit the effect of each measure to be separately determined. The attempt to do this also ignores the possibility that the effect of each measure is reinforced by the existence of the others so that their combined effect is greater than the sum of their individual effects—a conclusion frequently reached in situational crime prevention projects.

As for the third question, it is sometimes difficult to know the motivation of the hijackers, as Fidel Castro discovered; many of those claiming political motives for hijacking an airliner to his country seem to have been mentally disturbed or acting for their own criminal reasons. In any case, as we explained in Chapter 1, we reject any fundamental distinction between terrorists and criminals, especially in the strength of their motives. Both groups are rational actors in that they want to succeed and believe they have a good chance of doing so. Properly conceived and properly implemented passenger and baggage screening measures should cause both groups equally to reevaluate their chances of success.

HAVE TERRORISTS ADAPTED IN OTHER WAYS?

As explained above, displacement refers to an immediate change in the terrorists' behavior designed to circumvent new preventive measures. We have seen that there is little evidence of any such displacement after 1973 when the United States implemented measures to prevent hijacking of its airliners, and the very real achievements of these measures should not be overlooked. However, nothing lasts forever, and there is every reason to think that ways to defeat these successful measures might eventually be discovered—indeed, were discovered by the 9/11 hijackers. They correctly gambled on getting box cutters through the security screening—a feat that publicly exposed the inadequate screening at U.S. airports. Many experts complained about the inadequacy of this screening process, which had fallen well below that at airports in Europe. The U.S. authorities have now tightened up the security procedures at considerable cost. No doubt, they will be forced to tighten them further in the face of "complacency brought on by the monotony of the work and where the chance of successfully identifying a terrorist is perhaps more remote than finding a pearl in a restaurant oyster."[10] Even more important, U.S. authorities have had to rethink their whole approach to preventing hijacking since the 9/11 hijackers rewrote the book. The 9/11 terrorists were not seeking concessions, and they had no plans to escape. Nor did they plan to force the pilots to follow their bidding. Instead, they took over and flew the airliners themselves. They used them as weapons to destroy huge buildings and kill thousands of people, killing themselves in the process. In response to this new situation, the authorities have hired many more sky marshals, permitted pilots to carry guns, reinforced cockpit doors, forbidden passengers to move about the aircraft within 20 minutes of takeoff or landing, begun to scrutinize applications for flight training schools and undertaken many other new measures. These far-reaching situational interventions make it unlikely that terrorists could again take over airliners in the United States. Even if they did, knowing what was coming, the passengers and crew would likely fight back (as they did in the fourth airliner hijacked on 9/11) and the authorities might try to shoot down the plane.

So, although little short-term displacement followed the introduction of improved security, over the long term, terrorists adapted their approach to exploit weaknesses in the antihijacking measures. This is entirely to be expected and the authorities moved quickly to counter the new threat once it became a reality. But could they have anticipated the threat and preempted it? The answer is that, in view of the rise of suicide bombings in Palestine, authorities should have anticipated it. It was clear that many of the new generation of terrorists embark on their actions with the intent to commit suicide. However, it is less easy to say whether having anticipated the threat the authorities could have thought through the ways in which such an attack could be mounted, and whether they could have generated sufficient political will to institute sweeping new security measures in the face of a hypothetical attack. Box 4.1, which reviews the scope for dealing with the threat of terrorist attacks on airliners with shoulder-fired missiles, deals with these issues in more depth.

CONCLUSION

In response to a wave of airliner hijackings to Cuba from the United States, the two countries signed an antihijacking pact early in 1973. At the same time, because of the rise of airline hijackings in the Middle East, the United States also introduced the compulsory security screening of all passengers and their baggage. These measures removed the rewards and increased the difficulty and risks of hijacking. The data show that the measures were highly effective in reducing hijackings of U.S. airliners, and that the terrorists did not react by hijacking airliners from other countries or by turning to sabotage bombings instead. In retrospect, the reasons are fairly obvious. Why would dissatisfied Cuban nationals in the United States try to hijack airliners to some other destination? What would they have to gain by bombing U.S. airliners? Doing so would not enable them to escape to Cuba to a hero's welcome. And why would other terrorist groups turn from hijacking to sabotage, which

Box 4.1 The Potential Threat of Surface-to-Air Missiles

There is no question that U.S. airliners could be brought down by shoulder-fired missiles launched by terrorists. An estimated 700,000 of these missiles, known as MANPADS (man-portable air defense systems) have been produced worldwide since the 1970s. They are not difficult to purchase on the black market and are relatively inexpensive—some estimates put the price as low as a few hundred dollars for the older missiles. Many are now in the hands of terrorist groups hostile to the United States, such as Al Qaeda, the Taliban, Hezbollah, FARC, and insurgents in Iraq. Although these missiles have not so far been used against U.S airliners, they have been used by terrorists in various parts of the world to bring down more than 20 civil aircraft, including some airliners. They could certainly be used in single attacks against U.S. airliners that visit countries where terrorists operate. Conceivably, an organization such as Al Qaeda could also mount a coordinated attack within the United States using teams equipped with these missiles. Because of their small size and weight (typically less than 40 pounds and 6 feet), the missiles could easily be smuggled into the country inside one of the 20,000 shipping containers that are unloaded without being inspected at U.S. ports every day.

So, there is undoubtedly a danger of MANPAD missiles being launched against U.S. airliners. There are also many different preventive measures that could be introduced. These include onboard devices to divert or destroy attacking missiles; additional aircraft safety measures such as redundant flying controls and strengthened fuel tanks to resist fire or explosion; enabling and disabling locks for future missiles like those used for nuclear devices; international arms dealing agreements to prevent terrorists laying their hands on more of these missiles; international agreements to prevent the use of civilian aircraft to ferry troops into theatres of conflict; and security enhancements in the vicinity of airports and reduced takeoff and landing patterns.

However, none of these measures is fool-proof and many are also very costly; According to Rand, it would cost $11 billion to equip the fleet of 6,800 U.S. airliners with laser jammers and considerably more to maintain and support the jammers. This greatly reduces their chances of being implemented, particularly because there are so many unanswered questions regarding the threat posed by missiles. While they could undoubtedly be used to attack our airliners, they have not yet been used against the United States. Is this because there are, in fact, few real opportunities to use them against U.S. airliners overseas? And how likely is it that Al Qaeda would choose to bring down airliners in a concerted attack in the United States, demanding very considerable resources and organization, when with much less effort and risk, it could mount a frightening campaign of dirty bomb attacks against major U.S. cities? Imponderables such as these perhaps make it unlikely that any thorough attempt will be made to prevent the use of MANPADS against U.S. airliners, although Congress has designated $120 million to support a research and development program to test missile countermeasures for airliners. Everything would change, however, if a U.S. airliner were brought down by a missile.

Sources: Bolkom, Feikert and Elias (2005); Chow et al. (2005).

serves different objectives and which would require them to learn new skills, obtain new weapons and completely change their planning? Even if they wanted to, they might not have the financial or intellectual resources to reinvent themselves in these ways. In any case, not every terrorist is as determined as the 1970s hijacker, Leila Khalid, who underwent plastic surgery to prevent her recognition while attempting further crimes. Some of the thwarted hijackers might try to commit other forms of terrorism against new targets, but others might decide to pursue political rather than violent action. There is only limited truth in the saying, "once a criminal, always a criminal," and the same is true of the terrorist.

While we believe that the dangers of displacement are exaggerated, and that it is possible to bring about substantial reductions in terrorism at particular times and places, we are less sanguine about these reductions lasting forever. So, even when we are successful, we must remember two things: (1) security improvements wear out, especially those requiring vigilance, and (2) new groups of terrorists, with new skills and new energy, backed by new technology, can succeed in finding loopholes in our defenses and can successfully attack again. This does not mean we should give up the attempt to protect ourselves, but it does mean we must continually review our vulnerabilities to attack and continually renew our defenses (see also Figure 15.3). The lesson of 9/11 is that we can do this fast and effectively when we stare catastrophe in the face; it seems much harder for us to act decisively when death and damage are on a smaller scale. Complacency allows routine terrorism to get a hold and, over time, to inflict considerable damage on society.

5

Suicide Bombings, Step by Step

In This Chapter

> Suicide terrorism has a higher kill ratio than other kinds of terrorism, although its efficiency compared with other types of attack is questionable.
> Suicide bombing in Israel is typical of routine terrorism, which sets it apart from single incidents.
> In Israel, civilians and the places they frequent are the primary targets.
> Terrorist groups display distinct operational patterns in their attempts to routinize suicide bombing attacks.
> Step-by-step analysis of suicide bombings reveals important points of intervention and avenues for preventive action.
> Much more detailed information is needed to conduct a realistic analysis of how suicide bombing groups carry out their tasks.

ALTHOUGH USEFUL FOR everyday communication, "crime" and "terrorism" are words that can seriously confuse the analysis of preventive options. This is because both are abstractions covering a wide variety of different phenomena, each of which requires separate analysis if realistic preventive options are to be identified. Thus, drug trafficking, juvenile graffiti, car thefts and corporate frauds are all proscribed by law and are correctly referred to as "crime," but they have little else in common. They vary greatly in their seriousness and the punishments they attract. Each is committed by a different group of offenders, using different methods and with different motives (except to benefit themselves in some way). To talk about "preventing crime" in the abstract, leads one to ignore these differences and to focus instead on what they have in common, such as the offenders' lack of respect for the law or apparent imperviousness to the threat of punishment. In turn, this leads to preventive policies focused on offenders—those that attempt to teach them to be more law-abiding or to have more fear of detection. If instead, one talks more specifically about preventing car theft, for example, one is quickly forced to consider, in addition, the situational circumstances that facilitate car thefts, such as poorly secured vehicles or poorly lit streets. And if one breaks down car theft further into specific categories—juvenile joyriding, thefts of parts, theft for own use, theft for export and so on—then the preventive options become more highly differentiated.

This same is true of "preventing terrorism," because this general formulation glosses over critical differences among the variety of acts classified as terrorism and leads one to focus on the actors not the actions. This is why current "preventive" efforts are overwhelmingly focused on means of disrupting terrorist groups and "taking out" the most dangerous individuals. It is only when the preventive focus shifts to specific forms of terrorism (truck bombings of embassies, missile attacks on airliners, hostage taking of journalists) that the need for a situational approach becomes apparent. In fact, it is usually necessary to break down these categories of attack even further, because the modus operandi might vary quite significantly depending on the location, the terrorist groups' expertise, available weapons and so on. That is why in this chapter, in which we try to show how modus operandi can be unraveled using a situational approach, we choose a particular kind of suicide bombing for analysis—the kind in which a suicide bomber walks or runs without the aid of a vehicle, to place himself or herself in the right spot to detonate the bomb. We become even more specific by focusing our analysis on the suicide bombers in Israel, because locality plays an important part in the design and operation of a terrorist act. Indeed, we show in Chapter 15 that suicide bombings in Israel differ in many details from those undertaken in London in 2005 and that these details have important implications for prevention.

CHARACTERISTICS OF SUICIDE TERRORISM

Several kinds of modern terrorism use suicide as a method of attack, that is, the attacker is willing to give up his or her life to achieve a particular goal.[1] Apart from the well-known kamikaze attacks of World War II,[2] the most common suicide attacks of the twentieth century have been those in which the attackers ambushed the police or military knowing that their chances of survival were next to zero, having made no plans for escape. There have been others in which specific assassinations were carried out by individuals who knew that they could not escape, such as the assassinations of Indira Ghandi and Mahatma Gandhi. (Rajav Gandhi was later assassinated by a suicide bomber of the Tamil Tigers, the group that perfected the technique.[3]) There are other suicide missions, such as the bombing of the U.S. marine barracks in Beirut on October 23, 1983, during which a truck loaded with explosives was driven into the compound with no attempt by the driver to escape. This method of suicide attack using vehicles is now widely employed in Iraq.

All variations of suicide terrorism share certain characteristics that reveal the calculated, rational nature of these attacks. These are listed below:

Invincible superiority of the suicide attacker. The suicide terrorist attacks what the enemy loves most: life. The suicide attackers, by their very actions, show the "nobility" of their cause, treating their own lives as insignificant by comparison. They also demonstrate that the enemy's cause is less noble (inasmuch as the enemy is not prepared to die for it in the same way). Terrorist suicide attackers, therefore, expose the core weakness of the enemy. They become true monsters and a nightmare that amplifies the coercive effects of their terrorism. This gives them a tremendous psychological advantage.[4]

Suicide terrorism as an efficient means of warfare. In terms of the ratio of casualties of attacker to foe, suicide terrorism is far better than conducting any kind of battle. As the right hand man to Bin Laden, Ayman al-Zawahiri has said, "the method of martyrdom operations [is] the most successful way of inflicting damage against the opponent and least costly to the mujahideen in terms of casualties."[5] This claim is supported by Figure 5.1, which displays the deaths per incident for the most common types of terrorist attacks. Suicide bombing counts among the highest for deaths per incident, and it is likely that suicide also plays a part in other high kill ratio terrorist acts shown in Figure 5.1, particularly ram bombings, car bombings and ambushes.[6] However, if we take a broader measure of efficiency the argument that suicide bombing is more efficient is not so clear. Hostage taking and kidnapping have been shown to be much more successful in extracting concessions from the enemy. In one study, it was found that hostage taking offered a 79 percent chance that all members of the terrorist team would escape punishment or death, and in 40 percent of cases terrorists obtained concessions from the enemy, including the release of other terrorists.[7] The continued use of suicide terrorism demands a constant supply of suicide bombers and handlers. It is an act that also results in traces of the bomber being left behind. With continued progress in the technology of identification, the identities and other

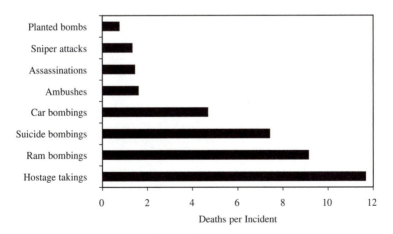

Figure 5.1 Deaths per Incident by Type of Attack
Source: Rand–National Memorial Institute for the Prevention of Terrorism.
Note: There are some uncommon, single terrorist acts that have a very high kill ratio, such as the 9/11 attack, which used suicide as a delivery mechanism.

information about suicide bombers are becoming easier to discover, as is evident from both the 9/11 and the 2005 London Underground attacks.

Martyrdom as propagating terrorism. Unlike soldiers in battle, suicide terrorists do not risk their lives; rather they willingly (it seems) give up their lives looking forward to a violent conflagration.[8] Their portrayal as martyrs therefore serves to encourage others to follow—others being not only new recruits who offer themselves up for certain death, but also terrorist groups that recognize its undeniable success as a recruiting technique. Some secular terrorist groups have copied the technique for its propaganda advantages.[9]

Nothing succeeds like success. While many deny it, there is good evidence to show that suicide terrorism works in that it extracts concessions from the enemy. It is well documented that the Palestine Liberation Organization (PLO) copied the suicide terrorism approach when it saw how successful Hamas was in extracting concessions from Israel. Perhaps the most commonly cited example of the effectiveness of suicide terrorism is the American withdrawal from Lebanon after the suicide attacks of Hezbollah on October 23, 1983.[10] The use of this technique has increased ever since, both in incidence and in lethality. And because these acts are copied by many different and sometimes competing groups, they give the impression of some kind of massively orchestrated, monolithic organization with a common focus and mission. The enemy, therefore, seems much bigger and better coordinated than it is.

Democracies are "soft targets." A comprehensive study of suicide terrorist attacks from 1980 through 2002 revealed that all suicide terror campaigns had been directed against democracies.[11] The reasons for this are perhaps obvious: (1) government policy is at the mercy of the public that traditionally has a low tolerance for casualties in war and especially for terrorism in which civilians are popularly viewed as the main targets; (2) there are legal constraints on the amount and kind of violence that democratic governments can use against terrorists; and (3) there is a free and open press that helps publicize the attacks and spread the propaganda and fear.

Suicide bombings are well-orchestrated political campaigns. The same study found that the overwhelming majority of suicide bombers were not motivated by religious fundamentalism but by patriotism; the bombers were looking to liberate their countries from what they perceived to be occupying forces. However, this motivation was facilitated by the presence of clear religious differences between the occupying force and the terrorists' perceived constituency.[12] These campaigns may be sustained and become routine, as we will describe below, depending on the location of the targets in respect to the operational base of the terrorist organization (see Part III).

Suicide terrorism depends on community support. More than any other kind of terrorism, suicide terrorism depends on the support of the local community in which its operations are based for its success. Many opinion surveys have demonstrated the almost universal support of local populations for the activities of suicide terrorism throughout the Middle East, where much of the suicide terrorism is undertaken.[13] There are three reasons for this: (1) the population's admiration of suicide bombers is needed to establish martyrdom as a convincing reason for violence against civilians; (2) the organizers depend on "walk-ins" and other volunteers from the local community to become suicide bombers or fulfill other roles necessary to orchestrate suicide attacks; and (3) almost total community support is necessary to avoid infiltration or detection by the government forces.

SUICIDE BOMBERS IN ISRAEL AND PALESTINE

When we begin to analyze a complete sequence of acts from beginning to end, we find that the suicide bomber who actually kills is more like the weapon of the *real* terrorist, the "handler" who prepares the bomber for the mission and sends him on his way. *The Economist* has succinctly described this arrangement:

> Such operations are rarely, if ever, the work of lone lunatics. Hamas, PIJ and the other Palestinian groups who practise suicide terrorism recruit, indoctrinate and train their bombers. They write the texts for the video testaments filmed shortly before each self-immolation (making them unreliable records of the true motives of the "martyr"), which the bombers themselves watch to redouble their resolve. They take the photographs that will later appear on propaganda posters. Then they deliver their foot-soldiers to pre-identified targets.[14]

So, when we speak about a "suicide bombing" we must begin to analyze all the actors at every stage of the process of carrying out this act. Other special features of suicide bombing in Israel are:

Routine suicide bombing. In Israel, suicide bombings of a similar kind are repeated often enough that they have become routine, probably because they have been so successful, judging by the slaughter accomplished (although the Israel government claims to actually thwart most of them—see Box 3.2).[15] However, it is also likely that special conditions are needed to be able to turn a specific type of suicide bombing into one that is routine. The frequency of bombings provides us with important clues about how the bombers are operating. For example, different groups manage to keep up their bombings on a more consistent basis than others. We see from Figure 5.3 that most patterns of bombings over time are sporadic, occurring in clusters, followed by a period of no bombings, followed by another cluster of bombings. This suggests that it is difficult to orchestrate bombings on a routine basis and that there may be economies of scale in doing several in a short time span, then taking the time to gather resources to do it again.[16] It is also possible that they occur in concordance with government responses.[17]

Simultaneous bombings. For heightened effects of fear and media attention, two or more bombings may be carried out simultaneously, giving the
impression of an invincible foe. Two or more bombings also increase the
chances of an overall successful mission, in case one of the bombers fails.
Simultaneous bombings also make it much harder for emergency response
teams to cope with the damage and injury, thus magnifying the effects of the
attacks.

People as the targets. The majority of targets in Israel are civilian,
although this varies according to the terrorist group, as Table 5.1 shows, and
probably according to various stages in the campaigns, which are executed in
reaction to the response of the Israeli defense forces and changes in Israeli
government policies.[18] In fact, Islamic Jihad and Hamas account for almost
all deaths of military and police, as seen in Figure 5.2, and more than half of
all victims of Islamic Jihad terrorists were military and police.

Structures and places as targets of suicide bombings. As noted above,
civilians are the main targets of suicide bombings in Israel. We should therefore expect that the main locations and physical places and structures where
bombings occur will be those where people are concentrated in a relatively
small area. We can see from Table 5.2 that this is well supported from our
own database of incidents for the period 2000–03.[19] Places of leisure and
transportation are by far the most popular targets for terrorists. This is of significant interest, because places of worship are not targeted. This suggests that
it is the qualities of the targets, as outlined in Chapter 7, that dominate terrorist planning and not the supposed religious extremism of the group.[20] The
different terrorist groups also differ in terms of the general geographic locations in which they work.

These data can be used only as a rough guide. Determining exactly which
target was intended by the suicide bombers is difficult, because the bombers

**Table 5.1 Suicide Attacks and Deaths by Terrorist Group, Israel, October
2000–August 2002**

	Hamas	Al-Aqsa	Islamic Jihad	PFLP	Jointly/ Unclaimed	Total
Number of attacks	22	16	12	3	7	60
Total deaths	168	38	31	3	22	262
Civillian deaths	153	36	12	3	22	226
Police/military deaths	15	2	19	0	0	36
Mean deaths per attack	7.6	2.4	2.6	1.0	3.1	4.4

Source: Adapted from Stork (2002, Appendix 2).
Note: PFLP = Popular Front for the Liberation of Palestine.

are, for all intents and purposes, "smart bombs." If they see a barrier to their target, they can turn to another target (if they have been well trained). In addition, a bombing may in fact reach two different kinds of physical targets at once. For example, in one incident a bomber detonated at the entrance to a busy market where there was a bus stop. The explosion killed many people because there were crowds exiting the market and waiting for the bus. So there were three targets: a crowd of people and the collateral targets of transportation and business. As for police and military victims, according to the Human Rights Watch database, most were not especially targeted, but were killed because they were in a crowded place with many other civilians (five incidents). In four other incidents, police and military personnel were killed at checkpoints or when a suicide bomber was stopped for identification (two incidents).

Ideological motivation of terrorist groups. The four terrorist groups identified in Figures 5.2 and 5.3 have well-known ideologies, are politically

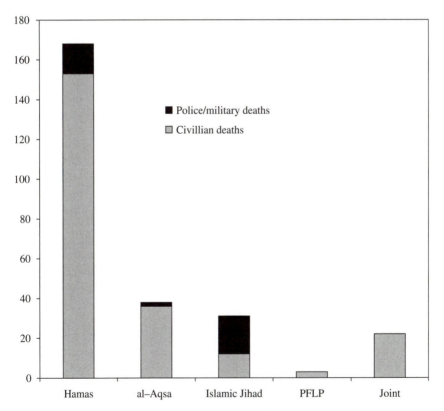

Figure 5.2 Civilian and Police/Military Killings by Terrorist Group, Israel, September 2000–August 2002
Source: Adapted from Stork (2002, Appendix 2).

Table 5.2 Populated Places as Targets, Israel Suicide Bombings, 2000–2003

Place	Bombings
Public spaces	
Places of worship	0
Institutions/Facilities	1
Infrastructure	1
Major public events	1
Pedestrian walkways, streets	16
Buses, bus stops	31
Cafes, bars, markets	33
Restricted spaces	
Infrastructure	0
Private residences	1
Security targets	5

Source: Authors' database of newspaper reports (see note 15).

driven and primarily are driven by religious differences rather than religious extremism,[21] Can we infer their ideological motivation from their choice of targets? It seems not, according to the data in Table 5.2, which indicates that no attacks were made against religious targets.[22] Furthermore, as noted above, with the exception of the Islamic Jihad, the groups did not primarily attack military targets, although the exact number of acts directed toward military targets is difficult to ascertain, because a number of acts seemed directed at civilians (a busload of people, for example) where members of the military also happened to be located. The differences in military and police targeting suggest not so much a difference in ideological motivation of the groups but rather an operational difference. Marighella's *Minimanual of the Urban Guerrilla*[23] advocated such a strategy of targeting specific representatives of military and government, which many terrorist groups have followed, including the IRA.

Characteristics of suicide bombers. With one exception of a 44-year-old father of eight who carried out a hotel bombing in December 2001, the age range for suicide bombers reported in the Human Rights Watch database was from 16 to 28, with the majority being 17 or 18 years old. The Merari database of suicide bombers during 1993–2004 reports that the mean age of the suicide bombers was 22.[24] Of the 183 Palestinian suicides in Merari's database, only 9 were women[25] and 91 percent were unmarried, reportedly because their handlers generally refuse married candidates. According to descriptions of the bombings, bombers typically dressed to fit in with the civilians they planned to blow up: one had "spiked" his hair and dyed it blond, another dressed as a member of the Israel Defense Forces (IDF), another wore a skull cap and so on. The young age of bombers fulfills two significant criteria: (1) they are more easily convinced that their martyrdom is for a higher cause, and (2) they more easily fit in with the civilian groups targeted, especially those in coffee houses and bars. The Chicago Project database also concludes that the suicide attackers were generally better educated than their peers.[26] What is clear from most research is that few, if any, could be characterized as mentally disturbed extremists or desperately poor. Their personality and lifestyle profiles are generally unexceptional.[27]

OPERATIONAL DIFFERENCES OF SUICIDE TERRORIST GROUPS

The process of training and preparing suicide bombers has been described by Merari as moving through three stages:[28]

1. Indoctrination. This stage may take anywhere from days to months, although when there is a demand for more bombings, the period of indoctrination may be shortened.

2. Group commitment. This is perhaps the most important stage, in which groups of young suicide attackers are formed into cells and make a mutual contract to each other to carry out the mission no matter what. It becomes a duty. This process has been used before, especially with the Japanese Kamakazi pilots of World War II.

3. Personal commitment. This commitment is achieved by the videotape made of the suicide attacker who expresses intention to carry out the mission. While this is used as propaganda by release to the media after the mission is completed, it also reinforces the candidate's personal commitment.

These stages of training and preparation take time and personnel, and thus organization. Figure 5.3 reveals that none of the groups were able to maintain a continuous barrage of attacks. Rather, the pattern of attacks is for a concentration of attacks within a particular time, reaching a peak and then suddenly dropping off. We conclude from this that operational needs dictated the frequency of attacks.[29] As we will see below in the step-by-step analysis of how terrorists carry out a suicide bombing, they need considerable logistical and other support to sustain routine attacks. The method of training, especially the stage of group commitment, probably results in bombings in clusters, coinciding with the graduation of each "class" of martyrs.

The ability of the groups to sustain frequent bombings is clearly different, with Hamas easily the most prolific and probably the most effective.[30] It is likely that the differences among the groups are related directly to operational factors, such as skill and experience of the handlers, readiness of the suicide bombers themselves, supply of willing martyrs and many more factors outlined in the step-by-step analysis that follows.

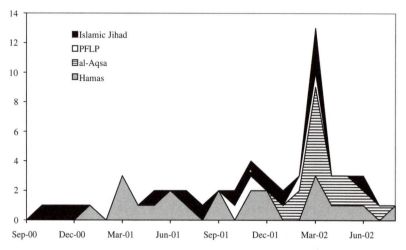

Figure 5.3 Suicide Bomb Attacks by Terrorist Group, Israel, September 2000–August 2002

Source: Adapted from Stork (2002, Appendix 2).
Note: PFLP = Popular Front for the Liberation of Palestine.

SUICIDE BOMBING, STEP BY STEP

Because the majority of suicide bombings in Israel are routine, that is, are repeated frequently against different targets, we will outline the necessary conditions for them to occur and the steps that must be taken to execute these attacks. There are two significant actors whose participation in the process of suicide bombing is essential for it to become a routine: the availability of a bomber and the presence of a handler, that is, the individual who trains the bombers and sends them on their way. We use the term "handler" to refer to one individual, although several people usually are involved in the preparation of the bomber, depending on the stage of preparation (indoctrination, group commitment or personal commitment), and different handlers are involved at different times. Other personnel must also be involved, such as those providing intelligence, those in charge of communications and those who select or find potential bombers. For our purposes in this exercise, we will simplify things by assuming that the two most immediate people involved in a suicide bombing are the handler and the bomber (the "shahid").[31]

For a suicide bomber to successfully complete the task, he or she must have the following:

- Explosives that can be concealed inside clothing
- Means of detonating the bomb
- Transportation: a means to get to the target, unless on foot

- A cell phone or means of communication with handler
- Knowledge of how to get to the target (map or memorized instructions)
- Knowledge of the target, preferably a previous visit, so he or she can dress accordingly and gain entry should that be needed
- Knowledge of an alternative target in case thwarted
- Dedication to the task

A handler must have the following:

- Safe house for operations
- Community support to maintain secrecy of preparations
- Supply of young zealots and organizational network for identifying them
- Skilled personnel to train and select bombers
- Reconnaissance capability: maps, intelligence for target selection, route to target
- Skilled personnel to write testimonials and shoot and edit videos
- Technology: Video cameras, computers to video edit last statement and so on
- Supply chain and warehouse for explosives and bomber suits

Following the work of Cornish and others,[32] we describe how a routine suicide bombing might be carried out, step by step, from beginning to end, and also include the resources and tools required to accomplish the act (see Table 5.3). We hasten to add that this must be speculative, because we simply do not have enough direct information about how suicide bombers and their handlers conduct their acts, although we have drawn on a small number of research projects that have included interviews with failed bombers, handlers and community supporters in Palestine.[33] Thus, even if our analysis is not as detailed as we would like, this exercise shows how points of intervention may be identified and possible responses made to thwart the attackers or to reduce the amount of harm. We have indicated reports or research that have referred to some of the interventions we identify, although we repeat that there is little, if any, definitive research that demonstrates whether these interventions have worked.[34] We have included all suggested forms of intervention, even though, from our point of view, some are not practical solutions that would give immediate results (e.g., trying to change community attitudes).

As noted earlier, we have had to guess at many of the choices that the terrorists must make in planning and succeeding in their task. But these guesses are reasoned ones, based on the assumption that the terrorists must plan their work and make logical choices if they are to be successful. We have only indicated possible interventions at this point. In later chapters (particularly Chapters 6 and 15), we will examine the techniques of intervention that can be applied to a variety of different kinds of terrorism. At this point, we seek only to demonstrate the preventive value of breaking down terrorist

Table 5.3 Steps in Suicide Bombing: Actions, Resources, Facilitating Conditions and Interventions

Steps	Action needed	Resources needed	Facilitating conditions[a]	Points of intervention
		Preparation		
1. Find safe house(s) for operations	• Identify friendly locality for safe house. • Arrange its use.	• House for HQ. • Warehouse for storing bombing apparatus (explosives, suits, etc.).	• Community collusion to support safe houses, provide information on housing market, who to ask, etc.	• Install surveillance to identify safe houses. • Identify friendly locations by interviewing unsuccessful bombers. • Reduce community support by exploiting community ambivalence about suicide bombing.[b]
2. Select target or targets	• Find attractive targets according to EVILDONE that fit mission Chapter 7). • Select targets who match bomber in appearance (e.g., young, mostly male). • Choose appropriate route to target. • Visit target to assess accessibility, etc.	• Maps and reconnaissance of target areas.	• Existence of attractive targets, especially those undefended. • Intelligence sources from target location and proposed route to target.	• Frequently change design of entrances at coffee houses—move doors, etc. • Construct barriers or walls.[c] • Install surveillance CCTV at key points. • Train guards at entrance to recognize bombers.

3. Select bomber candidates	• Use network to select candidate, maintaining secrecy. • Match candidate to target (male/female, youthful, etc.). • Begin indoctrination of bombers.	• Supply of young zealots. • Organizational network to secretly identify candidate. • Handlers to do indoctrination.	• Donations of money to support organization. • Payments to parents of bomber.[d] • Trusted volunteers to help in indoctrination.	• Trace payments and cut off money supply both to handlers and to families of suicides.[e] • Close down schools that educate young zealots; dismantle recruiting organizations.[f] • Locate handlers through interviews with failed bombers and their families.[g]
4. Specify exact location for detonation	• Choose location (e.g., "at bus stop X in front of busy market Y"). • Choose alternate location in case thwarted.	• Detailed information from local inhabitants at target location, or reconnaissance.	• Availability of maps, plans on Internet or libraries.	• Identify specific locations of detonation and fix accordingly (e.g., move bus stop from busy market).
5. Specify route to target	• Work out exact routes and methods of getting there (bus, taxi, walk). • Decide on best route and alternates.	• Detailed knowledge of target area and routes to target.	• Support of local inhabitants helpful.	• Change traffic flow, close off streets, divert pedestrian and car traffic on daily basis. • Close off streets to reduce number of possible routes terrorist can take to targets from point of departure.
6. Establish group commitment	• Group commitment sessions to bond bombers to each other, make mutual commitment.	• Trusted volunteers to encourage group commitment process.	• Network of trusted volunteers.	• Identify volunteers through interviews with failed suicides. • Dismantle training operations.

Table 5.3 (continued)

Steps	Action needed	Resources needed	Facilitating conditions[a]	Points of intervention
7. Train bombers	• Bombers must be familiarized with bomb vest, detonation procedures. • Must rehearse routes to target. • Familiarize with target and alternate locations. • Send bomber along routes and to targets as practice. • Learn to dress and behave to blend in with target setting. • Warn bomber against detonating too soon.	• Appropriate explosives and covering garments. • Detonators. • Safe house for training. • Bomb experts to assemble bomb vest, train bomber in detonation technique.	• Donations of money to purchase items. • Supplies of explosives from covert supporters. • Availability of light small-size explosives.	• Identify suppliers of explosives and shut down. • Identify stores of explosives and destroy. • Identify origins of specially sewn garments to cover explosives. • Identify sources/manufacturers of detonators mechanisms and shut down or cut off supplies.
8. Prepare propaganda, reinforce individual commitment	• Prepare poster with bomber's photograph, other announcements proclaiming his/her martyrdom. • Shoot video of bomber expressing commitment to carry out the mission.	• Video camera, computer and editing software. • Writing materials, cardboard for poster. • Photographs of bomber.	• Family may provide photograph, although usually does not know child has martyred himself/ herself until after act. • Suppliers of photographic materials and processing, etc.	• Work with video companies to track video cameras, provide means of identifying cameras. • Work with stores that supply services for photograph, poster needs. • Work to make sure families of candidates find out about their intentions before they can act.[h]

	Getting There			
1. Dispatch bomber	Get bomber from safe house to different location to begin journey to target.	• Intelligence on any recent changes in checkpoints, traffic patterns, etc. • Car or taxi for transportation of bomber to departure point.	• Friendly drivers and/or mechanics, car dealers, taxis.	• Change traffic patterns and check-points unpredictably and frequently. • Monitor traffic patterns in departure locations.
2. Reach target	• Bomber must move as directly as possible via agreed route to target. • Time taken increases risk of being spotted. • Time arrival to suit target (e.g., if bus, get to stop as bus pulls in). If café, arrive at busiest time.	• Detailed intelligence, careful training of bomber.	• Poorly designed buses. • Predictable bus schedules. • Poorly placed bus stops. • Poor building and venue security.	• Make entry to target area difficult. • Design bus[i] doors so they can be slammed shut immediately if driver suspects bomber. • Search entrants to cafes at busiest times. • Locate search and entry points at safe distance from café dining area.
	After the Event			
1. Claim responsibility	• Contact news media to claim responsibility. • Convey video of bomber's proclamation to media. • Post video on Web site. • Arrange payment for parents.	• Untraceable ways of contacting media. • Computer and ISP to post video on Web. • Money to pay parents.	• Donors to pay parents, untraceable money transfer system.	• Trace payments to parents. • Interview parents for information on handlers. • Surveillance of funeral events to identify possible handlers.

Table 5.3 (continued)

Steps	Action needed	Resources needed	Facilitating conditions[a]	Points of intervention
2. Review operation	• Assess whether bomber reached target and how. • Review approaches if thwarted. • Review criteria for selecting targets as appropriate.	• Detailed information on the attack process.	• Use cell phone to maintain contact with bomber up to point of detonation.	• Monitor cell phone use. • Study target selection and routes taken and entry methods; modify defenses accordingly.
3. Plan new attack	Return to start.			

Notes:

[a]See Orbach (2004) who argues that suicide bombing is spawned essentially by a range of facilitating conditions, not by the personal distress of the bomber.

[b]Bloom (2005); Dingley (2004); Merari (2004a, 2004b, 2004c)); Pape (2005).

[c]Merari (2004a, 2004b, 2004c). There is consensus, although no definitive study, supporting the claim that the fence built along the U.S.-Mexican border near San Diego substantially reduced the influx of illegal aliens in that region.

[d]For a survey of financial support sources for suicide bombers in Israel, see Stork (2002).

[e]Berman and Laitin (forthcoming); Ganor (2002).

[f]Ganor (2003).

[g]Merari (1998).

[h]Kimhi and Even (2004).

[i]Chan (2005).

acts into the small steps that make up the complete process leading to the act, carrying out the act and the aftermath.

CONCLUSION

While we do, perhaps, know more about suicide bombers than other kinds of terrorists, we still must learn more if we are to prevent suicide bombings.

- We need to interview unsuccessful suicide bombers to find out how they were trained, what happened to thwart them, the routes taken to their target, why they were chosen and so on.
- We need to interview handlers and other operatives to break down into smaller parts the necessary steps they take to plan, organize and routinize the missions.
- We need detailed information on the locations, times, routes to targets, selection of targets and the extent to which target selection dominates planning.
- We need to know the details of the targets selected, damage done, their accessibility to the bombers and so on. This information should be collected by police and assembled into a database that can be manipulated (analyzed) to reveal points of intervention.
- We need data to tell us whether any specific interventions (a fence, a wall, a change of traffic flow) affected the rate, targeting or use of tools and weapons of suicide bombings.

This kind of useful information and evaluation of the various interventions to prevent suicide bombing can only be obtained through research programs that fund the systematic collection of relevant information and employ sufficient numbers of trained researchers to conduct the work. In the final chapter, we detail the kinds of research programs that are needed to combat terrorist attacks.

6

Dynamics of Terrorist Decisions

In This Chapter

➤ Working in groups maximizes opportunities for terrorism, but terrorist decision making is constrained by the needs and conditions of the group.

➤ All terrorist groups are inherently volatile, containing the seeds of their own destruction, but out of that destruction new groups or factions may emerge.

➤ Conflicts inherent in the terrorist group inevitably lead to the operational demands of terrorism eclipsing idealism. Understanding the ideologies of terrorist groups will therefore give little insight into their selection of targets and tactics.

➤ The global reach of terrorist organizations such as Al Qaeda is achieved more through financial networks than ideological or social networks.

➤ Using situational prevention to increase the rates of terrorist group failure will speed up group disintegration.

➤ Group cohesion and morale can be undermined by such means as offering inducements for individuals to leave the group, by spreading rumors about infiltration of the group and, if possible, by seeking to remove the leadership.

WE HAVE SO far presented our thesis on the assumption that terrorists act as individuals. We have referred to terrorists as planning their missions on the basis of a limited rationality, meaning that their actions appear rational to them, and indeed are rational given the immediate goals that they want to achieve, such as placing a bomb in a particular location at a particular time. However, few terrorist missions are carried out by one person acting alone. In fact, with the exception of the lone assassin, most missions would be next to impossible to manage alone. And even those that may appear to be conducted by a single individual, such as a suicide bombing, often require many people to be involved in the planning of the mission. It is also likely that the process of decision making at the group level differs markedly at the individual level, especially in the perception of rewards, risks worth taking and valuation of outcomes.[1]

In this chapter, we outline the essential characteristics of terrorist groups that affect decision making. Working in groups maximizes opportunities for terrorists, but it also constrains them. That is to say, a terrorist group must reach agreement about every particular mission in which it will be involved and, if it does not, tension and confusion result. Such agreement is taken for granted by outsiders because it is assumed that the professed ideological commitment of the group ensures agreement with the overall goal of the group. However, it is the tension between the professed overall goal and the conduct of specific missions that makes decision making difficult for any terrorist group. There are several reasons for this tension:

- The operating principle for all terrorism (with the possible exception of cyberterrorism[2]) is the commitment to use violence to achieve its long-term goal, whatever that may be (usually either toppling a government or changing society in a radical way as in religiously motivated terrorism, or both).
- It is an article of *faith* that violence is essential to achieve this goal. While some terrorist groups proclaim a policy of "bullets and ballots" (e.g., Hamas, the IRA), the fact that they have great difficulty giving up on violence when they do win at the ballot box suggests that it is violence that has the upper hand.[3]
- It is extremely difficult, particularly in terrorist groups that reach the point of routine terrorism, to keep believing that the repeated acts of violence will actually lead to accomplishing the professed long-term goal (although short-term concessions may be obtained).

Governments, with rare exceptions, do not surrender their power easily, although they may show weakness and even give in to demands on occasion. They may suffer severe damage and disruption, but generally their overwhelming resources and sheer numbers are far too great for a small terrorist group. This is why many terrorist groups (with some notable exceptions) spend much time issuing communiqués that are designed not only to curry popular support, but also to convince themselves that their particular acts are leading to success.[4] This tension is played out over the life course of a terrorist group and, as we will see, is usually the reason for its demise. It is why few terrorist groups survive more than a year or two beyond their first attack. In fact, as we can see from Figure 6.1, the majority of terrorist groups listed in the Rand database fizzle out within the first few years of their activity.[5]

ENABLING AND CONSTRAINING CHARACTERISTICS OF TERRORIST GROUPS

The basic conditions that constrain or enhance group functioning, listed below, can be stated as a conflict of opposites—it is as though terrorist groups hold within them the seeds of their own destruction.[6]

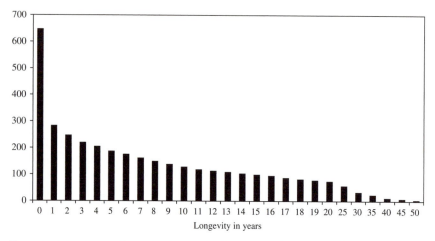

Figure 6.1 Number of Terrorist Groups by Longevity, Worldwide, 1968–2005
Source: Rand–National Memorial Institute for the Prevention of Terrorism.
Note: Longevity is defined as time between first and last recorded attack, incidents recorded 1968 through 2005.

Charismatic leadership—harsh discipline. The sociologist Max Weber described the charismatic leader as one who possessed special qualities that people admired or even worshipped, and that caused them to follow the leader blindly. There are many historical examples from Genghis Kahn to Mao Tse Tung.[7] All terrorist groups begin with such a "hero" who forms the terrorist group and shapes its ideology. To retain their charisma, these leaders must continue to demonstrate their power and usually do so with cruel and ruthless acts. Otherwise, according to Weber, the charisma dies away, and the group is left with a bureaucratic organization. A prime example is Abimael Guzman, former professor, who created the Shining Path in Peru. Guided by the writings of Hegel, Marx and others, Guzman constructed a unique ideology that advocated overthrowing the government of Peru through a peasant uprising (basically a Maoist ideology). Landowners and local government officials were ruthlessly murdered. Dissenters were not tolerated and individuals perceived as antagonistic to his cause were routinely killed. He established a very tight, self-contained terrorist organization, spending some five years preparing and organizing the group, before carrying out the first attack in 1980. In the first six years of its operation, it is thought to have been responsible for up to 12,000 terrorist attacks, killing as many as 10,000 individuals.[8] The group survived for some 20 years, but after Guzman was captured on April 5, 1992,[9] it gradually disintegrated, with only a small band left, now teamed up with drug dealers.[10]

Superior morality—hypocrisy in action. The function of all terrorist ideologies is to justify the use of violence as the means to achieving the group's ultimate goal. The usual claim is that "violence is a means of last resort." The group claims that it is forced to use violence because conditions of society or government are so bad, and the enemy is so recalcitrant that violence is the only way to achieve change. The contradiction is, of course, that the terrorists commit the very violence they condemn in their enemies. However, their advantage is the "freedom" they have in using violence in any way they choose, whereas in democracies the slightest government excess will be roundly criticized by the media. That is to say, democratic governments are constrained in their use of violence against terrorists, unless a state of war is declared.[11] Nondemocratic governments are not so constrained and have historically more than matched the violence of terrorist groups by adopting terrorist tactics themselves, for example, in Argentina's "dirty war" of the 1970s.

The moral hypocrisy of the terrorists' position, whether state sanctioned or not,[12] is thrust in their faces every day they commit violence. Thus, a powerful ideology is necessary to neutralize this conflict. If the ideology is essentially political, it will generate a perception of crisis, usually an imminent war, and attribute this crisis to the enemy. Thus, the terrorist group is "forced" to enter a war footing, where, of course, violence is morally permitted ordinary individuals:[13]

> Wars, war economy, a continuing economy based on arms: This is the central characteristic of the economy of imperialism.... militarism clearly appears as the lifesaver to which capitalism systematically clings....[14]

Where the terrorists' ideology is essentially religious, it is necessary to find authoritative interpretations of the religious teachings that justify the violence.[15] The neutralizing pronouncements of Al Qaeda and its affiliated groups justifying their use of indiscriminate violence are well known, as described in Box 6.1.

Entrance—exit. Some terrorist groups are not difficult to join, depending on how they are organized and the levels of membership available. A terrorist group may have many sympathizers, but few full members. This was the case with the Shining Path[16] and is purported to be the case with Al Qaeda.[17] In the case of routine terrorism that occurs close to the terrorist's base, entry must be made difficult because of the real danger of penetration by the enemy's intelligence. And if terrorism is to be conducted far away from the terrorist's base, extensive training will be necessary before an operative will be admitted, and very likely not at all, even if sent on a mission. This was the case with many of the 9/11 terrorists, who belonged to an Al Qaeda cell, but who were not full members of the inner core of Al Qaeda. To achieve full membership in Al Qaeda, an applicant must fulfill a list of 14 requirements outlined in the Al Qaeda training manual.[18]

Exiting a terrorist group is dangerous for both the individual and the group, because the person leaving immediately becomes the target of spies. Yet if a member remains in the group but raises his or her voice[19] against the

---

Box 6.1 Al Qaeda's Pronouncements

After Al Qaeda carried out bombings in Casablanca, Riyadh and Istanbul in 2003, killing many fellow Muslims, Al Qaeda made the following announcement arguing that their acts were justified according to Islamic law:

> Some claim that we consider most Muslims as non-believers and sanction killing them. How do we go everywhere to protect them and then sanction shedding their blood? This cannot be accepted by sound reason, let alone a Muslim who knows the rulings of God. We have repeatedly warned Muslims against approaching the places of infidels, and we now renew the warning. Moreover, it is impermissible, according to Shari'a ... to mix with those infidels, neither in their homes nor in work places, until they stop their crusading war against Islam and Muslims.

On February 23, 1998, Al Qaeda issued the following Fatwa, a declaration of war:

> All these crimes and sins committed by the Americans are a clear declaration of war on Allah, his Messenger, and Muslims. And ulema have throughout Islamic history unanimously agreed that the Jihad is an individual duty if the enemy destroys the Muslim countries.... On that basis, and in compliance with God's order, we issue the following Fatwa to all Muslims:
>
> The ruling to kill the Americans and their allies-civilians and military is an individual duty for every Muslim who can do it in any country in which it is possible to do it, in order to liberate the al-Aqsa Mosque [in Jerusalem] and the Holy Mosque [in Mecca] from their grip, and in order for their armies to move out of all the lands of Islam, defeated and unable to threaten any Muslim ... We—with God's help call on every Muslim who believes in God and wishes to be rewarded to comply with God's order to kill the Americans and plunder their money wherever and whenever they find it. We also call on Muslim ulema, leaders, youths, and soldiers to launch the raid on Satan's U.S. troops and the devil's supporters allying with them, and to displace those who are behind them so that they may learn a lesson.

Sources: These pronouncements were widely reported in the media. Our sources were Simon and Martini (2004–5, 141).

---

leadership concerning tactics (not likely to occur over ultimate goals), there is a good chance that he or she will be killed, or alternatively, will form a new faction and begin a competing terrorist group. The many factions fighting Israel in Palestine are testament to this fact,[20] as are the well-known competing branches of the IRA[21] and the loyalist factions in Northern Ireland.[22] It is this volatile nature of terrorist groups that makes it likely that, although they are short lived, they may nevertheless re-form into new groups.[23] Thus, as we discuss later in this chapter, eradicating terrorist groups by tracking down all their members is not likely to solve the problem.

For the cause—for the group. It seems obvious that terrorist groups are created *for* something. They form in order to achieve a greater goal of defeating an enemy. However, students of business and other kinds of organizations have argued that while a particular organization may originally be created for an instrumental purpose, once it has formed, it gains a life of its own. In fact, it becomes a mantra of the members of the organization to maintain its existence and prevent its decline.[24] The result is that the motivations of individuals in the group may often conflict with the stated or original purpose of the group. Thus, some terrorist groups may try to redeem themselves, not by trying to change the world that they despise, but by committing acts of self-sacrifice.[25] Over time, this may result in the terrorist actions appearing "inconsistent, erratic and unpredictable."[26] The overriding feature of the conflict is between "being for the group" as opposed to "being for the cause." Making rational decisions that link mission with immediate objective thus is made close to impossible.

This conflict is inherent in the circumstances of most terrorist groups because historic conditions change and societies evolve. To insulate against the pressures of history and societal conditions, a terrorist group must remain isolated and secluded (putting aside the defensive reasons against intelligence penetration). The Shining Path was a successful example of one such terrorist group. Guzman kept the terrorist group apart from society, even going so far as to rarely use the media—claimed by many to be a central feature of successful terrorism. A contrasting example was the 17 November terrorist group in Greece, which followed every act with lengthy communiqués dutifully published by the media, explaining its actions in obscure, Marxist-fascist-nationalist terminology. Throughout the 40 years of its existence—in terms of longevity a highly successful terrorist group—it carried out its terrorist acts while Greece, in spite of these, gradually moved toward democracy.[27] Although the 17 November terrorists' higher cause remains a mystery, it is clear that their own existence as a group took precedence and the purpose for which it was established seems never to have been achieved or even understood by its members.

The extent of the link between the terrorist group and the societal conditions in which it operates may be a significant factor in whether the group adapts to changing conditions (e.g., new technologies) or remains apart. The Shining Path terrorist group remained apart, using relatively elementary weapons, such as fire bombs and dynamite and small arms, even when more effective weapons were available. The 17 November group used signature weapons (a particular Colt 45 was used several times over many years—see Box 8.1) but also displayed sophistication in the use of explosives. Although it may be argued that the lack of connection between mission and society led these two terrorist groups to their demise, it must be also said that they lasted much longer than the majority of terrorist groups. Thus, their lack of adaptation may have prolonged the life of their group, but also may have hindered the possibilities of reaching their ultimate goal.[28]

Offensive—defensive organization. Terrorist organizations must accomplish two inherently conflicting tasks: (1) they must carry out acts of violence that require careful planning and implementation, which means that a well-organized group whose members know each other well and whose talents and capabilities fit together is essential; and (2) they must be organized in such a way that members possess little information concerning the structure and function of the organization of which they are a part and from which they receive instructions. Clearly, this is an impossible situation, particularly if the group is to endure over time and carry out repeated terrorist attacks that require continuous supplies of weapons, explosives and personnel (such as, for example, the level sustained in Iraq). Communication is key to the efficient functioning of any organization, which is why modern technology that enhances communication, making it possible to communicate without risking penetration by enemy intelligence, is perhaps the most important requirement of terrorist groups today (see Chapter 9). The Al Qaeda manual identifies three essential tools of terrorist operation: safe houses, secure communication and secure transport systems,[29] of which Al Qaeda identifies communications as the most demanding and most important.[30]

GROUP STRUCTURE: TRANSLATING DECISIONS INTO ACTION

We have outlined the basic conditions that constrain and enhance group participation in carrying out terrorist attacks. However, the organizational structure of groups may serve either to enhance group agreement or to insulate individuals from orders that may come from superiors. To make effective operational decisions and to ensure that missions are compatible with the overall goal of the terrorist group, some form of organization is necessary. Orders must be issued, and these must be transmitted from the originator to the frontlines. A loose organizational structure makes it possible for those on the frontlines to ignore orders, or adapt their operations to prevailing conditions. However, it also means that the operators may begin to act alone and, because of the operational demands of the moment, may stray considerably from the mission of the terrorist organization as a whole. In contrast, a strict military-like organization ensures that orders are carried out, but also suffers from poor adaptability to conditions at the front.

Much has been written on how, or how much, terrorist groups are organized. The theories range from speculations about hierarchical organizations similar to those adopted by organized crime (a model itself open to question) to the model of leaderless cells that operate independently, taking no orders from a single leader and deciding to act simply as a result of communications received on the Internet. The latter, the independent cell structure, has become a popular model for students of terrorism in the twenty-first century, but in the long run it remains highly doubtful.[31] We have seen that terrorist groups must have a charismatic leader, from whom flows the entire ideological underpinning of the group's cause, and the entire substrate of discipline. Thus, leaderless cells cannot function effectively for long.

Figure 6.2 displays in simplified form the basic types of organizational models adopted by different kinds of terrorist groups. These are discussed in more detail below:

Chain network. Most common in organized crime (and terrorist groups using their services or techniques) to move illegal products or services from source to customer. Product moves along the line sequentially. Each actor in the line acts like a buyer from the previous actor and seller to the next.

 Hub network. Typical of smaller terrorist groups or terrorist groups early in their creation. Examples include the Shining Path at its inception, the November 17 group in Greece. Communication occurs only through the leader and only occasionally among members when the leader is not present.

 All channel network. All members communicate on equal footing; a "leaderless" group. The modern version communicates freely via cyberspace. Examples include the ALF and ELF. Individuals act independently or in small temporary groups.

Hierarchical/cellular hybrid. The simplified model below represents the popular conception of Al Qaeda, the single leader at the top, layers of lieutenants beneath, each of whom manages various branch offices, that may in turn contain cells; described as a " global tribe." It is also similar to the mythical organized crime structure, a paramilitary hierarchy with semi-independent families running their own operations.

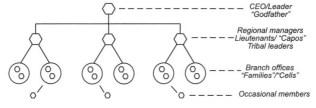

Figure 6.2 Simplified Models of Terrorist Group Networks

Sources: Portions adapted from Arquilla and Ronfeldt (2001); Ronfeldt (2005).
Note: ALF = Animal Liberation Front; ELF = Earth Liberation Front.

The chain network. The chain network is common in the smuggling of cars,[32] humans,[33] and guns and drugs[34] when individuals, often friends or relatives, come together to take advantage of a specific opportunity—usually to make money.[35] Recent research suggests that this is the most common form of organized criminal activity.[36] Small cells or groups made up of close friends or relatives have also been identified as significant aspects of Al Qaeda organization. However, these are characterized not so much by chain networks but rather dense cliques that remain tightly bound to in-group conformity and out-group aggression—perfect groups for suicide missions[37] for which operational decisions can rarely be questioned.

The hub network. While it is possible for a leader to maintain an organization of several cells separately connected only to him or her and not with each other (the *hub* network), this will limit considerably the size of the group and thus the range of missions it can conduct, unless there are managers at an intermediate level to administer groups of groups.

The all-channel network. The all-channel network[38] is dependent mainly on the Internet, which has made it possible for terrorists to communicate among themselves without actually forming a physical group or organization. For smaller terrorist groups with a limited field of operation, such as single-issue terrorists like the Animal Liberation Front, this form of organization works; however, so far, these terrorist groups are severely limited in what they can accomplish.

The hierarchical/cellular hybrid network. The hierarchical/cellular hybrid network comes closest to the way in which experts describe the Al Qaeda structure. The description is supposed to capture the innovative ways in which Al Qaeda operates. However, closer inspection reveals that its structure is very similar to that of most large organizations. All of the successful Al Qaeda operations have in fact been made possible by this quasi-business structure.[39] These are multinational corporations (or even national corporations) with regional managers, branch offices and local groups charged with particular tasks such as recruitment, sales, transportation and so on. This model was invented in the Godfather sagas and imputed to the Mafia mobs of New York City and Chicago, except that branch offices became "families" and branch managers were "capos." Others see Al Qaeda as "tribal"[40] at the branch level, with families of cells (to make them seem more clandestine) at the local level. Whatever the terminology, it is clear that this is not a new type of organization, but one that represents a multinational adaptation of the classic organized crime model. The literature, however, tends to exaggerate the global reach of Al Qaeda and its affiliates.[41] In addition to Al Qaeda, it is also likely that the more seasoned terrorist groups that have survived for decades, such as Hamas or the IRA, introduce management and structural features that mimic nation states: they develop political or diplomatic wings, army councils, operations, welfare, humanitarian aid and financial/banking divisions and even employee benefits schemes.[42]

Whatever the organizational form, it is clear that the communication of decisions from leaders to operatives is extremely complex, depending on the network structure of the groups involved, the porous or fuzzy boundaries of terrorist groups and the communication tools available.

IMPLICATIONS FOR POLICY

It has not been our intention to cover all of the complexities of group decision making in this brief chapter,[43] nor the complexities of network analysis of terrorist groups.[44] Rather, our purpose has been to identify the points of vulnerability of terrorist groups that might be susceptible to intervention. In the remainder of this chapter, we discuss four kinds of interventions: (1) taking out key members of the group; (2) disrupting terrorist recruitment; (3) situational measures to reduce the terrorists' chances of success and thus their morale; and (4) undermining group cohesion.

Taking Out Key Members

We believe that there is sufficient evidence that terrorist groups contain the seeds of their own destruction. This inherent fragility would suggest that the obvious response therefore is to track down and kill or capture the members of the group. Indeed, as we have repeatedly reported, this mindset tends to dominate the official law enforcement response to terrorism. We think that there may be some circumstances in which tracking down terrorists and killing them may have a direct preventive effect.[45] However, those circumstances are limited, and the long-term success of such a strategy is highly questionable. There are several reasons for this, as follows:

- When a terrorist group is disbanded or destroyed, it cannot be concluded that the threat has been eliminated. The "fuzziness" of terrorist group boundaries almost guarantees that remnants of terrorist groups will remain, even when the leaders are eliminated.[46] Indeed new groups may be formed as a defiant reaction to the failure of past leadership. This may have occurred in Bali where it is thought that the second bombing on September 30, 2005, was not undertaken by Jemaa Islamiyya, the group that undertook the first bombing and that the authorities believe was eliminated.
- The removal of one terrorist group, even if complete, does not guarantee that a new group with a different mission (or a similar mission with different strategies) will not emerge to take advantage of new opportunities that may arise. This is generally the history of organized crime, which has steadfastly resisted elimination. There are considerable similarities between terrorist groups and organized crime groups in the ways in which

they take advantage of the constantly changing opportunity structure that surrounds them.

- The complexity of some modern terrorist networks, such as Al Qaeda, means that it would take enormous resources to track down every single member of the network. In fact, given the loose connections among terrorist cells and among even terrorist organizations, it is highly unlikely that any effort to track them all down and take them out will even partially succeed. There is, therefore, the great danger of expending far too many resources in tracking down and identifying an amorphous terrorist network, resources that may better be expended on other approaches to prevention of terrorism, including the opportunity reduction approach we advocate.

That said, however, it does make sense to take out terrorists when two conditions are met. First, if it is known that the terrorist group is small and confined in its networking ability, and has a limited mission, it could be more efficient and effective to simply identify the members and remove them. Second, if there is a particularly charismatic leadership, such as Bin Laden and his top lieutenants, it is worth the effort to remove them, if the organization depends heavily on that leadership for its morale and for managing the day-to-day life of the group. The group may find a successor, but there is a good chance that the successor will not measure up to the original, charismatic leader.

Disrupting Terrorist Recruitment

The popular view of terrorist recruitment is that terrorists exploit those who are oppressed, and brainwash young innocents with propaganda, whether religious or political.[47] The response therefore must be to control the spread of these ideologies—thus, the call to close down the Madrassas in Pakistan and elsewhere to reduce recruitment by Al Qaeda. This approach appears to be entirely unrealistic for two reasons. First, the global avenues of communication today are so many that there is no way that any ideas, no matter how abhorrent, can be suppressed for long, if at all. There is already a growing literature on the terrorist use of the Internet and other advances of the twenty-first century to find possible recruits.[48] Second, we know from many historic examples that suppressing political or religious speech does not eradicate the movements that support them but pushes them underground. This is exactly what terrorist groups want, because recruitment is a risky undertaking for terrorist groups for it requires them to contact nonmembers, thus exposing them to the possibility of infiltration.

Another popular view of terrorist recruitment is that it occurs via family or social networks. This approach carries more weight, but also contains serious difficulties in implementation. Disrupting family or friendship groups is particularly difficult because they are, by definition, closed to outsiders. Because many modern terrorist groups are "fuzzy" organizations, with many members who are at the fringe and who may continuously move on and off that fringe, it is especially difficult to decide at what point an individual has been recruited. Furthermore, some terrorist groups, such as communist guerillas in the Philippines use a well-established procedure of infiltration of villages with the aim of supplanting traditional family networks, some using a combination of propaganda and coercion to gain recruits. Attempts to intervene in these methods of recruitment have proved very expensive, because intervention requires a heavy government presence in every far-flung village, and the heavy government presence may foster resentment from local citizens unless coupled with generous development aid.[49]

All in all, therefore, we see little promise in trying to disrupt terrorist recruitment using these approaches. We do think that it is likely that terrorist groups use different methods of recruitment, depending on their location, and we should learn much more about these methods. If the terrorists' base of operations is in inhospitable terrain, far away from their identified enemy, such as occurs in the Philippines, we would expect different points of contact and ways of induction compared with those used under the nose of one's enemy, such as by the IRA in Northern Ireland.

There is one respect in which social networks may be important and that is when they overlap with financial networks, such as may be the case in regard to the informal systems of money transfer (see below and Chapter 10). We also suggest in Chapter 16 that prisons offer many propaganda opportunities for terrorists and are ideal locations for intense indoctrination.[50] In principle, governments should have control over prison operations, so they should be able to implement procedures that reduce the opportunities for indoctrination by terrorists of other inmates. They often do not, however, control the publicity that surrounds the imprisonment of terrorists.

Reducing Chances of Success

Many terrorist groups have committed a startling, even awesome act for their first act of terrorism. The success of the first act fuses the violent means with the ideological end, making both appear morally justified. The challenge, for these terrorist groups, is to continue committing acts of similar dimension. This is where most terrorist groups fall short. It is difficult to keep up the same level of successful terrorist attacks; unless all the operationally demanding tasks are constantly fulfilled, idealism quickly recedes into the background. This is why the more we can do to reduce the successes of terrorist acts the greater the chance that the group will self-destruct. Failed terrorist attacks are extremely costly to terrorist groups both in terms of money and morale. As the Al Qaeda training manual says, "repeated failure of an operation lowers the morale of an organization's members themselves, causing them to lose faith."[51] Thus, the most effective means of combating terrorist groups is to make it difficult for them to succeed in every attack they attempt.

This can be achieved, as we have argued throughout the book, through situational interventions without knowing much about the international reach of the terrorists and without understanding the finer points of their ideologies. In Chapter 15, we undertake a comprehensive review of possible situational interventions and, here, we mention three that directly address group organization and decision making:[52]

1. Make group communication difficult. Control the availability of communication tools or make their use risky through technologies that track vehicles and cell phones (see Chapters 9 and 15). Making communication difficult will increase internal group conflict.

2. Improve international travel documents. Whether or not Al Qaeda has the global reach it is purported to have, it is obvious that for catastrophic attacks to be committed on Western countries distant from the base of operations, traveling to the country and transporting weapons is the major obstacle that must be overcome. Al Qaeda has clearly recognized this, having established entire sections of its organization that are devoted to collecting, stealing and forging passports, visas and other documentation.[53] Nothing short of an international effort to develop much more stringent document authentication procedures and use of new technologies is needed to make international terrorist travel more difficult.

3. Target terrorist financial networks. It is important to make it difficult for terrorist groups to move money and obtain financing (see Chapter 10). The distinction between financial networks and social/organizational networks is extremely important in this regard. Although the excellent social network analysis of terrorist organizations offered by current researchers is of considerable interest in terms of identifying the internal tensions and vulnerabilities of terrorist groups, financial networks are much more amenable to direct manipulation from the perspective of prevention.[54] In fact, as we note in Chapter 15, it is possible to introduce preventive techniques in banking procedures, for example, without needing to know who the terrorists are by name.

Undermining Group Cohesion

We have already discussed one way to undermine the terrorist group, which is to attack the leadership, especially the charismatic leader who expresses the higher cause for the group. Discipline, purpose and the daily life of terrorists are conditioned by the leader and his or her cause. Remove the leadership and the purpose and functioning of the group are severely undermined. But other things can also be done to undermine group cohesion, as follows:

Emphasize the hypocrisy of terrorists. Constantly use media or any other outlet to highlight the contradictions between the professed superior morality of the terrorists and the violation of these standards by the terrorists when they use violence. Repeated demonstration of these contradictions will place more pressure on the terrorists to constantly justify their actions. Of course, the effectiveness of this technique will depend on the audience reached. In most cases, this audience will be those whose opinion matters when it comes to supporting, both financially and politically, a nation's counterterrorism program (see Chapter 16) or the supporters of terrorists themselves.

Offer a way for terrorists to exit their group. The longer a terrorist group is in operation, the greater the likelihood that terrorists will be susceptible to inducements to leave their group. Offering reduced sentences to those captured may help group exit. Offering immunity from prosecution can sometimes help to end an uprising altogether. Events in Northern Ireland have shown how effective this strategy can be, and inducements to leave the group were used with success by the Italian authorities in breaking up the Red Brigade in the 1980s.[55]

Create a climate of paranoia for terrorists. This can be achieved by using media and other means to spread the word that spies and agents are operating throughout the group's sphere of operation.

Play for time. Time works against terrorist groups. The contradictory forces at play within their clandestine existence make it inevitable that the group will disintegrate. This does not mean that the problem will solve itself, however, because dissidents within the terrorist group may spawn other competing groups, as has occurred in Palestine, Northern Ireland, Peru and other countries where terrorism is widespread.

CONCLUSION

In this first part of the book, we have described how we must set about analyzing our vulnerabilities. We emphasized the need to understand the situational causes of terrorist acts and to focus on the four pillars of terrorist opportunity: targets, tools, weapons and facilitating conditions. We discussed the necessity to understand precisely how attacks are mounted using the example of suicide bombings. Finally, we explained the benefits of thinking like a terrorist and, because few attacks are carried out by a lone individual, we examined terrorist group decision making, with the intention of finding points of intervention. In Part II, we will examine more closely the four pillars of terrorist opportunity, looking again for effective ways to intervene. We ask what makes particular targets more attractive to terrorists than others? Why do terrorists choose particular weapons from the many that are available? What tools do they find most appropriate for what kinds of missions? This analysis inserts us into the decision-making process of the terrorists and points the way to establishing priorities for protection.

PART II

The Opportunity Structure of Terrorism

Targets

In This Chapter

- ➤ Terrorist ideology gives some insight into the choice of targets, but terrorists are forced to give priority to tactical issues over ideology.
- ➤ We do not have to protect every target to the same level, because not all targets are equally attractive to terrorists.
- ➤ EVIL DONE summarize the main features of the targets that terrorists choose. These are Exposed, Vital, Iconic, Legitimate, Destructible, Occupied, Near and Easy.
- ➤ Every chosen target ranks high on some of these criteria, but might not meet them all.

HOW CAN WE protect every school, railroad station, office building, bus or restaurant where large numbers of the public gather? How can we protect every bridge, reservoir, power station and port, which comprise the vital infrastructure of society? How can we protect military installations, vehicles or barracks from rocket attacks or bombs? Finally, how can we protect police, judges, politicians and other public officials from being targeted for assassination or kidnapping?

Brian Jenkins of the Rand Corporation long ago observed that terrorists spend a lot of time deciding on their targets, especially which targets are the most vulnerable,[1] and they also display remarkable consistency in their tactical deliberations over time.[2] This chapter asks what it is about a particular target that attracts the attention of terrorists. Why, for example, will they select a train to attack rather than a building? And why attack a particular building rather than another one? It is widely argued that "we can't protect everything" and, indeed, we cannot.[3] But in fact we don't have to protect everything because there is logic to the terrorists' choice of targets, and if we understand that logic, we can begin to think about how to prioritize targets for protection.

We have argued in previous chapters that terrorists *must* make choices because of the many constraints they face. There is always a reason why a particular target is chosen over some other, and the best starting place for thinking about these choices is the terrorists' objectives—what are they seeking to achieve by their actions? Trying to answer this question, however, takes us straight back to another of our constant themes, which is that the analysis of terrorist acts must always focus on specific forms of terrorism. This is because different forms of terrorism—assassinations, bombings, kidnappings, hostage takings—have different objectives and therefore focus on different targets. For example, the targets of terrorist assassinations are quite different from hostage takings. Individuals targeted for assassination are often representatives of the government, such as police, judges and politicians, whereas those targeted in hostage takings, as in hijacking of airliners, may be ordinary travelers. They may be citizens of the hated country and therefore "legitimate" targets for hostage taking; they may even hold important posts at home, but their principal value to the terrorists lies in the fact that their lives can be bartered for concessions from the enemy.

Many terrorist groups, especially long-lasting ones, develop an entire way of thinking, particularly ways of identifying their enemies and justifications for killing them.[4] These ways of thinking may range from naive to the highly sophisticated. Some groups do not get beyond committing a brief series of terrorist acts, without developing the thinking to go with them. That is to say, they get stuck in the tactics of specific operations, driven only by the vague notion that violence is necessary for their cause (as we described in Chapter 6). These terrorist groups usually have a short life.[5] Others, such as the IRA, develop principles then derive strategies from these experiences for identifying classes of targets. And these principles, strategies and objectives might change over time as a result of their varied success or other changes in a wide variety of other circumstances, including changes in the membership of the group. Thus, during its period of Marxist influence, the Provisional IRA (PIRA) targeted businesses and businessmen as well as its always favorite targets, the Royal Ulster Constabulary. At earlier periods, it was careful to attack only government personnel and not Protestants or loyalists per se. At other times, it contrived justifications to attack Protestants simply because they were Protestants.[6] Then, when the mainstream movement disavowed sectarian attacks, a breakaway wing (the "Real IRA") started targeting civilians, eventually killing 29 and injuring 200 in a single town center car bomb.

However, knowing the terrorists' objectives is only the starting point for understanding their choice of targets; this knowledge provides insight into the kinds of targets that the terrorists are likely to attack (e.g., in a particular case it might be airliners not government buildings), but it does not help us to narrow the choice. Probing more deeply into their minds or exposing the roots of their ideology may help a little—as the Northern Ireland example illustrates (different wings of the IRA had different priorities as did so-called "loyalist" terrorist groups). But within the general parameters of any terrorist group's general objectives, the form of attack must be within the operational capacities of the terrorist organization and target choice will mostly be determined by features that are intrinsic to the targets themselves. Identifying these features will help in undertaking two vital tasks: finding ways to change the features that invite attack and prioritizing targets for protection.

In the remainder of this chapter, we describe how to set about the task of identifying the determinants of target choice. In situational crime prevention, this is done by taking a large sample of the specific kinds of crime in question and carefully studying features of the targets. For example, a study of residential burglary might examine what distinguishes houses that are targeted by burglars from those that are not. Do the houses that have been burgled seem more affluent, do they have poorer security, are they hidden from the road by fences and bushes, or are they in deprived neighborhoods? Depending on the answers, it is usually possible to recommend preventive strategies. For example, it might be discovered that burglars operating in a particular neighborhood often break into homes through the patio doors. The police can then advise homeowners of this vulnerability and recommend ways to reduce it.

In the case of terrorism, the opportunities for undertaking these kinds of studies are limited because, with a few exceptions, such as attacks by paramilitaries in Northern Ireland or insurgents in Iraq, there are too few incidents of a specific type to analyze. True, it is possible to identify the main classes of terrorist targets by analyzing the various databases on terrorist incidents. For example, the Rand MIPT database shows that worldwide attacks on "transportation" constituted the main form of terrorism directed at infrastructure between 1968 and 2004 (Figure 7.1).[7] Presumably, these transportation attacks included ones on cargo-handling facilities (ports, ships, warehouses, trucks, railroad lines) as well as on passenger transport (trains, buses, stations, subways and so on). If the classification were more fine grained, and distinguished among different forms of transportation and its various components,

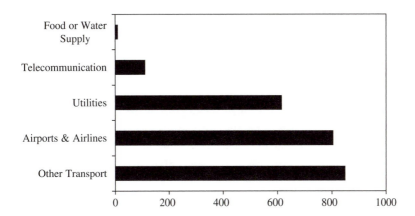

Figure 7.1 Infrastructure Attacks, Worldwide, 1968–2004

Source: Rand–National Memorial Institute for the Prevention of Terrorism.

the results could in principle help governments make risk-based allocations of protective resources. For example, in the immediate aftermath of the London Underground bombings, in 2005, a *New York Times* leader called for more resources to protect public transport, which it noted had been badly neglected compared with air transport.[8]

Unfortunately, the assessment of relative vulnerability is a good deal more problematic than the *New York Times* leader assumed. Thus, one could not simply count the number of incidents of terrorism in public and air transportation without carefully defining the events. How would we weight an explosion compared with a shooting? Would threats and attempts be counted, as well as actual incidents, and how would threats and attempts be defined, measured and weighted? Perhaps the comparison ought to be based on actual harm, but how would one compare, for example, destruction of property, disruption of commerce, the terror experienced by hostages, and actual deaths and injuries. Perhaps the most meaningful comparison would be based on deaths, but these comparisons should be related to the numbers of people at risk and the duration of risk. Thus, a hundred people killed in airline terrorism in any one year might represent a much higher level of risk than the same number killed by terrorists on public transport, simply because it could be (we have not made the calculations) that more people spend more time on public transport. In fact, we doubt that at this very general level of risk assessment, these problems can be solved—at least to the satisfaction of decision makers who have to take account of a much wider array of social and political considerations. In this connection, the same *New York Times* leader quoted above lamented Congress's failure to allocate the most protective resources to the most vulnerable regions of the country.[9]

In fact, the difficulties of comparing target vulnerability are greatest when comparing very different kinds of terrorism and very different kinds of targets. It is further complicated when we consider risk as well as vulnerability. By "vulnerability" we refer to the inherent features of targets that make them susceptible or attractive to attack by terrorists. By "risk" we encompass not only vulnerability but also the loss (material and otherwise) that may result from the terrorist attack—in other words, the features of the target from the point of view of the target or victim. For example, if a pylon that is part of a power grid is blown up, the entire grid might not be brought down if there is a system that reroutes the electric supply. While the London Underground was disrupted temporarily after the 2005 attacks, the entire system was not destroyed or even brought to a halt. This is because infrastructures, such as the Tube, are far more complex targets than single structures such as buildings (see "Does EVIL DONE Have a Wider Application?" below).[10]

Although still considerable, the difficulties are much reduced when comparisons are made among similar targets and among similar forms of terrorism. For example, the transport authorities in London could make valid risk or vulnerability comparisons between bus and tube travel or among different tube lines. But the more specific the comparisons become, the rarer the events, and we come full circle to the problem with which we began.

So how do we break this conundrum and try to identify different levels of risk and vulnerability when we have little or no empirical data to guide our analysis? We can only do this by trying to "think terrorist"—that is, examining the problem of target choice from the terrorists' perspective—and by drawing on the experience and research in situational crime prevention in regard to offender choice of targets.

TARGET ATTRACTIVENESS TO THIEVES: CRAVED

We described how situational crime prevention researchers would establish the preferred targets of burglars in a particular neighborhood. Another example of target attractiveness would be discovering products that are "hot" for theft. By surveying studies of various forms of burglary, theft and robbery, it is possible to establish the most vulnerable products—those most frequently stolen from among the many thousands produced—and, in fact, this has been done.[11] A short list includes cash, jewelry, liquor, cigarettes, cars and car parts, VCRs and CD players, cassettes and CDs, fashion shoes and clothing, contraceptives and some over-the-counter medicines and beauty aids. These products are particularly CRAVED by thieves because they are concealable, removable, available, valuable, enjoyable and disposable:

- **Concealable.** Things that can be hidden in pockets or bags are more easily stolen by shoplifters and other sneak thieves. Things that are difficult to identify or can easily be concealed after being stolen are also more vulnerable. This explains why we write our names in our books and why car thieves do not generally steal Rolls Royce's for their own use. Instead, they steal less valuable cars that blend into the surroundings.
- **Removable.** The fact that cars and bikes are mobile helps explain why they are so often stolen. Nor is it surprising that laptop computers and VCRs are often stolen, because they are desirable and easy to carry.
- **Available.** Theft waves can result from the availability of a new attractive product, such as the cell phone, which quickly establishes its own illegal market. Desirable objects that are widely available and easy to find are at higher risk. This explains why homeowners try to hide jewelry and cash from burglars.
- **Valuable.** Thieves will generally choose the more expensive goods, particularly when they are stealing to sell. But value is not simply defined in terms of resale value. Thus, joyriders are more interested in a car's performance than its financial value.
- **Enjoyable.** Hot products tend to be enjoyable things to own or consume, such as liquor, tobacco and CDs. Thus, residential burglars are more likely

to take DVD players and televisions than equally valuable electronic goods, such as microwave ovens or food processors. This also explains why the Apple iPod has reportedly sparked a wave of robberies in the subway and streets of New York.

- **Disposable.** Thieves will prefer products that are easy to sell. In fact, this characteristic may be the most important one in explaining volume thefts, such as commercial burglaries and hijacking of lorry loads.

Knowing which products are most vulnerable to theft helps us decide which ones to most carefully protect from thieves. Governments know which manufacturers to target in efforts to persuade them to "crime proof" their products.[12] Insurance companies know which warehouses must install better security as a condition of granting insurance. Police know which stores to focus on when trying to arrest shoplifters.[13] Stores know which of their products to protect by removing them from open display or guarding them in some other way. And private citizens know which products they should be particularly careful not to leave on the back seats of their cars.

CRAVED is only a general guide to what makes products attractive to thieves. Not all hot products exemplify every one of its features, nor to the same degree. For example, it does not fully explain why the Gillette Mach 3 almost always appears in newspaper stories of regularly shoplifted items, while other disposable razors are rarely mentioned. Nor does CRAVED explain every aspect of target attractiveness. For example, it does not fully explain why some of the most stolen products from American drugstores include remedies for intimate problems such as piles. We can only speculate that these products are stolen to avoid the embarrassment of purchasing them at checkout (an example of how effective "socialization" can cause as well as prevent crime).[14]

It is also the case that the circumstances of theft help dictate which aspects of CRAVED become salient for the thief. For example, "concealable" is a more important feature for the shoplifter than for the warehouse burglar. This interplay between desirable features and kinds of theft is both subtle and powerful. A few years ago, a very large study demonstrated that not only were some cars much more likely to be stolen than others, but that the models that were favored by thieves depended on the purpose of theft.[15] Thus, joyriders chose American-made "muscle" cars with powerful acceleration; those who broke in to cars to steal contents or components favored European models such as Volkswagens and BMWs with excellent radios that could easily be installed in other cars; and those who stole cars for resale favored expensive models such as Mercedes and Lincolns. Cars that were hardly ever stolen for any purpose were American station wagons. These were not only low value, but they had poor acceleration and terrible radios.

The fact that thefts are concentrated on a small range of products shows that thieves make careful choices about what they steal. Can the same observation hold true for the terrorists' selection of targets?

TARGET ATTRACTIVENESS TO TERRORISTS: EVIL DONE

We know that, out of the thousands, indeed millions, of possible targets that terrorists could select, only few are targeted and, even for those terrorist acts that are repeated regularly, the range of targets selected is limited. What characteristics single out these targets for attack? As already explained, there would be little practical benefit from answering this question for the whole range of terrorist attacks because, to be effective, preventive action has to be focused on specific kinds of terrorism. In any case, officials charged with preventing terrorism, in most cases, will have a limited number of targets to protect and a limited range of attacks to anticipate. Thus, the executives of pharmaceutical companies have a limited number of plants and laboratories to protect from a limited range of attacks, and the same will go for any other corporate, local authority or government agency.

In the illustrative exercise that we lay out below, we focus on the kind of single terror attack undertaken by foreign-based terrorists (see Chapter 11), such as the 9/11 attacks, using explosive force designed to kill large numbers of the civilian population in a large city. The prospect of these single attacks constitutes the most troublesome and worrying problem for a country's leaders, to whom people turn for protection.[16] In trying to understand what makes an attractive target for these spectacular attacks, we are hampered (mercifully, but almost by definition) by their relative infrequency; we do not have access to a large body of empirical data of the kind that helped to identify the CRAVED features of products. Instead, we have had to fall back on our knowledge of the few spectaculars that have occurred, supplemented by our attempt to see the problem of target choice from the terrorists' perspective. In other words, we have tried to "think terrorist." We stress that this is illustrative only and that for the purposes of this exercise we have focused on the least common but most politically and socially destabilizing attack that achieves maximum impact: attacks in which terrorists try to optimize benefits in terms of deaths, destruction, disruption and fear, as well as in terms of garnering admiration and support from their constituencies. This is the scenario in which the terrorist leadership might play an unusually direct role and for which the leadership organization would be inclined to invest an exceptional degree of time and resources.

We did not seek to produce a definitive list of target features that invite single attacks. Again, our purpose is illustrative, to show how to set about the task of identifying features that make targets vulnerable to attack. Also we stress that terrorism, like crime and most other human activities, is a dynamic process—it evolves over time. Thus, not only must the features of attractive targets be studied separately for each different form of terrorism, but they must be reexamined repeatedly over the months and years.[17]

We start with our acronym EVIL DONE and explain its elements below:

(1) Exposed. Any exposed, visible target that attracts attention is more likely to be attacked than a hidden one. This is the basis of camouflage and why antiballistic missiles were hidden underground in the cornfields of the Midwest. The 9/11 report noted that Bin Laden pressed for the White House to be the target of the 9/11 attacks, but this was resisted right up until the end by Atta, who considered it "too difficult." It was too small a target, very difficult to hit with a commercial airliner flown by a poorly trained pilot. In contrast, the twin towers of the World Trade Center stood out against the skyline of New York City like nothing else.

(2) Vital. Some targets are critical to a society's day-to-day functioning, one might even say its survival. These are commonly described as infrastructure such as electricity grids, computer networks, the water supply, rail systems and airline traffic systems. Pipelines are vital infrastructure to Iraq, so they have been a very attractive target to insurgents, in fact the third most popular target (see Chapter 12). The attack on the World Trade Center displayed intelligent planning: it was the critical center of the commercial district of Manhattan, where much of the stock market trading was conducted. This was a much easier way to attack infrastructure than to find where to hit an electricity grid, for example, which is a much smaller target and more difficult to hit with a passenger jet. The 9/11 attack not only disrupted the commercial operations of the United States and the world, but it also had many other ramifications. It disrupted tourism at home and abroad and paralyzed the airline system. Finally, it ushered in an era of costly new security.

(3) Iconic. The Statue of Liberty is perhaps America's best known icon. The planners of the 9/11 attack must have been very tempted to choose it as a target for this reason alone, but we can see that attacking the World Trade Center achieved much more in support of their goals. Not only was it an obvious, exposed target, but it was the symbol of capitalism. Similarly, the Pentagon is the symbol of America's military power. The Twin Towers were an icon simply of America and more specifically New York City, which itself is an icon. For Timothy McVeigh, the federal building in Oklahoma City embodied the government that he hated.

(4) Legitimate. One of the most difficult judgments for a terrorist is to anticipate public reaction to the attack—whether it will be perceived as powerful and audacious or whether it will meet with moral condemnation. An important indicator of the problem of legitimacy of targets is the constant necessity of terrorist groups, especially long-lasting ones, to explain their actions. The IRA developed these explanations almost into an art form. In fact, it was an integral part of the lives of IRA members to devote themselves to reading the classics of revolutionary thought, especially while in prison, and to writing lengthy tracts explaining, clarifying and justifying their actions and their cause.[18] To this day, Gerry Adams gives speeches that continue to do this.[19] The same may be said for Al Qaeda and Hamas,[20] and the communiqués issued by the 17 November terrorists in Greece.[21] These justifications are needed because some people are regarded as more "legitimate" targets for violence than others. Perhaps the least legitimate targets are children and, with the recent terrible exception of the school targeted by Chechnyan rebels, schools and other buildings populated by children seem to have been rarely chosen. When children have been killed, the terrorists responsible have issued statements "regretting" the deaths. At the other end of the spectrum, the most legitimate targets include soldiers, police and other functionaries of government "repression." Some of the most obvious targets of attack are the personnel and buildings serving the military, police and government functions of the hated country or government.

(5) **Destructible**. The target must be destructible. It must be seriously damaged if not utterly destroyed. Failure to inflict such damage, if that is the aim, or to kill targeted people, or to make off with hostages is a failure of the terrorist act. Thus, truck bombing the basement of the North Tower in the first attempt to bring down the World Trade Center failed because, as some argued afterward, the building was "indestructible." Tragically, these arguments were proven wrong by the airplane attack on 9/11. Although five people were killed in the blast, Mrs. Thatcher and her cabinet survived the bombing of their hotel in Brighton. The Semtex bomb had been planted behind a bath panel several weeks before by Patrick McGee who checked into Room 629 under an assumed name. After the bombing, the IRA issued a statement that made clear their disappointment: "Today we were unlucky, but remember we have only to be lucky once; you will have to be lucky always."

(6) **Occupied.** As the Brighton bombing shows, destroying structures is not always enough for the terrorists. It is better to kill people as well, because this is a necessary part of striking fear into the enemy, including civilians and those charged with the defense of the hated regime. Thus, any structures or places that contain large numbers of people or vehicles in which people are closely packed, such as buses, trains, airplanes and railway stations, are attractive targets. Once again, this is why the destruction of the World Trade Center, with its huge toll of life, caused such outrage and fear. Sometimes these targets are large (the World Trade Center, the Madrid Railway Station) and sometimes they are small but packed with people (e.g., buses blown up by suicide bombers in Israel, pubs bombed by the IRA in Northern Ireland and cafes attacked by Hamas in Jerusalem). These kinds of targets, where many people could be killed, should receive our closest attention, but we should try to distinguish among the kinds of people who might be killed as well as their locations.

(7) **Near.** Criminological studies of the "journey to crime" consistently show that offenders will select targets close to where they live, or if not close, easily accessible by mechanized transport, making them close in time. Like everyone else, criminals want to expend the minimum effort in reaching their goals, and terrorists are the same. Timothy McVeigh attacked the Oklahoma City federal building, relatively near where he lived, not a government building in Washington hundreds of miles away (see Chapter 13). The IRA mounted many more attacks on targets in Northern Ireland than

they did on the British mainland. It is apparent also that the selection of targets by Hamas to send in their suicide bombers is conditioned by the time it takes for the bomber to reach the target and the closeness of the target to his/her point of departure. This is why the Israelis have erected walls and barriers to force bombers to take a long or roundabout way and, in some locations, to go through a number of security checkpoints to reach their target. It has therefore been necessary for the terrorists to devise various ways of getting their bombers more quickly to the locations. It follows, of course, that the longer they take to get to their target, the greater the chance of their being seen and apprehended. The obstacles facing a terrorist group whose base is distant from the target, such as foreign terrorists seeking to strike a target in the United States are significant, so that the issue of international travel becomes central, as noted by the 9/11 report. We will examine the problems of terrorism near and far and their significance for policy in Part III of the book.

(8) Easy. Public buildings designed without security in mind (such as the federal building in Oklahoma City) can be an easy target for terrorists, just as houses without locks are prey to burglars. The Twin Towers were a relatively easy target of the first bombing, because the parking garage was poorly protected. But, given the improved security of the parking garage after the first bombing, and given that Bin Laden's objective was to topple one tower onto the other, they became a very difficult target. It took several years of preparation to make them reachable. Thus, increasing the protection of possible targets may sometimes make that target attractive. If it is a highly valued target, terrorists may be attracted to it because it is well protected. If terrorists can attack it successfully, they create an aura of omnipotence and fear.[22]

Not every target of a single attack will fit every attribute of EVIL DONE, but we hold that most targets will rank high on most of the attributes. Some of the attributes are more suitable for characterizing buildings, whereas other attributes may be suitable for transport systems or places where people congregate. However, in many instances, it is difficult to separate the people as targets from the buildings or locations in which they are targeted.

This complexity is what makes the choice of target for the terrorists so difficult. There are many target attributes that they must weigh and compare, and then they must decide which of those are important for the particular mission from a practical point of view and for achieving the group's prime objectives. They must also have a backup plan, if for some reason they cannot attack the chosen target. For example, the 9/11 planners considered the possibility of crashing the airliner into the midtown shopping district of Manhattan, should it happen that the pilot was unable to reach his primary target of the Twin Towers. This signifies how important it is to terrorists when they plan a single attack to choose a target that will present them with as many attractive features as possible.

In fact, we must go through a similarly complicated process in seeking to avoid attack. We must evaluate the likelihood that particular targets will be attacked—and then we must find ways of protecting those that seen most vulnerable. We know more about the latter than the former: there are many security specialists who can provide detailed, practical advice on the protection of particular classes of facilities (ports and cargo-handling facilities, for example) or protection from specific forms of attack (such as chemical or viral attacks). However, there is much less expertise to draw on when it comes to the task of assessing the comparative probability of different targets being attacked and, because we cannot protect everything from attack, of deciding which ones to protect and to what degree.

EVIL DONE IN WASHINGTON, D.C.

EVIL DONE is only the first step in identifying the most vulnerable targets.[23] It must be followed up by detailed studies of the actual targets of terrorism and with interviews with terrorists about their decision making. Meanwhile, we can do a rough rating of possible targets within cities using our EVIL DONE characteristics. In Table 7.1, we have taken the example of public buildings in Washington. We have rated their attractiveness to a foreign-based group planning to attack with a massive explosive force, such as a truck bomb or an aircraft loaded with fuel (no doubt the difficulties of the latter form of attack are much greater as a result of the security improvements introduced after 9/11). Note that these are all well-known structures that would be of relatively higher vulnerability than the hundreds of lesser-known public and private buildings in the city.

In making these ratings, we took account of the following:

- As explained, "exposed" has the two aspects of attracting attention and being easily identified. This latter aspect assumes considerable weight in this exercise, because we have included attacks from the air, which require the target to standout from its surroundings and be easily identified by an inexperienced pilot. Had we confined the exercise to truck bombings, this aspect would have been less important—which, again, illustrates the importance of analyzing highly specific kinds of terrorism.
- Clearly, the White House and the U.S. Congress perform vital functions for our country, but temporary arrangements could quickly be put in place to allow the president and Congress to carry on their work if these buildings were damaged or destroyed. In the case of the Pentagon, we assume few vital military operations are lodged only in the Pentagon, but are duplicated in many other places.
- The Washington Monument merits the label of iconic, but it is by no means as well-known overseas as the White House, the Capitol and the Pentagon.

Table 7.1 Ratings of Target Characteristics, Washington, D.C.

Target Characteristic	Capitol	White House	Pentagon	Washington Monument	Union Station	National Cathedral	Old Post Office	Georgetown University	National Zoo
Exposed	5	4	5	5	3	4	0	2	1
Vital	3	3	4	0	4	0	0	1	0
Iconic	5	5	5	2	0	1	0	0	0
Legitimate	5	5	5	5	3	1	2	1	0
Destructible	3	4	2	4	4	4	4	1	1
Occupied	4	4	3	2	4	1	2	3	3
Near	1	1	1	1	1	1	1	1	1
Easy	3	2	3	2	5	5	4	4	4
TOTAL SCORE	29	28	28	21	24	17	13	13	10

Note: 1 = Low; 5 = High

- The National Zoo receives a low rating on "legitimate" because many of the visitors are children and the permanent "occupants" are animals whose deaths would earn the terrorists considerable opprobrium from some quarters.
- It would be harder to destroy a dispersed target, such as the Zoo or Georgetown University, than most of the other targets on the list, which are relatively compact.
- Nearly all buildings have some occupants. In some cases, the occupants are few but of great importance (the White House), while in others they are many but of doubtful legitimacy (Georgetown University). Most of the targeted buildings on this list would be full at some times and empty at others (Washington Cathedral is full on Sunday mornings but virtually empty at other times in the week).
- For overseas-based terrorists, the targets in Washington are equally far, but for some cities (such as New York), it might be easier for terrorists to establish temporary bases in nearby immigrant communities (see Chapter 11).
- The ratings of "easy" are particularly problematic given that we are considering attacks by both aircraft and truck bombs. For example, the White House, the Capitol and the Pentagon might already have been secured against truck bombs, but the White House is not as easy to hit from the air (depending on the type of aircraft used) as the other two.
- While all the features of EVIL DONE are important in explaining terrorists' choices, they might not be equally weighted by them. We have not tried to apply differential weights in our table. This might explain, for example, why the Pentagon is rated overall as a less favorable target than the White House, even though it was successfully attacked, and not the White House, on 9/11.

It would be easy to argue with the ratings in Table 7.1, and we do not claim that each terrorist group would share the same priorities. The purpose of the exercise is to show that, in principle, it would not be difficult to develop a catalog of targets within each major city, rating them according to EVIL DONE criteria. It would be necessary to develop objective ratings scales for each of the EVIL DONE criteria, just as similar rating scales have been developed in other fields in assessing the security levels of parking lots or the criminogenic attributes of products.[24] The ratings must be made separately for different forms of attack, not just truck and airliner attacks, but also the kind of coordinated bomb attacks as occurred on public transport in London and Madrid. The next step would be to examine the kinds of targets within each city highly rated as vulnerable (e.g., train stations) to determine the kinds of protection that may be needed. In doing so, it might be necessary to repeat the EVIL DONE evaluation simply for that class of targets.

Some of the target characteristics would be difficult to change—for example, the iconic nature of the Capitol and its legitimacy as a target in the eyes of the terrorists. It is also likely that policymakers would wish to assign greater weight to one or more of the EVIL DONE characteristics, say, "occupied," because people are more important than monuments. There would be many other difficult decisions to make in turning EVIL DONE into a practical scale to assess vulnerability. However, it is better to face these difficulties to develop a systematic way of assessing vulnerability than to fall back on the unsystematic, politicized way of doing it, which is typical of current practice.

DOES EVIL DONE HAVE A WIDER APPLICATION?

Although EVIL DONE might provide a good starting point for evaluating the vulnerability of specific buildings to single attacks, we should ask whether it is more widely applicable and whether it can be used to differentiate among the possible targets of other forms of terrorism. We address this question in two stages. First, we apply EVIL DONE to two other forms of terrorism, one similar to that examined above (a single dirty bomb attack on a U.S. city by foreign terrorists) and one that is quite different (assassinations by a terrorist group). Then we see whether it can be used to help explain why infrastructures seem to be attacked relatively rarely.

The Targets of Dirty Bombs and Assassinations

As will be discussed in Chapter 10, most experts agree that it is only a matter of time before terrorists detonate a dirty bomb (a radiological dispersal device) in a city center in the United States.[25] Terrorists could make such a bomb with little difficulty and, because of its small size, could easily plant it somewhere in a city. Such an attack would cause widespread fear and might damage the health of large numbers of people. But which city out of many hundreds of possibilities would terrorists choose and can EVIL DONE help predict it? Although terrorists have not yet attacked a city with a dirty bomb, they have carried out many assassinations, the other form of attack we examine here. Again, we ask whether EVIL DONE can be used to help us understand who among the hundreds of possible targets (politicians, top officials and company executives) are most likely to be chosen.

Table 7.2 summarizes our answers to these two questions. It does seem that EVIL DONE would be helpful in analyzing the likely targets of both forms of attack, although not all of its components apply equally to both sets of targets. This is not surprising because the elements of CRAVED (the model for EVIL DONE) vary in importance in explaining the targets of different forms of product theft (e.g., burglary or shoplifting). Furthermore, we already found that "near" did not discriminate among the buildings in Washington, D.C., because they would all be equally distant from the base of an overseas terrorist group. In the case of a dirty bomb, we found that "easy" affords little discrimination among cities because they would all be easy to attack in this

Table 7.2 EVIL DONE Applied to Assassinations and to a Hypothetical Dirty Bomb Attack in a U.S. City

Target Characteristic	Dirty Bomb Attack in a U.S. City by Foreign Terrorists	Assassinations
Exposed	"Attracts attention" (not "easily identified") would be key here. The better known the city, the more attention that would be garnered by attacking it.	Well-known political figures are obvious targets. Lord Mountbatten was killed by the IRA and George Bush, Sr. was targeted by Saddam Hussein
Vital	Terrorists would choose a vital center of government or commerce because widespread disruption would result as residents fled.	Prime Minister Margaret Thatcher and her cabinet were targeted by an IRA bomb in a Brighton hotel in 1984.
Iconic	Terrorists would choose a city that embodies American life and values (e.g., New York, Washington, DC, Boston, San Francisco, Hollywood and Las Vegas).	The targeting of George Bush, Sr. requires no comment. The IRA targeted Mountbatten because he was related to the Queen and, although retired, was one of the British Empire's last colonial figures through his role in the independence of India.
Legitimate	Legitimate targets for terrorists would be New York (embodying capitalism); Washington (the seat of government); and Hollywood and Las Vegas (embodiments of moral degeneracy).	The IRA targeted soldiers of the British "occupying force" in Northern Ireland for sniper attacks and those who worked in government offices who were "aiding and supporting the enemy." On the other hand, communist terrorists in Italy killed about the same number of businessmen as police during 1970–82.[a]
Destructible	A dirty bomb would kill few but would endanger the health of many. The fear engendered by the attack might be out of all proportion to the real risk of permanent harm.	With the exception of personnel who may be wearing body armor, everyone is equally vulnerable to being killed by a bomb or bullet, but not everyone is equally open to attack (see "Easy" below).

Table 7.2 (*continued*)

Target Characteristic	Dirty Bomb Attack in a U.S. City by Foreign Terrorists	Assassinations
Occupied	Because a relatively small area would be affected by radioactivity, the city's population density would be more important than its size. New York is the densest U.S. city, but Washington and Boston have higher densities than larger cities such as Dallas.[b]	When assassins target the military or police, they try to kill as many as possible. A truck bomb killed 241 at the U.S. Marine barracks in Beirut in 1983 and another attack at the same time killed 55 paratroopers at the French barracks in the city.
Near	Overseas terrorists could reach some U.S. cities more easily (e.g., Hawaii is relatively close to the Philippines). More important might be the existence of an immigrant community near to the city where terrorists could prepare—but if sympathetic to the terrorists, it should not be put at risk of contamination.	Terrorists rarely attack military personnel in their own countries, but they regularly attack occupying forces.[c] A suicide bombing of an army mess hall in Iraq in 2005 killed and injured many American soldiers. The attack on the USS *Cole* by local terrorists resulted in the deaths of 17 sailors.
Easy	Some cities might be a little more difficult to attack than others. Thus, New York might be easier to defend from outside attack because of the limited number of points of entry by bridges and tunnels, but it could be attacked by boat and by air, of course.	It was easy for Indira Gandhi's politicized Sikh bodyguards to murder her. Most assassinations of important individuals occur close to their homes. Although they may alter their travel routines every day, one thing is predictable: "they must turn either right or left" when they exit their house.[d]

Notes:
[a]Drake (1998, 33).
[b]See, for an analysis, Gibson (1998). The definition of city area remains difficult and would be more precise using census tracts. We use these data only as an example, listing the most well-known cities.
[c]In fact, Pape (2005) argues that occupying forces are the preferred targets of attack by all terrorist groups.
[d]Drake (1998,105).

way and, in the case of assassinations, "destructible" has little discriminatory value because everyone could be killed by a bomb or bullet. Much more relevant for assassinations is the "legitimacy" of the target, because this is often questionable in these attacks unless they kill military personnel.[26] For example, when Mountbatten was killed, the attack was met with widespread condemnation and an outpouring of public sympathy. Ultimately, it might have harmed rather than helped the IRA, and this may help explain why targeted assassinations are comparatively rare.

Infrastructures as Targets

Government officials regularly demand that the infrastructures on which we depend for the comforts and necessities of everyday life should be given special protection. These infrastructures include:

- Transportation—air, sea, roads, rail, subways, ports, bridges and tunnels
- Food and agriculture—growing, processing and distribution
- Communications—telecommunications, postal service, radio, television and the Internet
- Water—reservoirs, distribution and purification
- Energy—refineries, generating stations, nuclear plants, electricity grids, oil and gas pipelines
- Industries and manufacturing—factories, warehouses, distribution centers, shops and retail outlets
- Public facilities—malls, restaurants, hotels, skyscrapers, stadiums and movie theaters
- Banking and finance—computer systems and offices
- Citizen care—public records of vital statistics, health, safety and social security systems, and property

It is clear from this list that infrastructures are essential for the economies—even survival—of all societies today and that their successful targeting by terrorists could indeed bring a government to its knees. In terms of EVIL DONE, they therefore satisfy its "vital" component. They also satisfy "near" because they span wide areas and terrorists might not have to travel far to find a vulnerable point to attack. (Internet access is of course "near" to anyone with an Internet connection). They meet the "exposed" criterion because many components of infrastructures, such as pylons or water towers, are highly visible if not obtrusive. They might be considered "legitimate" by terrorists because attacks on them may be unlikely to result in the deaths of "innocent" civilians, unless reservoirs are poisoned, or buses, subways, pubs and cafes are bombed. Finally, such attacks could be "easy" because national or federal governments are unable to protect infrastructures on their own, but have to rely on a patchwork of private and local government organizations to do this.[27] Coordinating this protection is an organizational nightmare.[28]

Despite these attractive features, terrorists have rarely attacked infrastructures worldwide,[29] and especially rarely in North America.[30] A notable exception is that soon after the occupation of Iraq the insurgents repeatedly attacked oil pipelines and electricity pylons and substations to show that the Coalition forces did not have control and were not improving conditions in the country. This made tactical sense in the specific context of that time and place. But worldwide, the MIPT database shows that of the 471 attacks on physical structures recorded from January 2004 through January 2005 only 29 percent were directed at infrastructure.[31] So, why are such apparently attractive targets not attacked more often?

We believe that the remaining components of EVIL DONE (i.e., iconic, destructible and occupied) can help to answer this question. First, with few exceptions, such as the Golden Gate or Brooklyn Bridges, infrastructures are rarely "iconic." Second, unless they directly serve the public, infrastructures are frequently not "occupied" and attacking them would not kill large numbers of people and deliver a body blow to a nation, one that causes extreme fear such as that resulting from the 9/11 attacks. Third, because infrastructures are so complex, terrorists would need extensive knowledge to discover how to bring them down. They are composed of systems that are interconnected in various ways (e.g., power grids, computer networks, rail networks, bus routes). To destroy an entire infrastructure would take much more planning, knowledge and reconnaissance than to destroy a specific building or conduct an attack in a specific location. Attacking a particular point or even several points of an infrastructure will not guarantee its destruction or even its extensive disruption.[32] In other words, infrastructures are not easily "destructible." This is particularly the case in modern societies, where redundancy is often built into the systems in anticipation of natural disasters. (This is why disasters such as earthquakes are far more deadly in less developed countries that do not have the level of finances or other resources to regulate the design and building of structures that can withstand earthquakes.[33]) Infrastructures can also span extremely wide areas, depending on the service provided. For example, power grids generally are regionally distributed; telecommunications are increasingly worldwide, although they depend on particular physical installations in particular locations (mobile phones, for example); water supplies tend to be regional and even local; food supplies are national and increasingly international. Terrorists can sometimes attack nearby infrastructure successfully, but they do not have the resources to attack entire infrastructures, at least when operating in a distant location far from their base. Rather, they must settle for one or two isolated attacks in specific locations, for example, specific stations within a subway system. These attacks characteristically cause temporary disruption, but subway systems are resilient and can quite quickly return to normal operation. True, the commuting public may be afraid for some time, but unless these attacks can be carried out on a regular basis, extensive disruption of the system is unlikely. And even in the case of continued attacks on public transport, such as Israel's bus service, because people must use the buses, the infrastructure itself will not be brought down. People

Box 7.1 Complexities of Infrastructure Protection: Pathways to and Through a Seaport

Although infrastructures have national and international links they also have extremely important local links. A seaport offers an excellent example of the local significance of infrastructure, the links it has to places far away and the pathways terrorists exploit to reach their targets and transport their weapons.

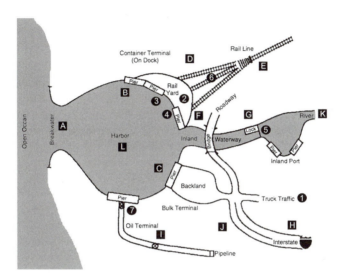

KEY:

A Target of Attack	**❶** Entry point/pathway to attack

A. Block harbor and channel entrance.

B. Sink ship in harbor or alongside pier.

C. Damage pier and terminal equipment.

D. Destroy cargo at terminal.

E. Break rail track within port area.

F. Topple a bridge restricting traffic.

G. Cause inoperable lock and close inland waterway.

H. Close interstate highway and divert traffic.

I. Break pipeline and disrupt flows.

J. Launch weapon from outside port to destroy facilities.

K. Poison, pollute river.

L. Blow up harbor and port with WMD.

1. Enter via truck; transport weapons, chemicals, explosives, people, drugs. Transport bomb, chemicals in truck.

2. Place nuclear, dirty bomb in container.

3. Enter terminal, get through immigration.

4. Bring bombs, weapons through customs.

5. Enter inland waterway.

6. Enter via rail line; transport operatives, drugs, weapons.

7. Enter via pipeline via liquid bulk cargo.

Source: Adapted from Price (2004).

will continue to use it, and preventive techniques to make it harder for bombers to attack the buses will be introduced.[34]

A final reason why infrastructures might not be attacked is that they are, in fact, also of great utility to terrorists. They can provide access to other targets and to the deployment of the tools and weapons they need to carry out attacks (see Box 7.1 and Chapters 7–10). In this respect, infrastructures might be less "legitimate" targets because terrorists depend on them as much as we do.

Before concluding this discussion of infrastructures, we should acknowledge that it breaks one of our cardinal rules—that analysis should be focused on highly specific kinds of attack and not on the many different forms of attack involving infrastructures. In fact, some of these forms—airliner hijackings and suicide bombings of public transport, for example—have at different times not only defined the public view of terrorism but have offered a highly tangible threat. This lack of specificity makes it difficult to reach any definitive conclusions from this discussion, but it does appear that EVIL DONE does help us to understand the reasons why infrastructures are not attacked as frequently as might be expected given their vital role in society.

CONCLUSION

We believe that EVIL DONE summarizes the main attractors of targets for terrorists. The influence exerted on target choice by each of its components will vary with the cultural background, organization and objectives of the terrorist group, and it will change over time. That, combined with a seeming infinity of potential targets (even when prioritized by EVIL DONE) can lead to a sense of futility, that there is no point in trying to anticipate the targets of attack. Such pessimism is unwarranted, however, because experience teaches us that systematic approaches are effective even when we are faced with an apparently impossible number of variables. We can see this in the successful efforts over the years to prevent industrial accidents. It is impossible to say where the next accident will happen. It could occur in manufacture, service, construction, transportation or any other sector. In any one of these sectors, it could be caused by falls, machinery, power failures or a host of other factors. It could take place in a company plant at home or overseas, operated by company staff or by subcontractors. On the face of it, then, the task is bewildering, but we know that a systematic, analytic approach is effective. This is why all accident fatalities and injuries are now a fraction of what they used to be. Industry is now required to undertake formal risk assessments of the sort we propose for terrorism.[35] EVIL DONE is a first step toward developing that risk analysis. Incidentally, we would disagree with those who might think that preventing terrorism is much harder than preventing accidents. Anticipating human logic should be no more difficult than anticipating human mistakes and structural failures.

We have said that all EVIL DONE features may be important to terrorists at various times throughout their planning, but we believe that, overall, the attribute of proximity to the target ("near") will have the most overwhelming influence on terrorist target selection. We put forward the reasons for this in Part III.

Weapons

In This Chapter

➤ Choice of weapon, like choice of target, is a crucial decision that faces all terrorists.

➤ The method of attack will depend on this decision

➤ The attributes of weapons that guide the terrorist's choice are summed up by the acronym MURDEROUS. The weapons are **M**ultipurpose, **U**ndetectable, **R**emovable, **D**estructive, **E**njoyable, **R**eliable, **O**btainable, **U**ncomplicated and **S**afe.

➤ Every weapon will contain, more or less, each of these attributes.

➤ The most important feature is that the weapon is easily obtainable, making it very familiar to the terrorist. Small arms and explosives are so obtainable.

➤ Switching from a routinely used weapon to a different weapon will be resisted, because it increases risk. Unconventional weapons, therefore, will be first used experimentally and for single attacks.

EVERY TERRORIST MUST choose a weapon, although there is one constraint, famously proclaimed by Donald Rumsfeld, the U.S. secretary of defense: "You don't go to war with what you would like, you go to war with what you have."

In fact, terrorists generally do have an advantage over those who must go to war: they have the time to get the weapons they choose, because they can generally choose when to carry out their missions, unhurried by tactical challenges posed by the enemy.

What factors, then, will contribute to the terrorist's choice of weapon? The first choice will depend on whether the terrorist has a particular target in mind. If the aim is to assassinate a particular individual who is highly protected, a high velocity rifle with telescopic sight may work. President Kennedy was killed in this way. However, the choice of weapon will also depend on other factors such as the availability of a trained marksman. The problem the terrorist faces then is how to get such a weapon, and how to find an individual who can use it. There are many other difficult contingencies involved in this choice, including whether the marksman is expendable. Terrorists who do not have at their disposal a trained marksman with a suitable gun may instead send a willing suicide to get close enough to the target and blow himself and the target up with a bomb (Sanjit Gandhi was so killed) or shoot the target at close quarters, knowing full well there is no chance of escape (the assassination of Mahatma Gandhi). Thus, the method of attack is contingent on both target selection and weapon selection. In the previous chapter, we described the distinguishing characteristics of targets that made them attractive to terrorists; in this chapter, we describe the attractive features of weapons.

As an elementary beginning, we suggest that there are three classes of weapons from which the terrorist must choose:

1. Guns and other small arms. It is surely obvious that the surplus of weapons in Iraq has enormously facilitated the actions of terrorists. In fact, the United Nations has complained that the world is awash in guns and other small arms. According to the Small Arms Survey,[1] the global value of such weapons is $7.4 billion, with huge stockpiles of 639 million small arms. The Survey was able to account for the transfer of only 50 percent of weapons internationally. The other 50 percent included dealings that were not reported to the United Nations by countries or by companies. Thus, the "gray-black" market in small arms is probably as large as the legitimate market. Not only have guns become increasingly available, but they have also become smaller and easier to use (see Table 8.1) and thus more attractive to terrorists.

2. Explosives. Guns are much easier to handle than explosives, which may explain why there were so many more terrorist shootings (35,794) in Northern Ireland between 1969 and 1999 than bombings (15,346).[2] On the other hand, although bullets can kill people, they generally do little damage to buildings and structures. This may explain why terrorists like to use explosives. These can damage structures, even bring down buildings, as well as kill people. The shock value of an explosion is therefore much greater. This has the advantage of creating more fear, especially as the newspaper and TV coverage of bomb damage can be so much more graphic than the coverage of a shooting. Indeed, Alex Schmid, former head of the U.N. Terrorism Branch

Table 8.1 Relative Size and Rate of Fire of Machine Guns, 1884–1970

Model and Year	Length (inches)	Weight (pounds)	Rate of fire (rounds/minute)
Maxim (1884)	46.50	40.00	600
Thompson (1928)	33.75	10.75	800
Uzi (1950s)	18.90	8.90	600
Ingrams MAC 10 (1970)	10.50	6.25	1,145
Uzi Mini (2005)	14.70	6.30	1,200

Sources: Adapted from Drake (1998, 94); Hogg and Weeks (1977, 101–2); http://www.uzitalk.com/.

has argued that the increasing incidence and lethality of conventional weapons and explosives has increased the shock value of terrorist acts.[3] In the United States, explosives account for 75 percent of all terrorist incidents recorded by the Federal Bureau of Investigation (FBI) for the period 1980–2001.[4] Improvised explosive devices (IEDs) are also commonly used by terrorists who, if short of money or equipment, may need to improvise with what is available. Depending on the availability of materials, these may range from elementary to highly sophisticated devices. In Iraq, they have become a major weapon and have increased in lethality and sophistication as U.S. forces have increased their defensive armor against them.[5] Clearly, the widespread availability of explosives and other bomb-making equipment in Iraq has facilitated the use and sophistication of these weapons.

3. Unconventional weapons. Experts usually explain the terrorists' widespread use of guns and explosives on the basis of their ready availability and familiarity.[6] "Unconventional" weapons, such as nuclear-related, chemical and biological weapons, have also become increasingly available, although still not as readily obtained as guns and explosives. These unconventional weapons offer special opportunities to terrorists, in particular the potential for mass destruction (called weapons of mass destruction, or WMDs). Their use by terrorists would, for the moment, probably have to be improvised, as is apparent from the various Al Qaeda manuals retrieved from Afghanistan,[7] although, as we will see in Chapter 10, their construction may be facilitated by the increased availability of technical know-how and nuclear materials throughout the world.

THE CHOICE OF TERRORISTS' MURDEROUS WEAPONS

We identify below nine attributes of weapons that will guide the terrorist's choice, which are summed up by the acronym MURDEROUS—multipurpose, undetectable, removable, destructive, enjoyable, reliable, obtainable, uncomplicated and safe.

(1) Multipurpose. Some weapons have a specific use, such as a high-powered rifle, while explosives have a much wider application from assassinations to conflagrations, but they cannot be reused, so their supply must be replenished. However, bullets must also be replaced, and there are ways to achieve the destructive effects of explosives, for example, by using dum-dum bullets and such weapons as rocket-propelled grenades and shoulder-launched missiles. These latter weapons combine the explosive force of bombs and the capacity to be aimed like a gun. Small arms such as revolvers, rifles and machine guns can be used over and over again. One weapon traced in the shootings carried out by the 17 November terrorist group in Greece was used in several different incidents that spanned some 20 years (Box 8.1).

Box 8.1 Staying with What You Know

For more than 27 years, 17 November was one of the most mysterious and successful terrorist organizations. Taking its name from a student uprising in 1973, the group claimed responsibility for the deaths of 23 American, British and Greek officials and business leaders. Its assassinations and attacks caused serious political problems for successive Greek governments, badly damaging the country's foreign relations. When the group's leaders and most of its members were apprehended in July 2002, it was striking just how small it was. With only some two dozen members (16 apprehended), 17 November based its terror campaign on a handful of guns. One of the revolvers recovered by Greek police had been used in at least six attacks.

* * *

Despite terrorist intentions, the group apparently had considerable trouble acquiring weapons and the expertise to use them. The arrests in 2002 stemmed from a botched bombing. They confirmed that the same firearms were used repeatedly. The group's most successful acquisition of weapons was a raid on an army depot on Christmas day in 1989 that yielded 51 antitank rockets, most of which have now been recovered. Whether the group was unable to use them or just unwilling to, they represented the limits of its interest in heavier arms.

Source: Graduate Institute of International Studies (2003).

(2) **Undetectable.** Because of the security procedures in place in many parts of the world, especially at airports, the weapon of choice might have to be concealable or undetectable. The Japanese and PLO terrorists who attacked airport terminals in Rome, Istanbul and Tel-Aviv in the 1970s used machine guns to mow down civilians. It is unlikely that they could do this today because of the security procedures in place to detect guns, although this security could be breached by some Glock handguns that are difficult to detect because of their largely plastic construction.[8] However, a handgun can kill only a limited number of people, unless the gun is used while an airplane is in flight. An explosive that is small and undetectable is much more lethal. That explosive is Semtex (or its American counterpart C-4 and other variations). This plastic explosive is highly stable and small amounts can do enormous damage. It took only 11 ounces of Semtex packed in an 11-inch Toshiba tape recorder to bring down Pan Am 103 over Lockerbie (see Box 8.2). Since then, Semtex has become the weapon of choice for many terrorists. Because it is so light and small, it serves as an ideal weapon for suicide bombers who must penetrate layers of security to reach their target.

(3) **Removable.** The weapons of terrorism must be portable, which means that they must be relatively light and reasonably small so they can be carried by one or two people, or at least lifted onto the back of a pickup truck. Their portability and size also make them very "stealable," because we know from

Box 8.2 Semtex: The Terrorist's Weapon

All explosives have important uses in modern life. They are used in mining, to build roads and tunnels through mountains and for many manufacturing processes. The controlled explosion of Semtex is used to harden steel (especially the hardened steel of missile nose cones, which must withstand extremely high temperatures).

Invented in Czechoslovakia during the Cold War era, reportedly at the request of North Vietnam to obtain an explosive equal to the American C-4 plastic explosive, Semtex is now widely used by terrorists around the world. Thousands of tons of it have been sold to many states, some of which are, or were, supporters of terrorist groups. Between 1975 and 1981, Czechoslovakia shipped Libya several hundred tons of Semtex, some of which Libya then supplied to the IRA and various other terrorist groups. The IRA has used Semtex in all bombings carried out since at least 1986.

Given the enormous popularity of the explosive around the world for commercial as well as destructive purposes, attempts have been made to modify the explosive to shorten its shelf life from the currently estimated 20 years to 3 years. However, the makers of Semtex claim that this is not possible technically, and that the shelf life of Semtex (and other similar explosives) is generally unknown, but it is probably around 100 years or more. They also say that to shorten its shelf life would place Semtex at a competitive disadvantage with its competitors.

Semtex does leave an identifiable trace after its explosion, but it has been recently modified to remove these traces. There are also devices for detecting unexploded Semtex and like substances, but it is only a matter of time before versions of Semtex that are undetectable by these detectors will emerge.

With the technological solution to reducing the usefulness of Semtex to terrorists limited, another approach has been tried, and that is to control the sale and distribution of Semtex. The European Union has set up a monitoring system to take over its distribution and sales, but the effectiveness of this intervention is yet to be demonstrated.

There is one small drawback to using Semtex as a compact bomb in, say, an airplane, which is that it requires a small explosion to detonate it. This is how the shoe bomber Richard Reid was caught when trying to light a fuse on his sneakers on a trans-Atlantic flight in 2001. This is, however, a small technical problem that a more skilled terrorist could overcome.

studies of "hot products" (see Chapter 7) that objects of high value that are portable are those that are most often targeted by thieves. Thus, when high-quality stereo equipment was still very expensive, it was a favorite target of burglars for many years. Of course, the value they saw in these products was in their disposal for cash. To a terrorist, the value he or she sees in the weapon is in its utility for the terrorist mission.

(4) Destructive. It is beyond doubt that the weapon of choice by many terrorist groups is an explosive device that causes as much damage as possible. A possible exception to this rule is the IRA's use of guns at a much higher rate than bombs in the early 1970s (see Figure 8.1). This might be explained by the

IRA's strategy at the time, which was to target specific individuals identified as the enemy (Loyalists, Royal Ulster Constabulary, politicians)—a strategy that was informed by the writings of Carlos Marighella who advocated selective killing of specific members of the colonial or occupying force.[9] Guns may be a more efficient way to kill targeted individuals and, incidentally, guns were also much more useful in the many armed robberies carried out by the IRA to raise money for their activities. In this respect, therefore, the choice of weapon depends on both the specific mission and the overall strategy of the terrorist group.

While the number of shootings declined rapidly in the second half of the 1970s, bombings continued to be undertaken at a fairly steady rate throughout the 1980s and early 1990s (Figure 8.1). In 1979, the technology of remote detonation became available to the IRA, and in the 1980s they received shipments of Semtex from Libya.[10] Furthermore, their shootings received much less coverage in the media than did their bombings for which they are most well known. This is probably because more people are killed in bombings than in shootings.[11] It may well be that for the purposes of media effect and infliction of fear on the public, bombings achieve a much greater return to terrorists than do shootings.

(5) Enjoyable. Terrorists are clearly attracted to their weapons, seeming to get much excitement and pleasure out of their use. In fact, it is not just terrorists who enjoy weapons. Many ordinary people do too. However, ordinary people are limited in the amount of firepower they can purchase in a weapon and the destruction they can legally cause when they use their weapons. Children (and adults) delight in fireworks and delight in playing with them, even though they are dangerous. This is why laws have been passed in many countries and various states of the United States banning their sale. There are no

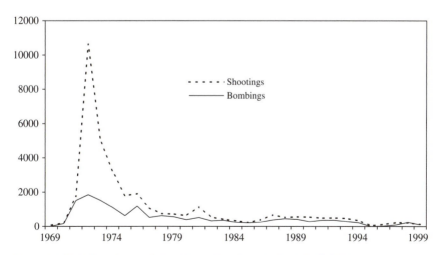

Figure 8.1 IRA Shootings and Bombings, Northern Ireland, 1969–1999
Sources: Adapted from Alexander (2002, 202). Data taken from Statistics and Research Agency, Royal Ulster Constabulary.

such felt restrictions on terrorists, unless, of course, their mission calls on them to show restraint (which may well occur, for example, in holding off on firing or detonation until just the right moment). Furthermore, some societies in which terrorists operate tolerate much more public use of quite powerful weapons, for example, the accepted practice in Middle Eastern countries of shooting guns in the air using live bullets at celebratory functions.

(6) Reliable. We have all seen movies in which the gun jams at the critical point. A weapon must be highly reliable, which is the reason why new military recruits require thorough training in caring for the weapons that they might have to depend on in extremely dangerous situations. Users of a weapon find out whether or not it is reliable by gaining familiarity with it. If they have used the weapon, or one like it, many times before, they are likely to favor that weapon over another. This means that unconventional weapons, of unknown reliability, will be shunned unless the mission cannot be accomplished in any other way. It is also very likely that, in situations of routine terrorism, unconventional weapons or weapons with which the terrorists have little experience will be rejected in favor of those that are routinely used. In fact, the most feared unconventional weapon has never been used in a terrorist attack (that is, a nuclear bomb), although others, such as Sarin gas, have been used on a limited basis, which were basically botched attempts. The 1995 Sarin attack in the Tokyo subway was the second such attempt by the same terrorist group, which had previously carried out an experimental attack. It will take many such attacks for any terrorist group to develop a reliable and trusted methodology for deploying unconventional weapons on a regular basis.

(7) Obtainable. This is, perhaps, the most important of all characteristics. How easy is it to get the weapon? Can it be bought easily? Can it be stolen easily? Or can it even be manufactured in-house? As we noted earlier, the world is awash in small arms, which are the most widely used weapons of terrorists. And because there are so many of them, there are plenty of places from which to steal them—probably the most common way in which terrorists obtain their weapons.[12] Semtex and other plastic explosives are probably the most widely traded or stolen weapons.[13] As noted in Box 8.1, many tons of Semtex have been sold to terrorist-friendly states, which have passed it on to terrorist groups. In 2003, journalists from the London *Daily Mirror*[14] even posed as terrorists and bought 13.5 kilograms of Semtex from terrorists in Kosovo for £10,000. They were also offered three shoulder-to-air missile launchers and an antiaircraft gun. Other weapons are also freely available and cheap. In 1994, a standard Chinese-made hand grenade cost about $5 compared with a European-made one that cost $16; a Soviet-made AK-47 costs $100 compared with about $700 for a similar West European rifle.[15] In contrast, unconventional weapons are rarely used by terrorists, partly because not nearly as many are available in the world. They have become much more available than they once were, but they have a long way to go to reach the wide availability of conventional weapons.

(8) Uncomplicated. A weapon's user-friendliness determines how much training is needed for terrorists to operate it successfully. Even seemingly simple weapons such as a handgun require practice and training to use properly (see Box 8.1). A complicated weapon or one that demands considerable skill to use effectively, such as a free-flight armor-piercing missile, will rarely be used. In fact, when these have been used by terrorist groups, they have often proved unsuccessful because of incorrect use.[16] The more widely used particular weapons are, the more easily available will be personnel who are trained to use them or who can train others to use them. Again, therefore, we see that the bias is heavily toward weapons that are widely or commonly used, both legally and illegally. A weapon that requires extensive training for its use also increases the preparation time for an attack, reduces the number of individuals available to use it at any point in time, increases risk of discovery because of time needed for training in secret locations, and time needed for individuals of the terrorist group to be physically together for the training. This is why the training camps of Al Qaeda were at risk of attack: although located in remote locations, their existence was, in fact, known by U.S. and other intelligence agencies. We would also add, by the way, that unconventional weapons are also complicated in construction and delivery, and for this reason alone may not be adopted easily by terrorist groups unless such groups are of considerable longevity with considerable financial resources.[17]

(9) Safe. The use of bombs as weapons is inherently more dangerous than the use of other weapons. It is common to hear of terrorists blowing themselves up while preparing a bomb and there are a number of recorded instances.[18] In fact it is claimed that during the period 1969–93 one-third of PIRA members were blown up by explosives that detonated prematurely.[19] This also means that preparing bombs for an attack, even using the much safer Semtex and other more stable explosives such as the American C-4, still requires expertise. In fact, Israeli intelligence reports that all bombs used for suicide bombings in Israel are made by a handful of technicians, each of whom has his own identifiable method of bomb construction.[20]

SWITCHING WEAPONS

We can see from the foregoing, particularly Box 8.1, that it takes a lot to get terrorists to switch weapons, especially in regard to routine terrorism such as suicide bombings in Israel. The setup costs are so high that a change in weaponry would have to be forced on the group because of some change in operating conditions or because the new weapon offered a considerable advantage over the old, making it worth the risk to change. In fact, this is exactly what happened with suicide bombing in Israel. The early attacks against Israel by Hamas and other groups were carried out using truck bombs, sometimes with suicide ram bombings and sometimes with placement of the truck bomb near the target. However, as the Israeli Defense Force developed preventive measures, especially ways of detecting dynamite, and as it narrowed the check points and entries into Israel so that more thorough searches could be conducted, it became increasingly difficult to get a truck laden with explosives through to the target.[21] It was at this point that Hamas turned to Semtex, a much smaller and more stable explosive that was easier to conceal and get through Israeli checkpoints. The change in weapons was thus forced on Hamas by new security procedures and by the highly attractive features of Semtex.

The example of the switch to suicide bombing is an example from routine terrorism, a significant feature of which is the longevity of the terrorist group. It is only in terrorist groups that last for a long period that the capacity exists to improve on the original technology. For example, the IRA greatly improved its detonating techniques and even created a type of grenade to penetrate armored vehicles. It could not have done this if the group lasted less than a year, as do most terrorist groups (see Chapter 6).

OVERCOMING COMPLEXITY

Group longevity will also contribute to overcoming the complexity of weaponry. However, it will still require considerable investment in time, money and personnel, and, as noted earlier, it increases the risk of exposure. Unfortunately, some terrorist groups have been able to overcome this difficulty by contracting out to "free-agent" terrorist groups that may specialize in the use of particular weaponry.[22] It is also apparent that the use of complex weapons in Iraq (e.g., rocket-propelled grenades) has been made possible because many of the terrorists are apparently former members of Saddam Hussein's military guard, who may have been well trained in the use of such weapons.

Finally, the opposite of group longevity, the advent of the "leaderless resistance" movement—advocated by Louis Beam[23] of the right-wing militia movements, in which individuals are called on to act alone and depend only on themselves—causes these leaderless terrorists to fall back on their own resources.[24] This is why Timothy McVeigh used a primitive (though very effective) bomb, which he had to make himself with some help from his associates. In all 20 of the terrorist attacks within the United States recorded by the FBI in 2000 and 2001 the weapons used were relatively primitive, including those used on 9/11. In at least 4 of the 18 domestic incidents of terrorism, which were carried out by lone individuals or tiny groups emulating the Beam "leaderless resistance" approach, several of the incendiary devices failed to detonate. When individuals are forced to rely on their own devices, without organizational or other support, the sophistication of weaponry suffers.

In the next chapter, we continue our analysis of the opportunity structure for terrorism: the tools that enable terrorists to make their attacks.

Tools

In This Chapter

- ➤ The tools that terrorists need almost always include cars and trucks, credit cards and cash, cell phones and information about the target for attack.
- ➤ Many of these tools are "hot products"—sought by ordinary criminals; terrorists also acquire most of these illegally.
- ➤ We can modify these products to make them less easily used by criminals and terrorists, we can make them more difficult to obtain illegally, and we can track their use.
- ➤ Measures to prevent terrorism are more likely to be implemented if they also reduce ordinary "volume" crimes or organized crimes.
- ➤ We should carefully evaluate every proposed measure for its social and economic costs before introducing it.
- ➤ We must expect that the terrorists will try to find ways around any new preventive measures we introduce.

IN THE PREVIOUS two chapters, we spelled out what we mean by targets and weapons, and defined those features that made them attractive or not attractive to terrorists when planning their attacks. In this and the following chapter, we will describe the two major factors that bring weapons and targets together. These are the tools and facilitating conditions that enable terrorists to get their weapons or enhance their effectiveness, and that help them select or reach their targets.

There is an important distinction between tools and facilitating conditions. Tools such as cars and trucks, credit cards, stolen IDs and cell phones are tangible products (like weapons) that terrorists use in their attacks;[1] facilitating conditions, on the other hand, are societal features and systems that make it easier for them to mount these attacks. However, both of these characterizations require some qualification. Some tools rely on broader systems for their effectiveness. For example, a cell phone is a tangible product, a valuable means of communication for the terrorist, but its operation depends on an underlying system of wireless communication. This wireless system is what might be called a facilitating condition. Another similar example would be a false credit card that might be used by a terrorist organization to obtain goods and services, but this would only be possible if it passed muster with the broader credit system on which these cards depend. Weapons also share a common attribute with tools in that they are products, so that many of the techniques to control the acquisition of tools as "hot products" may also apply to them. However, weapons are a special kind of tool because they have a much more specific function in terrorist attacks, which is why we examined them separately in the previous chapter.

Both cell phones and credit cards are, of course, tools of everyday life with a multitude of legitimate users. Because these tools are part of our everyday life it is difficult to make them less readily used by terrorists. We take the wonderful conveniences that they provide for granted. We overlook the ways they can be exploited by terrorists and only become aware of these possibilities when we are victimized by criminal exploitation of these advantages, for example, by identity theft.

THE TOOLS OF TERRORISM

We discuss a short list below of the tools (i.e., tangible products) that are often used in the course of a terrorist attack. In keeping with our usual precept, we might have made up a list for each different form of terrorism, but for the purposes of this chapter we have chosen to discuss the tools that are needed in most forms of attack. This may be less practical, but it avoids a detailed discussion of the many different forms of terrorism simply to make a point that holds for all. At the same time, it allows us to meet our general objective—which is to lay out a methodology for thinking about reducing opportunities for terrorism without being waylaid by the details of applying the methodology.

We should also be clear that our discussion does not specifically include rare occurrences, such as the attacks of 9/11 (even if much of what we say is still relevant to those events). Nor do we include greatly feared attacks that have not yet occurred or have occurred only very rarely (nuclear, chemical and biological attacks). Finally, we have not tried to foresee the possible nature of future attacks, although we discuss the need to do this later in the book. Rather, we have limited ourselves to the most common kinds of terrorist attack that occur frequently around the world, such as ram bombings, car bombings, drive-by shootings and targeted assassinations. As far as we can see, these attacks generally require the terrorists to have access to the following tools: cell phones or other means of communication and control; cars or trucks to transport the terrorists and/or their weapons; money—either cash or (false) credit cards; false documents—for example, driver's licenses, passports or visas, and vehicle registration documents; and, finally, maps, plans, addresses, photographs and other information about the target. In what follows, we discuss these tools in a little more detail and begin to speculate on possible ways to control them or make them less useful to the terrorists.

1. Cell phones. We know that mobile phones have facilitated the organization of drug dealing on the street,[2] and without cell phones the terrorists of today would be hamstrung. They are used as timers to detonate bombs (the 2004 Madrid train station bombing), to communicate with the media to claim responsibility for their deeds and increase the attendant publicity and, perhaps much more useful, to communicate among themselves. The existence of cell phones makes it far easier for loose organizations to communicate with each other.[3] A rigid structure of command is unnecessary and constricting. Cell phones allow for the organization of a project to be done on the fly, should unexpected barriers to carrying out an attack arise. Their importance must be enormous to terrorists who still, as far as we can determine, use them although they know that there is a good chance that intelligence agencies might be eavesdropping.

2. Cars and trucks. In most major terrorist attacks against American targets both at home and overseas, cars or trucks have been the main tool for delivery of explosive. An exception is the 9/11 attack, although a truck was used to deliver the explosive in the first attack against the World Trade Center. Without cars or trucks, where would terrorists be? They would be limited to sending letter bombs through the mail, sending in suicide bombers on foot or using rocket-propelled grenades or other high-powered weaponry. While such weaponry is frequently used in Iraq because of its easy availability there, in the United States and other Western democracies, getting hold of such a weapon and using it on a regular basis offers a far greater challenge, and far greater risk, than using a truck filled with explosives.

3. Cash and credit cards. Innovations of the past 40 years, such as bank cards and credit cards, have made financial transactions much easier and more convenient. Unfortunately, the massive amount of credit card and other banking information stored on computers has made this information a ripe target for criminals. Used in conjunction with false or stolen identities, criminals and terrorists can access the bank and credit card accounts of individuals and use this money to pay for their expenses and to cover their tracks (charging the rental of a truck, for example, to a false or stolen credit card, as occurred in the first attack on the World Trade Center).[4] Although some terrorist organizations have been financed by various benefactors, many are not, or many need more money than they have. This has led some organizations to engage in drug trafficking and other forms of organized crime to obtain funds, while others, such as the IRA, have committed armed robberies on a regular basis. (According to Royal Ulster Constabulary records, the IRA was responsible for just under 21,000 armed robberies in Northern Ireland from 1969–99).[5]

4. False documents. Documents that record the identity of people include birth and marriage certificates, passports and visas, social security cards and driver's licenses. All individuals in Western democracies carry with them one or more cards that contain some of this information. The information attests to who they are and is used on many occasions to authenticate their identities. These systems make our lives easier in ways that we take for granted and that seem simple even though they are complicated. Ways of efficiently identifying and authenticating individuals in a modern society are crucial. It is because these identifying systems are taken for granted, however, that terrorists can exploit their weaknesses without our realizing it. The irony is that the very systems developed to track individuals—where they live, who they are—provide terrorists with the opportunities to hide among us. If any of the systems that track or identify people are lax in their administration (or use old technology), then holes will be quickly found and exploited by criminals or terrorists. As we now know, the majority of the 9/11 hijackers were operating under false or stolen identities, made possible by lax procedures for issuing identity-related documents.

5. Target information. During the cold war, it was difficult to obtain detailed maps of Soviet-block countries and in World War II road signs were removed in Southern England to make it difficult for the expected German invaders to find their way around. Just as the military needs maps and methods to find their targets so, too, do the terrorists. For a letter bomb to reach its intended victim, they need the victim's address. When targeting a specific building, they need a map to know where to put the bomb or how to bypass security, and when targeting a specific individual, they need an account of the target's daily routines, a photograph or, at the very least, a detailed description. It is hard to see how in peacetime any of this information could be kept out of the hands of terrorists, although tightening up regulations on where photography is permitted might help achieve this. Airports are progressively introducing such controls and the London Underground does not permit photography in some of its stations.

CONTROLLING TOOLS

Some general points relevant to control emerge from this brief review of the tools of terrorism, as follows:

1. Hot products. Any list of "hot products"[6]—things that criminals target for theft—would include many of the tools we have identified. This is certainly true of cars and trucks, cash and credit cards, passports and cell phones.

2. Electronic systems. Many of these tools, especially credit cards and cell phones, depend on underlying electronic systems for their authenticity or operability. This means that our prevention efforts must be focused as much on these systems as on the products themselves.

3. Theft and fraud. The terrorists probably steal most of the tools they use, or acquire them illegally in other ways. We know that terrorist groups (such as the IRA) commit armed robberies for cash. They might also manufacture their own passports and credit cards, but they are just as likely to acquire them from organized crime groups. Indeed, the distinction between organized crime and terrorism is often quite murky. For example, it has been documented that terrorists in Central America serve as couriers for drug traffickers ("narcoterrorism")[7] and it is claimed that the IRA is morphing into an organized crime group as its terrorist role diminishes with advances in the Northern Ireland peace process.[8]

4. Inadequate controls. The acquisition of many tools is made easier by lax and inadequate controls on international trade and financial transactions. The international dealing in weapons benefits greatly from clandestine markets that flourish in spite of national and international laws limiting the sale of many powerful weapons.[9] The complex regulations and conflicting laws of many countries make it easier for terrorists to sidestep usual banking procedures and to launder money in many innovative ways,[10] often using a parallel system to regular financial markets (see next chapter).

What these facts imply is that our existing efforts to prevent theft of hot products, to disrupt the operations of organized crime and to close loopholes in banking and other regulations exploited by transnational organized crime groups will also make life more difficult for the terrorists. How exactly we should go about doing this is beyond the scope of this chapter, because it would involve a detailed technical discussion of each one of the tools that we have listed and the electronic record keeping and authentication systems that underpin their use. It would also preempt our discussion of the general principles of prevention that we set out in detail later in the book. However, we can say that there are three general approaches to tightening up controls on tools: (1) we can modify them to make them more difficult to convert to terrorist use; (2) we can tighten up their supply or reduce their accessibility to terrorists; and (3) we can track their distribution so we know who has acquired them.

In respect to the first option, modifying the tools themselves, there is already a long history of doing this in preventing crime, beginning at the end of the seventeenth century with the introduction of milled edges for silver coins to prevent them from being "clipped" to collect enough silver for another coin.[11] Ever since then, the technology of cash and banknote production has been progressively evolving in response to developments in the forgers' techniques. The same story can be told with developments in the security of automobiles, which when first available had no ignition locks or even doors. Now all cars sold in the European Union and Australia, and many sold in the United States, come with built-in electronic immobilizers that are difficult for thieves to defeat.[12] In fact, attempts have already been made to modify practically every one of the tools of terrorism to make them less readily usable by criminals and thus also by terrorists.

Unfortunately, we have been playing catch up with products and systems in trying to prevent misuse by criminals—and now terrorists. For example, the United States did not anticipate the explosion of cloning that followed the introduction of cell phones, although the problem has now been resolved by new technology (see Box 9.1). In the same way, we did not anticipate the problems that would arise with the Microsoft Windows operating system, which was designed to make using computers easy for everyone. There was not the slightest inkling that security of the system should be built into its

---

Box 9.1 The Rise and Fall of the Cloned Phone

When cell phones became popular, criminals found ways to clone them so that they could use them without paying any bills. They used scanners near airports and hotels to capture the numbers that each phone transmits to send and receive calls. They then created "clones" of the original phones by reprogramming the numbers into phones they had stolen. The original phone would then be charged for calls made by the clone. This rapidly became big business. The top line in the figure shows that the cloning losses for all cell phone companies increased quite rapidly from June 1992 to June 1996 when they totaled nearly $450 million for the previous six months. (The losses were the charges that the phone companies wiped off the bills of legitimate subscribers whose phones were cloned.) At this point, the phone companies began to introduce a variety of technologies that made it much more difficult to steal phone numbers and to use a clone. There was a rapid reduction in cloning so that, by December 1999, it was all but eliminated (see boxed figure). Incidentally, the second most common form of cell phone fraud, "subscription fraud" (opening an account with a false name and address), did not skyrocket when cloning was closed down, as displacement doomsters would predict. This could be because cloning was easy to "mass produce" by organized criminals, whereas subscription fraud is not.

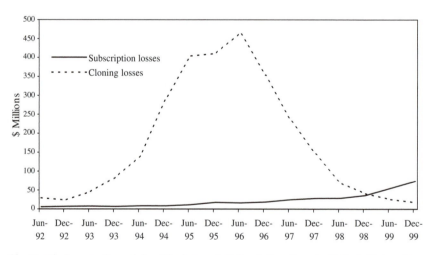

Six-Month Losses Caused by Cloning and Subscription Fraud: United States, June 1992–December 1999 ($ millions)

Source: Clarke, Kemper and Wyckoff (2001).

design. Now it is obvious that criminals and terrorists can hack into computer systems and wreak havoc, exploiting the holes found in the Windows operating system. Microsoft is hard at work retrofitting security into the system. What Microsoft should have done at the very beginning was not at all obvious. It has only become obvious with the passing of time. What we must do, therefore, is try to anticipate what will become obvious in the future. In fact, we must not only catch up, we must get one step ahead of the terrorists (see Chapter 15).

The second approach to reduce illegal access to tools has perhaps an even longer history. We have already mentioned that safe cracking and bank robbery have been greatly reduced by improvements in bank security and safe technology. In the long run, the slow and inexorable move to a "cashless" society, driven by convenience shopping, will probably result in the complete removal of cash as a tool and target of crime.[13] This process would be hastened if banknotes were produced in denominations no larger than $20, which has sometimes been suggested as a means of disrupting money laundering. This would make it more difficult for terrorists to move around large sums of cash—$1 million in $20 bills weighs about 115 pounds and fills two suitcases. Nowadays, there can be few legitimate reasons for people to carry around large bills, and the anonymous purchasing power they provide assists organized crime as well as terrorism.

The third general strategy for controlling the tools of terror—tracking products and even people—probably has the most potential—thanks to the electronic revolution. Following are some examples of what could be done:

- Transponders routinely fitted to all vehicles, together with monitoring points on highways and city streets, could make it much more difficult for terrorists to obtain and use stolen cars and trucks. These would have the additional benefit of monitoring compliance with traffic regulations and licensing requirements. But this could only work if the systems for recording, insuring and licensing vehicles were considerably improved (see Box 9.2).
- RFID (remote frequency identity) tags in all packages sent through the mail and courier services could make it much harder for terrorists to mount a campaign using letter bombs or chemically laced parcels.
- "Smart cards" encoded with individuals' personal details, photos and other data could serve as all-purpose driver's licenses, passports and credit cards. Such a proposal always invokes protests from the spokespersons for civil liberties, but the convenience they could afford ordinary citizens in their everyday lives is considerable, and we believe that the introduction of new forms of electronic identification are inevitable. Given the equal dangers of their misuse, especially by terrorists, we believe they would not be launched without careful security design considerations governing their manufacture and distribution.[14]

Box 9.2 Loopholes in the United Kingdom's Vehicle Licensing and Registration System

The United Kingdom has one of the highest rates of car theft in Europe. About 340,000 cars are stolen in the United Kingdom every year, of which about 120,000 are never recovered. It has long been suspected that loopholes in the vehicle licensing and registration system operated by the Driving and Vehicle Licensing Authority (DVLA) are systematically exploited by criminals to provide stolen cars with a new identity. (Again, it is ironic that the very system established to track individual owners and drivers of vehicles should be exploited by criminals (and terrorists too) who hide in the cracks of these systems by obtaining false driver's licenses or stealing motor vehicles.) The U.K. government commissioned a study of the system to find ways of closing these loopholes, which produced the following recommendations:

A. To reduce database inaccuracy

1. Registered owners remain liable for their vehicle until a change of ownership is notified to DVLA.
2. Buyers to show reliable proof of identity (identity card/photo ID and proof of current address) when registering as a new owner.
3. Move to a single virtual database by 2004.
4. Key details (vehicle and owner identification) verified and updated at each relevant contact with vehicles/owners.
5. Police and other appropriate enforcement agencies to have secure, online access to relevant parts of the database, leaving an audit trail for data protection purposes.
6. Insurance industry and car dealers to supply relevant information to the database electronically within one working week by 2004 and move to real time by 2007.
7. The government to commission a review of insurance arrangements with respect to whether the person or the vehicle should be insured.

B. To reduce insecurity of vehicle identification systems

8. The government should plan to introduce electronic vehicle identification before the end of 2007.

C. To strengthen enforcement

9. An enforcement capability should be established funded out of increased tax and insurance receipts.

D. To remedy lack of strategic overview

10. A Vehicle Licensing Implementation Group and a Vehicle Licensing Futures Group should be established.
11. Crime prevention should take a higher priority within DVLA.

Source: Laycock and Webb (2005).

CONCLUSION

We have not sought in this chapter to list all the tools that terrorists use. Nor have we sought to explore all the possible ways that these might be controlled. But even from our brief review of possibilities, it is clear that much more could be done to make life difficult for the terrorists by developing controls on the many products that they routinely use. We have noted that many of these products are favored by ordinary criminals as well also by organized crime. Concentrating preventive efforts on them would therefore not only impede terrorism, but would also reduce crime. Others have noted that antiterrorism measures that carry some such "dual benefit" are more likely to be adopted, and we return to this theme in Chapter 17. Meanwhile, we should also anticipate another theme, which is that there is a multitude of ways to reduce opportunities for terrorism. Each time we consider a proposed prevention measure we should carefully evaluate its social and economic costs and compare it with other ways of serving the same ends. This applies to everything we have suggested—including having only $20 banknotes, transponders in vehicles and smart identity/credit cards. Subjecting each of these suggestions to this careful process of evaluation should ensure that we do not impose on ourselves undue burdens of cost or unnecessary restrictions of our day-to-day freedoms.

Unfortunately, many conditions facilitate terrorism beyond those of the availability of tools and weapons for use in terrorism. These conditions prevail internationally and in particular societies, both developed and less developed. In the next chapter, we turn to a review of these facilitating conditions, and do this within the context of the threat of nuclear terrorism.

Facilitating Conditions: The Nuclear Example

In This Chapter

➤ "Facilitating conditions" are the social and physical arrangements of society that make specific acts of terrorism possible.
➤ Analysis of these conditions helps to identify preventive options.
➤ Five categories of facilitating conditions can be distinguished—those that make terrorism **E**asy, **S**afe, **E**xcusable, **E**nticing and **R**ewarding (ESEER).
➤ Facilitating conditions must be identified for each stage of a specific type of terrorist attack (this chapter uses the example of terrorists constructing and deploying a crude nuclear bomb).
➤ It is not possible to address every facilitating condition; analysis must identify those most amenable to change and those that will bring the greatest preventive benefits.
➤ Those with the most potential for yielding preventive benefits must be studied in detail to determine the best ways to increase the risks and the difficulty of this form of attack, reduce its rewards and remove excuses and enticements.

IN THIS CHAPTER, we consider the fourth pillar of terrorist opportunity, "facilitating conditions"—the social and physical arrangements of society that make acts of terrorism possible. We have already given many examples of facilitating conditions for various forms of terrorism, including the advantages of airliners for hostage-taking, the widespread availability of shoulder-fired missiles on the illegal arms market and the porous borders of targeted countries. In this chapter, we use the example of nuclear terrorism to explore the concept in more detail, to illustrate its uses and to provide a framework for analyzing facilitating conditions. We begin our discussion by looking at the U.S. Department of State's criteria for determining whether a particular country has a "money-laundering problem,"[1] because this has been a facilitating condition widely acknowledged as utilized by terrorist and organized crime groups. This is especially the case with Al Qaeda, which has transformed many of these conditions into a well-oiled parallel financial system (see Box 10.1 that offers a simplified schematic of how money laundering works to facilitate terrorist activity in a global economy). The criteria below are a shopping list of attributes that money launderers (including terrorists) would look for in choosing an offshore-banking center—in other words, the facilitating conditions for money laundering. These include the following:

1. A criminal justice system that has failed to criminalize money laundering or failed to enforce any money-laundering offenses
2. Law enforcement that has limited asset seizure or confiscation capabilities and/or limited narcotics and money-laundering enforcement capabilities
3. Bank regulatory agencies that are understaffed, underskilled and underpaid, and that have limited audit authority over foreign-owned or controlled banks
4. A government and civil service that is prone to, or ripe for, official corruption
5. Rigid bank secrecy laws
6. Few identification requirements to conduct financial transactions and the ability to use anonymous, nominee or numbered accounts
7. No mandatory disclosure of the beneficial owner of an account or of the beneficiary of a transaction, and no mandatory reporting of suspicious transactions
8. Lack of effective monitoring of currency movements and no recording requirements for large cash or near-cash transactions
9. Use of bearer monetary instruments

Box 10.1 Following the Terrorist Money Trail

Almost all banks of the twenty-first century maintain their accounts electronically. This means, among other things, that all transactions are, in principle, automatically recorded and so can be traced to their sources. Thus, terrorists and organized crime groups spend much time covering up their money trails, and the globalization of finance in the twenty-first century has made this easier for them. They therefore set up shell companies and shell banks that become correspondent banks with major international and national banks. These correspondent banks are used by the major banks when they do not have bona fide branches of their own in the particular locality. While in theory they should be carefully vetted by the major bank, the vetting is often cursory. Terrorists can thus move money through many different banks and venues before it reaches its desired destination. The simplified diagram below displays some of this complex movement of finances identified for Al Qaeda by various researchers.

Although in a formal system of banking all transactions can be traced, the degree of anonymity afforded the customer of banks in the twenty-first century is considerable. Much banking can be done anonymously, just as most transactions on the Internet can be carried out anonymously. However, the task of imposing an international regulation of banks that will ensure that they "know their customers" is daunting, and probably impossible, because (1) legitimate banks and their host countries have a heavy interest in attracting as much money into their markets as possible no matter where it comes from—in fact, some experts have argued that the laundering of money forms a significant part of the gross domestic product of Western countries, and (2) it is unlikely that all countries everywhere will comply with all or even part of any international banking regulations. The FATF (Financial Action Task Force) set up by the G-7 countries has achieved some success into pressuring and shaming noncompliant countries, especially by setting up a "black list." There is still, however, a long way to go.

The U.S. Patriot Act has attempted to impose restrictions on countries with which it deals, requiring banks to adopt a KYC (Know Your Customer) policy and holding them responsible for providing services to terrorists. Unfortunately, the United States has avoided actually defining what a terrorist group is, except by placing groups from time to time on their terrorist list. This hardly suffices, because it is common for the United States in one year to move a country or group on and off its terrorist list, depending on the politics of the moment. However, because the U.S. Patriot Act requires that banks "know their customer"—that is, use standard identity authentication procedures so that they can verify who their customer is—it has become more difficult for terrorists to cover their money trail. This is why they also use the other much older methods of moving finances around the world—for example, couriers carrying cash, Hawala systems of exchanging money that ensures anonymity of sender and receiver, and bartering with products and precious metals.

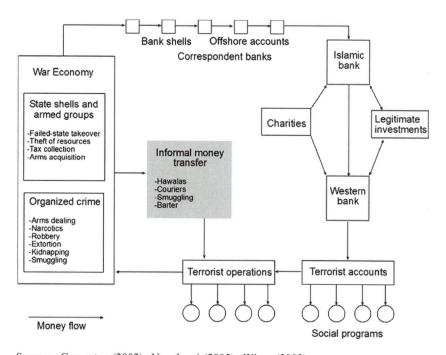

Sources: Gunaratna (2002); Napoleoni (2005); Winer (2002).

10. The ability to use American dollars in the local economy and a significant trade in gems, particularly diamonds
11. Well-established non-bank financial systems
12. Ease of incorporation, including the use of shell corporations, shareholder nominees and/or bearer shares
13. A domestic banking system that allows foreign banks to control, own or freely use domestic banks
14. Access to free-trade zones, such as the Colon Free Zone in Panama

This list of "facilitating conditions" is not intended to help money launderers find safe off-shore banking centers, but rather to help the U.S. State Department identify centers likely to be used for money laundering, which should be flagged for closer monitoring of transactions originating in the United States. In addition, the list suggests specific ways in which the banking procedures and the governing legal framework should be changed to reduce the risk of money laundering.[2] It is this second, preventive purpose that is the focus in this chapter. We provide a standard framework designed to assist analysis of the facilitating conditions for any specific form of terrorism, and then illustrate the application of this framework using the example of nuclear terrorism.

HOW FACILITATING CONDITIONS MAKE CRIME "ESEER"

Like much of our thinking, the framework for analyzing facilitating conditions is drawn from the field of situational crime prevention, specifically from the five principal techniques of opportunity reduction. These are discussed in more detail in Chapter 15, but they consist of techniques that (1) increase the effort needed to commit a particular kind of crime, (2) increase the risks of the crime, (3) reduce the rewards, (4) remove excuses for committing the crime, and (5) remove specific temptations or provocations. These opportunity reducing techniques correspond to five categories of facilitating conditions—those that make crime Easy, Safe, Excusable, Enticing and Rewarding (or ESEER). With regard to the list of facilitating conditions for money laundering, it could be said that the first four make it safer, the middle four make it more excusable and the last five make it easier. Number 14 (access to free-trade zones) makes it easier and more rewarding, and perhaps therefore more enticing as well, because it permits avoidance of taxes on the laundered amounts.

This is not meant to be a hard-and-fast classification;[3] indeed, as in the case of free-trade zones, it is not always possible to categorize a particular facilitating condition under one of the five techniques because it might assist crime (and terrorism) in more than one way. The distinction between making crime rewarding and making it enticing or tempting is particularly problematic, but it is easy to understand that, while theft might usually bring financial rewards, it only becomes tempting under certain conditions—for example, when there is almost no risk of being caught, when the rewards are especially high, when it demonstrates daring or contempt for authority, when the object is personally useful, when it is committed against an organization not an individual, and so forth.

CONDITIONS THAT FACILITATE NUCLEAR TERRORISM

The prospect of nuclear terrorism strikes fear into everyone—more even than the prospect of biological or chemical attack—because of the massive potential for death and destruction, the suddenness of the attack, the inability to escape and the lingering aftereffects of the explosion. In fact, "nuclear terrorism" encompasses many different forms of attack (Friedrich Steinhausler of Salzburg University lists 16 "attack modes"[4]) with different potentialities for damage and varying likelihoods of occurrence, but the main possibilities are accommodated by the following:[5] (1) terrorists steal or purchase a ready-made weapon or are given it by a rogue state; (2) terrorists construct a nuclear weapon of their own; (3) terrorists sabotage a nuclear power plant or attack it with an aircraft or a truck bomb; and (4) terrorists plant a radiological dispersal device (popularly known as a "dirty bomb") in a city center. In terms of our distinction between "near" and "far" terrorism, in each case, the terrorists are more likely to be from afar because of the potential for indiscriminate damage and destruction. For example, the radioactive particles from a dirty bomb detonated in Israel could easily drift over to Palestine.

Most experts agree that of these various forms of nuclear terrorism detonation of a dirty bomb is the most likely to happen. To date, this is the only form of recorded attack—an unexploded dirty bomb planted by Chechen separatists was discovered in a Moscow park in 1995—and many experts even think it is inevitable that such an attack will be made in one of the cities of the United States.[6] They think that terrorists could relatively easily acquire the materials for making such a device, that making it would not be difficult and that, because of its small size, smuggling and planting it could be easily accomplished. Fortunately, a dirty bomb would be likely to result in relatively little harm to the population of a city because most of the radioactive materials would be dispersed harmlessly in wind and water. The much larger release of radioactive materials resulting from bombing a nuclear facility would cause much more harm than a dirty bomb, but this would be much harder to accomplish, particularly in the wake of the tightened aircraft security following the attacks of 9/11. Of the other varieties of attack, experts think it is unlikely that a rogue state would go to all the trouble of acquiring a bomb, only to give it to terrorists. They also believe that it could be easier for terrorists to construct a crude nuclear bomb of their own, rather than to steal or purchase a ready-made one. This is because existing nuclear weapons, even in the former Soviet Union, are considered to be more tightly controlled than the materials, technology and expertise needed for their construction.[7] For these reasons we have chosen to examine below the facilitating conditions for this one form of nuclear threat—terrorists constructing their own bomb.

CONDITIONS FACILITATING THE CONSTRUCTION BY TERRORISTS OF A NUCLEAR BOMB

We should begin by looking a little more closely at the application of ESEER to acts of terrorism, because these differ in some ways from acts of crime. In general, terrorism is more carefully planned than crime and is committed by more determined and well-organized individuals, often working in cooperation with others. It is never "easy" or "safe," which some crimes can be. This means that these terms cannot be applied to acts of terrorism unless an implicit comparison is made to the risks and difficulty of some other acts of terrorism, or of the same acts at some other time or place. Nor do "enticing," "excusable" or "rewarding" have quite the same meanings when applied to terrorism as they do when applied to crime. Generally speaking, crime brings some direct (often financial) reward to the perpetrator, but this is rarely the case for terrorism. The rewards of terrorism are less material and consist of obtaining satisfaction from "serving God's will," humbling, taking vengeance on or destroying the enemy, and gaining prestige in the organization and in the supporting community. Just as with crime, rewards become enticing when they hold the promise of being beyond the ordinary. For example, nuclear terrorism might be enticing because of the tremendous logistical and security challenges it poses to terrorists. As for excuses, criminals must invent these for themselves, but the terrorist usually has them supplied ready made, unless his or her actions harm "innocent" people (as defined by his or her critics). In such circumstances, the culpability of victims can be redefined or intentional harm might be denied (as in instances in which the IRA has apologized for killing ordinary people with its bombs).

Assuming that they had obtained the nuclear material, terrorists could make an elementary nuclear weapon in less than a year.[8] Such a weapon would be relatively small and might be crude by present-day military standards (see Box 10.2). It would be relatively easy to transport and smuggle and, despite its lack of sophistication, could still cause major devastation. Before identifying conditions that would facilitate the construction of such a bomb, we should spell out the minimal technical requirements that would have to be met. According to Steinhausler[9] these would include the following:

- Scientific knowledge of physical and chemical properties of uranium and plutonium

---

Box 10.2 Weapons of Mass Destruction: Contrasting Needs of Terrorists and the Military

Weapons of mass destruction (including nuclear weapons) for terrorist use can be produced to much lower standards than for military use. This considerably affects any assessment of the likelihood of terrorists constructing and using these weapons. These contrasting requirements are as follows:

Military Requirements	Terrorist Requirements
Mass producible	Single or small-run production
Deliverable by normal military means	Deliverable by truck, motorboat or small plane
Effective against properly equipped enemy combatants	Effective against unprotected civilian targets
Rugged and reliable	Improvised and unsophisticated
Adequate shelf life	Just-in-time production
Highly predictable effects	Less precision
Operable by soldiers	Operable by trained individuals

Source: Falkenrath, Newman and Thayer (1999).

- A sufficient quantity of nuclear weapons-grade material and Kryton switches
- Access to an advanced workshop
- Machining capabilities for production of complex shapes
- Ceramic crucibles, electric furnace, argon-filled enclosure, Freon gas and vacuum pumps

Because the workshop facilities and tools are widely used in manufacturing, the last three on the list would be relatively easy to satisfy. The first two requirements would pose more difficulties, but Alex Schmid, former officer-in-charge of the U.N. antiterrorist branch, has noted some conditions that would facilitate them.[10]

- Nuclear research institutes and facilities in or near areas of intense terrorist activity (e.g., the Caucuses or Pakistan) could be used to produce nuclear weapons.
- The increasing civil use and production of nuclear devices and technology has resulted in increased shipments of plutonium and uranium and an increase in the number of facilities holding these materials; in turn, this has increased the number of possibilities for theft of these materials.

- Organized crime could assist in the procurement and transport of nuclear materials and in at least one case has already done so.
- The information revolution, particularly information posted on the Internet has increased the likelihood of people getting access to critical information.
- Large numbers of trained physicists, chemical engineers and biologists are able to use this information and there is little doubt that terrorist organizations such as Al Qaeda or Aum Shinrikyo could succeed in recruiting individuals with this knowledge.

This list of facilitating conditions is far from complete. It contains nothing about the rewards and enticements of a nuclear attack that we mentioned earlier, nor anything about the excuses for such an attack on the United States or other countries (including the invasion of Iraq). It deals only implicitly with conditions that might reduce the risks of attempting to construct a bomb (e.g., the greater the sources of supply of fissile materials, the greater the choice of materials that pose fewer risks) In fact, the list covers only one of the components of ESEER—the ease or difficulty of making a nuclear device—and only the first step in making a terrorist attack with a homemade bomb—assembling the necessities to construct the device. It does not deal with subsequent stages of transporting, smuggling, deploying and detonating the device. Nevertheless, this partial list is sufficient for our present purpose, which is to illustrate the kind of analysis of facilitating conditions that is needed to inform preventive efforts. We therefore now proceed to the next stage of analysis, which consists of choosing which conditions to address.

DECIDING WHICH FACILITATING CONDITIONS TO ADDRESS

It is clear that our society cannot protect itself from every possible form of attack. There are just too many possibilities and the resources to deal with them are too limited. This means that we must make hard choices about which preventive steps to take and we must prioritize these for action. Protecting ourselves from nuclear terrorism must surely come high on the list of priorities. We have seen that it would be difficult but not impossible for terrorists to make their own bomb, and it would not be impossible to deploy these bombs successfully. True, it has never happened, but experts would not rule it out. The consequences are so appalling that one might think we would do everything in our power to prevent such an attack. So, for example, why has the international community not moved more swiftly to secure the facilities holding fissile materials[11] or to ensure the security of these materials in transit?[12] Part of the answer concerns the financial costs[13] and the political difficulties of taking this action, and part concerns the inability of individuals and society to take preventive action against a threat that has never materialized.[14] Another set of reasons concerns the assumed costs and benefits for terrorists of a nuclear attack. Thus, some experts believe that chemical and biological weapons would be much easier and cheaper to obtain[15] and would meet many of the terrorists' objectives. Others argue that the revulsion caused by a nuclear attack could result in a loss of support for the terrorists' cause.[16] Such arguments sap our resolve to take action, despite the warnings about nuclear terrorism that date from the mid-1940s.[17] However, just as important as any of these reasons is that we do not have the capacity to address every facilitating condition for a nuclear attack and we must make choices about where to place our efforts.

The fact is that not all facilitating conditions are of equal importance and some we can do very little about. So an assessment must be made of the chances of successfully mitigating a facilitating condition and the benefits of doing so. If one considers Schmid's list, the prospects for intervention seem limited in respect to nearly all the conditions listed. For example, the knowledge needed to produce a nuclear weapon has already been disseminated,[18] all those engineers, chemists and other scientists have been trained, and our society has chalked up few successes to date in dealing with organized crime. The same could be said of Steinhausler's list of technical requirements for producing a bomb: the tools and the knowledge needed are too widely available to control. The one exception in both lists concerns the availability of fissile materials.[19] Without these materials, no bomb can be made and tightening up controls on them does not seem impossibly ambitious, even if some uranium and plutonium has already disappeared or been stolen.[20] We can only hope that these materials have not ended up in the hands of terrorists willing and able to use them.

There is one other important consideration in choosing the facilitating conditions on which to focus: does the condition also facilitate other forms of terrorism apart from the one being analyzed? For example, the smuggling into the United States of 9 pounds of plutonium or 35 pounds of uranium needed to make a terrorist bomb,[21] both of which emit only faint radiation signals, would be facilitated by (1) the extremely porous borders with Mexico and Canada (more than 1 million illegal immigrants from Mexico are apprehended each year near the border[22]); (2) the 7 million cargo containers that arrive each year at U.S. ports of which only 5 percent are opened for inspection;[23] and (3) the cursory checks made of vehicles at dozens of border entry points. But these conditions also facilitate the unlawful entry of other weapons of terrorism and even of terrorists themselves. Two other examples of conditions that facilitate many different forms of terrorism are the capacity to launder money and the existence of large immigrant communities that, unwittingly or not, provide cover for terrorist activities (see Chapter 11). Taking account of the benefits of multiple forms of terrorism might seem to violate one of our cardinal principles, which is that preventive analysis should always focus on a specific form of terrorism. It would be foolish, however, to ignore the wider preventive benefits of tackling a particular facilitating condition when choosing the ones to address.

The choice of a facilitating condition having been made, it must then be subjected to a more detailed analysis to guide the intervention. Let us take further the example of the proliferation of facilities and laboratories holding quantities of uranium or plutonium. Not all of these facilities will be equally at risk of theft, because some, perhaps most, will already have adequate security in place. In fact, whenever the crime risks of a range of facilities are studied, it is always found that a small minority of the facilities in the sample account for the great majority of incidents and that most of the others have very low rates of crime or none at all.[24] This greatly simplifies the preventive task, because the interventions can be concentrated where the risks are greatest. Comparing the high-risk with the low-risk facilities can also help identify practices and procedures that protect facilities or expose them to risk. Other data about actual incidents of theft or attempts (when did they occur, who was involved, how were the thefts undertaken, how were they thwarted and so on) can provide additional information to guide the choice of preventive strategies. As will be discussed in Chapter 15, these strategies seek to increase the risks and difficulty of terrorism, reduce its rewards and remove excuses and enticements.

We will discuss the next vital step of implementing the preventive measures in the final chapters of the book. Suffice it to say for the present that this step presents considerable difficulties with many opportunities for failure. The greatest single difficulty is getting those who are competent to act to accept their responsibility to do so. This is a general difficulty encountered in crime prevention endeavors, but it is greatly magnified in the arena of terrorism by the need for international collaboration and the political and cultural barriers to achieving this goal.

CONCLUSION

We have not sought in this chapter to provide an exhaustive list of the conditions facilitating the various forms of nuclear terrorism. This would have been tedious and beyond our expertise and would not have served our purpose, which was to illustrate a general approach to the analysis of facilitating conditions for any form of terrorism. We chose to focus on the specific threat of terrorists constructing their own nuclear device and detonating it in the United States or other Western country. We looked in detail at only one step of this process, namely the construction of the bomb, not transporting or deploying it. We suggested that the analysis of facilitating conditions would be assisted by thinking about how these conditions make the act easy, safe, excusable, enticing and rewarding—ESEER. We explained that the analysis of facilitating conditions was not intended to assist prediction of the act in question, although we do believe that it helps in providing some broad assessment of the risks of its occurrence (an assessment needed for helping to determine its priority for prevention). Rather, the purpose of analyzing facilitating conditions is to expand the possibilities for successful intervention. Laying out these conditions in detail, while at the same time examining the targets of each form of terrorism and the tools and weapons typically employed, enables a systematic and comprehensive study of the points of intervention.

As explained, the process of analyzing facilitating conditions must proceed in a series of sequential steps and we close this chapter by listing them below:

1. Carefully define the specific form of terrorism that is the focus of analysis—down to the nature of the targets and their location.
2. List the steps that must be taken by the terrorists to complete the act.
3. List as many facilitating conditions as possible for each step, using ESEER to ensure that the listing is exhaustive.
4. Identify those conditions that seem to be modifiable.
5. Closely scrutinize each of these to determine the ones that seem the easiest to change and that will significantly reduce the opportunities for this form of terrorism.
6. Conduct detailed studies to determine the best ways of increasing the risks and the difficulty of executing this form of terrorism, reducing its rewards and removing excuses and enticements.

PART III

Vulnerability at Home and Overseas

Targets—Near and Far

In This Chapter

> ➤ Proximity to the target is the most important target characteristic to terrorists.
> ➤ Being close to the target makes routine terrorism possible.
> ➤ When routine terrorism is not possible groups will resort to single, spectacular attacks.
> ➤ Being distant from the target forces adaptations to overcome the inefficiencies introduced by distance.
> ➤ To overcome distance, foreign-based attacks exploit immigrant communities within the target country.
> ➤ Although routine terrorism has occurred in the United States, it has not endured over time.
> ➤ Domestic-based terrorism in the United States is limited mostly to single-issue terrorism, causing fewer fatalities.
> ➤ Different preventive policies are needed to respond to domestic attacks as against attacks from afar.

OF THE EIGHT EVIL DONE characteristics of targets that we spelled out in Chapter 7—Exposed, Vital, Iconic, Legitimate, Destructible, Occupied, Near and Easy—we think that the decision to strike a target that is near or far is likely to dominate terrorist planning in important ways. The history of many terrorist missions is replete with examples of proximity dominating planning, perhaps the most obvious being the kidnapping of Canadian Pierre Laporte, deputy premier of the Quebec liberal government, by a cell of the FLQ (*Front de libération du Québec*) in 1970 simply because he lived close to the terrorists.[1] It is not surprising that proximity to target is of great importance to terrorist planning because we know from research on "the journey to crime" that criminals are much more likely to commit crimes close to home than in more distant places.[2]

THE ADVANTAGES OF TARGET PROXIMITY

We read in Chapter 5 that the journey to the target for the suicide bomber was a crucial part of the planning. It also played a role in the responses

Table 11.1 IRA Terrorist Incidents, Northern Ireland and England, 1969–98

Year	N.Ireland	England	Year	N.Ireland	England
1969	83	0	1984	1,292	1
1970	383	0	1985	995	0
1971	3,760	0	1986	1,485	0
1972	14,415	1	1987	2,013	0
1973	7,856	1	1988	1,738	0
1974	5,674	4	1989	1,590	1
1975	3,763	10	1990	1,335	1
1976	3,989	0	1991	1,474	1
1977	2,292	0	1992	1,616	0
1978	1,881	0	1993	1,408	2
1979	1,796	1	1994	1,125	0
1980	1,509	0	1995	473	1
1981	2,351	0	1996	555	2
1982	1,572	2	1997	719	0
1983	1,509	1	1998	823	0

Sources: Numbers for Northern Ireland are adapted from Royal Ulster Constabulary data reproduced in Alexander (2002, 202). The total incidents include shootings, bombings and armed robbery. The number of incidents for England have been compiled from various media sources and may be incomplete. Each separate bomb was counted as a separate incident. Thus, if two bombs went off at the same time, but in different locations, these were treated as two separate incidents, although the perpetrators may have been the same.

developed by the Israeli Defense Forces, who constructed barriers and walls and deployed other techniques to make the bomber's journey to the target more difficult. Furthermore, because the suicide terrorist planners were close to the targets, it enabled them to establish a base of operations, making it easier for them to keep a ready supply of the tools and weapons they needed, such as specially adapted explosives. This meant that they were able to mount suicide attacks on a routine basis (although some Palestinian terrorist groups were better at this than others).

The patterning of IRA terrorist attacks illustrates how this simple principle affected their operations. Northern Ireland terrorists (whether loyalists or republicans) operated close to their home bases, keeping to familiar territory, taking advantage of being able to retreat quickly.[3] Table 11.1 shows the incidents committed between 1969 and 1998 by the IRA in Northern Ireland and England. These incidents include the three main types of terrorism used by the IRA: shootings, bombings and armed robbery.

The very large number of incidents in Northern Ireland contrasts with the few and spasmodic attacks in England. With a well-established organization right on the scene in Northern Ireland, it was possible to orchestrate many attacks on a systematic and continuous basis. In England, the IRA began in earnest in the 1970s with the bombing in 1974 of the Parachute Regiment headquarters in Aldershot in reprisal for the shootings by its soldiers of demonstrators in Londonderry. The IRA subsequently placed "sleeper cells" in England to perpetrate additional acts. However, it is clear that it was unable to sustain the number of attacks anywhere near that of its attacks in Northern Ireland. The obvious reason is that, to carry out these attacks, it takes a great deal of local support, organization and management of resources. Indeed, some of the attacks were botched, resulting in arrest and conviction of several operatives.

OVERCOMING TARGET DISTANCE

To make up for the inability to carry out routine terrorism in England, the IRA altered its strategy as follows:

- It used increasingly large bombs, on the assumption that one very large bombing compensated for many routine smaller bombings as done in Northern Ireland. In fact, the bombing in Manchester in 1996 was the single largest peacetime bomb ever detonated in England and Wales[4] since World War II.
- It targeted high-profile individuals (e.g., Margaret Thatcher, Lord Mountbatten).
- When neither of these tactics worked, in the 1990s it targeted the financial district of London, with the clear aim of causing the United Kingdom severe economic difficulty.
- It stopped targeting civilians. Because public opinion had turned against the IRA since it began targeting civilians, it targeted physical structures in London's financial district in the evenings when few people were at work (the district having a low-resident population). In fact, for many of these bombings, the IRA even sent coded messages to warn where and when the bomb would go off.
- To make up for the lack of routine bombing, the IRA sent threatening letters to many businesses in the financial district informing them that, no matter how much security the London authorities put in place, they could easily break through it.[5] This tactic created a great deal of fear and uncertainty on the part of businesses and put a lot of pressure on the London authorities to "do something." The tactic had the effect, therefore, of exaggerating the psychological influence of the still rare and infrequent attacks.

These adaptations in IRA methodology give us a hint about why the 9/11 attack in the United States happened the way it did and, in fact, why there have been few terrorist attacks of any magnitude carried out on U.S. soil. Al Qaeda had "sleeper cells" in the United States, but it took them years to develop the capacity to carry out an attack. The first attack on the World Trade Center in 1993 was, in fact, a failure, given that the aim was to topple the one tower onto the other. The 9/11 attack made up for the shortcomings of the first, by devising a method of attack that increased the violence of the attack (similar to the IRA adaptation) and thus was able to kill as many people in one hit as it took the IRA to do over 30 years (at least 2,000 people killed in Northern Ireland by the IRA from 1969 to 2005, depending on the source).[6]

It also explains why Al Qaeda and other terrorist groups have traditionally targeted U.S. targets overseas. These targets are closer to their bases of attack and easier to get to. Certainly, the early attacks on the U.S. embassies and military barracks were even easier, because they were poorly guarded, with minimal security (see Chapter 12). It is also why the USS Cole was attacked where it was—in a place close to operational bases of terrorists, on familiar territory. It also explains why terrorists attacked Australian targets in Indonesia, particularly the Bali bombing—the target was in local, hospitable territory where it was much easier to plan and carry out an attack, rather than trying to attack targets in Australia (see Box 11.1).

Box 11.1 Close to Home

Of the 43 terrorist groups officially listed by the U.S. Department of State in 2001 all but one (The Japanese Red Army) routinely carried out attacks either within the country of their home base, or in countries bordering their home base. Only 10 terrorist groups carried out attacks in countries not adjacent to the country of their home base.* Of these, only one (JRA) had not established an operation of routine terrorism close to home. The age of these nine groups was above the median for all groups. Thus, longevity and a history of routine terrorism may be important indicators of ability to mount overseas attacks.

*These were (1) Mujahedin-e Khalq Organization (MEK or MKO), (2) a.k.a. The National Liberation Army of Iran (NLA, the militant wing of the MEK), (3) the People's Mujahedin of Iran (PMOI), (4) the Japanese Red Army (JRA), (5) the National Council of Resistance (NCR), (6) the Muslim Iranian Student's Society, (7) the Palestine Liberation Front (PLF), (8) Popular Front for the Liberation of Palestine-General Command (PFLP-GC), (9) Al Qaeda, (10) Provisional Irish Republican Army (PIRA). It should be noted that the State Department uses a restrictive definition of terrorism, so the database of terrorist groups is not as complete as other databases of terrorist groups. In addition, the official list of terrorist groups changes from year to year depending on political circumstances and events.

Source: U.S. Department of State (2001, Appendix B).

Thus, the proximity of targets to terrorist spheres of influence helps distinguish the American problem of terrorism from many other countries that have experienced routine terrorism over many years. In fact many West European countries (England, France, Germany, Greece, Italy, Northern Ireland, Spain), and many Central and South American countries have lived with terrorism for years, including Mexico on America's southern border.

To mount an attack against the United States from the outside (that is to say, orchestrated by terrorist groups whose primary base is not within the United States), the terrorist must overcome many obstacles. The most obvious way to overcome distance is by using airline travel. However, this requires many steps. Obtaining the documents and other necessities for travel is a major operational challenge for terrorists. As the 9/11 report shows, Al Qaeda developed an extensive system for overcoming these obstacles of documentation to get its operatives across unfriendly borders.[7] There is also the added difficulty that, until 9/11 at least, the security surveillance was much greater for air travel than for other forms of travel. There are also additional challenges for conducting an attack from afar, as noted in part by the 9/11 report.[8] These include:

- Communications to enable planning and management of a complex enterprise from afar;
- Availability of personnel at the location of attack sufficiently trained and indoctrinated;
- Intelligence to identify the enemy's strengths and weaknesses;
- Ability to move people around (travel);
- Availability on location of the necessary weaponry; and
- Ability to raise and move money as needed.

The inability to overcome all these obstacles was why the attempt in 1999 by Ahmed Ressam to bomb Los Angeles airport was unsuccessful.[9] Not only was he caught at the border, but also he attempted this operation alone because his coconspirators could not get all the necessary travel documents to join him. It is significant, however, that he used as his operational base a country (Canada) that was adjacent to the United States. He had overcome, in part, the distance problem. This problem was also overcome in the first attack against the World Trade Center, because it was possible to use, as an operational base, a small Islamic community in New Jersey, a community that was also used by some of the terrorists who carried out the second attack. This observation informs us that externally based terrorists will mount their attacks from locations that are as close as possible to the target. These locations will be selected according to the extent to which operatives can obtain the necessary local support to carry out their tasks. We do not necessarily mean communities that are sympathetic to their cause, but rather communities that help any immigrants settle into their new country. This issue deserves further elaboration because it is easily misunderstood and mistaken for a kind of "profiling."

FOREIGN TERRORISM AND THE IMMIGRANT SUPPORT SYSTEM

Do immigrant communities support terrorism? Unfortunately, the answer is yes, although not because immigrant communities want to or conspire to support terrorism, but rather because their very existence is used by terrorists as an opportunity. We read earlier that even the most successful terrorist groups have difficulty in sustaining repeated attacks that are distant from their home base. Those that manage to bring off such attacks depend on the existence of immigrant communities in the distant country to provide them with contacts— for example, where to rent a house, how to get a driver's license, where to open a bank account, how to get a credit card. These are everyday necessities taken for granted by those who have access to them, but they represent a challenge for someone confronted by them for the first time in an unfamiliar setting. The need for immigrant support is even more important when the host country's language is not spoken by the immigrant (or terrorist operative). The informal network of support of immigrant communities that reaches both inside the host country and across to the immigrant's home country has been well documented by sociologists at least since the classic *The Polish Peasant in Europe and America*,[10] which studied Chicago's immigrant communities in the early 1900s. Immigrant communities therefore provide a ready-made support system for those wishing to commit terrorism or crimes of an international nature, such as international trafficking in stolen vehicles,[11] drug trafficking,[12] human trafficking[13] and organized crime of various kinds.[14]

It follows that this kind of family, friend and community support (e.g., church or mosque) is exploited by terrorists who want to operate close to the immigrant community. Of the nine terrorist groups identified by the U.S. State Department[15] that have carried out attacks in places distant from their home base, all but one has confined its operations to countries that not only are relatively close to home, but also countries that have significant immigrant or ethnic populations that match their own ethnic or cultural backgrounds. For example, the Kurdistan Workers' Party (PKK) has attacked not only in Turkey but also in Europe where there are significant Kurdish minorities; Al Qaeda has attacked U.S. interests in Middle Eastern countries and in African countries containing significant Islamic populations. In the case of Al Qaeda, we mentioned that the first Twin Towers attack was carried out with the support of operatives who were embedded in an immigrant community in New Jersey close to the Twin Towers. Although the second attack used operatives from further afield in the United States, all nevertheless lived in areas that have a high density of immigrants that matched the assailants' ethnic and national backgrounds: New Jersey, Florida, Chicago and Boston.[16]

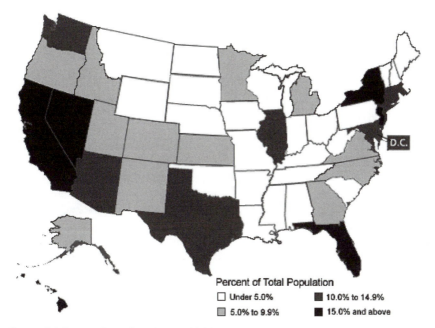

Figure 11.1 Foreign-Born Population, 2000

Sources: Data from 2000 U.S. Census; map adapted from Bean et al. (2000).

Figure 11.1 depicts areas in the United States that are more likely to be places where terrorists will target. Although the measure of immigrant communities as "foreign born" is rough, it does give an indication of how we may begin to narrow down places in the United States that are more at risk than others. Thus, not every densely populated city in the United States has an equal chance of being targeted by a foreign-based terrorist group.

The cities at risk, therefore, are those in or near the states of Florida, Hawaii, California, Nevada, New York and New Jersey. Close behind them are cities in or near Texas, Arizona, Maryland, Washington, D.C. and Illinois. This leaves a large portion of the United States at a low risk of foreign-sponsored terrorist attack. Of course, domestic terrorism—that is, terrorism that is near to the terrorist base—will have its own mission and its own attractive targets as we will read below.

The most important implication of our analysis is that we can make intelligent guesses as to the involvement of immigrant communities in terrorism without inventing any conspiracy of sympathizers living in the immigrant community. The immigrant community is a great benefit to foreign terrorists or any others who first enter a strange land and need to find their way around. By adopting this perspective, we also avoid the temptation, displayed by the U.S. State Department, to inflate the numbers of any particular terrorist group by calling unnamed numbers of an immigrant community as "supporters" or "sympathizers." Not that they do not exist, and indeed they are important, particularly for purposes of raising money and sending it to the terrorist group. In fact, of the 43 terrorist groups officially listed by the U.S. State Department as of 2001, 24 received external support of money, training, weapons or safe refuge, and those groups receiving external support generally remained in action longer than those that did not.[17]

In fact, terrorist groups that wish to survive for a long period require two types of support: external financial support and internal operational support. It is important to note, however, that the financial support given to terrorist groups usually does not come from the location from which they primarily operate, that is, their permanent base. Rather, it comes from ethnic or other communities from places far away. We also know that foreign terrorists have received financial support indirectly, because charities within local immigrant communities have sent money abroad to support various terrorist groups. This is not surprising. It is well known that U.S. sympathizers sent vast sums of money to the IRA to support its activities,[18] which enabled it to continue its attacks over many, many years. And the extensive revenue-raising operations of Al Qaeda through charities and mosques in immigrant communities are well documented.[19]

Finally, we should note that the use of an unconventional weapon, such as a dirty bomb or some other weapon of mass destruction, may alter the target preferences of the attackers from afar, although it is likely that it would simplify the selection of targets to one in which the most people possible could be killed. The problem for the terrorist here, however, is that the use of an unconventional weapon against densely populated cities would result in unknown casualties, very likely harming the immigrant communities on which the terrorist group depends. Thus, in the case of an attack that aims to kill as many people as possible, the type of weapon would probably be limited to a large conventional weapon, the destructive power of which is known, and with which the terrorist group has experience. Once again, the creativity of the 9/11 attack is revealed: the weapon was certainly "unconventional," but the destructiveness was relatively confined to a small geographic and densely populated area, adjacent, but not harmful, to an immigrant community with some supportive members just across the river in New Jersey.

TERRORISM THAT IS NEAR: DOMESTIC TERRORISM IN THE UNITED STATES

According to the Rand MIPT database, 98 domestic terrorist incidents occurred over the period 1998 through 2004, reaching a peak of 36 in 2001 and a low of just 6 in 2004. In recent years, the number of foreign-based attacks on U.S. soil has been minimal—in fact, just four, occurring in 2001

Table 11.2 Terrorist Attacks by ALF and ELF, U.S. Regional Distribution, 1998–2004

	West	Great Lakes	Northeast	Other
ELF	20	8	15	2
ALF	4	3	2	0
Total	24	11	17	2

Source: Rand–National Memorial Institute for the Prevention of Terrorism.

and 2004. However, the fatalities resulting from attacks within the United States are minimal compared with those in foreign attacks. For the period January 1998 through April 2005, the Rand terrorism database reports 177 deaths in the United States resulting from domestic terrorism and 2,817 deaths from foreign terrorism (i.e., incidents in the United States by externally based terrorist groups).[20] Thus, it is important to understand that although few foreign-based attacks have occurred in the United States, their lethality has been far greater than domestic attacks. As we have explained, the ability to carry out frequent attacks is severely limited by distance from the target, so it is compensated for by making a single attack far more lethal.

In the United States, three kinds of terrorism occur from within (i.e., not perpetrated by externally based terrorists):

- Spasmodic attacks by single-issue terrorists (e.g., ecoterrorists, antiabortionists, various hate groups, militias)
- Spates of disconnected attacks, such as those that occurred in 1994 against the White House, by particular individuals
- Incipient routine attacks

Spasmodic attacks. Table 11.2 displays the total number of terrorist attacks in the United States executed by two of the most active groups in recent years, the Animal Liberation Front (ALF) and the Earth Liberation Front (ELF). The majority of attacks for both groups occurred in just three main geographic regions, the West, the Great Lakes region and the Northeast. These incidents were spasmodic, verging on rare, although 70 percent of the ELF attacks occurred in just three years (2001–03). Looking more closely at the timing of ELF attacks in California, there were three attacks in 2001, none in 2002 and five in the first eight months of 2003. These data are highly suggestive that, once again, the targets of terrorist attacks are conditioned primarily by their proximity to the group's base of operations.[21] Because the incidents are split between the east and west coasts, it is unlikely that a single group can travel from one coast to the other to carry out its attacks. Rather, these activists are not tied together into one well-organized and directed

Box 11.2 Journey to a Bombing

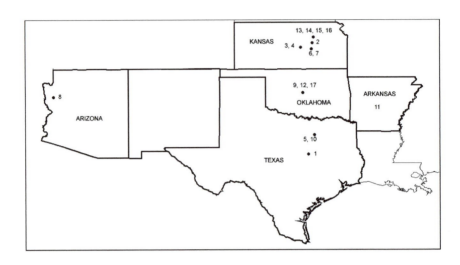

Key to Map

1	March 1993	McVeigh travels to Waco to see firsthand the standoff between the Branch Davidian compound and the ATF. The Waco incident is said to have fueled his decision to attack the federal building in Oklahoma City.
2	September 22, 1994	McVeigh rents a storage unit in Herington, Kansas. McVeigh and Nichols collect materials for a bomb and use the unit to store them before eventually assembling the device.
3	September 23, 1994	McVeigh purchases 10 bags of fertilizer from the Mid-Kansas Coop in McPherson, Kansas.
4	September 30, 1994	McVeigh and Nichols purchase 40 fifty-pound bags of ammonium nitrate in McPherson, Kansas.
5	September 30, 1994	McVeigh purchases three drums of nitromethane at $950 each from V.P. Racing located south of Dallas.
6	October 1, 1994	McVeigh and Nichols steal explosives from a storage locker in Marion, Kansas.
7	October 3, 1994	McVeigh and Nichols steal sticks of dynamite, 544 electric blasting caps and 93 nonelectric blasting caps from the Martin Mariette Quarry, Marion, Kansas.
8	October 3, 1994	They transport the stolen explosives to Kingman, Arizona, where McVeigh rents a storage locker.

9, 10	October 10, 1994	McVeigh and Nichols drive through Oklahoma City headed to buy nitromethane at a race track in Dallas. They drive by the Murrah Building and estimate the walking time from the building to where McVeigh would be when the bomb went off
11	November 5, 1994	McVeigh and Nichols rob a firearms dealer in Arkansas.
12	December 18, 1994	McVeigh, drives with old friend Mike Fortier to the Murrah Building and confirms the building as the target. They had previously rejected a building in Kansas City and in Little Rock.
13	April 14, 1995	McVeigh checks into room 25 of the Dreamland Motel in Junction City, Kansas.
14	April 15, 1995	McVeigh places a deposit on the rental of a Ryder truck at Elliott's Body Shop in Junction City.
15	April 17, 1995	McVeigh picks up the 20-foot Ryder truck.
16	April 18, 1995	McVeigh and Nichols build the truck bomb at Geary State Fishing Lake, 10 miles south of Junction City.
17	April 19, 1995	A few minutes before 9 a.m. CDT, McVeigh lights the fuses on the bomb and parks the Ryder truck outside the Alfred P. Murrah Federal Building in downtown Oklahoma City.

Sources: CNN chronology available at http://www.cnn.com/CNN/Programs/people/shows/mcveigh/timeline.html (accessed on May 30, 2006); documents prepared by McVeigh's attorney, available on PBS Web site: http://www.pbs.org/wgbh/pages/frontline/documents/mcveigh/ (accessed on May 30, 2006).

group, but act independently of each other, using the information and rallying cries found on various Web sites.[22] Both ELF and ALF are described as international groups in the Rand MIPT database, but they are only international in the sense that the Internet is international. It is doubtful that they receive any financial or operational support from foreign sources (although they may receive inspirational support from the Internet). It should be added that none of these attacks resulted in fatalities, although all have caused considerable destruction to their targets.

Fatalities have resulted from other single-issue terrorists, such as antiabortionists,[23] survivalist or hate groups. Commonly one or two individuals who are inspired by the slogans of particular groups carry out such acts. Timothy McVeigh is the major example of this type of terrorist,[24] and proximity to target also explains why he chose a target in Oklahoma City. McVeigh traveled around four adjoining states in the U.S. heartland—Colorado, Texas, Kansas and Oklahoma—looking for a target. The chronology of McVeigh's journeys shown in Box 11.2 demonstrates how proximity to the target was important in carrying out the attack, once the target had been chosen. The attack also occurred in the general geographic area that helped fuel his motivation to attack the federal government, because Waco, Texas, was the site of the botched Bureau of Alcohol, Tobacco and Firearms (ATF) operation that ended in the deaths of Davidian women and children trapped inside their burning compound. Getting a physically large bomb to a government building in Washington, D.C., would have been much more difficult than placing it at a government building in Oklahoma City. Not only was the building closer, but also it was easy: access was a snap, the ability to park the truck within eight feet of the building, and no other apparent security to speak of. Even so, this "simple" bombing required considerable planning and many steps to carry it out (see Box 11.2, which describes, in highly simplified form, McVeigh's journey to crime).[25]

Spates of disconnected attacks. The history of attacks on the White House most clearly reflects this type of attack. All such attacks have been disconnected events carried out by individuals. Here is a brief chronology of events:

- February 17, 1974—Private Robert Preston steals a helicopter and lands it on the south lawn of the White House.
- December 25, 1974—Man claiming to be the Messiah crashes a car through northwest gate of White House complex, claiming to have explosives (they were flares) strapped to his body.
- 1976—Stephen B. Williams attempts, unsuccessfully, to ram his pickup truck through the new northwest gate.
- September 12, 1994—Man with a history of alcohol and drug abuse steals a small aircraft and crashes it into the White House, just beneath the president's bedroom.
- October 29, 1994—Lone gunman opens fire on the White House with a semi-automatic rifle.
- December 20, 1994—White House struck by bullets fired from somewhere south of the White House grounds.

This pattern is not confined to terrorist attacks; it also has been observed in other kinds of attacks, such as school shootings, that are widely publicized in the media.[26] Those who emulate these acts do so when they see that they are possible. Thus, it is no coincidence that there were three attacks on the White House in 1994, the first from the air, the other two using long-range weapons. To attack from the air requires that the attacker be able to fly a plane. But the fact that it was achieved, creates the perception that attacking the target is certainly possible, and those who tried to copy that incident could not fly a plane, so they used the weapon they had available and that could also bypass White House Security—that is, a weapon that could be fired at long distance. We learn three important lessons from the observation of these sporadic attacks on the White House:

1. A target of high iconic value will attract attacks from a wide range of sources that may or may not be terrorist. Thus, studying the ideological or psychological motivations of various groups and individuals will not tell us how to secure this target.
2. Because we know that a target of high iconic value will attract attacks, we need to concentrate our analysis not just on how to protect it, but *how much* to protect such targets. We deal with this problem in Chapter 13.
3. Understanding technology is essential in anticipating how it will be used by terrorists and others to attack targets. The types of attacks made against the White House over the 20-year period reflect the changes in technology. In the nineteenth century there were no trucks to drive at high speed and crash through fences such as there were in the twentieth century. Yet it was not until 1976 that a strong wrought iron fence was erected around the White House grounds to prevent such an attack (and indeed it did prevent an attack in that year).[27] And obviously, it would have been very difficult to attack the White House in the middle of the nineteenth century by air. With rare exceptions, we tend to play catch-up with criminals and terrorists: it is only after an attack that we realize that particular technologies provide opportunities to terrorists or criminals to carry out their tasks in new ways. We will examine this issue again in Chapters 15 and 17.

Incipient routine attacks. In recent times,[28] routine terrorism on the scale of Northern Ireland or Palestine and even parts of Europe has never seriously taken root in the United States, although there have been occasional signs of it and there are some conditions that from time to time make its eruption possible, even likely. The clearest example is the FALN (Fuerzas Armadas de Liberacion Nacional), the terrorist group that campaigned in the 1970s for Puerto Rican Independence. It killed a number of people in fairly low level attacks against banks and other commercial establishments using firebombs and small bombs.[29]

If we examine the activities of the Puerto Rican separatist groups during their heyday in the 1970s, we see a typical patterning of routine terrorism, similar to those of the suicide bomber groups in Palestine (Chapter 5) and those of the IRA in Northern Ireland (Table 11.1), with the exception that the Puerto Rican groups were unable to last for longer than one decade. The FALN's busiest year, 1977, was one of sporadic attacks, requiring downtime for preparation between each spate of attacks (Table 11.3). There were no attacks in January, 16 attacks in February, March and April, none in May, one

Table 11.3 Timeline of FALN Attacks, 1977

Jan	Feb	Mar	Apr	May	Jun	Jul	Aug	Sep	Oct	Nov	Dec
0	5	3	8	0	1	0	4	0	4	0	0

Sources: Rand–National Memorial Institute for the Prevention of Terrorism; Sater (1981).

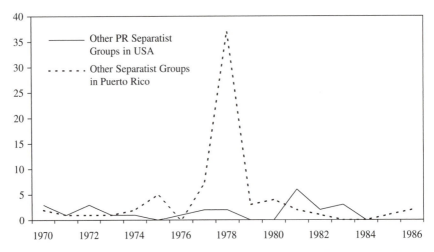

Figure 11.2 Attacks by Non-FALN Terrorist Groups in Puerto Rico and the United States, 1970–1986

Sources: Based on data in Sater (1981), Appendices A and B, and Rand–National Memorial Institute for the Prevention of Terrorism.

Note: Incidents include attacks only, not threats, 98 percent of which are usually false. In 1981, New York City was receiving typically 25–30 bomb threats each day. After the bombings of 1981, which occurred within days of each other, the NYPD received 170 bomb threats in one day (*New York Times*, May 20, 1981, A1).

in June, none in July, four in August, none in September, four in October and none in November and December. Five separate attacks in February of that year were all carried out on the same day. This accomplishment was not to be repeated in any subsequent attacks. More than 95 percent of FALN attacks occurred in New York or New Jersey and Chicago. These are all locations with strong Puerto Rican and Latino immigrant communities. However, after reaching a peak of almost 30 attacks in the United States in 1977, the number of attacks declined rapidly to zero in 1981, and sporadic attacks thereafter. The FALN was never able to sustain frequent attacks in Puerto Rico. It was numerically a very small group. Once its leaders were caught, the movement became inactive. Other independence terrorist groups (mainly the Macheteros) took up the cause in the United States for a brief period (1981–83) after the FALN ceased operations, as can be seen in Figure 11.2, but they were unable to continue on a routine basis. It is likely that the Macheteros and other groups were composed of previous FALN members who were, for whatever reason, disaffected with the FALN or who had already split from that original group.[30] In sum, the Puerto Rican terrorist groups went through periods of "death" and "rebirth" into newer groups that would take advantage of any facilitating conditions that favored routine terrorism. Compared with the FALN, however, these groups were able to sustain attacks at home but not abroad.[31]

It is of particular interest that the FALN was able to sustain a level of attacks much higher in the United States than in Puerto Rico, which seems counter to our argument that near is much easier than far terrorism. There are several reasons for this, the prime one being that the FALN was much better organized under the leadership of Filiberto Ojeda Ríos, who had been trained in Cuba, and less hampered by internal strife compared with the other groups. The FALN was therefore able to take better advantage of the fact that Puerto Ricans have statutory citizenship of the United States, so they can travel, work and reside in the United States with ease. Thus, they face few of the hurdles that other foreigners face in coming to the United States. Furthermore, Puerto Ricans began settling in New York City as far back as the 1940s, so the FALN could draw upon a well-established immigrant support group. It is also clear from Figure 11.2 that the group could not maintain the same level of attacks in Puerto Rico at the same time it was carrying out attacks in the United States.

Conditions that favored routine terrorism by the FALN and similar groups within the United States were as followed:

- A long history of grievances related to demands for independence (somewhat like the IRA).
- The fact that the majority of countries colonized in the eighteenth century were liberated, some by revolution, during the second half of the twentieth century offered a model for terrorist ambitions.
- A substantial Puerto Rican immigrant population in New York City and Chicago provided conditions to establish local operational bases.

Current conditions that are favorable to the rebirth of Puerto Rican terrorist groups in the United States are as follows:

- A number of past operatives imprisoned for their terrorist activities in the United States are now released as a result of the controversial pardon by President Clinton. Again, this is a similar condition to the IRA but on a much smaller scale.
- Ready availability of guns throughout the United States, especially among the gangs in the cities of New York, Los Angeles and Chicago.[32]
- The recent morphing of some terrorist groups into criminal gangs and the potential morphing of some gangs into terrorist groups.

Of the above points, possibly the last two are of greatest concern. The attacks by the FALN and other Puerto Rican separatist groups during the 1970s were relatively primitive affairs, mostly using homemade firebombs. Indeed, it is remarkable that we have not seen more lethal attacks in recent years by one or other of the separatist Puerto Rican groups, given the ready availability of lethal weapons over the last 20 years among the Latino gangs in many major U.S. cities.[33]

The same may be said concerning organized crime, which is, after all, also composed of violent gangs. We have noted elsewhere the morphing of the IRA into organized crime, but this is not an isolated case. We know that there is a strong link between terrorist groups in Afghanistan and the drug trade. Recently, it has been estimated by the U.S. military that some 80 percent of the Iraqi insurgency is conducted by assassins or terrorists for hire.[34] The link between the Colombian terrorist group FARC (The Revolutionary Armed Forces of Colombia) and Colombian drug barons is well established.[35] There is some speculation that gang activity in Los Angeles is ripe for morphing into terrorism, fueled by the U.S. deportation of criminals back to Latin America who then establish international networks with compatriots remaining in the United States. Gangs composed of former paramilitary extremists from El Salvador (Mara Salvatrucha) are now established in Los Angeles,[36] although within the United States, it is unclear what cause would justify their terrorist acts.[37]

CONCLUSION

Terrorists are constrained by geography. Like criminals, they will choose targets that are close to their operational base (or, alternatively, they may shift their operational base close to their targets). However, if their ideology forces them to choose targets that are considerably distant from their operational base, they must make adaptations to overcome many obstacles that stand in the way of their reaching the target. Because carrying out operations distant from the operational base is so difficult, these kinds of attacks are comparatively rare, although they are usually more spectacular and destructive. Because terrorists have but one opportunity to carry out their attack, they seek to extract as much from this one attack as they can. This has been demonstrated by the considerably higher explosive power of the bombs set off by the IRA during its England campaign in the 1990s and by the Al Qaeda attacks on the U.S. embassies and on the World Trade Center in 1993 and 2001. It is worth noting, however, that terrorists who carry out attacks from afar also gain the benefit of geography: their home bases are more difficult to track down and destroy if their main organization is a great distance from the targeted country. Just as terrorists in a foreign country may stand out, so too may their pursuers if they try to penetrate the terrorists' foreign base of operations. Obviously, this is the advantage held by Al Qaeda with its members dispersed around the globe and its headquarters in a remote region of Pakistan.

In contrast, terrorism that is frequently carried out close to the home base of terrorists becomes routine and is typically composed of many attacks against relatively predictable targets over a long period of time. However, this means that local terrorists must therefore live close to their mistakes, especially if these result in the capture of their operatives or the penetration of their operations by the enemy's intelligence. In this case, discontent and paranoia may spread among the terrorist groups, resulting in conflict and disintegration (see Chapter 6). It is also likely that disciplining cadres who are close to home is easier than disciplining those who are operating far away in a foreign country.

The different operational conditions of routine terrorism versus single attacks from afar will require different strategies and policies for prevention. Two questions must be addressed in developing such policies: *what* targets must we protect, and of those, *how much* should they be protected? Before we begin to answer these questions, however, there is one final wrinkle in the near and far appraisal of terrorism. When a country such as the United States has a strong and significant presence throughout most countries of the world, its outposts become targets. In this case, the question of near and far targets becomes more complex, because the targeted country moves its targets closer to the terrorists, as is the case with many U.S. foreign interests, which we demonstrate in the next chapter.

Taking It to Them—When Far Is Near

In This Chapter

➤ When one country occupies another, ideal conditions for routine terrorism are created. The typical recent example is the U.S. occupation of Iraq.

➤ However, all countries must to some degree maintain interests and facilities abroad, so they are at risk depending on how close they are to operational bases of terrorism.

➤ Foreign embassies and other facilities are natural targets for terrorists who cannot reach targets in a country's homeland.

➤ Attacks against U.S. embassies range from sporadic to almost routine.

➤ Defending against attacks that are distant from the homeland is more difficult because prevention ultimately depends on the friendliness of the host country.

➤ In the case of U.S. embassies, even when money was made available, bureaucratic and policy reasons inhibited preventive efforts.

➤ Research based on the four pillars of terrorist opportunity is needed to develop an effective protocol for risk assessment of facilities abroad.

THIS CHAPTER EXAMINES the situation in which a country actually increases opportunities for terrorism because of political necessities or strategies of choice that provide new targets or more accessible targets to terrorists. These opportunities appear when a nation places its facilities closer to the base of terrorist operations, thus losing its advantage of being distant from foreign terrorists. There are two basic international acts a nation takes that decrease its advantage of distance, one of necessity and one of choice. First, it must maintain embassies and other government facilities abroad to manage its international affairs. Second, it may decide, for whatever reason, to occupy a country and thus place its facilities and personnel in the backyard of the terrorists. All countries are faced with the first disadvantage. Many countries have and continue to place themselves at the second disadvantage, such as Israel, the United States, Russia and China. In addition, many business enterprises, such as airlines, are closely associated with their home country and are often thought to represent that country.

In this chapter, taking the United States as an example, we first examine the disadvantages faced by a country in defending itself when it occupies another country. Next, we briefly review the history of American attempts to protect embassies and government personnel employed overseas.

ROUTINE TERRORISM IN IRAQ

Soon after 9/11 President Bush announced that the United States would "take it to them," meaning that the United States would track down the terrorists and wipe out their bases of operation. This resulted in the invasion of Afghanistan, followed a year later by an invasion of Iraq. In various speeches, President Bush has claimed that by "taking it to them" it was better to fight the terrorists on their own soil rather than on that of the United States. It is unlikely, however, that providing terrorists in Iraq with plenty of American targets means that terrorists will not attack the U.S. homeland again. Rather, it has engaged in an additional battle, one providing many more opportunities for terrorists to target Americans.[1]

We have seen that routine terrorism flourishes when the target government is close to the terrorists' base, ideally their own government in their own country. While there are some disadvantages for the terrorists in living close to one's enemy—indeed, in the midst of one's enemy in some cases such as in Northern Ireland or Palestine—these are far outweighed by the advantages. It is possible to make full use of a supportive community and targets are close at hand. Also at hand is an intimate knowledge of the country's institutional support, such as banking, document authentication and issuance; government and military bases and arms dumps; purchase, sale or rental of property; and so on. Full use can be made of members of the group who are captured by obtaining propaganda advantages, claiming ill treatment and torture of prisoners. And if the government can be provoked into conducting sweeps through residential areas and breaking into homes, support for the government will be eroded as well. Imagine how much of an advantage the terrorists have if the government they are fighting is a foreign government, that is, an occupying force that must make great effort to learn the ways of the local communities that it occupies, especially its language. It does not take great insight to consider how Americans would feel if foreign troops occupied U.S. soil. Indeed, even when troops are welcomed, as were the British soldiers by Catholics in Northern Ireland, a protective force soon runs the risk of being perceived as an occupying army.

The U.S. occupation of Iraq transported Americans away from a protective environment, the United States, to an environment in which they were open to attack. The failure of the United States to secure or destroy the many weapons caches found in the aftermath of the invasion resulted in the massive availability of weapons to the Iraqi insurgents (or homegrown terrorists). The use of poorly armored Humvees during the early stages of the occupation also increased the vulnerability of Americans to attack. If we examine the number

of terrorist incidents that have occurred in Iraq since the beginning of the
U.S. occupation through May 2005 (Figure 12.1), we see the familiar pattern
of routine terrorism, with one exception: there are few gaps in activity. In
fact, even when there are down times, a substantial number of attacks still
occur with the exception of March 2004, when attacks ceased briefly just as
the new government was elected. The levels of attack are far greater than
those of suicide bombers in Israel and Palestine described in Chapter 5. Furthermore, we can see that the number of incidents has been consistently ris-
ing, which suggests that the abundance of targets, weapons, tools and ideal
facilitating conditions (e.g., porous borders) make terrorism in Iraq a relatively
easy undertaking.

Domestic terrorists also have the time and facilities to attack a range
of different targets depending on the strategies or opportunities available.
Table 12.1 demonstrates clearly the variety of targets attacked by the Iraqi
insurgents during the period of U.S. occupation, although it also shows a
clear preference for police and government targets. However, this table is
slightly misleading in regard to the targeting of private citizens. The numbers represented in this table only show incidents that are specifically targeted at private citizens and do not include incidents in which many
citizens were killed because they were unlucky to be in the area of the
attack against other targets. Figure 12.2 shows more clearly the deaths of
Iraqi citizens. When compared with Figure 12.3, this reveals that many

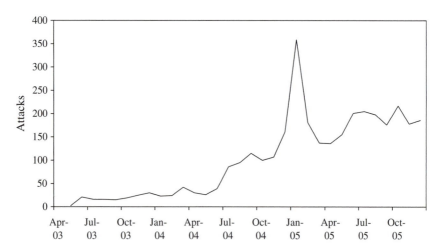

Figure 12.1 Terrorist Attacks in Iraq, April 2003–December 2005
Source: Rand–National Memorial Institute for the Prevention of Terrorism.
Note: These data are based primarily on media reports. It is likely that there are many attacks
that are not reported to the media, so this representation of routine terrorism should be seen as an
underestimate, possibly by a considerable margin. The media reporting of terrorist activity by
number of deaths also shows a similar pattern.

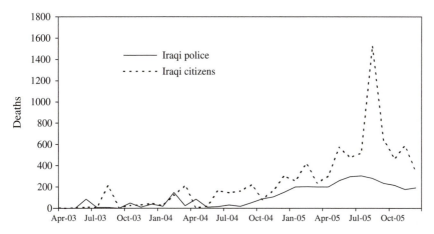

Figure 12.2 Iraqi Civilians and Police Killed in Terrorist Attacks, April 2003–December 2005

Sources: Rand–National Memorial Institute for the Prevention of Terrorism and http://www.ica-sualties.org.

more Iraqis were killed (4,249) than the U.S. military and contractors (1,604) for the period covered by the graphs. In sum, the occupation of Iraq may not have displaced terrorist attacks from the United States to Iraq, but rather it created new attractive and easy targets close to terrorist bases of operations.

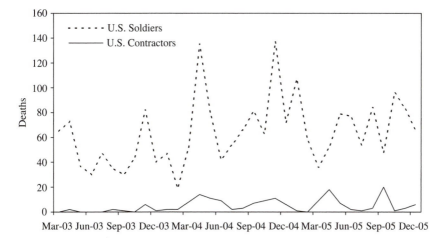

Figure 12.3 U.S. Military and Contractor Deaths in Iraq, April 2003–December 2005

Source: http://www.icasualties.org.
Note: Military deaths include deaths from accidents and friendly fire.

Table 12.1 Terrorist Attacks in Iraq by Target, March 2003–December 2005

Target (persons or facilities)	Attacks
Police	1,059
Government	807
Utilities/infrastructure	228
Business	174
Private citizens	168
Religious	150
Journalists/media	69
Diplomatic	65
Educational	53
NGO	22
Military (Iraqi and U.S.)	37
Other/unknown	472

Source: Rand–National Memorial Institute for the Prevention of Terrorism.
Note: The low military count may indicate the definition used by the MIPT in classifying many attacks on military as military attacks rather than terrorist attacks. Similarly, private citizens who are not directly targeted, but are corollary victims, are not counted. Data are mainly from media reports, so many incidents may be omitted. See Figure 12.3 for a more complete count.

The extreme conditions in Iraq have given considerable advantage to the terrorists. These advantages include the following:

- Ready availability of a range of powerful conventional weapons
- Many civilian, government and infrastructure targets from which to choose
- Constant supply of jihadists to replace suicide bombers and other insurgents killed in action
- Ready availability of tools for carrying out attacks, including cell phones and vehicles
- Entrenched support among communities that can give terrorists cover
- Friendly countries on at least two sides making it easier to move people, weapons and money across porous borders
- Global, but especially regional, media coverage that widely reports all successful attacks
- Removal of stability—although dictators like Saddam Hussein are detested by many citizens, they exert a greater grip over internal conflict than a democracy can readily impose
- U.S./Iraqi government use of drastic techniques such as encircling areas and towns (e.g., limiting entrances to Baghdad in May, 2005, an extreme version of the Belfast "ring of steel," see Chapter 13) and systematically

searching private households, a method used in Northern Ireland with mixed results

There are, however, some telling disadvantages to the insurgents, which include the following:

- There are fewer legal obstacles to government use of force because of the quasi-war setting.
- Infiltration and payment of informers is made possible because of the many unemployed Iraqis, who need money to support their families.
- Greater access to and higher recruitment of informants might create a climate of paranoia among terrorists, thus increasing possibility of internal conflict.
- The targeting of civilians by terrorists may not be seen as legitimate by local communities so may erode community support for terrorists.
- Spectacles of terrorist violence may backfire, especially beheadings and hostages pleading for their lives, leading to erosion of popular support.
- The semblance of a democratic government has been established, making it possible for the United States and its allies to talk of withdrawal. However, the United States has resolved to "stay the course" until the Iraqi government requests withdrawal.

ATTACKS AGAINST U.S. EMBASSIES AND OTHER FACILITIES

If we turn to the problem of defending a country's embassies and other interests against terrorist attacks in foreign countries, the problem is smaller in scale, but in one respect it is more complicated to solve. That is, the options for making changes to improve security are limited in a country in which one is a guest rather than an occupier.

The United States has been attacked abroad by terrorists on many occasions, for several obvious reasons:

- U.S. embassies, military barracks and business interests abroad are closer to the bases of operations of foreign terrorists and are easier to reach.
- Some countries may offer support to terrorists even harboring terrorist cells or bases of operations.
- In almost all countries, buildings and businesses that are American stand out and are easily identified as such.
- As a whole, Americans are easily identified in foreign countries, and so are the places they frequent (bars, schools, churches and so on).

Terrorist attacks against U.S. embassies have decreased over recent years as can be seen in Figure 12.4. There is no identifiable pattern of attacks, which is to be expected because they occurred in many different countries

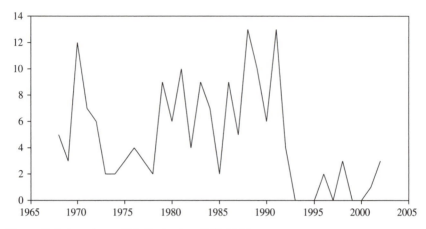

Figure 12.4 Attacks on U.S. Embassies, 1965–2002
Sources: Rand–National Memorial Institute for the Prevention of Terrorism; U.S. Department of State, Bureau of Diplomatic Security (1987–2002).

and were carried out by a wide variety of groups and individuals. Unfortunately, because of the lethality of a small number of attacks, the number of people killed in recent years has been much higher, although the number of actual attacks against embassies has gone down. Contrary to the popular view of terrorism as directed primarily against civilians, deaths of U.S. government personnel were equivalent to civilian deaths[2] from 1970 through 2002 (430 and 426, respectively). Of these numbers, it is significant that close to half of each is accounted for by a few attacks. These attacks include the following:

- U.S. Marine barracks, Beirut, Lebanon, October 23, 1983: 241 killed[3]
- Bombing of Pan Am flight 103, December 21, 1988: 270 people killed
- Bombing of Khobar towers housing complex, Saudi Arabia, June 15, 1996: 19 U.S. servicemen killed
- Bombing of U.S. embassies in Nairobi, Kenya and Dar Es Salaam, Tanzania, August 7, 1998: 224 people killed of whom 12 were Americans

However, if we consider the geographic distribution of terrorist attacks against U.S. embassies, we find that they occurred principally in South and Central America and the Middle East, followed by Europe and then by Canada and Asia (see Figure 12.5). Particular countries such as Peru (20) and the Philippines (6) accounted for a disproportionate number within their regions. Spain and one or two other European countries also report higher levels of attacks, reflecting, possibly, Europe's long history of terrorist activity. Proximity most likely explains the selection by terrorists of embassies in all of these regions as targets.

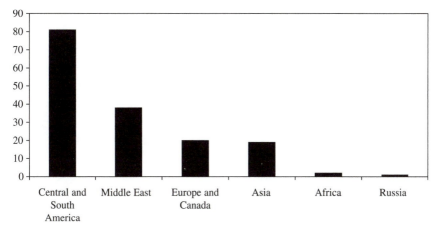

Figure 12.5 Worldwide Distribution of Attacks on U.S. Embassies, 1968–2005
Source: Rand–National Memorial Institute for the Prevention of Terrorism.

Where repeated attacks are mounted on a particular embassy, this is probably due to the routinization of terrorism in that country. Peru, the top-ranking country for terrorist attacks against U.S. embassies, is one example. We can see in Figure 12.6 that the pattern of terrorism looks similar to the patterns we have seen of incipient routine terrorism in England by PIRA and in the United States by Fuerzas Armadas de Liberación Nacional (FALN) and other Puerto Rican terrorist groups—spurts of activity followed by lulls while the terrorist groups prepare for the next attack. This is only a rough indication, however, because this pattern persists over a period of years, with few attacks in each year. The typical routine terrorist attack pattern shows a frequent pattern of monthly, and in the case of Iraq, daily attacks. In the case of Peru, because of the extremely high levels of attacks throughout the country by the Shining Path terrorist group over the 40 years of its existence, the many attacks on the U.S. embassy is but a small part of the overall levels of routine terrorism sustained by the group. In any event, these data demonstrate that not every embassy is equally at risk to attack. We should also note once again that the number of attacks does not reveal their lethality. The attacks in Tanzania and Kenya, for example, did not raise that area to that of a high terrorism region, but the numbers killed were considerably greater than most other terrorist bombings against U.S. embassies.

THE AMERICAN RESPONSE

Over the years, the United States has tried four basic approaches to respond to terrorism against its interests abroad. These have been as follows:

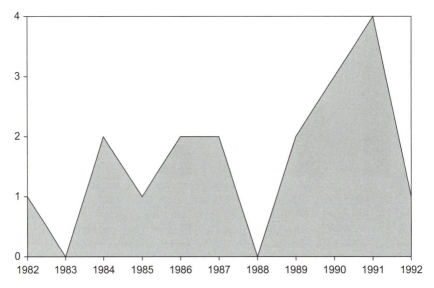

Figure 12.6 Attacks on U.S. Embassy by Terrorist Groups in Peru, 1982–1992
Source: Rand–National Memorial Institute for the Prevention of Terrorism.

1. Reactive strikes, such as the bombing of Libya in 1986, in response to the attacks on American interests, especially the bombing of the discothèque frequented by American servicemen in West Berlin, or the bombing of the supposed chemicals factory of Bin Laden in Sudan in response to the first World Trade Center bombing
2. Introduction of increased penalties for terrorist acts in U.S. law in the 1980s, followed by considerable increases in penalties and surveillance possibilities in the legislation that followed the 9/11 attacks
3. Trade and economic sanctions and embargos, which have been widely used
4. The fortification of embassies using standard security procedures, such as concrete barriers and bomb and metal detection machines at entries to embassies, beginning largely as a response to the takeover of the American Embassy in Iran in 1979

It is likely that reactive strikes did not reduce terrorism in the long term, although in the short term, they may have caused immediate increases in retaliatory attacks by the terrorists.[4] In general, economic analyses have concluded that negative sanctions such as reactive strikes or increased penalties (e.g., increased prison terms, sanctions against offending countries) do not reduce terrorism.[5] Evaluating the effects of increased penalties, however, is fraught with methodological difficulties, mainly because the penalties are too vague both in definition and in application. In all criminal justice systems, there is only a weak or distant link between the actual specific acts of an apprehended offender and the ultimate punishment.

In regard to protecting embassies, the situation is a little different because the link between the preventive action (improved security of buildings) and the result (a reduction in successful attacks against U.S. embassies) should be easier to make. In fact, attacks against embassies have decreased, but as we shall see below, the reasons are not entirely clear.

A Short History of Embassy Protection

Significant resources were provided for improvements to the security of U.S. embassies and other facilities abroad throughout the 1980s as a result of the Inman report,[6] which surveyed the state of U.S. embassy security throughout the world in response to the Iranian embassy hostage affair. One important recommendation resulting from this report was that no embassy officials be located on the ground floor of an embassy, thus making it difficult for terrorists to penetrate sufficiently into the building to take hostages. Since then, no further U.S. embassy takeovers have occurred—a success for the preventive approach that we advocate.

However, it is clear that the U.S. State Department resisted fortifying its embassies because of concern that they would appear like citadels, disconnected or isolated from their host countries. Furthermore, what improvements were made did not anticipate explosions as large as the 1998 truck bombings used against the U.S. embassies in Tanzania and Kenya. These bombings resulted in yet another security survey of U.S. embassies conducted by Admiral Crowe, delivering yet another set of guidelines for security improvements, many similar to those advocated by the Inman Report a decade earlier.[7]

Follow up of the Crowe report has revealed that although Congress provided adequate funds to the State Department to address the security shortcomings of embassy buildings and security procedures, much of the money was not spent appropriately. Some 80 percent of U.S. embassies were not in compliance with even one basic guideline for the setback of buildings from the perimeter of the embassy grounds.[8] The most telling finding of the Crowe report was that both embassies bombed in 1998 were located immediately adjacent or close to public streets and were especially vulnerable to large vehicular bombs. The report concluded:

> The Department of State should radically reformulate and revise the "Composite Threat List" and, as a part of this effort, should create a category exclusively for terrorism with criteria that places more weight on transnational terrorism. Rating the vulnerability of facilities must include factors relating to the physical security environment, as well as certain host governmental and cultural realities.[9]

Claims of Displacement

While it is clear that more recent improvements have been made to protect embassy facilities, the State Department reports that this has led to terrorist groups switching their attention away from embassy buildings and onto embassy officials and personnel. In response to Government Accountability Office (GAO) criticism[10] that the Department of State had made little progress in responding to this problem, the State Department established the Bureau of Diplomatic Security Office of Intelligence and Threat Analysis, which constructed the Security Environment Threat List (SETL). This protocol assesses the threat levels of all U.S. posts according to several categories, including political violence, crime and terrorism. Produced twice a year, this list is classified, so there is no way to tell how it is constructed and upon what specific criteria. Certainly the categories political violence, crime and terrorism, as we have already indicated at the beginning of this book, are far too vague to allow for any meaningful analysis of threat[11] for specific targets. The best assessment of vulnerability that can be derived from the SETL is shown in Figure 12.7. This is much too general to be any use at all for developing a program of protection.

The GAO criticism focused specifically on the protection of embassy officials outside embassies. The claim by the State Department, among others, was that Al Qaeda, faced with increased protection of embassy facilities, had shifted its targeting to embassy officials outside the protection of embassies. It is not clear whether this supposition is true. Indeed, as we read in Chapters 3 and 4, research shows that the displacement of attacks onto other targets is not automatic and should never be assumed. If we look at Figure 12.8, we see that there has been a recent rise in U.S. officials killed. However, the numbers are small, and it is more likely that the reason for the increase is related to

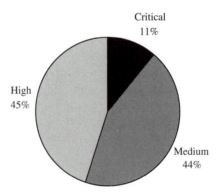

Figure 12.7 Approximate Percentage of U.S. Posts by Terrorism Threat Levels

Source: U.S. Government Accountability Office (2005, 7).

Note: GAO analysis of Department of State information. Calculations are based on 260 posts abroad. Threat levels indicated are for transnational terrorism.

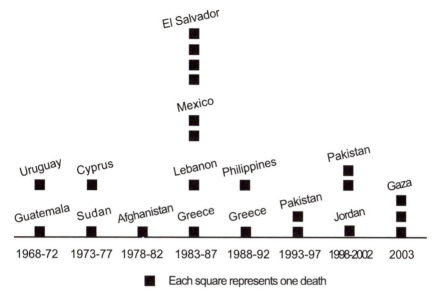

Figure 12.8 Number of U.S. Officials Killed by Terrorist Attacks Outside Embassies, 1968–2003

Source: U.S. Government Accountability Office (2005, 2).

specific local problems, as was the case in El Salvador in 1985 during a period of civil strife, rather than displacement caused by increased hardening of U.S. embassies.

Protecting Soft Targets Abroad: An Impossibility?

The GAO also expanded the definition of "soft target" to cover all Americans overseas, regardless of whether they were embassy personnel or not. The State Department vociferously opposed this expansion, arguing among other things that it had no legal authority to restrict the behaviors of American citizens abroad (such as taking basic steps to prevent one's victimization), although at the same time it had to admit that it was concerned for the safety of all Americans. It is surely obvious that the responsibility for protecting all Americans abroad is way beyond the capabilities of U.S. embassies that have proven unable to protect even themselves. One of the clear difficulties in implementing even the simplest protection at federally owned office buildings is that there are many agencies involved in providing this protection—in fact, 22 in all, according to a GAO survey in 2002[12]—and these often include facilities that are leased from private companies. The problem was, and continues to be, determining whose responsibility is it to develop a strategy for protection of facilities and citizens abroad, and whose responsibility is it to see that such a strategy is implemented. We discuss this problem in the final chapters of this book.

CONCLUSION

Professor Robert Pape has argued that the major motivation of suicide bombers throughout the world has been to free their countries from an occupying force. He backs this up with data showing that in almost every instance the attacks have occurred in countries where an occupying force was present.[13] Another interpretation of such data is that these attacks occur with higher frequency in countries where there is an occupying force because it is easier to carry out such acts when the target is closer to the terrorists' home base. Nevertheless, the political solution he recommends, that of "off-shore balancing," follows logically from the analysis of the great advantages terrorists have in being able to commit routine terrorism. It is, in fact, the policy that has been followed by several previous U.S. administrations. It consists basically of keeping U.S. forces out of the three main oil producing countries—Iran, Iraq and Saudi Arabia—but keeping them available off shore, in case trouble arises, and maintaining friendly relations as far as possible to ensure that there is an infrastructure in each country that would make it easier for military action should it be necessary.[14] This argument rests, of course, on a foreign policy that is primarily driven by protection of America's oil and other economic interests and of maintaining the balance of power in the area. While we claim no expertise on foreign policy matters, this particular policy fits logically with our analysis of the advantages of routine terrorism.

Should troop withdrawals be militarily or politically unfeasible, many alternative strategies are available, depending on geographic locations. There is a strong case to be made for the U.S.-led military and police in Iraq to adopt many of the techniques of prevention outlined throughout this book, even giving precedence to this approach over the current policy of taking out as many terrorists as possible. We have argued in previous chapters that such a policy has never worked with crime, and, given the seemingly endless supply of terrorists in Iraq, we fear it will not work there either. What has, mostly, worked in Iraq has been the establishment of a secure zone (the "green zone") in Baghdad. This strategy has been applied in other cities faced with the threat of terrorism, although with different degrees of intensity. In the next chapter, we examine this strategy and ask how one determines how much protection is appropriate to a given threat.

Unfortunately, off-shore balancing does not guarantee that terrorists in these countries will not perceive American embassies or even commercial facilities in their countries also as "occupation." However, whether or not they do is mostly irrelevant in deciding how to go about protecting such facilities. Rather, the key lies in the development of a systematic method of assessing differential vulnerabilities of government and nongovernment targets in all foreign countries, regardless of any speculation about the overall motivation of would-be attackers. In other words, we must focus on the opportunity structure for terrorism in each country and less on trying to identify particular terrorists or potential terrorists, a quest likely to fail given the political risks involved, as well as the financial cost. And when there are limited finances available, it is more prudent to use them for systematically assessing the vulnerability of targets and implementing the amount of protection needed in each case.

As we have said many times, not everything has to be protected equally. If the vulnerability assessment has been sound, implementing differential protection policies will be more easily accepted by those who must live with them, because not everyone will have to comply with the strictest protection policy all the time. This helps managers and policymakers because they can achieve the following:

- Announce clearly to staff that not all facilities can be protected to the same level, nor should they be, and demonstrate why based on presentation of the data that have been collected during the research phase.
- Settle on a basic level of security for all facilities, using established guidelines such as the U.S. Department of Defense minimum antiterrorism standards for buildings.[15]
- Work with private companies and government agencies to develop agreed-on acceptable levels of risk. Identify those locations that will require additional protection, such as if they are close to the base of operations of known terrorist groups.[16]
- Use established and proven methods of prevention such as CPTED (Crime Prevention Through Environmental Design) for securing buildings.[17]

This chapter demonstrates the need for operational research, based on an understanding of the four pillars of terrorist opportunity, to develop a rational program for anticipating and preventing terrorist attacks on a country's overseas facilities and citizens abroad. However, we have not examined how, given the differential assessment of vulnerability, one matches the amount of protection to the amount of threat. The following chapter examines how three cities in the U.K. responded when faced with different degrees of near and far terrorism. Each city faced a different threat, and each developed its own measured response.

Terror in Three English Cities

In This Chapter

- ➤ Belfast, London and Manchester have experienced different kinds of terrorism according to how distant they were from the terrorist group's home base.
- ➤ Each city developed a different response according to how it perceived the threat of terrorism, which ranged from routine to single attacks.
- ➤ In the case of Belfast, walls and barriers—"the ring of steel"—were an obvious and effective preventive response.
- ➤ London introduced a "ring of plastic" that limited entry into its financial district ("The City of London") to a few points and that paved the way for reducing traffic congestion, requiring tracking of all vehicles entering and leaving London's inner core.
- ➤ Manchester quickly rebuilt its business district, keeping overt surveillance to a minimum.
- ➤ While all of these responses appear to have been effective, they were so only against the specific type of terrorism faced, and they would not be effective against a different type of terrorist attack, such as, for example, the London Underground bombings in 2005.

WE READ IN Chapter 11 that the patterning, modus operandi, target selection, choice of weapons and choice of tools are conditioned by whether the terrorists are near to their targets. When the targets are close and there is a supportive community, such as in Palestine or Northern Ireland, terrorists can mount systematic and frequent attacks; they can make them routine. And they use fairly routine, conventional weapons that are widely available. When they attack targets that are distant from their base, they must use different tactics and weapons and overcome many other obstacles. We would expect that these two different scenarios would require or elicit different types and intensities of responses. In this chapter, we review the differing responses to terrorism in three U.K. cities: Belfast, a case of routine terrorism at very close range; London during the 1990s when it was attacked by the PIRA; and Manchester, which suffered a massive single attack by the PIRA during the same period. Each of these cities suffered a different kind of terrorist attack, and each developed its own set of responses.

BELFAST AND THE "RING OF STEEL"

The early years of the "troubles" in Northern Ireland of 1968–70 were those when bombings and shootings became the order of the day. The situation seemed permanent. Then, in July 1970, a large bomb exploded in Belfast's business district, which previously had not been targeted. This represented a significant shift in IRA tactics. It came at a bad time for Belfast, which was coping with the decline of retail business in the city center because of the rise of shopping malls elsewhere in Belfast and population movement away from the city center—a familiar pattern in many large cities throughout the Western world. As we saw in Figure 8.1, attacks reached a peak in 1972 and, in response to the bombings, Belfast established a cordon around the city core. This was composed of new traffic restrictions, barbed wire fences across some main streets, and checkpoints manned by the British Army.

There was much disagreement among the business community concerning this response. Some 300 retail businesses collapsed and close to one-quarter of the retail space was lost. Business leaders were concerned that the besieged appearance of the city center would drive customers away.[1] On July 21, 1972 (Bloody Friday), the PIRA detonated 22 bombs within 75 minutes of each other in and around the Belfast's city center. This occurred three days after the cordon had been placed around the business district. It was taken as evidence that the cordon had worked, because most of the bombings occurred outside the cordon. It also supported the claim that preventing terrorist acts in one place may displace them to another (outside the cordon). However, this displacement was short lived as we shall see below.

By 1974, the barbed wire fences were replaced by steel gates (thus the "ring of steel"). By 1976, there were only two vehicle entry points, and all other openings were exit only. The downtown center was divided into secure segments, with gates to each, and checkpoints and searches conducted upon entry. The success of the ring of steel is well documented. In 1974 there were 62 bombings, in 1984 just 3. There was an overall decrease in IRA attacks in Northern Ireland from 1972 to 2000, with a quite precipitous decline soon after the rings of steel were introduced (see Figure 8.1). One final important action was taken by the city: it encouraged and arranged for considerable investment in the redevelopment of the Belfast downtown area. By the 1990s, as the business district began once again to flourish, the outer cordons were gradually dismantled, leaving a small central ring of steel. The loosening of the cordon was not accompanied by any increase in bombings.

LONDON FOLLOWS

The IRA had targeted England for many years. Its campaign in the 1990s against the business district of London (known as "The City of London" or more simply, "The City") is of special interest because of the way in which London this time responded to the attacks by following the example of Belfast's ring of steel. However, there were significant differences in the characteristics of the terrorist attacks in London compared with those of Belfast. First, as we have noted on a number of occasions, it was not possible for the PIRA to mount a routine series of attacks on London, such as to make the situation appear permanent, as it did in Belfast. Second, unlike Belfast, the prime targets were not civilians who were in the downtown area but business institutions themselves, attacked when there were few people inside. Warnings were also issued. And as we noted in Chapter 8, the terrorists made important changes in their methodology to make up for the impossibility of establishing their attacks as routine or "permanent."

The London authorities responded as though they saw the PIRA attacks as a permanent fixture. They were anything but routine, but a series of bombs did occur throughout the decade in London's central area. Then, a mortar attack on 10 Downing Street, the prime minister's residence, on February 7, 1991, and the Bishopsgate bomb in 1993 helped set the scene for a climate of fear, and the perception by the business community and media that the PIRA was unstoppable. The chronology of the City of London attacks was as follows:

- July 20, 1990—Bomb in Stock Exchange
- February 29, 1992—Explosion at Crown Prosecution Services, Furnival Street
- April 10, 1992—Van bomb at Baltic Exchange, St. Mary's Axe
- June 25, 1992—Device explodes under car in Coleman Street
- April 24, 1993—Vehicle bomb in Bishopsgate
- August 28, 1993—Device recovered from Wormwood Street near Bishopsgate

It was not until the St. Mary's Axe bomb in 1992 that the City of London police began to respond in any direct way to the terrorists by putting an additional 100 police officers visibly on patrol. However, at the same time, a development plan had been prepared for the revival of the downtown area. Recommendations included introducing pedestrian malls, reducing traffic congestion, controlling parking and other traffic management techniques. Closed-circuit television (CCTV) was introduced to aid in traffic management. The City of London Police wanted to set up permanent vehicle checkpoints on all entrances to the City, but this was rejected on the basis that it would frighten people even more and make London look like Belfast. However, subsequent bombs, especially the Bishopsgate bomb in 1993, changed all that. In the months preceding the Bishopsgate bomb, the City of London officials had communicated extensively with the Royal Ulster Constabulary, which had overseen Belfast's security cordon. The City planners saw the destruction caused by the Bishopsgate bomb as an opportunity to redevelop the area.

The media, however, demanded stepped-up security, a "ring of steel" based on the Belfast model. Eventually, by July 4, 1993, a security "ring" was in place around the City of London square mile, but it looked nothing like the steel gates and barriers constructed in Belfast. Rather, as some called it, it was a "ring of plastic." It relied on high-tech CCTV, plastic traffic markers that guided traffic in required directions and careful planning to close off entries into the city, while maintaining customary traffic flow through the city.

By the end of the 1990s, CCTV was recording the license plate of every vehicle entering the city. By 2002, not only was this vehicle checking used as security, but it also readied London for the introduction of the much publicized "congestion charge"[2] that all vehicles have to pay on entering the core of the city. Similar to EasyPass in the United States and elsewhere, the license plates of all cars entering the congestion charge zone are automatically read and checked against records of prepayment. It is a matter of dispute whether this congestion charge and introduction of sophisticated tracking of vehicles was introduced for reasons of traffic congestion or security against terrorism. The unfolding of events remains complicated. The best conclusion is that concerns about congestion existed well before the terrorist bombs, and the necessary technology was increasingly available. The bombings simply happened at this propitious moment in City planning and development.[3] There is little doubt, though, that the City of London police commissioner was very vocal in demanding increased powers to stop and frisk anyone he wanted on any pretext.[4] There was an increasingly strong and visible police presence, particularly at the checkpoints at entry into the City.

One important corollary to the City's response was its campaign to persuade businesses and other financial institutions to install basic security equipment and procedures for the protection of their own establishments. They were urged to install CCTVs of their own, and the City pressed insurance companies (unsuccessfully) to give reductions in premiums to businesses that installed security measures.

It is not clear whether the ring of plastic succeeded in reducing terrorism or not. Certainly it is well documented that ordinary crime decreased during the decade after the ring of plastic was installed.[5] The assumption clearly was that it was working, because the cordon was gradually extended to cover an even greater area. Today, London has the greatest density of CCTV cameras compared with any other city in the world. The control of traffic congestion is looked upon as a considerable achievement. The tracking and recording of vehicles and drivers by CCTV and other means has become increasingly sophisticated. The number of Northern Ireland terrorist attacks in the City has decreased to zero, but so have they generally in the United Kingdom, despite a small rise elsewhere in England in the 1990s, possibly because it became too difficult to undertake them in London.

Was this massive response to a series of terrorist attacks necessary since the attacks were not and could never become routine? We doubt it. Although the beginnings of the cordon were warranted as an immediate response, the establishment of the ring of plastic in fact made the effects of the attacks permanent, by making the security cordon permanent. It may be argued that the cordon was extended after the 1990s and made technologically much more effective and sophisticated because of the 9/11 attack. However, the 9/11 attack was essentially a single event, not part of routine terrorism. The City of London officials needed instead to assess whether there was any evidence for the rise of a homegrown terrorist group other than the PIRA (who, although effective, have not managed to make attacks routine in London as they did in Belfast) to sustain permanent or routine attacks. If not, we think that a different policy is needed, one that addresses the problem of single rather than routine attacks.[6]

MANCHESTER FOLLOWS ITS OWN

On June 15, 1996, the largest peacetime bomb in the history of England and Wales was detonated in the city center of Manchester, the largest shopping center in Northwest England. The day chosen was a Saturday, the busiest shopping day of the week. Amazingly, no one was killed, although 220 people were injured. The low number of fatalities is attributed to the fact that a warning was given 75 minutes before the blast. However, over 670 businesses were displaced and roughly a third or more of the retail space was destroyed or rendered unusable.

Manchester acted urgently to bolster business confidence and tried to get as many businesses back into the shopping center as soon as possible, even as repairs and improvements were being made. It capitalized on the support, outrage and defiance that people displayed when they visited the bombsite. An appeal was launched for money to help businesses get up and running again and to help with refurbishing the shopping center. As far as security is concerned, the underlying assumption was that there could be no absolutely safe city. Additionally, security is more closely related to how people feel about terrorism than any assessment of risk.[7] Thus, the approach taken was to reduce fear by getting things back to normal as quickly as possible, helping businesses to reopen and reporting successful reopenings and developments in the media.

Although the Belfast and London models were rejected from the outset, security was improved. CCTV cameras were widely installed, but their visibility was carefully reduced. The emphasis was on establishing normality in everyday life. While some concerns have been expressed about the long-term impact of the bombing on confidence in the city as it competes with other large cities in England and Europe, Manchester is currently touted as the "UK's second most popular location for retailers outside London."[8]

CONCLUSION

The stories of these three cities reinforce the importance of knowing whether the terrorists are homegrown, and therefore offer a persistent threat, or whether they are foreign based and therefore can only mount infrequent but possibly more catastrophic attacks. We see in Belfast that, because of the persistent nature of the attacks, the draconian security steps were necessary and were highly effective. In London, the attacks were spasmodic, but the PIRA managed to make them seem as though they were a persistent and permanent threat. Although less draconian than the Belfast defenses, the "ring of plastic" was probably effective in bringing a halt to the spasmodic PIRA bombings, but it did not succeed in preventing the single attack from an Al Qaeda–inspired terrorist group that occurred in July 2005. Because the security ring was directed at controlling car traffic, it was ineffective against attacks on the subway system or the buses.[9]

The response of Manchester to the attack on its center was rather different from that of London. Manchester seems to have decided that the PIRA would not succeed in repeating the attack, and it sought quickly to reestablish business confidence and reinforce this with upgraded but unobtrusive security. Mercifully, to date, this approach has paid off. Manchester has avoided the mistake of responding to the attack as though it were homegrown and has not introduced more security than was needed.

No ring of plastic or even of steel around New York would have been of any use in preventing the 9/11 attack on the World Trade Center—although it might have prevented the 1993 attack, which was mounted using a truck rented in New Jersey. The rings of concrete and steel now around the White House would not have protected it from the fourth hijacked airliner had it reached Washington. We make these observations not to decry the security measures that were put into place in the three cities, but to emphasize that a systematic assessment of terrorist opportunities is needed to prepare for the diverse array of attacks that might occur and to ensure that we do not expend more resources than are necessary to achieve protection. In the next chapter, we review the history of attempts by the U.S. government to protect the White House and the Olympic Games event in Atlanta—two targets it deemed highly vulnerable to terrorist attack. As we shall show, the confusion of terrorism from near and far has hindered the development of a rational program of homeland security in America.

Confusing Near and Far: Crisis Planning in the United States

In This Chapter

> The American government's preventive strategy has been dominated by a law enforcement mindset of worst-case scenarios, resulting in overreaction to the threat of terrorist attacks.

> Overreaction may result in unnecessary restrictions on civil liberties.

> Separate policy guidelines for near and far are not only possible but necessary in developing a rational homeland security policy.

> Failure to recognize the distinction between near and far terrorism leads to misallocation of money and expenditure on unnecessary protection.

> While we can learn from all terrorist attacks everywhere, prevention interventions must be tailored to the specific form of attack and location.

IN THIS CHAPTER, we examine two cases of the American response to terrorism, the first concerning protection of the White House from attack and the second concerning protection of the Olympic Games venue in Atlanta. We choose these two cases because they vividly demonstrate the problems that stand in the way of developing a rational homeland security policy in America. In the second part of the chapter, we list the preventive interventions that emerge from our analysis of near and far in this and the previous three chapters, showing how for the most part these policies differ significantly from each other.

CONFUSION AT THE WHITE HOUSE

The question of how much to protect the White House has been an issue almost since it was built. No president of the United States has ever been killed in the White House, and only one president (President Tyler in 1841) was ever actually attacked there. Even the attempt to blow up President Truman did not occur in the White House, but in Blair House where the first family was residing during renovations to the White House. The difficulties—and the confused thinking that surrounds the protection of the White House—are most clearly demonstrated by events that occurred in the 1980s, none of which actually were attacks on the White House. These events were as follows:

- The 1981 attempt to assassinate President Reagan (carried out about a mile away from the White House)
- A series of car and truck bombings of American targets in the Middle East, culminating in the 1983 truck bombing of the U.S. Marine barracks in Beirut
- The 1983 explosion of a small bomb outside the Senate Chamber of the Capitol
- Intelligence reports that pro-Iranian terrorists were planning to attack major U.S. installations.

In 1983, the U.S. Secret Service, whose primary mission is to protect the president, responded to these events by placing large trucks filled with sand at various security points around the White House grounds as a defense against truck bombs. Within two weeks, these temporary installations were converted into permanent concrete walls (so-called Jersey barriers) and were added at various intersections surrounding the White House grounds. Soon, iron bars that rise out of the ground when the gates to the White House are closed were also installed, as were additional concrete barriers, masonry piers and advanced electronic sensors around the perimeter of the grounds. Surveillance was established from the White House roof. The following incidents in the 1990s provoked further security changes:

- The 1993 bombing of the World Trade Center
- Three disconnected, nonterrorist attacks on the White House in 1994, including an aerial "attack"
- The 1995 Oklahoma City bombing

As a result of the aerial attack in 1994, a commission was formed later that year to examine security issues concerning the White House. The commission recommended that Pennsylvania Avenue be closed off at 15th and 17th Streets, the main fear being that a large truck bomb similar to that used in Lebanon could damage the White House and its occupants. According to the Rand assessment[1] of this closure and subsequent decisions in 1995 to close off Pennsylvania Avenue to all traffic, it was the Secret Service and other law enforcement agencies related to presidential and White House protection that forced the "temporary" closure that later became permanent. The White House initially rejected the recommendation because it served to separate the president from the people and broke with a long tradition of making the White House the "peoples' house." However, the Oklahoma City bombing changed all that, and the closure became permanent. As the Rand study clearly points out, this decision was made on two faulty assumptions. First, it assumed that the circumstances of the Lebanon bombing and the Murrah Building bombing were the same, which they were not. The Lebanon bombing used a suicide attack with advanced explosives; the Murrah bombing used volatile, primitive explosives that were left in a parked truck that was less than 10 feet from the Murrah Building.

Second, as the Rand study revealed, the U.S. Secret Service and other White House–related law enforcement agencies insisted on the total closure of Pennsylvania Avenue, although the standoff distance from the Pennsylvania Avenue side to the White House (some 325 feet) was greater than that even recommended in standard explosive assessments.[2] Additionally, because of the low structure and design of the White House, it was unlikely that a large truck bomb from such a distance would produce catastrophic results. The law enforcement response to security design was, as it typically is to other threats, the maximum, as if the sky were falling. These were not measured responses. The process of deciding how much protection was needed was never carefully orchestrated. The Rand study notes the following:[3]

> This action [the closing of Pennsylvania Avenue], which does not appear to have involved any independent, outside consultation, has unilaterally created an almost "sacred precinct" of security around the White House unlike that at any other federal government building or historic landmark....

The law enforcement agencies have, in fact, established a ring of steel around the White house, not unlike that adopted in Belfast to cope with IRA routine terrorism, as we read in the previous chapter. Furthermore, once they had established this extreme response to terrorist threat, they tried to expand their ring of steel to encompass more and more of the surrounding area of the city. It could be argued that something positive resulted from the security installations: the iron railings were tastefully done and visitors now gain a more serene view of the White House unobstructed by traffic on Pennsylvania Avenue. However, the central issue is whether the amount and kind of response was justified by the threat, particularly when the costs were high: financial costs, traffic congestion and the dilution of the time-honored perception of the White House as the "peoples' house."

CRISIS IN ATLANTA

In 1996, based on various intelligence reports, Richard Clarke,[4] chair of the White House Counter Terrorism Security Group, became concerned that Iran might be planning attacks on the United States. He formed a team to examine "how we could move to deter and prevent ... attacks" by Iran. Three significant events occurred around this time that completely dominated the team's planning. These were as follows:

- On March 1996, four suicide bombings within the space of nine days killed 62 people in Israel. The Hezbollah terrorists who carried out the attack were probably funded by the government of Iran.
- On June 25, 1996, a truck bomb destroyed part of the Khobar towers housing project in Dhahran, Saudi Arabia, killing 19 U.S. servicemen and many civilians. The attack was by terrorists probably funded by the government of Iran.
- On July 17, 1996, two days before the Atlanta Olympic Games opening ceremony, TWA flight 800 exploded minutes after taking off from New York's JFK airport, killing all on board. Conspiracy theories abounded, but the disaster was eventually termed an accident.

The security team decided that one possible target could be the Olympic Games in Atlanta scheduled for August of that year.[5] Within weeks, the team descended on Atlanta to review the security planning for the Games and was appalled to find that there was virtually none. Access to events would be handled by volunteers, without any surveillance or metal detection equipment. There was nothing in place to prevent an attack from the sky and nothing to prevent attacks on rail transportation, much of which passed through Atlanta in tunnels directly under the city. The Olympic Village encompassed a large portion of the Georgia Tech campus, which also contained a nuclear reactor. Millions of dollars later, Clarke had cobbled together an aerial defense network, orchestrated the diversion of dangerous cargo by rail away from Atlanta and moved hundreds of Secret Service personnel to vet those entering the Games venues. What came to be known as the "security blanket" descended on Atlanta, just as it would later be applied to other major public events, such as the Republican and Democratic national conventions and the United Nations 50th Anniversary in New York.

Then, on July 27, a bomb placed in a trash can exploded in Atlanta's Olympic Park, killing one and injuring many others. It had been the work of Eric Rudolph, a lone terrorist.

In their obsession, Clarke's security team, which was locked into a "sky is falling" mindset, constantly operating in crisis mode, constantly planning based on the worst-case scenarios, overlooked the most obvious threat—a domestic threat of small proportions. We have read in the previous three chapters that the ability for a foreign group to carry out suicide bombings in the United States is extremely limited even today, let alone in 1996 when suicide bombings were only just beginning as a routine form of terrorism in Israel. Clarke also claims to have been concerned then about a terrorist group crashing a plane into the Olympic stadium. We also know that to carry off such a feat takes years of planning and special supporting conditions, which Al Qaeda managed to do against the World Trade Center only after several years of preparation. But we must also ask why Al Qaeda or an Iranian terrorist group would attack the Olympic Games in Atlanta. Surely there would be better and easier targets? The PLO suffered a severe setback in legitimacy as a result of the hostage taking and murder of Israeli athletes in the Munich Games. Furthermore, planning and implementing an attack from afar on a brief event such as the Olympic Games is a much more difficult enterprise than an attack on a building such as the World Trade Center in New York City.[6]

It is easy to criticize Clarke's team in hindsight, but we raise this example to demonstrate how a particular law enforcement mindset, one that plans protection based only on worst-case scenarios, leads to enormous expenditure of effort and money on protecting the wrong target in the wrong way. This mindset also confused planning the protection of targets with planning for actions of first responders. Had the team thought in preventive terms, it would have systematically assessed the vulnerability of the entire surroundings and environment of the Olympic Games, including the placement of trash cans (a standard security concern). This might not have stopped the attack, but it may have avoided the waste of millions of dollars and manpower protecting against the imagined unlikely event of an attack from the sky by an Iranian terrorist group or a Palestinian style suicide bomber. Nevertheless, Clarke linked the above very different terrorist attacks in very different locations together as if they were the same, and they clearly were not. As he said, "from where I sat, Khobar, TWA 800, and the Atlanta Olympics bomb had given the impression of a renewed wave of terrorism against the United States...."[7]

He continues to admit that, even if it turned out that the attacks were not connected (and how could they be, we repeat!), "it was a good time to play the Washington game of increased funding."[8] He requested, and got, a little over $1 billion emergency terrorist protection funding. Among some of the unwarranted expenditures that would result from this was the purchase of special decontamination trailers for coping with biological or chemical weapons fallout for many police departments across the country. These are still being purchased today, at a cost of many thousands of dollars, even by police departments that are nowhere near large population centers.[9]

CONCLUSION: PLANNING FOR TERRORISM FROM NEAR AND FAR

As the two cases above demonstrate, planning for prevention against terrorist attacks in the United States is driven by the powerful law enforcement mindset advocating a prevention policy that assumes the worst-case scenario. It begins with first responder scenes of disaster and moves directly to drastic prevention, thus ensuring that the preventive response to terrorism will be excessive in most cases. It treats all terrorist acts as the same, assuming that one terrorist attack somewhere in the world can and will be easily replicated anywhere in the United States. As FBI Director Mueller stated on May 25, 2002, suicide bombing attacks similar to those in Israel are "inevitable" in the United States.[10]

Table 14.1 summarizes the essential difference we see in the operational features of terrorist attacks from afar compared with attacks from within. Of course, these are general differences that are chosen for emphasis. There will be many circumstances in which both types of attacks are mixed, such as when a well-equipped and organized terrorist group is able to place operatives or develop cells within a country that is distant from its base and have them operate as though from within. Such was the case with the 9/11 attacks on the

Table 14.1 Operational Differences between Near and Far Attacks from the Terrorist's Perspective

Attacks from Afar	Attacks from Within
Cities are likely targets	Cities themselves are not targets
Cities with attractive locations or buildings may be preferred	Particular buildings, locations or people are targets according to tactical necessities
All civilians are potentially targets	Specific civilians or government personnel are likely targets
Unexpected or surprise targets are preferred	Targets often announced in advance; routine terrorism develops predictable patterns and range of targets
Unconventional weaponry, or innovative use of conventional weapons	Conventional or "homemade" weapons
Attack of high-impact, great destruction and maximum casualties	Limited destruction; multiple simultaneous attacks
Single attacks	Routine attacks, spasmodic attacks, rashes of unrelated attacks
Travel obstacles must be overcome	Travel is less problematic
Requires immigrant support group at target location or site of operation	Requires active support group to sustain longevity, can blend into local population.
Innovative use of tools (e.g., airplane as bomb)	Use of easily available tools
Choice of weapons dictated by difficulty in reaching target	Choice of weapons dictated primarily by ease of availability
Single acquisition of weapons for single job	Supply line of weapons, operatives and tools required
Organization may be loose, or temporary, sufficient for single attack.	Organization and division of labor needed to sustain attacks over time
Group usually does not exist long enough to breed informers	Dealing with informers becomes major distraction

United States in 2001 and the bombings against London's Underground in 2005. Nevertheless, even here, because of the infrequency of the attacks, the disadvantages of operating at some distance from home base are clear.

In Table 14.2, we offer some guidelines for developing terrorism prevention policy based on the distinction we have drawn between near and far. We hasten to add that these are rough guidelines and recognize that there are many political and philosophical debates embedded in them. We seek at this point simply to indicate how a careful assessment of the different kinds of terrorism and the different responses called for terrorism from near and far provides for the development of a rational homeland security policy. In the next chapter, we delve further into the ways in which many different techniques of crime prevention can be applied to preventing terrorism. And, in subsequent chapters, we discuss the difficulties in implementing policy guidelines and specific techniques of intervention, and their implications for a secure society in general.

Table 14.2 Policy Considerations for Near and Far Attacks

	Attacks from Afar	Attacks from Within
Infiltration	Terrorists distant from their target are also distant from their enemies, so infiltration and informing is more difficult. However, their presence may be more easily noticed by indigenous populations.	Local operations place terrorists not only close to their targets, but also close to their enemies. Thus, infiltration by spies and informants is easier.
Interviewing offenders	Interviewing offenders is difficult because there are too few in the country that is targeted, and many may be killed in the action.	Interviewing offenders for operational information helps to uncover their decision-making processes, and thus the points of weakness.
Surveillance	Must rely on electronic surveillance via satellite, monitoring communications, unless there is a well-established network of informers.	Surveillance, human and electronic, is easier because of proximity of terrorists to enemy. Monitoring communications within the United States and other democracies may be limited by privacy regulations.
Prevention	Prevention planning must rely on assessment of target attractiveness and allocation of resources accordingly, without the benefit of learning from many prior attacks.	Prevention planning is better informed as to likely targets because (1) single-issue terrorists often name their targets or they are obvious and (2) routine terrorists will display preference for particular targets and routes to targets, so their patterns of activity become predictable.

Table 14.2 (*continued*)

	Attacks from Afar	Attacks from Within
Infringement on freedoms	Over-reaction to major terrorist events is likely because of public fear fanned by media shock and awe coverage. Heavy-handed government response often followed by media outrage at government incursions into citizen freedoms.	Routine terrorism becomes an established part of life, and security responses that curtail freedoms are more easily accepted. Sporadic single-issue terrorism is dealt with like traditional crimes of arson and so on without media frenzy.
Security	Basic security probably insufficient to protect against an innovative attack	Basic crime prevention procedures used by individuals, governments and businesses may also serve to protect against terrorism.
Retaliation	Retaliatory attacks are difficult to direct specifically at major perpetrators and probably provoke more attacks against different targets.[a]	Retaliatory attacks provide propaganda advantages to routine terrorists who are near, but may cripple a terrorist group if it is newly formed.[b]

Notes:
[a] Enders, Sandler and Cauley (1990).
[b] Wolf (1989, viii). The effects of retaliatory strikes against routine terrorists are mixed. While capturing operatives obviously depletes the numbers, especially if leaders are captured, the constant replacement of operatives and leaders serves to rejuvenate the group. As well, propaganda of torture and ill treatment of terrorists serves to gain support from local citizens. See also Chapters 5, 6 and 16.

PART IV

Responding to the Threat

A Framework for Prevention

In This Chapter

➤ The 25 techniques of situational prevention seek to reduce specific forms of crime by increasing the effort, increasing the risks, reducing the rewards, reducing provocations and removing excuses.

➤ Their use has resulted in many crime prevention successes and they are adaptable to preventing terrorist attacks.

➤ Situational interventions cannot be translated from one kind of terrorist act to another without taking careful account of the similarities and differences between them.

➤ The Haddon matrix, a public health model for injury prevention, helps in identifying the variety of interventions available and which ones to choose.

➤ While we may not be able to protect everything, we certainly can protect large classes of targets by learning from past terrorist attacks and by anticipating the form of future attacks.

➤ We must always choose from a range of alternative interventions, taking into account their effectiveness, monetary costs and intrusiveness.

SO FAR IN this book, we have described how to analyze terrorism from the perspective of situational prevention. We have described the opportunity structure for terrorist attacks and have identified preventive interventions where they seemed to flow easily from our analysis. In fact, it is a major advantage of the situational crime prevention approach that it always leads to action. It does not try to do the impossible—to uncover the root causes of crime—but rather seeks to remove the opportunities for offending and to mitigate the effects of the crime if it is not prevented.

In this section, we build on our analysis in the previous chapters to construct a comprehensive framework for the situational prevention of terrorist attacks. In our view, such a framework should achieve the following:

1. Provide a way of identifying the opportunity structures of different kinds of terrorist attacks

2. Provide a methodology to link preventive interventions to the specific opportunity structures of terrorist attacks
3. Help anticipate and identify new opportunities for terrorists that arise as technology and society change
4. Identify a means for implementing the identified preventive responses, that is, translating the ideas into action
5. Provide for an assessment of the effectiveness of responses, once implemented

The first of these requirements was dealt with in Part II. This chapter elaborates on the second and third requirements. Chapter 16 illustrates the second requirement by applying the principles and techniques of situational prevention to the use of publicity in preventing terrorism. Chapters 17 and 18 deal with the fourth and fifth requirements, respectively.

THE 25 TECHNIQUES OF SITUATIONAL CRIME PREVENTION

The 25 techniques of situational prevention have evolved over the years in step with developments in theory, technology and crime prevention practice. Although they were originally developed to deal with traditional crimes such as burglary and various kinds of theft, the techniques have proven to be highly adaptable to dealing with a broad range of crime, including e-commerce crime, identify theft and child sexual abuse.[1] Their principal value is to broaden consideration of the repertoire of possible responses in dealing with a specific form of crime. We believe they can perform the same role for terrorism.

There are three steps in applying situational prevention to terrorism:

1. We must match the 25 techniques of situational crime prevention reproduced in Table 15.1, to the opportunity structure of specific types of terrorism that we have identified throughout the book.
2. We must identify the sequence of events that produce the terrorist attacks and link the appropriate techniques of prevention to each step. (We began to do this in Chapter 5 where we analyzed suicide terrorism step by step.)
3. We must assess the possible interventions in terms of their practicality, costs, intrusiveness, public acceptability and so on.

What follows is a general prescription for identifying a range of preventive interventions. These should be considered separately for each specific type of terrorist attack. We will illustrate later in this chapter how such responses may sometimes apply and sometimes not apply to seemingly similar terrorist acts that occur in different settings, using the example of suicide bombings in Israel and in the London Underground.

The 25 techniques arrange the repertoire of possible preventive responses into five main approaches that research has shown are effective in changing the decision-making process of the offender or would-be offender. These are as follows:

- Increase the effort
- Increase the risks
- Reduce the rewards
- Reduce provocations
- Remove excuses

The techniques seek to modify the circumstances that encourage offenders to commit crime in specific situations and that make it possible for them to carry through their crimes to completion. As we have noted, not every technique is applicable to every type of crime. Each specific type of crime must be analyzed according to its own internal logic, and only then can the appropriate technique from the range offered in Table 15.1 be applied.

It is likely that many of the 25 techniques could help prevent terrorism because, as we have seen, many terrorist acts also involve specific crimes (e.g., stolen passports, money laundering, theft of weapons). A cursory look at the 25 techniques reveals that many of them have direct relevance for the various aspects of terrorist activity. For example, if we look at the first column, increasing effort, we find that target hardening, controlling access to facilities, exit screening, deflecting offenders and controlling tools and weapons have direct relevance to terrorist missions we have reviewed throughout this book.

In Table 15.2, we adapt the five main approaches underlying the 25 techniques of situational crime prevention to the opportunity structure of terrorism, which comprises targets, tools, weapons and facilitating conditions. This results in a wide array of techniques, many of which are already used in various locations as a means of preventing crime. While most of the examples given are self-explanatory, a few clarifications and some general observations should be made about each of the five approaches.

Increasing the Effort

The more difficult we can make it for terrorists to reach their targets, obtain their weapons, use their tools, exploit facilitating conditions and maintain their organization, the more effort they require to succeed. If we can raise the level of effort high enough for some of their tasks, we may see them either give up on a particular target or take much longer to execute their terrorist missions. Thus, barriers, walls, tough ID authentication and extensive ID requirements for opening bank accounts in immigrant communities all raise the level of difficulty for terrorists.

Table 15.1 25 Techniques of Situational Crime Prevention

Increase the Effort	Increase the Risks	Reduce the Rewards	Reduce Provocations	Remove Excuses
1. Target harden • Steering column locks and immobilizers • Antirobbery screens • Tamper-proof packaging	*6. Extend guardianship* • Take routine precautions: go out in group at night, leave signs of occupancy, carry phone • "Cocoon" neighborhood watch	*11. Conceal targets* • Off-street parking • Gender-neutral phone directories • Unmarked bullion trucks	*16. Reduce frustrations and stress* • Efficient queues and polite service • Expanded seating • Soothing music/ muted lights	*21. Set rules* • Rental agreements • Harassment codes • Hotel registration
2. Control access to facilities • Entry phones • Electronic card access • Baggage screening	*7. Assist natural surveillance* • Improve street lighting • Defensible space design • Support whistle-blowers	*12. Remove targets* • Removable car radio • Women's refuges • Prepaid cards for pay phones	*17. Avoid disputes* • Separate enclosures for rival soccer fans • Reduce crowding in pubs • Fixed cab fares	*22. Post instructions* • "No Parking" • "Private Property" • "Extinguish camp fires"
3. Screen exits • Ticket needed for exit • Export documents • Electronic merchandise tags	*8. Reduce anonymity* • Taxi driver IDs • "How's my driving?" decals • School uniforms	*13. Identify property* • Property marking • Vehicle licensing and parts marking • Cattle branding	*18. Reduce emotional arousal* • Controls on violent pornography • Enforce good behavior on soccer field • Prohibit racial slurs	*23. Alert conscience* • Roadside speed display boards • Signatures for customs declarations • "Shoplifting is stealing"

4. Deflect offenders	9. Utilize place managers	14. Disrupt markets	19. Neutralize peer pressure	24. Assist compliance
• Street closures • Separate bathrooms for women • Disperse pubs	• CCTV for double-deck buses • Two clerks for convenience stores • Reward vigilance	• Monitor pawn shops • Controls on classified ads • License street vendors	• "Idiots drink and drive" • "It's OK to say No" • Disperse trouble-makers at school	• Easy library check-out • Public lavatories • Litter bins

5. Control tools/weapons	10. Strengthen formal surveillance	15. Deny benefits	20. Discourage imitation	25. Control drugs and alcohol
• "Smart" guns • Disabling stolen cell phones • Restrict spray paint sales to juveniles	• Red light cameras • Burglar alarms • Security guards	• Ink merchandise tags • Graffiti cleaning • Speed humps	• Rapid repair of vandalism • V-chips in TVs • Censor details of modus operandi	• Breathalyzers in pubs • Server intervention • Alcohol-free events

Source: Cornish and Clarke (2003).

Table 15.2 Situational Prevention Techniques Applied to Terrorism

	Targets	Tools	Weapons	Facilitating Conditions
Increase the effort	• Identify vulnerable targets • Prioritize targets for protection • Close streets, build walls and barriers • Security training for VIPs • Control dissemination of weapons technology	• Reduce supply of cash • Design electronic products to prevent use as detonators, timers • High tech passports, visas, driving licenses • National ID cards	• Restrict weapons sales • Hold contractors liable for stolen explosives • Reduce explosive's shelf-life • Bomb recognition publicity • "User-unfriendly" weapons • Restrict information on weapons use	• Tighten identity and credit authentication procedures • Tighten border controls • Destroy safe houses/training camps • Disrupt recruitment (e.g., Madrassas)
Increase the risks	• Strengthen formal and informal surveillance through CCTV, citizen vigilance, hot lines	• Technology to identify and locate cars, trucks, cell phones • Internet surveillance • RFIDs for parts on vehicles and electronic products • GIS chips in terrorist tools	• RFIDs/GIS chips to track weapons • Screen incoming cargo for weapons • Outlaw technology to circumvent screening	• "Know your customer" bank policy • Track all financial transactions • Monitor foreign student activity • Promote ties between local police and immigrant communities

Reduce the rewards	• Conceal or remove targets • Bomb-proof buildings/Kevlar curtains • Design guidelines to reduce injury from explosions • Swift cleanup of attack site	• Anticipate terrorist innovation in use of tools	• Use publicity to isolate terrorist groups from community • Use publicity to portray hypocrisy, cruelty of terrorist acts • Anti-money-laundering regulations
Reduce provocations	• Unobtrusive public buildings at home and abroad	• Clear and consistent rules of engagement	• Work closely with immigrant communities and host community abroad • Clear rules for public demonstrations • Avoid provocative announcements ("bring them on")
Remove excuses		• Avoid use of controversial weapons (e.g., phosphorous bombs)	• Avoid maltreatment of prisoners • Clear rules for interrogation

Increasing the Risks

By far the most important group of techniques to increase risk for the terrorists are the new tracking technologies that become cheaper and more effective every year. The miniaturization and mass production of RFID (remote frequency ID) chips coupled with GIS (global information system) technology now make it possible to track just about anything with considerable accuracy, from products and parcels to pets, cattle and humans.[2] Thus, the tracking of electronic products that terrorists use as tools shows considerable promise for prevention. In the case of attacks from afar, it is clear that, apart from increasing the effort through tightened border controls, tracking technologies and systems are needed for individuals once they get through the border. Smart cards, national ID cards and other means of ID verification and authentication are just a few of the possibilities. Tightening up procedures for issuing documents such as driver's licenses, health cards and birth/death certificates increases the effort needed to obtain a false ID, but also increases the risks of getting caught. In addition, as we will see below, these measures offer the added benefit of making identity theft more difficult.

Reducing Rewards

The most effective and feasible way to reduce the rewards is to implement as many protective measures as possible to make terrorist attacks unsuccessful. Not only can these techniques prevent attacks from happening, but they can also mitigate their effects later—for example (as we will note in more detail in the following chapter), by using publicity that emphasizes the futility of the attacks and highlights their extremist, hypocritical nature. This would include ways of avoiding any show that the terrorist group may be making progress, such as never acknowledging or giving in to terrorist demands,[3] remaining resolute in the fight against terrorist propaganda and representing terrorist acts as failures. This denies the group its rewards, and presents it with the challenge that its mission cannot be achieved except over a long period of time, if at all. Part of the reward for terrorists is the destruction of buildings and injury of people. Making buildings bombproof and indestructible, and designing public places to reduce injury from bombs therefore reduces those rewards. A more general technique would also reduce the rewards of being a terrorist: immediate retaliation against successful attacks may reduce rewards, although at least one study in Israel suggests that it may also provoke additional attacks.[4] An attraction to would-be recruits to a terrorist group is the idealistic mythology that surrounds it. Highlighting incidents in which terrorists either kill each other because of internal disagreements, or accidentally kill themselves such as occurs in bomb preparation, may help demythologize the terrorist group, making it look less attractive.

Reducing Provocations

Convincing terrorists that the barriers to their success are considerable without provoking them into making greater efforts can be difficult. For example, touting the great advances in screening technology may also challenge some terrorists to prove that the technology can be overcome, or claiming a building to be indestructible may challenge terrorists to prove otherwise. In this sense, every innovation we introduce to prevent terrorist attacks also invites the dedicated terrorist to overcome it. This is why we must constantly anticipate how terrorists will respond to our interventions, as we note further below.

Nothing can be done, of course, about the greatest provocation of all to such terrorist groups as Al Qaeda—the very existence of the United States. The United States (whether government or corporate) is subject to many more attacks abroad than it is at home, for the simple reason that its facilities are much more exposed in foreign countries. However, efforts should be made to make the facilities and its personnel blend more easily into the local surroundings.

Removing Excuses

Using violence in response to terrorist attacks is not only a provocation to terrorists to respond in kind, but also offers them an excuse for using violence as their central method of achieving success. "If the enemy does it, why can't we?" There is also the very strong enticement for the terrorists to provoke the enemy, when it is a government, into overreacting to their terrorist acts, resulting in deprivations of freedoms for ordinary people. Again, as we demonstrated in Chapter 6, this feeds the terrorists' underlying justification that the government's dependence on violence is far greater than their own. Similarly, the slightest heavy-handed treatment of terrorists in prison provides sufficient provocation and thus, in the terrorists' eyes, justification, for their violent behavior, and provides substance for powerful propaganda. Finally, refusing to talk or negotiate with terrorists also supports their basic justification for violence as a means to achieve change. We should note, however, that talking and negotiating with terrorists does not mean that one should give in to them, because that would increase their rewards.[5] Rather, the aim of such talks should be to identify any legitimate terrorist complaints and offer nonterrorist alternatives to solving those complaints.

WHY SPECIFICITY MATTERS: THE ISRAEL AND LONDON UNDERGROUND SUICIDE BOMBINGS

In Chapter 5, we demonstrated the need to break down terrorist attacks into their component parts to uncover the opportunities that these attacks exploit. We used the specific case of a suicide bomber reaching a target on foot in Israel. We saw that sending a suicide bomber on his or her way involves a long and complex process that makes it difficult to sustain these attacks repeatedly and that provides many opportunities for preventive interventions. In fact, the detailed scripting of suicide bombing from beginning to end also

Table 15.3 Suicide Bombings in Israel and in the London Underground

	Israel (2005 and earlier)	London Underground (2005)
Targets	Targets close to base of operations, but bombers must evade security checks.	Targets close to base of operations; no routine security checks to avoid.
Tools	Variety of tools such as cars, taxis, false IDs, various disguises, used to gain access to or reach target.	Train system provides access to Underground. Maps of subway and bus system freely available.
Weapons	Explosives and bomb vests from supply line readily available.	Bombs manufactured in safe house, perhaps with foreign advice.
Facilitating conditions	Supportive Palestinian refugee communities; money from charities, corruption and friendly countries used to support attacks.	Well-established immigrant communities close to target site; extremist clerics able to openly recruit terrorists, preach violence.
Group organization	Routine terrorism established. At least four terrorist groups claim responsibility for various suicide attacks over several years.	Group probably fragile, brought together only for specific attacks. Routine terrorism not developed as yet.
Success	At their height, bombings perceived as successful, although Israel Defense Force claims that 75% or more thwarted (see Box 3.2).	Successful first attack. Second attack failed because of inexperienced bomb-making; no foreign-based terrorists involved. Further successful attacks unlikely for some time.

demonstrated that the different groups involved in suicide bombings in Israel differed in their operations, in their target selection and in the numbers of attacks they could sustain. It would not be surprising, therefore, if the suicide bombings in Israel and those in London in 2005 differed in ways that would make the Israeli response to suicide terrorism inapplicable in London. Differences between the Israeli and London suicide bombings are listed in Table 15.3.

Perhaps the main difference is that the London suicide bombings were discrete events, whereas those in Israel have been routinely and repeatedly committed. In fact the main ways of combating suicide terrorism by the Israel Defense Forces (IDF) are designed to deal with repeated attacks and consist of a combined approach of the following:

- Building walls, barriers and checkpoints to make reaching the target difficult
- Retaliation for every successful suicide bombing attack
- Use of intelligence to identify managers and handlers of the suicide bombing operations and to conduct incursions to kill or capture these individuals
- Reducing the rewards to families of suicide bombers by bulldozing down their houses
- Training citizens in detection of possible suicide bombers en route to their targets

It is not known which of these approaches contributes most to the reduction and prevention of suicide bombings,[6] but our analysis above suggests that they mostly cannot or should not be transferred to London. The suicide attacks on the Underground have not become routine and might not do so because the conditions for routine terrorism in London do not exist.[7] There are no "occupied" adjacent ethnic/nationalist territories, there is little support for terrorism in immigrant communities, and there is no evidence of a sustained supply line for terrorist activities (weapons, bombers and tools).

Thus, while the IDF responses to suicide bombings may be appropriate to the Israeli conditions, they should not be imported wholesale into the London. Drawing on recommendations made in Chapter 11, responses appropriate for London would include the following:

- Restrict movement of terrorists into and out of the United Kingdom—that is to say track and control entry and exit of known terrorists and individuals who visit countries that are either sympathetic to terrorists or harbor terrorists
- Foster close working relationships with supportive immigrant communities; conduct training and educational sessions on identifying possible terrorist activity (e.g., banking, money laundering and so on)
- Introduce smart IDs, smart passports and national ID card and integrate into the Underground ticket machines
- Redesign buses and railway carriages to make it possible to exclude possible suspects (in Israel, doors on buses can be slammed shut if the driver thinks he or she has identified a possible bomber, and some buses have turnstiles at the rear entrances to prevent people from boarding without passing the driver); build in bomb-detection equipment; where possible, relocate bus stops to places that are less crowded[8]

London authorities could commission a study to improve detection of potential bombers at entry points to the Underground or other public transport facilities, including training personnel in the detection of possible bombers.[9] However, the costs of introducing these preventive techniques may be out of proportion to the likelihood that routine use of suicide bombing will develop in the United Kingdom. Because the Underground is a complex part of London's infrastructure, destroying or even disrupting it for a long period is unlikely unless frequent attacks can be mounted. For reasons outlined in Chapter 7 concerning the difficulties in attacking infrastructure as a target in itself, the maintenance of a successful campaign against this complex target is very difficult for a terrorist group, even when it is close to home. Israelis still ride their buses, although they are frequently attacked.

In sum, the London suicide bombings were more like the 9/11 attack than an indicator of the beginning of routine terrorism as in Israel or Northern Ireland. We saw in Chapters 11 and 12 how there are substantial differences between terrorist attacks that occur near to the terrorists' base compared with those perpetrated far away. All the differences spelled out in that chapter apply to the distinction between the London suicide bombings and those in Israel. It is likely, if we had more details concerning the ways in which attacks were carried out and planned, that more differences specific to the locations of the attacks would be uncovered. It follows that great care should be taken when importing responses to terrorist attacks even of the same class, from one country to another. Perhaps this is an obvious point. Yet, as we saw in the previous chapter, the U.S. government counterterrorism task forces planned their security on at least two occasions (in respect of the White House and the Atlanta Olympic Games) on the assumption that the same types of terrorist attacks carried out abroad would also occur at home.

CHOOSING TECHNIQUES: THE HADDON MATRIX

Choosing the most appropriate intervention, or rather set of interventions, is not a simple task, and for help in its solution we can turn to the field of public health, which has a long history of studying how to protect people from injury. Particularly useful in this context is the Haddon Matrix,[10] which was originally developed to reduce the trauma resulting from car accidents (see Figure 15.1).

Four important insights followed from this matrix, as follows:

1. It shows that the human factor—that is, the driver—is only one of many factors that contribute to the injury resulting from a car accident. This was contrary to the received wisdom of the day,[11] which viewed the major cause of accidents to be driver behavior.
2. By examining accidents as a sequence of events, Haddon identified the "second crash" in the crash phase—when the occupant of the car was propelled into the frame of the car or ejected from the car during impact. The conclusion from this observation—now seemingly obvious, but not at the time—was that cars should be designed to reduce injury resulting from

	Factors		
Phases	Human	Vehicle and equipment	Environment
Precrash			
Crash			
Post crash			

Figure 15.1 The Haddon Matrix

Source: Taken from Graham (1989), although it is available from a wide variety of sources. See, for example, Rechnitzer (2000).

the second crash. Seat belts should be fitted, steering wheels should be made collapsible and hard metal dashboards should be padded.

3. This insight pointed in a radically new direction for a solution: the car manufacturers.[12]

4. Perhaps most significant, the Haddon matrix suggests that the solution to a problem may not follow from what seems to be its primary cause. That is, the careful analysis of the specific phases of the accident diverted attention from the central actor in the event, the driver, to the car and therefore to a "cause" of considerable distance in time and space from the accident event—the manufacturer. By changing the design of the car, innumerable injuries in millions of accidents were prevented.

The same thinking about prevention also applies to crime and terrorism. For example, in the case of one of the first "chemical attacks" in the United States (the poisoning of Tylenol capsules resulting in several deaths), the solution to preventing further killings did not depend on catching the murderer/ terrorists—the "obvious" cause of the deaths. Rather, it led to the introduction of tamper-proof packaging by the manufacturers of Tylenol. The enormous, far-reaching effects of this simple solution can be seen today in the fact that almost every consumer item is now contained in some form of tamper-proof packaging (see Box 15.1).

The Haddon matrix has been applied to preventing deaths of illegal migrants crossing the Mexican border to the United States (see Box 15.2) and its application to terrorism provides a way to link important elements of the terrorist opportunity structure to specific terrorist acts as shown in Figure 15.2.

In fact, the dissection of the terrorist act into a sequence of events underlies our step-by-step analysis of suicide bombing in Chapter 5. We emphasize again that, even though we must begin with the detailed analysis of a terrorist act, very often the solution may (as in the case of the Tylenol killings or in the case of preventing road deaths) have far-reaching effects on a whole class of events. We need constantly to be reminded that, while "we can't protect everything," we may, if we find the right solution, effectively protect a huge number of targets, as the Tylenol case clearly demonstrates.

Box 15.1 The Tylenol Poisonings: A Preventive Solution with Multiple Benefits

In 1982, seven people died in Chicago as a result of swallowing cyanide-tainted Tylenol. The event caused widespread fear about the safety of personal products that were displayed on open shelves in stores and spurred a number of copycat incidents with the aim of extorting payments from stores. The U.S. Food and Drug Administration moved with unprecedented speed to develop regulations that required tamper-resistant packaging for many cosmetic products and over-the-counter drugs. This change heralded widespread adoption of secure packaging of everything from lipstick to soft drinks.

Catching the people responsible proved to be impossible, and their motivations were never revealed. Today, this act would be labeled an act of terrorism. It was a chemical attack by faceless unknown assailants who sneaked into a drug store and targeted random victims. (We should note that the choice of drug store and way of delivering the poison was not random). This example illustrates several of the important points of this and the following chapter:

1. Tamper-proofing was a massive, national intervention designed to prevent a rare crime that was extremely successful at the local level.
2. It is often argued that we cannot know where terrorists will strike and therefore we cannot protect everything. This example demonstrates otherwise. Tamper-proofing has removed an easy and tempting target for terrorists or criminals.
3. The intervention has had other benefits apart from preventing poisoning of products on open display, including preventing pilfering and damage of smaller items; reduction of tampering during manufacture; and reduction of counterfeiting by using technology such as attachment of holographic or other unique identifying labels.
4. The so-called copycat crimes that followed over the next eight years revealed a wide variety of motivations (from spouse killing to extortion). Most of these terrorists, in contrast to the original Tylenol killers, were caught because tamper-resistant packaging made completing the task much more difficult. This clearly demonstrates that it is possible to prevent or reduce a serious form of terrorism (a chemical attack) without knowing who the perpetrators will be and what their motivations might be.
5. Tamper-proof packaging has become a standard part of everyday life, accepted by the public and viewed by manufacturers as an attractive marketing feature for their products.

Source: Clarke and Newman (2005b).

EVALUATING THE EFFECTIVENESS OF INTERVENTIONS

We must always seek to evaluate our interventions, but traditional evaluation methods have significant drawbacks in deciding which preventive interventions are the most effective for the following reasons:

	Factors: Terrorist Opportunity Structure				
Phases	Targets-victims	Weapons	Tools	Facilitating conditions	Group organization or decision making
Pre attack					
Attack					
Post attack					

Figure 15.2 The Haddon Matrix and Terrorism
Source: Adapted from Graham (1989).

- Many terrorist acts are isolated, rare events, although of dramatic destructive proportions. Measuring effectiveness of a particular intervention against these rare events cannot be done by counting the number of attacks before and after the measure was introduced. In some situations, however, there is little need to evaluate an intervention. For example, we do not need a study to tell us that installing concrete barriers to prevent a truck full of explosives from parking eight feet from a government building, as was the case in the Oklahoma City bombing, makes that building safer from attack[13] (although we might need a study to tell us whether they prevent other kinds of vehicles from overcoming the concrete barriers). Nor did we need a study to establish that tamper-proof packaging would prevent more Tylenol cyanide murders. It would quickly have become apparent if this measure had not been effective.

- When there are multiple attacks, waiting for them to occur so that we can evaluate the effectiveness of particular interventions means ignoring the fact that many people may be killed while we carry out our scientific studies.

- Measuring the effects of one intervention at one particular point in time tells us little about the long term effectiveness of the intervention because, as we will note in the following section, protecting our targets from terrorists is a constant cycle in which we try to outsmart the terrorists and they, in turn, try to outsmart us.[14] For example, we may introduce concrete barriers to prevent trucks from getting close to a building, but the terrorists may then attack from the air. This does not mean that the barrier was not effective: it was effective against trucks but not against aircraft.

Wider Consideration of Costs and Benefits

There is never just one way to prevent a specific form of terrorism. Rather, there are many different possibilities that vary in their practicality, their cost effectiveness, their public acceptability and so on. This further complicates the task of deciding which preventive measures to introduce because we must consider these other variables, not just effectiveness.

Privacy. Perhaps the most common criticism leveled against situational prevention techniques is that they rely too much on increased surveillance and other intrusions into citizens' privacy.[15] We certainly would not shrink from

---

Box 15.2 Preventing Deaths of Illegal Migrants

Each year, some 300 migrants die in tragic circumstances crossing the U.S.-Mexico border—for example, by drowning in canals and rivers, by heat exposure in desert regions or as result of vehicle accidents. By tracing the steps that illegal migrants take in crossing the border and trying to understand the circumstances that lead to loss of life, Rob Guerette of Florida International University came up with a number of life-saving suggestions. He classified these suggestions in a two-way grid:

- Across the top, he followed Haddon and sorted the preventive suggestions into those that applied before, during and after the life-threatening event.
- Down the side of the grid, he followed the "crime triangle" (a method of analyzing crime events; see http://www.popcenter.org) and sorted measures by whether they were aimed at (1) the migrant or the "victim," (2) the "coyote," who is employed by migrants to get them safely across the border (the "offender"), and (3) the "place" or environment (i.e., desert, rivers, urban areas and so forth).

Some of these suggestions were extensions or improvements of measures already in place, but others were novel, which shows the value of his approach. Most of the suggestions are self-explanatory, but more background is needed to understand some of them (the numbering follows the table below):

1. His research showed that proportionately more females die from heat exposure.
3. Migrants typically gather in staging towns close to the border in Mexico where they make contact with coyotes.
4. When highly trained search-and-rescue agents are dispatched to make a rescue, Guerette found migrants are more likely to survive than when regular line agents are dispatched.
5. To prevent immediate attempts to recross the desert in the very hot months, migrants apprehended in the Arizona desert during these times were repatriated in 2003 to Mexican towns near the Texas border. This experiment was effective in saving lives.
6. In 2004, the Mexican authorities agreed to accept repatriations from Arizona to destinations in the interior of Mexico.
14. Motorists in Arizona commonly see small bands of illegal migrants attempting to cross the desert in the hot months. This campaign would seek their aid in saving lives by calling a 1-800 number to report the sighting.
15. Border Patrol agents in Arizona told Guerette that they often had great difficulty in locating a migrant reported to be in distress by other migrants, whom they had apprehended. This is because large swathes of the desert are quite featureless and the directions given by apprehended migrants are often vague. A systematic program of temporary desert markings using color coding or symbols could ameliorate this difficulty.

	Before life-threaten-ing event	During life-threaten-ing event	After life-threatening event
Migrant	1. Inform female migrants about dangers of cross-ing the desert 2. Implement alert system for haz-ardous conditions	3. Distribute instructions in staging towns for migrants to fol-low when in dis-tress 4. Expand Border Patrol search and rescue capacity	5. Lateral repatria-tion 6. Interior repatria-tion
Coyote	7. Implement alert system for haz-ardous conditions 8. Warn coyotes of prosecution in event of migrant deaths	9. Target coyote for arrest	10. Create task force to prose-cute coyotes when deaths occur
Environment	11. Target problem-atic times and places 12. Erect barricades at dangerous crossing points 13. Post visible warning signs in risky areas	14. "Save a life/ report a migrant" pub-licity campaign 15. Desert markers	16. Continually review data to detect new pat-terns of hazard

Source: Guerette and Clarke (2005).

advocating, for example, improved authentication of citizens' identities or the electronic tracking of weapons and tools to reduce opportunities for terrorists. We consider this controversy to be largely moot, because in advanced market economies people are voluntarily surrendering their anonymity (and therefore privacy) at a rapid rate to enjoy the increased conveniences of shopping and managing their everyday affairs. In the United States, for example, the use of credit cards for purchases surpassed the use of personal checks in 2005. The electronic payment of tolls for freeway use, and thus the tracking of citizens, is another example of a measure that has been accepted by citizens with little complaint (after teething troubles were overcome) because of the convenience it offers.[16]

In fact, many conveniences of modern life cannot be managed without effective authentication of identities: driver's licenses, birth certificates, death certificates, passports, visas, vehicle identification numbers and many others. All of these forms of identification have been exploited by terrorists and criminals alike. The rise of Internet access has taught criminals and terrorists how to exploit weaknesses in identity authentication. There were, for example, 14 million victims of identity theft and fraud in the United States in 2004. We think, therefore, that increased tightening of identity authentication of both people and products is not only inevitable but also desirable. The stakes are too high, especially because it is possible for terrorists to perpetrate a single attack of immense proportions facilitated by the use of false or stolen identities. Furthermore, by tightening up identification procedures, we also help reduce many kinds of crime, not just identify theft, but also other frauds and thefts of vehicles and many other products.

It may be the case that governments and businesses will abuse this information resulting in the violation of individuals' civil liberties. However, we think that violations of civil liberties are less likely using situational prevention than when seeking to "take out" terrorists, which requires the collection of large amounts of information about individuals. The techniques we advocate, however, do not primarily depend on the identification of individuals or classes of individuals based on a particular profile of those most likely to become terrorists or carry out a terrorist attack. The majority of the techniques are directed at strengthening and tightening identification procedures so that they may not be exploited by potential terrorists. In this case, we do not need to know the names or identities of such people. Indeed, we would argue that it is next to impossible to know who may or may not become a terrorist in the next week, month or year.

This is the primary difference between the intelligence-led policing approach and the situational prevention approach. We can put in place many barriers to make terrorist planning and implementation more difficult without having to know the names or individual characteristics of the potential terrorists. At the simplest level, putting up a concrete barrier does not require that we know the identities of the terrorists (although it may require that we know their preferred modes of attack). Intelligence-led policing, however, necessitates the collection of enormous amounts of information without any way to assess its relevance in predicting which individuals may commit the next terrorist attack. It requires the manipulation of massive databases of individual transactions and histories, looking for the veritable needle in a haystack.[17] The U.S. government's attempt to amass such an enormous database collapsed not only because of public outcry but because it was, in fact, impossible to analyze.[18] Worse, the focus on collection of this information about individuals is inevitably led by speculations about the race, ethnicity or other profiles of attackers.

While it makes sense to focus attention on supportive immigrant communities that foreign terrorists may exploit, it makes no sense to assume that everyone in that community is a potential terrorist. Rather, as we noted in Chapters 10 and 11, we need to focus on the conveniences of everyday life in immigrant communities that facilitate the activities of terrorists from abroad, such as opening bank accounts, renting cars, obtaining credit cards and obtaining driver's licenses. Thus, while the situational prevention approach would collect a great deal of information about how terrorists exploit local communities in carrying out their attack, it would not depend on collecting personal information about all individuals in that community. On the other hand, there may be circumstances in which the identification of networks of various kinds may be important (see Chapter 6)—for example, in identifying the networks that facilitate human smuggling, money laundering and drug dealing. Yet even here, it may be easier, more effective and efficient to tighten up borders, improve ID authentication or identify the local conditions that facilitate drug markets.[19] Research comparing different techniques is clearly needed, for although there are issues of privacy or civil liberties involved in regard to choosing a technique, these decisions cannot be made in a vacuum: we need to know how effective interventions are and compare these with the costs to civil liberties.

Financial costs. This ought to be self-explanatory, but it is not. It is difficult to explain because too few alternative interventions are considered under current antiterrorism policy, so there is the tendency to put massive amounts of money into just one or two approaches. For example, the Pentagon allocated $54 million to the total information awareness program mentioned above.[20] We probably will never know how effective this program, or others like it, might be because of the high degree of secrecy given to all such take-them-out programs. We are generally forced to take the word of the program directors that they thwarted a particular attack or several attacks. But, as we note in Chapter 18, secrecy more often than not is a cloak for incompetence. We know that "taking them out" is an important component of any antiterrorism policy, but we must have a way of assessing the effectiveness of these programs. We have been forced to accept them on faith for too long, even though it has been shown in the field of crime control that "taking them out" cannot be the sole solution to crime.

Feeling safe. It is difficult to establish a feeling of security among the public if we (1) conduct frequent disaster response practices in schools and other venues, (2) announce daily terror threat levels that stay "elevated," (3) encourage people to "be vigilant" for things they cannot identify, and (4) trumpet the killing or capture of a terrorist or would-be terrorist, which may signify that reprisals are coming and reminds the public that catching a few terrorists does not solve the problem. A prevention technique must therefore take into account how it will affect the public perception of safety, or the extent to which the public will adapt to the presence of physical indications in the surrounding environment, such as the presence of heavily armed guards. The public quickly adapted to CCTV[21] and even to concrete barriers around prominent buildings. But it may not adapt to checkpoints supported by iron bars or fences when entering a part of the city (see Chapter 13). Public perceptions of their safety and acceptance of techniques of intervention must be considered when choosing among alternatives.

Dual benefits. We have noted above that improved identity authentication procedures have the dual benefit of preventing identity theft as well as preventing terrorists from using false documentation to slip across borders or into controlled spaces. A more tangible example of added benefits can be found in the far-reaching effects of the tamper-proof packaging introduced to prevent more Tylenol cyanide killings (see Box 15.1). The change in packaging of the product not only eliminated that type of random killing, but also spawned an entire industry that promoted secure packaging of a huge variety of products—resulting in much greater safety for the public and also less theft. (We discuss dual benefits more fully in Chapter 17).

Competing solutions. Some solutions or techniques may compete or even conflict with each other. For example, we noted earlier the Israeli practice of destroying the houses of families of suicide bombers. While this intervention fits neatly into a situational prevention technique of reducing the rewards of terrorist acts, it also risks provoking terrorists into further action. However, negative sanctions are also important to give the risk of detection sufficient bite. For example, improved identity authentication increases risk for the terrorist or criminal. But the risk only matters if there are negative consequences to getting caught. For the terrorist, there mostly are consequences. For the identity thief, however, there often are not.[22]

ANTICIPATING FUTURE ATTACKS

Resourceful offenders and smart terrorists are constantly on the look out for new opportunities. It is essential, therefore, that we develop a capacity to anticipate the features of products, targets, weapons and other systems that provide new opportunities to terrorists. In fact, as societies change and technology affects all aspects of everyday life, new opportunities arise for crime, and for terrorists.[23] The Internet is obviously the prime example of such an opportunity in the twenty-first century. How can this problem be overcome?

There is no simple answer, but experience of preventing the theft of "hot products"[24] suggests two approaches to adopt:

Retrofit products, targets and tools. Retrofit the product, target or tool so that its attractiveness to the terrorist is decreased. Thus, the introduction of large concrete barriers makes it more difficult for the terrorist to place a bomb close to the target.[25] Or, the redesign of cell phones made it more difficult, in fact impossible, to clone cell phones, thus removing a hot product for criminals and a useful tool for terrorists.

Create new designs. Design the product or target in such a way to eliminate its attractiveness. For example, the new tower to replace the World Trade

Center will be set far enough back from the street to withstand a car bomb, which was not the case for the original building.

These are two parts of what should be an ongoing strategy that constantly feeds back information concerning design and redesign of products, tools, weapons, targets and systems. It must be an ongoing strategy because, in point of fact, we can never be completely successful in predicting how a terrorist will find an opportunity in a target, particular tool or weapon. As technology and society change rapidly, new opportunities are constantly arising for terrorists to exploit. Worse, products that have been around for a long time and have never been seen as possible tools or weapons for terrorists may be used in innovative ways that overcome existing defenses. The second attack on the World Trade Center is an example of terrorists taking advantage of existing products and systems. They converted airplanes full of fuel into extremely powerful weapons. This explains why no solution can ever be final in situational prevention. The best we can do is constantly analyze attacks and retrofit, redesign and reevaluate (see Figure 15.3). Using this process, we cannot *predict* a specific attack, but we can *anticipate* kinds of attacks and, accordingly, design security into targets, weapons, tools and other products.

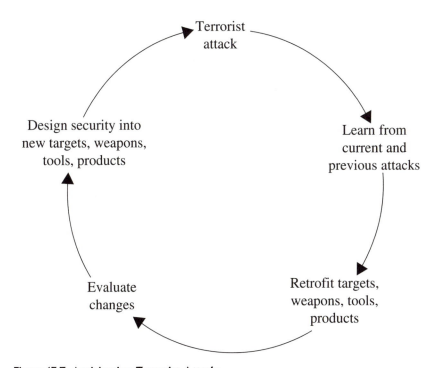

Figure 15.3 Anticipating Terrorist Attacks

We are aware that the complicated and demanding process of what amounts to a massive application of operational research (see Chapter 18) to a vast range of products and systems would be a huge undertaking. How can this be done? And who should do it? It has been difficult enough to get it done in the sphere of reducing the criminogenic properties of common retail products—in fact, the effort is still in its infancy.[26] The enormity and complexity of the problem already tells us part of the answer: clearly governments can't do it alone. We explore the implications of this fact in Chapter 17.

CONCLUSION

In concluding this discussion of the application of the 25 techniques of situational prevention to terrorism we should emphasize four points:

1. The array of techniques displayed in Table 15.2 is only indicative of the *method* of finding ways to respond to specific forms of terrorism. When separate forms are studied in detail and analyzed according to our framework, a range of specific interventions will be revealed.
2. However, we will not know, until we experiment, which techniques are likely to be more effective than others and even which techniques may turn out to be counterproductive.
3. Some techniques may conflict with others. For example, identifying and destroying terrorist safe houses and training camps to increase the effort needed by terrorists to carry out their missions may conflict with reducing provocations; indeed, they may be highly provocative.
4. Some of the techniques may not be feasible because their political, social or economic costs may exceed the benefits of prevention that they promise. There is little point in attempting to introduce a technique that will result in public outcry, or whose cost would be prohibitive (e.g., trying to protect every target regardless of risk level to the same extent). Thus, the ultimate measure of whether a particular technique should be introduced (e.g., national ID cards) will depend on the public's tolerance of inconvenience or intrusions (perceived or real) into their privacy.

Situational Techniques and Publicity

In This Chapter

> Their commitment to violence and the need to constantly justify its use puts terrorists at a considerable disadvantage in the media.

> Thus, it is unnecessary to restrict or control how media portray terrorism.

> This is impossible anyway for reasons of globalization and new technologies such as the Internet.

> Situational prevention has shown that offender-targeted publicity can prevent crime under specific circumstances and enhance techniques of intervention.

> Governments should exploit the media to target terrorists with messages that apply the techniques of situational prevention.

> Official media responses to terrorist events should be guided by long-term preventive strategies.

IN THIS CHAPTER, we adapt the techniques of situational crime prevention as outlined in the previous chapter to develop some principles for preventing terrorist attacks using publicity as the tool. Much has been written on the role of publicity in terrorism, most analyzing it from the terrorist's perspective, especially the advantage that it gives them. Some argue that terrorism is a form of psychological warfare and claim that publicity is an essential part of a terrorist act—for example, the notion that "terrorism is aimed at the people watching, not the actual victims. Terrorism is theater."[1] In fact, terrorist groups vary in their use of publicity (the IRA and 17 November groups embraced it; the Shining Path avoided it) and the publicity that accompanies terrorism also varies according to the type of act. For example, hostage taking usually commands considerable publicity simply because it continues for an extended period of time and may involve public demands by terrorists accompanied by public pleading by the families of victims, if not the victims themselves.

Yet all terrorist acts that are violent involve publicity of some form. It may be argued, for example, that the dreadful violence of the Shining Path terrorists was itself enough to publicize their acts by word of mouth.[2] In this case, violence is its own publicity.[3] If we consider the variety of media available in the twenty-first century for publicizing one's cause, using violence appears as a primitive form of publicity. Al Qaeda understands this, which is why it uses television and the Internet so extensively. And it is worth noting that the Internet empowers word of mouth so that geographically distant groups can spread "the word" easily, and most important, cheaply.

Whether or not publicity aids and abets terrorists has been the focus of most previous research on this topic. While still controversial,[4] the general conclusion is that it probably does spread fear and stress in the public[5] (an assumed goal of terrorist acts), creates the possibility for others to copy terrorist acts (whether these others are terrorists or simply criminals who see an opportunity),[6] and manages to publicize political or religious causes (whether intended by the terrorist group or not).[7]

In support of the research, the policy responses have almost always assumed that publicity does aid the terrorists. Thus, the inclination of governments is to clamp down on publicizing terrorist acts (e.g., the prohibition of television interviews or appearances of IRA members during the 1970s and 1980s). When they do this, however, governments, especially in Western democracies, risk being seen as "doing what the terrorists want"—that is, infringing on civil liberties.[8] In the decades toward the close of the twentieth century, much of the literature was full of these arguments,[9] and even in the United States resulted in the media adopting voluntary standards for publicizing terrorist acts.[10] However, in the twenty-first century, many of these arguments are largely irrelevant, simply because the Internet provides so many outlets for publicity and there is no way any government can put the lid on publicity of these acts.[11] Globalization has also ensured that no government has control of the media, so the popular arguments of critics that governments can control the meaning or portrayal of terrorism, because journalists depend on the government for information, are now less valid.[12]

In sum, the literature on terrorism and publicity tends to be split into three camps: one that claims that the government controls the entire media image of terrorism,[13] another that it is the terrorists who do the controlling and the government that is made helpless,[14] and the third that the media organizations are essentially in control. We are inclined toward the third camp, with some qualifications. Until the turn of the twentieth century, when mass media in Western democracies was under the control of big media networks, it was reasonable to conclude that they acted as gatekeepers and therefore controlled much of how the media portrayed all news. With globalization, the rise of Internet access and the plethora of new media organizations worldwide, however, the mass media networks no longer monopolize information as they once did.

If terrorists have found the media to be a useful tool, so too have governments, most of whom in Western democracies have extensive media relations departments with experts who attempt to engineer media reports as favorably as possible to their policies.[15] We should expect, therefore, that the media, if used expertly, is potentially of great power in combating terrorism. Accordingly, we offer in this chapter some suggestions, based on situational prevention, of how publicity might be used against terrorists. We hasten to add that these can only be very general, because we have little control over how news is interpreted and reported in distant places and through different media. Messages aimed at terrorists in Afghanistan may be different from those played to academics in New England, and an emphasis which plays well to the gallery in small town Ohio may cause resentment in Riyadh. Indeed, as we saw in early 2006, a newspaper cartoon of Mohammed as a suicide bomber that seemed mildly amusing at best and unremarkable at worst in Denmark, caused seething anger, riots, demonstrations, arson and killings in the Middle East. Thus, the familiar theme throughout this book—the distinction between near and far—is equally important to consider when designing interventions using publicity. And the Internet may call for different responses than, say, network television.

The incredible complexity of publicity and its effects also suggest that we should start in the simplest, most direct way, which is to aim it at a target that we can identify—in crime prevention, particular offenders carrying out particular offenses, such as car theft, and in terrorism, particular terrorists or terrorist groups carrying out particular attacks, such as suicide bombings. We recognize that a "media war" pervades the mass media, including the Internet, with many hoping to convert religious zealots, some trying to press moderates into extremism, others trying to win the hearts and minds of supporters of terrorism. However, we view these attempts at influence as far too vague, unpredictable in effects and lacking in specificity: The suggestions we make below are targeted at offenders, not their supporters or ideologies. Although they are modest, they still take many things for granted and oversimplify what needs to be done.

USING PUBLICITY AGAINST TERRORISTS

With respect to the media, terrorists have some advantages: (1) what they do, by its nature, is shocking and likely to garner publicity; (2) they stage the terrorist event and have the advantage of knowing where and when it will take place,[16] and (3) mass media, especially television, magnifies the importance or significance of terrorist events. However, publicity is a complex medium, and if it is to be used with effect, its different modes and contexts need to be understood and carefully exploited. We think that terrorists, because of their situation and the nature of their enterprise, are at a serious disadvantage in answering two questions that lie at the heart of using publicity to further ones cause: what should we say and what should we do in public?

Because terrorists rely so heavily on violence, they are at a serious disadvantage in answering these questions.[17] This is why, depending on the group, terrorists spend a great deal of media time justifying their acts of violence.[18] And their commitment to violence dictates, in large part, their answer to the first question. The more violent and indiscriminate or horrendous are the acts, the more "explanation" they must give to the public, the more they must argue that it is a "state of war" that demands their violence. Furthermore, they will seize on any act of violence by their enemy, no matter how minor, and exaggerate it, or if there is no such act, they will hope to incite it or invent it.[19] A final disadvantage suffered by terrorists in using publicity is that their relations with official or major media outlets must usually be clandestine, so that refinements in developing and dealing with media contacts will be limited. In contrast, government agencies, including politicians and various law enforcement personnel, who must make statements to the public in response to terrorist acts (past or anticipated), have many more choices available to them and some have vast media resources themselves. They may carefully weigh their answers to the above two questions and choose those answers according to what research suggests will make the lives of terrorists more difficult, and carefully pick and choose their media outlets.

The use of publicity in crime prevention is not (or at least should not be) reactive to a particular crime event.[20] The most important principle is to focus on the long term—the objective should be to make it more difficult for the particular terrorist group to repeat its terrorist acts or continue its enterprise.[21] Prevention looks forward, so when publicity is used, it should take a longer view than merely reacting to a newsworthy crime of the moment. The long-term approach includes assessing the weaknesses of terrorist groups and uses publicity to exacerbate those weaknesses. Any public statement made in response to a particular terrorist act should be guided not by the details of that particular event, but by the details of repeated events and knowledge of the terrorist group, its field of operations and so on. This is particularly challenging, because much of the terrorist event gains its power from precisely the intense focus by media on the event and its immediate aftermath. It bears repeating that it is the long-term view of prevention that offers the strongest advantage to governments. And we repeat the caution that the problems of publicity near and far must be constantly scrutinized: the target audiences must be clearly in focus, whether they be the terrorists themselves, local communities close to the site of the attacks or local communities close to the terrorist base of operations. The challenge of controlling what news is spread, how it will be interpreted and who it will reach is daunting.

Research in the field of situational crime prevention can provide some indications about what kinds of publicity will work and what will not. While more elaborate classifications have been proposed,[22] crime prevention publicity campaigns are divided into two kinds: those that seek to influence the behavior of potential offenders (e.g., by advertising higher penalties or the existence of new crime prevention initiatives) and those that seek to change the behavior of potential victims (such as "lock your car" campaigns). While evaluations have been mixed, they have generally found that campaigns focusing on victim behavior are less effective than campaigns focusing on

Box 16.1 Offender-Targeted Publicity to Reduce Gun Violence in Boston

In 1996, law enforcement and their crime reduction partners began a project to reduce gun violence and youth homicide in an inner-city Boston area. Because they knew that a major portion of the violence was perpetrated by a small number of identifiable offenders who were gang members, they focused their crime reduction techniques on those individuals and groups. As well as adopting a "zero-tolerance" policy toward violence perpetrated by those individuals, they also mounted a publicity campaign to communicate their zero-tolerance policy. The message conveyed was "a promise to gang members that violent behavior would evoke an immediate and intense response." The methods of communication included sit-down meetings with gangs, speaking at assemblies in schools and discussions with inmates of juvenile correctional facilities. Although there was initially no significant reduction in gun violence as a result of the zero-tolerance policy by police, after the publicity campaign was implemented, there was a 63 percent decrease in youth homicide and a 25 percent reduction in gun assaults.

Source: Kennedy, Braga and Piehl (2001).

offenders, especially when advertising the existence of new crime prevention initiatives.[23] (An example of the successful use of offender-targeted publicity in reducing gun violence is presented in Box 16.1.) Accordingly, we focus below on using the media and publicity in the attempt to affect the behavior of the offender, that is to say, the terrorist.[24]

APPLICATION OF THE 25 TECHNIQUES

As we reviewed in Chapter 15, the research on situational crime prevention has identified 25 techniques that are aimed at reducing opportunities for offenders to commit their crimes.[25] These are all based on the notion, outlined in Chapter 2, that crime and terrorism are both the products of offenders taking a rational course of action, involving a specific sequence of steps to complete an offense. And we demonstrated this approach in Chapter 5 using suicide bombing as our example. Applied to terrorism, many of these intervention techniques may be enhanced by publicity of various kinds, as summarized in Table 16.1.

The rationale for the effectiveness of the publicity approaches listed in Table 16.1 is as follows:

1. Increase the effort. Some argue that we should not publicize new procedures to, say, protect particular buildings, because it only provides the terrorists with information they can use against us by devising ways around our protective procedures. We know from situational prevention that individual terrorists are likely to decide that the effort to carry out an attack against

Table 16.1 Publicity That Targets the Terrorist

Technique	What Should We Say?	What Should We Do?
Increase effort	• "Random searches will be conducted on people entering the subway."	• Invite media to accompany searches.
Increase risks	• "CCTV cameras have been installed in all subway stations." • Spread false rumors about infiltration of terrorist groups by informants. Never admit to poor intelligence. • Ask for public assistance in tracking down terrorists.	• Show subway cameras to press, refer to other covert surveillance. • Show handcuffed offenders caught by surveillance camera. • Show raids on terrorist's home. • Establish hot line for reports.
Reduce rewards	• "These latest attacks strengthen our resolve." • Announce rewards for defection.	• Be seen speaking with religious, political and ethnic leaders. • Have victims speak on television (e.g., London bus driver of July 9, 2005).
Reduce provocations	• Don't say, "Bring 'em on!"	• Avoid televised scenes of violence attributed to authorities in response to terrorism.
Remove excuses	• Don't refer to "The war against terrorism!" Avoid war rhetoric, which terrorists use as their excuse for violence.	• Visuals of revered religious, political or public figures denouncing terrorist acts.

Note: The introduction of random search squads at subway entrances in New York City depends largely on publicity to spread the word that there is a chance (rather low) that one's bag will be searched. The legal challenge to this practice further enhanced the publicity of this tactic. See Chan (2005b, B3).

a highly protected target is too great, and they will look for other ways to commit terrorism that involve less effort and less risk. Furthermore, when a new intervention is announced concerning particular crimes, it has been found that the crime rate may drop, even before the intervention is introduced.[26] Thus, publicity does not necessarily (and perhaps should not) reveal the full scope of prevention programs, thus adding uncertainty to the terrorist's choice of targets. Crime may even drop in nearby locations or for similar targets—a phenomenon known as diffusion of benefits.[27] We have argued in Chapter 3 that similar results might well be achieved with terrorism.

2. Increase the risks. Publicity is, of course, entirely about perception, so the focus will be essentially on increasing the *perceived* risk, although any way to clearly link such publicity to actual risk of getting caught will no doubt enhance the effectiveness of this strategy. There are many ways in which heightened risk may be conveyed to terrorists: publicizing efforts that reduce anonymity (e.g., access passes for subways), random searches at subway entrances, installation of surveillance cameras and tracking of cars through checkpoints. In addition, we saw in Chapter 6 that terrorist groups, particularly those that have lasted over time, live in fear of being infiltrated. Information can be spread announcing the successful infiltration of the group or the enlistment of informers. This information, if effectively communicated to the terrorists, makes recruitment more difficult for them and generally undermines the trust among terrorist group members, thus hastening the disintegration of the group. Information can be obtained from arrested or convicted terrorists and this information can be used in publicity to create tension within the terrorist group, for example, by (1) announcing knowledge of the organizational structure of a group and names of group members and (2) letting it be known that reduction in sentences or punishment are available for those terrorists who provide information on the group (i.e., make exiting the group rewarding).[28]

3. Reduce rewards. If homeowners place their most valuable items, such as jewelry, in banks, they will deny burglars the rewards that they seek. Thus, we need to place the rewards of publicity for the terrorists as far as possible out of their reach. This may seem impossible when we see the jubilation of crowds throughout the Middle East upon hearing the news of the 9/11 attack and see the difficulty inherent in trying to shape such events in the media to one's own advantage. Clearly, violence provides considerable reward to terrorists and their sympathizers. However, the *strategic* reward to terrorists is not the violence (to which they are deeply committed), but the successful completion of missions that take them one step closer to reaching their goal. Publicly characterizing a terrorist event as unsuccessful should be the approach taken, regardless of the extent of violence perpetrated. In fact, the more violent, the more *unsuccessful* one may argue it is. This is because the strategic link between violence and achieving the ultimate goal of the terrorist group is poorly understood by terrorists (see Chapter 6). Thus, any publicity that undermines this presumed link between violence and the goal will reduce the rewards of any particular terrorist act, no matter how jubilant the sympathizers may be when they see it on television. Public statements in response to a terrorist act should therefore always focus on the impossibility of the violent act leading to any sort of satisfaction for the terrorists in achieving their mission. In addition, the quicker and more efficient authorities are in (1) cleaning up the site of the terrorist attack and (2) catching the perpetrators will reduce, retrospectively, the perception of the success of the terrorist attack. Any terrorist acts that are not completed successfully or are thwarted at any point along the way should be highly publicized and repeatedly so.

Lastly, if terrorists depend on the cover provided by immigrant communities, as described in Chapter 11, working with these local communities to spread the view that the terrorists are extremists, will further drive any terrorist cells into isolation and reduce the rewards of being a member of the terrorist group. The news footage of the bus driver, obviously from an immigrant community, denouncing the violence of the terrorists after the London Underground bombings in July 2005 is an extremely powerful example.

4. Reduce provocations. A major strategy of terrorist groups is to provoke authorities into violence or overreaction so that they can use these acts to justify their own acts of violence. Authorities also do the same, especially those that are less democratic. It is an inherent element of violence that it invokes violent reactions.[29] The "cycle of violence" as it is called, once established, is difficult to break, as is obvious in the occupied territories in Palestine. Israel's practice of destroying the houses of families of suicide bombers, for example, while designed to reduce the financial rewards to the family of having a member carry out a suicide mission, nevertheless can be nothing but provocative when aired on television. It is likely, therefore, that this intervention of reducing rewards is neutralized by the provocative publicity that it produces. On the other hand, it is especially important for the authorities not to show "weakness" in the face of terrorist affronts. For example, it can be argued that the lack of U.S. retaliation to terrorist attacks on its embassies in the 1990s emboldened Bin Laden to continue and broaden his attacks (see Chapter 12).

5. Remove excuses. Excuses are probably the greatest prop that supports and sustains terrorist groups and their members. Because terrorists must constantly justify their actions, they spend a large part of their own publicity campaigns doing just that, attempting to explain away the death and carnage they inflict on their victims. We know that many terrorist groups are concerned about the perception of the legitimacy of their acts by the public and their sympathizers (Chapters 6 and 7). Thus, people in authority in government must constantly harp on this theme, pointing out calmly and consistently with each terrorist incident, how utterly callous they are, how hypocritical the terrorists are in claiming that what they are doing is forced on them because there are no other alternatives. In fact, the mantra of terrorists is that they are forced into fighting a "war" as a last resort. This suggests that the authorities should avoid the claim that dealing with terrorism is a war, because this reinforces the main excuse used by the terrorists for their actions. On the other hand, the war rhetoric might help to obtain public support for spending a lot of money fighting terrorism. The government must carefully strike a balance between these two results of war rhetoric. In the case of those who claim that they are acting in the name of a religion, such as Al Qaeda and Islam, constantly hammering home the hypocrisy of their violent acts, contrasting them specifically to the peaceful messages of Islam will help undermine the confidence of operatives, make recruitment more difficult and eventually undermine their supporters. Offering dialog with the terrorists also undermines their argument of lacking alternatives.[30]

CONCLUSION

The complexity of media is beyond the manipulation of any single organization in regard to the portrayal of the "meaning" of terrorism. The vast number and variety of media outlets and organizations ensures that competition among them produces multiple images of terrorism. However, we also know that the media is a highly effective way of selling ideas. Terrorists are limited to one way of selling themselves: violence. In contrast, government has at its disposal many ways of conveying its messages and is able in principle to direct its messages to specific target groups. In sum, the development of a publicity strategy against terrorists requires

- A careful analysis of the terrorist events and terrorist organizations that lie behind them
- Identification of their points of weakness guided by the known techniques of situational prevention
- Construction of a schedule of public statements and deeds
- Selection of specific media for effective delivery

Implementing a Program of Situational Prevention

In This Chapter

- ➤ In dealing with the threat of terrorism we must not repeat the mistakes of the 1960s and 1970s, when we were too slow to retrofit security in response to growing crime.
- ➤ Governments must take the lead in reducing opportunities for terrorism and must rapidly develop expertise in this field.
- ➤ Governments must plan separately to protect their citizens from attack at home and overseas.
- ➤ Governments must work directly with the private sector to reduce access to weapons, to make tools less easily used and to reduce facilitating conditions for different forms of attack. Wherever possible, "dual benefit" solutions that also help reduce crime should be adopted.
- ➤ The responsibility for protecting targets must "cascade" down from the highest level of government to progressively lower levels (and to corporations and businesses).
- ➤ Governments must develop risk-based systems for allocating prevention budgets to state or regional levels. In turn, these levels of government must make risk-based allocations to local levels of government.
- ➤ All preventive planning must be done within the context of these budgets, which must be continuously reviewed as risks change.

SOCIETY'S CURRENT LACK of preparedness to deal with the risk of terrorism reminds us of its similar lack of readiness to deal with the increased crime of the 1960s and 1970s. We begin this chapter by reviewing society's response to the increase in crime, and we argue that the major (but usually unacknowledged) factor in securing the subsequent reduction was the vastly expanded use of security affecting virtually all aspects of everyday life. Businesses and industry led this "retrofitting" of security, while governments stayed largely on the sidelines, preoccupied with trying to improve the effectiveness of police and the criminal justice systems. We should not repeat this mistake in our efforts to deal with terrorism and, in this chapter, we outline a plan for retrofitting security to protect us against terrorism. This plan envisages that from the beginning governments will form partnerships with business and industry to accomplish the task.

THE CRIME INCREASE IN THE 1960s AND 1970s

When crime began to increase in the 1960s, most criminologists and policy pundits blamed the rise on increased drug use, the breakdown of family values, the destruction of neighborhoods, the growth of the underclass and so forth. These explanations focusing on the supposedly more criminal population were entirely consistent with the "dispositional" theories of the day. However, in line with other situational prevention theorists,[1] we would blame instead the increases in the opportunities for crime that were ushered in by the consumerist society. There was a huge increase in the availability of personal possessions (particularly electronic goods) and a similar vast expansion of leisure, travel and entertainment possibilities.[2] Owning these goods, traveling more and spending more leisure time out of the home all exposed people to a greater risk of theft and other forms of criminal victimization. To help purchase these new goods and services, more women entered the labor force, which resulted in many more unguarded homes in the day and unsupervised teenagers out of school hours.[3] The fact that more people spent more time away from their homes in places such as malls, holiday resorts and entertainment areas also meant that they were presented with opportunities to commit crime with little chance of being recognized. Finally, economic competition forced the providers of goods and services to cut costs wherever they could, which led to severe reductions in the numbers of "unproductive" service workers, such as bus conductors, park attendants and school janitors, whose presence had helped reduce crime in the places where they had worked.

The response of the authorities to the increased crime was to pour huge amounts of money into experimental programs in poor neighborhoods designed to prevent the development of delinquency and into correctional programs to find ways of rehabilitating offenders. Despite the variety of experiments and the energy with which they were implemented, crime continued to rise and those treated continued to offend. This eventually led to disenchantment with social and psychological intervention strategies, and governments turned to a series of "get tough" measures, such as "three strikes and you're out" and mandatory imprisonment for drug dealing and possession. Whatever their impact on crime, the get tough measures resulted in substantially increased prison populations in some countries, particularly America. Somewhat later, traditional models of policing that relied on vehicle patrols, rapid response and detective work, and which had not fared well in evaluations, began to be replaced by "community policing" models, such as "broken windows," and later still by the COMPSTAT

(Computer Statistics) model for reporting and acting on the geographic distribution of crimes, which was developed in New York City.[4]

THE CRIME DROP

Property crimes began to decline in the late 1970s and violent crimes followed suit some 10 to 15 years later, but criminologists in the United States—where the reductions were most marked—still argue about the reasons. One camp believes it was a result of the criminal justice policies introduced; the other believes that it was the result of various social changes, such as the reduction in the crack/cocaine epidemic, a reduced proportion of young people in the population, a decline in teen pregnancies and even a moral backlash against the permissive ideals of the 1960s and 1970s.[5] The difficulty with both sets of explanations is that they mostly do not hold for other Western countries where crime has also declined. For example, most of these countries had not been infested with crack/cocaine to anywhere near the same extent, their use of imprisonment was much lower than in America, and they generally had not embraced COMPSTAT and other American policing models. In fact, the only thing in common among all these countries (including the United States) is that they have all made a huge investment in security during the past 25 years, affecting almost every aspect of everyday life.[6]

Business and industry, not government, made this investment, the most obvious manifestation of which was the huge increase in private security guards.[7] Many other changes were also made, however, to retrofit security to homes, cars, stores and parking lots, to mass transit and public housing, to schools and hospitals, to offices and other work places, to entertainment venues and sports stadiums, to airports and seaports, and to warehouses and transportation terminals. New technology was harnessed to produce burglar alarms, video surveillance cameras, breathalyzers, red-light and speed cameras, bar coding and electronic article surveillance (shoplifting tags), metal detectors, baggage screening systems, PIN numbers, instant credit card verification, steering locks and vehicle immobilizers, and a host of other devices and systems. Relatively few of these security services and devices have been evaluated,[8] but situational prevention specialists have conducted many evaluations of opportunity-reducing projects,[9] and police services in the United States and the United Kingdom have reported hundreds of other projects to control specific crime problems using situational techniques.[10] Most of these projects have been local and small scale, but effective action has also been taken on a broader scale to reduce important categories of crime (Box 17.1 provides some evaluated examples).

It is impossible to identify the distinct contribution of security to the crime drop, because it was improved at the same time as other actions were taken to reduce crime. However, it would strain credulity to argue that this

Box 17.1 Security Improvements of National Scope

1. Governments and consumer and insurance groups have prodded car manufacturers into taking numerous measures over the years to improve the security of cars. These measures have included the fitting of steering columns locks to all cars in the early 1970s in the United Kingdom and the United States and, in the 1960s, in Germany, and the fitting of ignition immobilizers in the 1990s to all new cars sold in the European Union and some other countries. Evaluations have shown that these security improvements have contributed to the decline of auto thefts in many countries.

2. Many housing authorities in this country and abroad have taken radical action to improve public housing in response to criticisms by Oscar Newman and others in the 1970s that the design and layout of projects increased the likelihood of crime. Hundreds of high-rise blocks have been demolished in this country and overseas, and more human-scale housing designs have been introduced that allow residents to exercise some control over the public and private areas of the projects. While crime and disorder problems still remain, evaluations have shown that these improvements have helped to reduce the number and the seriousness of incidents.

3. Thousands of stores throughout Western society have introduced a wide range of anti-shoplifting measures, including CCTV, electronic article surveillance systems, ink tags and now RFID devices. Several small-scale evaluations have shown these measures to be effective and, although shoplifting is a poorly measured offense, there can be little doubt that shoplifting has cumulatively been made more difficult.

4. Credit card issuers have taken many steps to reduce fraud, including tightening up the delivery and receipt of cards, improving point-of-sales verification, using PIN numbers and now using embedded chips in cards. Evaluations conducted over the years show that these measures have been highly effective, although new problems have arisen with the growth in their use for online purchases and the forgery of cards by organized criminals in Asia.

5. The U.S. cell phone industry wiped out a problem with cloned phones that was costing hundreds of millions of dollars per year in the mid-1990s in unbilled calls by implementing a series of technological measures. These measures made it difficult to "steal" the numbers of legitimate phones and to use the clones of these phones when the numbers had been reprogrammed into them.

6. Banks have largely eliminated the "heists" commonly committed by criminal gangs in the 1970s and 1980s by the widespread introduction of CCTV cameras, security guards, reduced cash in tills, time release safes and bullet-proof screens. Most bank robberies nowadays are committed by lone offenders, many of whom are addicts, who net small amounts from robbing individual tellers.

7. CCTV cameras are now widely used in offices, campuses, parking lots, schools, airports, bus stations, subway systems and many other places. In the United Kingdom and some other European countries, they are widely deployed in city centers and shopping complexes. They serve both a preventive and an investigative function—the latter dramatically illustrated by footage of the suicide bombers embarking on their deadly mission in the London Underground in July 2005.

vastly expanded security, costing huge sums per year, undertaken by almost every one of society's important institutions, has had no effect on crime. In fact, we believe (but cannot prove) that the security measures we have described have a much wider effect on crime than might be expected from their often narrow focus because they have a cumulative effect in reducing opportunities for crime. They have made it more difficult to engage in "a life of crime" because career criminals depend on committing a wide range of bread-and-butter offenses that yield regular amounts of money to support their lifestyles. The systematic reductions in the opportunities for shoplifting, burglary, robbery and car theft mean that these criminals can no longer rely on a steady stream of income. Without this income, they cannot routinely make use of drugs, gamble and drink, or purchase sex from prostitutes, which are all activities that provide income for other groups of offenders. Nor will they have the leisure to plan and undertake more ambitious crimes that provide greater rewards. Altogether, a life of crime becomes less attractive and those who would otherwise pursue it must find alternative ways of making a living.

LESSONS FOR RESPONDING TO TERRORISM

It is quite remarkable that the vastly increased investment in security is hardly ever mentioned in the various criminological discussions of the crime drop.[11] To us, this is further evidence of the dispositional bias of most current criminology: the blame for crime is put squarely on the offender, not on situational temptations and opportunities, and the cure for crime is changing the offender, not improving security. This mistake must not be repeated in our antiterrorism policies. As we have said repeatedly in this book, governments must put as much effort into developing a program of situational prevention as into interdicting or taking out terrorists. They must act quickly to ensure that the responsible public and private agencies improve security and they must help them to spend available resources to achieve the best effect.

Before we discuss the requirements of such a program, however, we should note two important differences between the crime rise of the 1960s and 1970s and the present increased threat of terrorism. The first and most obvious of these is that the reasons for the increases in crime and terrorism are different. In the case of crime, we have placed the blame on the rise of the consumerist society that significantly increased the opportunities for many forms of crime, while at the same time removed many of the controls. In the case of terrorism, however, the rise of religious fundamentalism, and possibly also of nationalism, has greatly increased the numbers of individuals ready and willing to engage in terrorism.[12] While we should do everything possible to combat these trends, this is not the subject of our book. Instead, we are focused on reducing opportunities for terrorism, which we believe have greatly expanded in the past few decades as a result of globalization and developments in technology. Together these have made it easier for terrorists to travel and move money, as well as to gain access to the tools and weapons they need. In fact, the increased opportunities for terrorism and the increased motivation go hand in hand. The easier it becomes to commit terrorism, the more will individuals be drawn into it as a way of life.

The second important difference is that in the 1960s and 1970s society was confronted with not merely a *threat* of increased crime but with an actual increase in crimes, amounting to hundreds of thousands of offenses per month, across a wide range of different crime types—a situation that demanded a response from all those directly victimized. The case of terrorism is rather different. There has not been a huge rise in the number of attacks in the United States, although the few attacks that have succeeded have claimed many lives and caused widespread fear. This has had enormous consequences, not least in terms of military action in Afghanistan and Iraq as well as hastily expanded legal powers in several Western democracies to deal with suspected terrorists. It has also led to demands for reducing our vulnerabilities to attack, to which this book responds. To date, however, there has been no repetition in the United States of the 9/11 attacks and, consequently, the pressure to reduce our vulnerabilities is waning. It would of course be renewed if another attack occurred, as indeed was the case in the wake of the London Underground suicide attacks in July 2005.

In the face of the enormous cost and difficulties of retrofitting security against terrorism, it is tempting to argue that it makes little sense to protect all potential targets, the vast majority of which would never be attacked; that it is more efficient to strengthen the security forces' capacity to deter, capture or kill individual terrorists who pose a threat; that it is not only a more economical approach, but also one that seems to be working.

This is a seductive line of argument, but it neglects several important facts. First, we know from bitter experience that preemptive action by the security forces cannot succeed in taking out every potential terrorist who might attack the country. Second, the United States and other countries face their greatest risks of attack when their soldiers, diplomats and businesses are operating overseas. These must all be directly protected because it is even more difficult for security forces to take out terrorists overseas than it is at home. Third, no government can leave itself open to the criticism of doing too little to protect the country from attack. This means that all governments must take action to reduce the country's vulnerabilities to attack—the only issue is how this can be done effectively and efficiently, without squandering financial and human resources. Finally, businesses and corporations will leave themselves open to expensive law suits in the event of a terror attack, if they have failed to take preventive action. In the next section, we lay out the requirements for a program of situational prevention to meet these needs.[13]

A PROGRAM OF SITUATIONAL PREVENTION

Before describing what governments must do to implement a program of situational prevention, we should first rehearse the elements of the approach. It consists essentially of analyzing and reducing opportunities for terrorism. This must be done separately for each separate form of attack and should focus on targets, weapons, tools and facilitating conditions. The principal means of reducing opportunities is by physical changes to make terrorism more difficult and risky, and less rewarding. This will often require government and law enforcement agencies to enter into partnerships with businesses and corporate entities, because these entities own so many of the facilities and infrastructures that might be targets for attack. Because it is impossible to eliminate every opportunity, ways must be found to identify those that are most attractive to terrorists. This can sometimes be done by analyzing past incidents, but it will always be necessary to "think terrorist," that is, to examine the task of completing a terrorist attack from the perspective of those planning it. The reaction of the terrorists to reducing opportunities must always be anticipated, although experience in preventing crime has shown that short-term displacement is less common than longer-term adaptation.

This apparently simple formula translates into a complex set of requirements for any government embarking on a program of situational prevention. We discuss these policy requirements in the remainder of the section.

Governments must develop expertise in situational prevention. The first and most urgent policy need is for governments to develop in-house expertise in reducing vulnerabilities to terrorism. Without this expertise, it is doubtful that governments can play their proper role in encouraging and coordinating action to reduce a nation's vulnerabilities.[14] It is important that government experts understand the role of opportunity in terrorism and also understand why most people find it hard to accept that terrorists can be stopped by situational means. They must be able to explain that terrorists are not fanatically driven to commit acts of terrorism. Most of them will not persist in this objective if the balance of risk, effort and reward shifts in an unfavorable direction for them. Many fewer young men might be attracted to terror groups if they perceive the likelihood of success as low.

Governments must develop plans to prevent attacks both at home and overseas. We have shown in Part III that Western societies are generally more vulnerable to attacks overseas, near the terrorists' bases of operation, than at home. Providing protection overseas to businesses, embassies and the military presents a different set of problems, involving a different group of agencies, than protecting from terrorist attacks at home. Governments will have to establish specific capacities and separate budgets to provide this protection.

Governments must work directly with corporations and industry to deal with weapons, tools and facilitating conditions. As will be clear below, action to protect targets must often be taken at the local level. However, governments usually must work directly with the relevant business interests to reduce access to weapons, to make tools less easy to use and to reduce facilitating conditions for different forms of attack.

Governments must develop a methodology for prioritizing protection of targets. Because it is impossible to protect every target, governments must make hard choices in deciding where to put preventive resources.[15] Political considerations will influence these choices, but as far as possible, they should be based on the risk of attack. It has been repeatedly demonstrated by situational prevention researchers that the risk of crime is not distributed evenly throughout society; rather, it is heavily concentrated on particular places, targets and victims.[16] This concentration seems to be an example of the "80/20 rule" that holds widely in the social and natural world: a small proportion of entities produces a large proportion of total output. Thus, only a small proportion of land is fertile, a few people hold most of the country's wealth, a small group of police officers produce the majority of arrests, a relatively few academics produce a large proportion of published papers and so on. We would argue that the same phenomenon holds for terrorism: a few targets attract most of the attacks and a few tools and weapons are disproportionately useful to terrorists. (We have already seen that the World Trade Center attracted two deadly attacks.) Indeed, this principle governs the attempts we have made in earlier chapters to identify the targets, tools and weapons requiring the most attention. As explained, our attempts, such as EVIL DONE, were merely illustrative of the work that needs to be undertaken and, in the final chapter, we spell out an agenda of research to refine the methodology for allocating government funds, based on risk, not on population.

Detailed plans must be developed for "cascading" responsibility for the protection of targets from central government to progressively more local lower levels. The groups and agencies at these "lower" levels include county and municipal authorities, as well as local police agencies,[17] who should all be encouraged to think about vulnerabilities in their particular spheres of responsibility. They should analyze the principal vulnerabilities within their immediate jurisdictions and develop a plan for reducing them. For example, a municipality must ensure that the local schools, reservoirs, malls and entertainment venues have developed contingency plans. In this way, responsibility *cascades* down from central government to involve every government level below. These plans, at all levels of government, will need to be periodically reviewed on a schedule determined by government budgetary disbursements.

Budgets should determine the scale of protection. We have said above that risk should determine preventive priorities, but this leaves open the question of the precise *level* of risk that would demand preventive action. In fact, this question cannot be answered in the abstract, except perhaps for very low or high risks of imminent attack. For other levels of risk, it is impossible to know where to draw the line. The only realistic option we can see is for each responsible public and private entity to work within a predetermined budget that would include government subsidies. This will force them to allocate priorities for prevention according to their assessments of risk, which, in effect is what businesses have always done to protect themselves from crime. They have not tried to protect themselves from every form of criminal attack, but, within the limits of a defined budget, have generally sought protection only from those attacks causing the most damage. Of course, it is much easier for businesses to write off other losses against profits (or tax) than it would be for the government to admit that, because of budgetary constraints, it had failed to protect a target from terrorism that was eventually attacked. However, if the government has pursued a clear and agreed-on policy of protection, within an established budget and has made use of the best available measures of perceived risk, it should be able to protect itself from accusations of neglect and incompetence.

Governments must treat business and industry as vital partners in protecting targets. Businesses and corporate entities own so much of the country's vital infrastructure (reservoirs, chemical plants, transport systems, ports, airliners, communications and so on) that they are almost always collateral victims of terrorist attacks, if not in many cases the prime targets.[18] Such attacks have the potential for major loss of life as well as for considerable disruption to the economy and everyday life. They can also be devastating for the companies concerned. This means that businesses and corporations have a dual role in protection: if they protect themselves from attack, the rest of us reap the benefits. In theory, nobody understands the vulnerabilities of their property (and the costs and the difficulties of protection) better than businesses do themselves. We say "in theory" because the fact is that, despite attempts to treat it as a "revenue generator," in-house security (in contrast to businesses that sell or provide security technologies and services to clients) in many corporations and businesses is often regarded as a necessary and unwanted cost of doing business.[19] Consequently, security procedures in businesses, especially crime prevention efforts, are given little real attention by senior managers and are largely overseen by former police or military officers, who are untrained in crime prevention and whose mindset remains one of tracking down and arresting offenders or potential offenders.[20] Businesses therefore will need to make a considerable investment in training and hiring of qualified personnel if they are to take advantage of up-to-date situational prevention techniques and fill their role in the prevention of terrorism.[21] But there is also another way in which businesses must become much more attuned to their role of preventing terrorism, and that is to address the negative externalities that sometimes result from their business practices. Corporations have been slow to recognize their responsibilities here, although much progress has been made in recent years in the field of environmental pollution, perhaps the most widely acknowledged negative externality of corporate activity. In regard to terrorism, for example, businesses that manufacture arms have been shown to have saturated markets with their weapons, thus contributing to the widespread availability of weapons to both criminals and terrorists.

THE CHALLENGE OF INVOLVING BUSINESSES

Governments will face many difficulties in getting businesses and industry to take on more responsibility for protecting themselves (and us) from attack. Principal among these difficulties is the mindset among the public at large that dealing with crime (and therefore terrorism) is the sole responsibility of the police and elected authorities. There are deep historic reasons for this completely unrealistic public perception of the police role,[22] but it must be taken seriously if some of the responsibility for preventing crime and terrorism is to be shifted away from government and onto the private sector. The public must be convinced that they will benefit from more comprehensive protection if the private sector is fully engaged. This will require a transparent and highly public partnership among all levels of government and businesses, publicizing what is being done and why. Public, systematic and realistic assessments of risk, together with information about what is being done to reduce these risks, will engender more public confidence than will news items of local sheriffs in tiny towns purchasing decontamination chambers for hundreds of thousands of dollars, exhortations to the public to "be vigilant" or vague terror threat levels announced daily.

Added to the unhelpful public mindset about the responsibility for dealing with crime is that the private sector in countries with open-market economies is usually suspicious of government motives when the government presses them to act in certain ways. And we know that the public remains suspicious when the government works too closely with business. The solution is the same as we mentioned above: it is for government to adopt a clear set of organizational guidelines for the protection of targets that is widely publicized and widely acknowledged by all relevant sectors of society, and that identifies clearly which businesses are most vulnerable to what kinds of terrorist attacks and which businesses are best situated to implement preventive measures.

A third set of difficulties relates to the complexity of the task of involving the private sector in prevention. On the one hand, there is the complexity of government itself. Businesses are regulated in many ways by a host of government departments and orchestrating the links between these departments and their respective private sector constituents will take years of patient and persistent effort. Without a clear set of goals and planning tools (like those we have begun to develop in this book), this could even produce negative results. On the other hand, there is the complexity of the business and corporate world. This is much larger than government and is not organized in the same tidy, hierarchical fashion. Finding the right people at the right levels to meet with and persuade would be a difficult challenge for the government, but concentrating on those businesses and corporations most at risk would reduce the effort. These fall into four main groups: (1) those responsible for vital infrastructure, such as reservoirs and power stations; (2) those responsible for facilities in which large numbers of the public gather (transit authorities, entertainment complexes, malls); (3) those that have the potential for causing vast damage if attacked, such as chemical or biological plants and nuclear facilities; and (4) those that are located near large concentrations of recent immigrants. This excludes a vast amount of private sector activity, including large sectors of the manufacturing and distribution industries (automobile plants, furniture and appliance manufacturers, consumer electronics and office supplies, haulage and shipping companies and so on), and considerably narrows the task for government.

The government does have at its disposal various tools and instruments that it can deploy in getting businesses to act. We have reviewed these in previous publications dealing with government efforts to get businesses and manufacturers to change products or services that are exploited by criminals.[23] They range from appeals to "corporate social responsibility," through regulation or legislation (both punitive and remedial), to various kinds of incentives, usually tax related. All these approaches could be used in persuading the private sector to take action against the risk of terror attacks, but we found that in getting manufacturers to change their products most success resulted from the provision of incentives. In the most startlingly successful cases, there has been a clear and unambiguous business benefit to the corporation or company in adopting a particular preventive technique.[24] In other cases, such as car safety, it has taken years of acrimonious exchanges among various and often-conflicting arms of government (i.e., the U.S. Congress, White House, the Federal Trade Commission), car manufacturers and consumer groups to reach the point at which car safety has become a significant marketing tool for car manufacturers. We cannot afford years of acrimonious debate before businesses adopt measures that are needed to prevent terror attacks. We therefore think it is inevitable that the government will have to provide them with subsidies or incentives to do so—although always within the limits of the defined budgets that we discussed above.[25]

Much of what corporations must do to prevent terrorism will have the additional benefit of preventing crime. Where they are the victims, this will improve profits; where the public are the major beneficiaries, this will have benefits in terms of a public perception of improved corporate social responsibility. But the major beneficiary of reduced crime will often be the government because of reduced demand on the police and criminal justice system. We would argue, therefore, that government should put particular emphasis on corporate action that has the *dual benefit* of preventing terrorism and crime,[26] and it should be open to promoting these benefits through various kinds of incentives. Table 17.1 gives just a few examples of the dual benefits

Table 17.1 Dual Benefits for Prevention of Crime and Terrorism from Corporate Action

Preventive Intervention	Dual Benefits		Considerations for Business
	Impact on Terrorism	Impact on Crime	
Banking regulations—"Know Your Customer"	Makes terrorism financing more difficult	Interferes with organized crime, money laundering and drug dealing	*Negative*: Closes off lucrative source of customers *Positive*: Ensures identity of customer so may avoid losses from bad loans
Smart cards, improved identity and document authentication	Exposes terrorists to greater risk of being identified	Makes identity theft, credit and bank card fraud more difficult	*Negative*: Costly to introduce new technology *Positive*: Reduction in losses from fraud and theft
Product marking and tracking	Terrorists' tools and weapons become traceable, thus exposing them and their organizations to greater risk of capture	Increases the risks of burglary, theft by employees, shoplifting and customer fraud	*Negative*: Costly to introduce; difficult to get business clients to change systems *Positive*: Drastically improves inventory control; improves after-sales service fostering new sources of income
Improved physical security	Reduces terrorist access to targets; reduces theft of tools and weapons	Reduces theft, burglary and robbery	*Negative*: Poorly designed physical security may interfere with public perception of "privacy rights" *Positive*: Businesses and clients benefit from a safer working environment

we have in mind. It also indicates some of the reasons why corporations may resist such changes.

CONCLUSION

It is clear from the discussion above that governments (in the United States and other Western countries) face a daunting amount of detailed work in developing a comprehensive plan for reducing opportunities for terrorism. This must be done by separately analyzing the different forms of attack, by formulating separate programs for home and overseas protection, and by working closely with lower levels of government and with business and industry. Only our greatest vulnerabilities should be reduced; otherwise the task of reducing opportunities for terrorism becomes overwhelming and nothing will be done. The extent of the protection introduced should be determined by the budgets allocated, which will need to be continually reviewed as risks change. To support the detailed administrative work needed to reduce opportunities for terrorism, the government must commission a program of applied research. This program is discussed in the next chapter.

Becoming Smarter

In This Chapter

- ➤ We must learn how terrorists carry out their attacks, how they choose their targets and how they select weapons and tools. We must evaluate the effectiveness of our defenses and determine what more we must do to protect ourselves.
- ➤ Governments should commission this research from universities, think tanks and other nongovernmental agencies. If this research is to influence policy, there must be a collaborative, open and equal relationship between those commissioning the research and those undertaking it.
- ➤ Those commissioning the studies must ensure their relevance, keep them on track and feed their results into the policy process. Those undertaking the research must judge their results by the effect on policy, not by the usual academic criteria.
- ➤ Procedures for granting access to data for research must be made less cumbersome and ways must be found to build trust between researchers and those who must assist them.
- ➤ Those undertaking the research could also serve as consultants to assist the police, security forces, local authorities, businesses and corporations in the task of thinking through ways of reducing the vulnerabilities to attack.

SECURITY SERVICES ARE constantly working to identify and "take out" the most dangerous terrorists, and the police and emergency services are continually refining their plans to reduce the loss of life in the event of a terrorist attack. However, insufficient progress is being made on the third essential element of protection from terrorism: the development of a systematic approach to identifying and closing our vulnerabilities to attack. The U.S. 9/11 Commission identified this need in the preamble to its final recommendation[1] when it wrote the following:

> The Department of Homeland Security was established to consolidate all of the domestic agencies responsible for securing America's borders and national infrastructure, most of which is in private hands. It should identify those elements of our transportation, energy, communications, financial and other institutions that

need to be protected, develop plans to protect that infrastructure, and exercise the mechanisms to enhance preparedness. This means going well beyond the preexisting jobs of the agencies that have been brought together inside the department.

The former members of the Commission recently rated the U.S. government's progress in implementing the recommendation as "unsatisfactory,"[2] and although the government might have made more progress than the rating suggests,[3] we should not be surprised if it had not. It might not be very difficult for security forces to refocus their energies on terrorists rather than on organized criminals or foreign agents, and police and emergency services might not have to respond very differently to terrorist attacks than to other kinds of disasters. But there is little experience to guide officials in thinking about how to protect people, infrastructure and buildings from clandestine attacks launched by malevolent and well-organized adversaries.[4] Our book brings to bear one important source of relevant experience provided by the field of situational crime prevention, but the tools and concepts that it offers must be refined and developed in real-world applications, guided by a comprehensive research plan, if they are to be routinely useful in practice. This requires a sustained investment in situational prevention research, and in this final chapter, we discuss the studies that are needed and the conditions that must be created to ensure that this research properly contributes to counterterrorism policy.

Before proceeding, we should return to a question mentioned earlier in our discussion concerning the proper balance between taking out terrorists and protecting vulnerable targets. As we have noted, some would argue that the former is clearly more important than the latter when the risk of terrorist attack is low—as it has been historically, for example, in the United States. In these circumstances, it makes little sense to protect all potential targets—the vast majority of which would never be attacked. Rather, it is argued, it makes more sense to strengthen the security force's capacity to deter, capture or kill individual terrorists who pose a threat. Not only does this approach seem to be working—at the time of writing there has been no repeat in the United States of the 9/11 attacks—but, in principle, it seems the more economical one. Although we have a multitude of enemies, they can only enter our countries in small numbers, and we should be able to intercept them and turn them back at our borders. If they succeed in entering, we should be able to track them down.[5]

These arguments neglect the fact that the greatest risks of attack are when Americans and the nationals of other Western countries are overseas, engaged in tourism, business, diplomacy or military action. It is considerably more difficult for security forces to take out terrorists abroad than at home, and governments must therefore do more to reduce our vulnerabilities overseas. The political reality is, in fact, that governments must also try to do this at home. As the events of 9/11 made tragically clear, governments cannot depend on the security forces to take out all the dangerous terrorists, and they cannot leave themselves open to the criticism of doing too little to protect their countries from attack. Above all, they cannot run the risk of a repeat attack as devastating as that of 9/11. So they will have to do as much as they can to reduce the most obvious vulnerabilities.[6]

RESEARCH NEEDS

Situational prevention studies must always be focused on specific forms of terrorism, if they are to provide the detailed information needed to inform policy and practice. We should also recognize that it is difficult to apply the normal quantitative methods of situational prevention to very rare events such as terrorist attacks at home, and researchers must be prepared to experiment with new and less familiar methodologies. The studies needed are listed below.

Systematic interviews with terrorists about their decisions. The objective would not be to gain intelligence on terrorist organizations, but to help find ways to make terrorist acts more difficult, risky and less rewarding. The studies would also help anticipate displacement or adaptation by terrorists.

Systematic interviews with terrorism experts. These interviews, including but not limited to academic experts, would obtain some of the same information. These are needed because of the difficulties of interviewing terrorists.

Systematic ratings of the attractiveness of different targets. These ratings for specific forms of attack would be established by police, security experts, and government and corporate administrators. This will help in prioritizing preventive resources.[7]

Detailed problem-solving exercises of the scope for controlling specific tools and weapons. Such exercises could be conducted, for example, for credit cards or Semtex. Situational prevention provides a methodology for guiding such research and for choosing among possible control measures.

Studies of the journey to terrorism. These studies will help to understand how distance from the targets or from supportive immigrant communities complicates the task for terrorists and makes it difficult for them to mount routine attacks.

Empirical analyses of databases and newspaper accounts of incidents. These analyses include such incidents as IRA shootings and Iraq roadside bombs. Such research can help to pinpoint and remove specific vulnerabilities regularly exploited by terrorists.

Analyses of thwarted attacks. How many attacks have been thwarted compared with completed attacks and what factors led to failure?

Analysis of operations to close down opportunities for organized crime rackets. These analyses can be used to glean lessons for terrorism prevention.

Studies of implementation failures and successes. Preventive measures that are agreed and funded are sometimes not implemented or not implemented properly. Understanding the reasons should make future implementation more certain and less troublesome.

Cost-effectiveness studies of implemented measures. We need to know what works, and at what cost, if we are to make the best use of limited preventive resources.

Some people will question whether this research is really needed. Is it not the case, they might ask, that those with the direct responsibility for protecting our population and infrastructure—the police, business and corporate heads and a host of others—are already trying to answer these questions? Is it not also the case that their down-to-earth practical approach will be more useful than research studies undertaken by "ivory tower" researchers, who are removed from the problems and have no direct responsibility for prevention?

The answer to these questions is that research is not a substitute for the efforts already being made to reduce vulnerabilities to attack, but it can assist these efforts in many important ways. Indeed, one important benefit of commissioning such research would be the creation of a cadre of researchers with detailed knowledge of terrorism who could be called on as consultants to assist the police, security forces, local authorities, businesses and corporations in the task of thinking through new ways of reducing vulnerabilities to attack. Given the magnitude of the task, it is vital that such a body of knowledgeable consultants be available if only to challenge entrenched beliefs and attitudes. We have found repeatedly in our own work on problem-oriented policing that police find it difficult to break out of mindsets that prevent them from abandoning ineffective traditional approaches and adopting new solutions. For example, most police continue to believe in the deterrent value of random patrols and crackdowns when research has consistently shown these have temporary benefits at most.[8] Allied with the faith in patrols and crackdowns is defeatism with regard to displacement. Police nearly always believe that raising the risks for criminals in a particular location will simply result in them moving elsewhere to commit their crimes, when the research shows that this displacement is by no means inevitable (see Chapters 3 and 4).[9] Faith in such entrenched beliefs can only be shaken by empirical evidence forcefully presented by researchers who have established their credibility in the fields concerned.

Experienced researchers can help to improve policy and practice in some other ways. They know how to collate, assess, summarize and communicate knowledge and can therefore serve as a repository of reliable information about ways of assessing vulnerabilities and responding to them. Second, they routinely communicate across international boundaries and can therefore serve as a conduit for information among different countries. This is particularly valuable in the case of terrorism where policy differences might separate these countries. Third, they can provide concepts and theories to assist in interpreting and make generalizations about existing experience. This is vital in responding quickly and effectively to new or emerging threats of terrorism where current experience seems not to provide any guide to action. Fourth, they know how to evaluate preventive projects and programs and can therefore provide the evidence base for policy and practice. Finally, by undertaking focused research studies, they can produce the new information needed to improve and refine policy and practice.

GETTING THE RESEARCH DONE

Unless governments commission the studies we have outlined above, most would never be undertaken. There are simply too few researchers with a background in situational prevention to undertake the necessary volume of work on their own initiative. Other researchers might be attracted to conduct such work by the availability of new research funds, but governments must first be persuaded of the need for such research. In the United States, the Department of Homeland Security to date has not called for these kinds of studies. Its externally funded research program consists of six Centers of Excellence:

1. The National Center for Food Protection and Defense (NCFPD), which is focused on protecting food production, storage and transport
2. The National Center for Foreign Animal and Zoonotic Disease Defense (FAZD), which emphasizes protection against foreign animal diseases
3. The Center for the Study of High Consequence Event Preparedness and Response, which conducts research into responding to disasters, including terrorist acts
4. The Center for Advancing Microbial Risk Assessment (CAMRA), which deals with protecting human life from biological threats
5. The Center for Risk and Economic Analysis of Terrorism Events (CREATE), whose mission is to evaluate the risks, costs and consequences of terrorism, and to guide economically viable investments in countermeasures
6. The Center for Behavioral and Social Research on Terrorism and Counter-Terrorism (START), which spans work on the causes of and responses to terrorism and the psychological impact of terrorism on society

The first four of these centers seem to be undertaking mostly technological and scientific work, which is different from the situational prevention research we have advocated. Later in this chapter, we say more about these differences when we discuss the wartime operational research done in the United Kingdom, but we might illustrate the point by considering the work of the fourth center, CAMRA, concerned with biological threats. Presumably this center develops improved technologies to detect and counter such threats. Situational prevention researchers would have little to contribute to that work, but they could help by assessing the likelihood of terrorists employing the various forms of biological attacks and how they might seek to counter the technology. The fifth center (CREATE) is concerned with risks, costs and consequences of terrorism but, judging from the partner institutions, only from an economic perspective. The sixth center (START), for behavioral and social research on terrorism, could undertake the kind of studies we call for, but it currently possesses only limited expertise in situational crime prevention.

Before long governments will recognize the need for the studies we advocate and will begin to commission them. Given the novelty of this approach, the commissioning officials might have difficulty in ensuring that the research produces what they want and, indeed, they might have unrealistic expectations about what it can produce. At the same time, those being commissioned might exploit the situation to undertake studies that further their own research interests and not those of the contracting agency. In the remainder of this section, we discuss ways that governments and researchers must work together to ensure that the investment in research is not squandered and that it really does help to reduce the country's vulnerabilities to attack. We begin with governments.

Commissioning the Research

Government departments should not undertake the research in-house, because this would militate against the open sharing of information with universities, think tanks and other nongovernmental agencies that we believe is essential to reduce the vulnerabilities to terrorist attack (see below). Instead, these departments should develop strong in-house units capable of commissioning, monitoring and assessing the research that is needed. To prevent them from being manipulated by academic contractors, these units should be staffed by well-qualified and knowledgeable officials, who must be able to see through vague promises about the preventive benefits of certain lines of work. They must also insist that the studies commissioned have a realistic chance of producing preventive benefits in the short term, not in the distant future. They must constantly monitor the research to ensure that it does not drift from its initial goals, but at the same time they should have the flexibility to adjust the terms of the research funding if it becomes clear that a change in direction is needed. Finally, they must insist that the research is reported with a clear and succinct statement of the implications for prevention.

It will be important for them to understand the ways in which situational prevention research can complement more technical or scientific research. For example, it would be vital to undertake field evaluations of the accuracy of new forms of detection or surveillance, such as biometric or DNA screening, before these were widely deployed. It would also be important to conduct research into the ways that terrorists (and criminals) might adapt to the deployment of the new equipment and perhaps neutralize its effectiveness. If these latter kinds of studies were funded out of the same budgets and managed by the same units as the basic scientific and technological work, there is a real danger that they would be sidelined. This is because they require relatively few resources compared with scientific and technological research, which needs large well-equipped laboratories. It would be natural therefore that management would give correspondingly less attention to work consuming fewer of their resources.

The distinction we have drawn between research needed to develop new technologies and that needed to evaluate their effectiveness when deployed in the field is a familiar one. During World War II, for example, the field of operational research was created by the British to assist in assessing new weapons, in comparing the costs and benefits of similar kinds of military equipment and in assessing various offensive and defensive strategies and tactics. Box 18.1 lists some of the products of this work, which materially assisted the war effort and which repaid its relatively small cost many times over.

It is not hard to see why this wartime research was so effective. The operational researchers were under tremendous pressure to find ways of staving off defeat by the Germans. Many of them were among the best scientists of the day. They were located in government or military units and could ask for, and expect to receive, extensive cooperation from the civil authorities and the armed services. Their analyses were often facilitated by the availability of large data sets. On occasion, their work was personally endorsed by Winston Churchill, the country's prime minister. Even without these considerable advantages, however, we believe the research we advocate would be of great value in protecting the country from attack (but this time by terrorists) because, like the wartime operational research, it would constantly have to meet the test of practical relevance; it could not survive on the vague promise of improving our understanding of terrorism.

Conducting the Research

We have said this research would have to be commissioned by governments but be undertaken by universities and think tanks. We have described the kinds of studies needed and we have suggested ways for governments to ensure that the research commissioned produced policy-relevant results. The researchers themselves, especially those in universities, must also play their part in ensuring that their studies do, in fact, contribute to the goal of reducing the country's vulnerabilities to attack. This would demand some changes in the usual academic ways of doing business, and the principles that should guide them are as follows:

- Never propose studies without immediate policy application. Judge the impact of the research by the effect on policy, not by the usual academic criteria of publication and so on. On the other hand, do not take on work that could not be published and thus could not contribute to the store of knowledge on preventing terrorism.
- Never conduct research that does more to advance personal research agendas than meet the expectations of the commissioning agency.

Box 18.1 British Operational Research in World War II

Operational researchers made many contributions to the British war effort. They used a combination of methods that included direct observation, interviews with service personnel, and mathematical and statistical analysis. Among the many facts of great importance that they established were the following:

1. The chances of ships escaping U-boat attack could be substantially increased if they sailed in large convoys (of 150 ships or more) rather than in a larger number of small convoys.
2. Coastal Command aircraft should be painted white rather than black, because they would be significantly less visible to surfaced U-boats and would thus be more capable of launching an attack before the U-boat submerged.
3. Coastal Command aircraft were more likely to sink U-boats if they aimed their depth charges directly at their conning towers, not at some point in front of the submarine in an attempt to compensate for its forward motion.
4. To take best advantage of the limited supply of radar-sighting devices, anti-aircraft guns should be deployed in batteries of eight rather than in batteries of four guns, as was the existing practice.
5. The higher claimed "hit" rates of coastal anti-aircraft batteries were due to the fact that their claims could not be checked against downed aircraft, because these fell into the sea not onto the land. More incoming bombers would therefore not be shot down if anti-aircraft batteries were relocated to the coast from further inland.
6. The number of fighter missions flown could be doubled if all serviceable aircraft were flown whenever required, rather than ensuring that 70–75 percent of fighters were always serviceable, as was the existing practice.
7. The chances of a fighter aircraft intercepting an incoming enemy bomber could be substantially improved using a simple geometric formula (a "vector") based on the different starting points of the two aircraft and their different speeds.
8. Despite wide claims to the contrary, there was very little empirical evidence that fighter bombers could be deployed effectively against tanks.
9. It was highly cost-effective to deploy a portion of the bomber fleet in a specially trained "pathfinder" role. Their task was to find the target and illuminate it for the main bomber force with fires and flares.
10. Enlarging the escape hatch of the Lancaster bomber by two inches would substantially increase the crew's chances of bailing out successfully when the bomber was shot down; in fact, this increased the proportion surviving from about 15 percent to about 21 percent. (A total of 12,790 airmen successfully escaped from Lancasters that were shot down during the war)

Source: Kirby (2003).

- Do not regard the commissioning agency simply as source of funds, but see it as vital partner in conducting relevant work. Meet with the agency as soon as results begin to emerge from the study. Listen carefully to questions raised in the discussions to see whether the work can be adapted to provide answers. Be prepared to write frequent and timely policy briefings.
- Always allow the problem being addressed—not a favored methodology or theoretical framework—to determine the research approach.
- Adopt the motto of the British wartime operational researchers: "Second best—but tomorrow!"[10] This means working to shorter time scales and undertaking more short-term "rapid appraisal"[11] work. Terrorists continually adapt their methods as opportunities and technologies change, and as the authorities introduce new countermeasures. Although terrorist activity at one point in time might best be described by lengthy and detailed research, from a policy perspective, it might only provide yesterday's answers to today's problems.
- If it becomes clear before completion that the original research design was misconceived, inform the commissioning agency. Work with the agency to modify the research so that it can provide more useful and relevant results.
- Deliver what is commissioned—or something more relevant to policy.

BUILDING TRUST

One of the sharpest lessons of 9/11 is that the work of the security forces must be more publicly accountable because secrecy is often a cloak for incompetence and time-serving ritual. In fact, this is true of any professional, government or business activity: the more protected it is from public scrutiny, the more likely it will be that self-serving and exploitive practices flourish. This is why we believe that the research we advocate must be contracted outside government. We have discussed the research management difficulties of such an arrangement, but not the greater difficulty of building trust between researchers and the practitioners who must facilitate their studies and implement the results. These people include personnel who hold the data needed for research, such as records of attacks and failed attacks, actions taken to prevent attacks, transcripts of interviews with arrested terrorists, descriptions of the methods used in attacks and so forth. They also include a wide range of people who can help researchers to collect their own data about such matters as the vulnerabilities of targets, the precautions and security in place, the capabilities of terrorist weapons, the vulnerabilities of tools and facilitating conditions and so on. In some cases, providing this access or assistance to researchers might involve much cost and inconvenience and it might be tempting to refuse cooperation on the grounds of possible breaches of security. In some cases, businesses might object to releasing information on the grounds that this could jeopardize their market position.

Confidentiality, in fact, can be safeguarded and secrecy maintained when granting access to sensitive information. In any case, researchers do not usually need information about current operations, and they rarely need to know the identity of suspected individuals. But if research is to play its full part in policy development, it cannot be delayed by extended negotiations to provide the needed information and access. Commissioning agencies will therefore have to devote considerable effort to developing protocols for granting access to needed data for research, to speeding up security clearance for researchers and to developing ways of building trust between the researchers and those who must assist them. It will also have to act quickly to resolve the kind of access problems that sometimes obstructed the vital wartime research referred to above. The findings of that research were sometimes brushed aside because they were produced by scientists with supposedly little understanding of military and practical realities. If this happened in wartime, we can expect it to happen again in the fight against terrorism. This underlines the need for great care in commissioning relevant studies, in keeping them on track and in feeding their results into the policy process. Done properly, this will amply repay the investment in research by helping to find effective and efficient ways of reducing our vulnerabilities to terrorist attacks.

Notes

Chapter 1

1. Clarke (1980); Clarke (1992); Clarke (1997); Clarke (2005); and Newman et al. (1997).

2. The popular view is that suicide bombers are deeply committed to their higher (religious) cause and that this is why they do what they do. There are at least three reasons to doubt this portrayal of the bombers' motivation. First, it is well known that they must be carefully trained and prepared to carry out their task. They are, in fact, trained just like soldiers in regular battle are trained to risk their lives for the cause. That they must be trained to do it means that it is never assumed that the motivation to risk one's life runs deep. Second, theirs is a one-time act and a one-time commitment. They do not have to be committed in the long term, unlike soldiers, police officers or the handlers who train suicide bombers. Third, the fact that the families of suicide bombers in Palestine are routinely given large payments in lieu of their son's or daughter's sacrifice undermines the claim that these suicide bombers carry out their acts only for a higher religious cause.

3. We are indebted to Nick Ross for this formulation.

4. There are other similarities between terrorism and crime: (1) terrorists, like criminals, are disproportionately young males; (2) sustained levels of terrorism or crime in particular locations undermine the social fabric of the community; and (3) some types of crime resemble terrorism and even war, such as gang violence and some types of organized crime. See Lafree and Dugan (2004, 54–56).

5. For an excellent example, see Bajpai and Gupta (2005, 301–09).

6. Recent studies of suicide terrorism identify the resentment of Islamic nationals against occupation by the foreign forces, particularly Russia and the United States as contributing to the overall motivation of terrorism. See Pape (2005) and Bloom (2005), chap. 4.

7. This is not meant to excuse the failures of our intelligence services.

8. For a review of this case see Hartocollis and McGeehan (2005). The cost to government is further complicated by the current and future role of the Terrorism Risk Insurance Act that provides for the U.S. government to cover up to 90 percent of insured losses after a deductible is met. The act, due to expire December 31, 2005, was renewed with small adjustments in November 2005 for another two years. See Carroll et al. (2005). For a discussion of ways to assess terrorism risk, see Willis et al. (2005).

9. Throughout this book we have relied heavily on the Rand MIPT database. However, this database, like all other general databases on terrorism available at present, is incomplete. Some researchers such as Ricolfi have augmented it with data from other databases. The difficulty in merging different databases on terrorism is that the databases use different definitions and categorizations of their incidents. See Ricolfi (2005, 117–19) for an excellent appraisal of the MIPT and other terrorism databases. Ricolfi has found that it contains only 70 percent of suicide missions. However, the data on the success of suicide missions are also supported by Pape (2005) who assembled a data set of all suicide bombings from 1980 to 2003. In general, there is a remarkable concordance of findings concerning the characteristics of suicide bombers across most of these databases. For an appraisal of the eight terrorism databases available as of 2004, both regional and worldwide, see Schmid (2004).

Chapter 2

1. March and Simon (1958) invented the term "satisfycing" to express the idea that decision making was always bounded or limited by the constraints of the individual's situation. Cornish and Clarke (1986) adopted the term to explain the limitations on rationality of offenders when they planned and carried through their acts.

2. Clarke and Cornish (1985); Cornish and Clarke (1986); Clarke and Cornish (2001).

3. Ekblom (2001–02) has argued that, in the absence of events to analyze, we must "think thief" to imagine what methodologies they will adopt in the future when they adapt to the changing conditions of everyday life.

4. In any case, this has many drawbacks as a preventive policy, not least that the criminal justice system has had limited success in detecting and imprisoning habitual offenders (or "career criminals" as these are called) and many rapes and house break-ins are committed not by career criminals but by opportunistic and less committed offenders.

5. An exception to this difficulty is that terrorists tend to publicize what they do and attempt to explain publicly why they act the way they do, as we note in Chapters 6 and 16. This gives us information that we normally do not get from thieves who prefer to remain furtive, although they will divulge their techniques to skilled interviewers once caught (Walsh 1986).

6. And as we will see in Chapter 16, countering propaganda is a complex undertaking that should also be based on sound situational crime prevention principles.

7. Thanks to John Eck and Nick Ross for suggestions that helped us to develop Table 2.1

8. Patil (2003).

9. Hesseling (1994); for fuller discussion, see Chapter 3.

10. This illustrates another important lesson of crime prevention. Even when security measures are successful for a while, constant probing for weaknesses and experimentation by criminals (and by terrorists) can eventually require that the measures need to be revised and strengthened.

11. The role that Madrassas play in producing terrorists is complicated. There is evidence that many suicide bombers and other jihadists may have attended Madrassas, but the claim that enrollment in these schools in Pakistan has increased wildly in recent years, especially since 9/11, appears to be exaggerated (Andrabi et al. 2005).

12. See "The Northern Ireland Conflict" on the BBC Web site, available at http://www.bbc.co.uk/history/timelines/ni/internment.shtml.

13. National Commission on Terrorism Attacks upon the United States (2004), 344.

Chapter 3

1. Clarke and Lester (1989).

2. BBC News (2000). Legislation introduced in 1998 required paracetamol to be packaged in packets of 16 or fewer in supermarkets, and 32 or fewer in pharmacies. Overdoses fell by 21 percent after the new packaging was introduced.

3. Clarke and Mayhew (1988).

4. Langan and Farrington (1998).

5. Shover (1991).

6. Hesseling (1994).

7. Clarke and Weisburd (1994).

8. Ekblom (2001/2002).

Chapter 4

1. Paul Ekblom has developed the concept of adaptation. See Ekblom (1997, 2001/2002); Ekblom and Tilley (2000).

2. Adapted from St. John (1991)

3. Dobson and Payne (1982), quoted by St. John (1991, 40).

4. St. John (1998) sorts countries into four groups according to their policies for dealing with hijackers: retaliation (Israel and United States); no compromise (Britain, France, Holland, India, Jordan, Kuwait, South Korea and West Germany); flexibility (Belgium, Canada, Egypt, Sweden and Switzerland) and concession and accommodation (Austria, Cypress, Greece, Italy, Japan, Malta, Spain and Thailand). He notes that most of those falling into the "no compromise" group by 1998 had formerly pursued less hard-line polices.

5. The question of which had the greater effect is relevant only to American not worldwide hijackings.

6. Because relatively few hijackings (15 percent) are thwarted, Merari (1998, 23) has argued that "... the blunt fact is that the effort to protect commercial airliners from attacks has by and large failed." It is true that once they find a way to board the aircraft, hijackers generally achieve their objectives, but many fewer of them can get past this first hurdle. In making this argument, he therefore discounts the deterrent effect of the increased security. This seems a perverse conclusion to an otherwise careful analysis.

7. Wilkinson (1998).

8. Jenkins (1998).

9. See, for example, Cauley and Im (1988); Chauncey (1975); Dugan, LaFree and Piquero (2005); Enders and Sandler (1993, 2000, 2006); Enders, Sandler and Cauley (1990). For a review, see Lum, Kennedy and Sherley (2006).

10. Choi (1994, 7).

Chapter 5

1. Defining suicide attacks or missions is difficult. For a particularly provocative account of the definitional problem see Gambetta (2005). This volume offers an excellent review of the main forms of suicide missions. In this chapter, we have avoided these definitional difficulties by focusing on a specific type of suicide bombing in a specific place.

2. Hill (2005).

3. For a detailed description of the Rajav Gandhi killing, see Cutter (1998). For a general background of the LTTE (Liberation Tigers of Tamil Eelam) in Sri Lanka, see Gunaratna (2001). While the LTTE are pioneers of this method of attack, they are also unusual in their use of women as suicide bombers (Bloom 2005).

4. For an excellent account of the strategic advantages of suicide terrorism, see Pape (2005).

5. *The Economist* (January 8, 2004).

6. The high kill ratio of hostage taking is misleading because the kill ratio is computed as number of killings per incident. However, hostage taking is a labor-intensive crime, usually requiring many more terrorists to participate in the key operation of taking the hostages and subsequently keeping them in a safe place. Thus, in terms of efficiency as described by Al-Zawahiri, this is probably not an efficient way of doing business (although the method may have instrumental advantages, such as extortion or manipulation of the media).

7. Milbank (1978).

8. We use the term "martyrdom" in a secular manner, because research suggests that it is not any particular religion per se that dictates the use of this technique. The motivations of suicide bombers, that is, what they are trying to achieve personally through their act, are complex, although probably tied to issues of identity that confront all teenagers and young adults. See, for example, Harrison (2004), Merari (1998), Pape (2003, 2005). Regardless of the personal issues involved, however, at least one study found that it is facilitating conditions that make suicide bombing possible or likely, not the personal stress of the bomber (Orbach 2004).

9. The Popular Front for the Liberation of Palestine (PFLP), for example, which is a secular organization (Bloom 2005). Hopgood (2005) has argued convincingly that religion cannot explain the emergence of suicide terrorism of the Tamil Tigers in Sri Lanka. Pedahzur (2005) has convincingly documented the political effects of suicide bombings on governments, particularly those responding to Hezbollah, Hamas, Fatah, LTTE and the PKK. At the same time, however, he has also shown how government responses (the capturing of PKK's leader Ocalan and the building of walls in Israel) resulted in significant decreases in suicide bombings.

10. The measure of success of suicide bombing in general is difficult, of course, as Pape (2005) has well argued. Pape's study of all suicide bombings from 1980 to 2002 has clearly demonstrated that most campaigns were successful in extracting concessions from the nations or governments that were the objects of their campaigns. However, the overall success, whether the governments were forced to make concessions in regard to issues of their own national interest is questionable. The reality is that national governments are much more powerful and resilient than are terrorist groups.

11. Pape (2005).

12. Pape (2005).

13. For the most recent surveys, see Bloom (2005); Pape (2005).

14. *The Economist* (January 8, 2004).

15. As Pape (2005, 239) recounts, the campaigns of Hamas and Heizbollah were successful in extracting a number of concessions from the Israeli government.

16. This phenomenon complicates attempts (for example, Dugan, LaFree and Piquero 2005) to study whether terrorist events are contagious, that is, whether they lead to imitation.

17. Pedahzur (2005).

18. Pape (2005).

19. The list is composed of attacks that occurred since the outbreak of the most recent conflict, known as the Al-Aqsa Intifada, which erupted on September 28, 2000. The data set includes incidents up to December 2003. These parameters were chosen because of the high frequency of suicide bombing incidents occurring in that region during this time period. Information about the individual attacks was gathered from five newspapers. Two of the newspapers are published in English; these include *The New York Times* and *The Jerusalem Post*, published in Israel. The remaining three newspapers, *Ha'aretz*, *Maarive* and *Yediot Acharonote*, are published in Israel and are written in the native Hebrew language.

20. In fact the religious makeup and political views of these groups is quite diverse as clearly demonstrated by Pape (2005).

21. Pape (2005) argues that suicide bombers are generally driven by political motivations of liberation from a perceived foreign occupier rather than religious extremism. Of his worldwide sample of suicide bombers, 43 percent were religious and 57 percent secular. The comprehensive account by Pedahzur (2005) also supports this view.

22. However, our measure was narrowly defined as "places of worship." The Human Rights Watch database lists two incidents that occurred in the high orthodox area of Jerusalem, one in a public place and the other at a Bar Mitzvah. However, a recent study found that 52.8 percent of suicide missions from October 1981 to September 2003 were carried out by secular terrorist groups, which suggests that it is not religion that drives the selection of suicide missions as the method of attack (Gambetta 2005, 262).

23. Marighella (1971).

24. Merari (2004a, 2004b, 2004c).

25. Women have been found to be more committed and are less often searched, suggesting the need for female security guards (Beyler 2004).

26. Pape (2005, 214).

27. Pape (2005, 214).

28. Other research based on interviews of handlers and of preempted or failed suicide bombings generally reports a similar process of indoctrination and group commitment. See Hassan (2001, 2004). Ricolfi (2005, 79) reports that 5–10 percent of the executed missions in his database failed.

29. Other possible explanations are that their frequency responds directly to (1) political events in the "peace process" or (2) competition among rival terrorist factions. Pedahzur (2005) and Ricolfi (2005, 84–105) offer some evidence for the former, although it is difficult to account for the variations in frequency by each group. Looking at the groups combined, however, offers a plausible explanation for the linkage between political events and bombing frequency. Our routine explanation fits the bombing frequency more closely, especially when viewed in light of the routine patterning of IRA attacks, as we will see in later chapters.

30. Bloom (2005, 19–44) argues that there is intense rivalry among the different terrorist groups that results, among other things, in some terrorist groups claiming responsibility for attacks that they did not carry out. It is therefore possible that the data in Figure 5.3 are affected by these false claims.

31. This analysis is supported by findings of a number of research projects. See Argo (2004); Atran (2003).

32. Cornish (1994); Lacoste and Tremblay (2003).

33. Argo (2004); Hassan (2001); Merari (2004a, 2004b, 2004c); Pedahzur (2005); Post, Sprinzak and Denny (2003); Shiqaqi (2002).

34. Merari (2004a, 2004b, 2004c). Also, if we examine Box 3.2, we see that IDF responses have been largely successful, although it is impossible to say which intervention was most effective. It was a combination of solutions that appears to have worked.

Chapter 6

1. As Dugan, LaFree and Piquero (2005, 1059) note, "... traditional deterrence-rational choice models in criminology have been primarily aimed at understanding the behavior of individual offenders. A rational calculus at a group level may look very different. For example, a group level calculus may privilege outcomes such as publicizing group grievances, countering feelings of hopelessness and humiliation, and obtaining international status ahead of the perceived individual costs of certainty and severity of punishment. Even among individual measures, there is much difference between concern about legal punishment versus the attractions of martyrdom or eternal bliss."

2. But even cyberterrorism is committed to destruction or at a minimum severe disruption of networks, which could result in violence or death, such as the disruption of a power grid, water supply or nuclear power plant operations, air traffic control and so on.

3. As we write, Hamas has won a significant victory in the Palestinian election, but has so far refused to renounce the use of violence. Factions of the IRA still hold out on surrendering weapons, and pointedly continue the use of violence even as victory at the ballot box was in the offing.

4. Cordes (2001).

5. And of those lasting for more than the first year, only 50 percent last for more than decade. See Hoffman (1998, 170); Jackson et al. (2005).

6. The irony is, of course, that Marx, so often the ideological master of terrorist groups, identified similar internal contradictions of capitalism.

7. Charismatic qualities also help many politicians to get elected in democratic societies. It is reasonable to speculate that the underlying ruthlessness of the charismatic, authoritarian personality represents a continuous threat to all democratic societies. Terrorist groups of course are not democratic organizations, although their forms and structures vary considerably as we describe in the second part of this chapter.

8. McCormick (2001, 109).

9. Guzman's conviction was overturned in 2003 and his case sent for a new trial. See Gotkine (2004).

10. In the case of successful terrorist leaders, the cult of hero worship may continue long after the leader is gone, although the followers may gradually disengage their mission from the original leader's ideology, as is the case in China today regarding Mao Tse Tung.

11. In this respect, an occupying force, such as the United States and its allies in Iraq, can justify force that normally would not be justifiable or possible under their own laws because of the suspension of the rule of law in the occupied country, making it easier to argue that the situation really is one of war.

12. There is an extensive literature on the psychodynamics that the state-sanctioned terrorists used to justify violence and torture in Argentina's dirty war. See, for example, Taylor (2002).

13. Ferracuti (1982, 136).

14. Communique from Direct Action (1984).

15. Yehuda Etzion advocated active redemption for Israel, a force that was to dominate the actions of the Israeli underground terrorist group Gush Emunim: "The State of Israel was granted in Mercaz ha-Rav, an unlimited and independent credit. Its operations—even those that stand in contrast to the model of Israel's Torah—are conceived of as 'God's will', or a revelation of his grace..." (cited in Sprinzak 2001, 205). The Gush Emunim group meticulously planned an attack on the Dome of the Rock, the holiest place for both Judaism and Islam in Jerusalem. However, it was so conflicted by the use of violence that it consulted three Rabbis to obtain their approval, and not receiving it, did not carry out the mission.

16. McCormick (2001).

17. Gunaratna (2002, 3).

18. Gunaratna (2002, 73).

19. Hirschman (1970).

20. Bloom (2005).

21. In fact, Bin Laden went one step further. When he disagreed with his mentor Abdullah Azzam, founder of the Afghan Service Bureau, over the fundamental direction of Al Qaeda, he had this spiritual leader of the international Islamists killed (Gunaratna 2002).

22. See, for example, Cairns (2002); Mcauley (2004).

23. This pattern of disintegration, dispersal and reformation into new groups has also been identified in an exploratory study of domestic terrorism in the United States that analyzed FBI data (Smith and Damphousse 2002).

24. Hirschman (1970).

25. Wilson (1973).

26. Crenshaw (2001, 27).

27. Kassimeris (2001).

28. The Rand Corporation's study of terrorist group learning argues that adaptation is essential for terrorist group survival (Jackson et al., 2005). The longevity of Shining Path and 17 November suggests otherwise.

29. Gunaratna (2002, 79).

30. Sageman (2004).

31. Louis Beam (1992, 5), charismatic United States militia spokesman, argued that the cell model of terrorist organization was open to infiltration and penetration from the outside because it still required at some level direct communication between someone higher up and the cell selected for the task, a lot of money and outside support. Thus, he argued for the unstructured model, that is, no organization at all, with individuals, small in number, highly committed, able and willing to operate on their own, relying on no one. The great advantage of this, argued Beam, was that those who were not up to it would be winnowed out (Damphousse and Smith 2004). However, the weakness of this nonorganization is that individuals are thrown on their own resources, which are usually meager, so that the choice of target and choice of weapon will be severely limited and the means of reaching the target much more difficult. This is not to say that they cannot carry off a terrible act of destruction. The McVeigh bombing attests to this, but it also demonstrates the difficulty in devising a weapon that will work.

32. Clarke and Brown (2003).

33. Raymond and Hughes (2001); Ryf (2002); Salt (2000).

34. Eck and Gersh (2000).

35. Groups now involved are quite different from the traditional "mafia" of the textbooks. Instead, many more small, loosely structured networks of criminal entrepreneurs have arisen, often with specialized knowledge, that come together to exploit specific opportunities for crime such as credit card fraud or counterfeiting banknotes. The existence of these opportunities, which permit substantial illegal sums of money to be made, encourages the development of these networks. See Andreas (2001), Brown and Clarke (2004), Eck and Gersh (2000), Finckenauer (2001), Guerette and Clarke (2005), Levi and Naylor (2000), Natarajan and Clarke (2004), and Spener (2001).

36. Recent research in the Washington-Baltimore area during 1995–97 revealed a "cottage industry" of "many small groups of traffickers that form and break-up easily," rather than a "concentrated industry" of a "relatively small set of large, hierarchically organized distribution networks" (Eck and Gersh 2000, 241).

37. Sageman (2004, 156–57).

38. The extent to which terrorist groups organize themselves in this manner is yet to be demonstrated, although in the early 1980s, the U.S. Congress and the office of the U.S. attorney general beefed up their war on terrorism based on this assumption. This impetus led to the arrest and prosecution of Louis Beam, leader of a right-wing militia, and his compatriots (Damphousse and Smith 2004).

39. Sageman (2004) points out that, in many respects, Al Qaeda broke its own rules concerning isolation of cells and so on in all its successful terror attacks. In all cases, it is how most of the perpetrators who carried out the actual operation were caught. Furthermore, of those operations that were failures (and there have been many), all could be attributed to individuals or small cells acting without clear guidance from the hierarchy (Sagemen 2004, 167–68).

40. Ronfeldt (2005).

41. The global reach was also made possible by the casual attitudes of governments in liberal democracies regarding the organization, money raising and preaching the Al Qaeda ideology throughout the 1990s in Britain, Holland, France, Italy, Germany, Australia and the United States. See, for an excellent review, Gunaratna (2002).

42. Recent documents released from the trove of documents retrieved in Iraq and Afghanistan during both invasions reveal, according to the *Wall Street Journal* (2006, A10), "that al Qaeda functioned like a corporation in some ways, with fixed terms for employee benefits such as family leave."

43. See Drake (1998, 168–72) for a brief review of the group decision-making research applied to terrorist groups.

44. The study of network analysis to uncover points of vulnerability of terrorist networks is in its infancy. The main difficulty is obtaining sufficient information to allow construction of network diagrams that can be used for prevention purposes. The majority of attempts to map terrorist networks rely on publicly available information, usually resulting from the prosecution of particular terrorists. For a promising start in using such information for preventive purposes, see Krebs (2002). This study also identified the facilitating conditions, strategy and goals, and demands of the task around which networks arose—all operational aspects of carrying out a terrorist act that we describe through this book. The additional feature that Krebs identifies is *trust*, the glue that binds all these networks together and makes them last over time. Techniques to undermine this trust (such as perceived or actual infiltration by informers) therefore would be an additional mode of preventive intervention to reduce the longevity of the group.

45. The one documented example of eradication of a terrorist group by removing its leader is that of the PKK in Turkey (Bloom 2005; Pape 2005). Attacks, however, are still carried out under a different name, which are attributed by some to the Kurdistan Workers' Party (PKK) and others to Turkish military agents (Schmid 2006, personal communication).

46. Sageman (2004, 151).

47. Forest (2006).

48. Gruen (2006); Weimann (2006).

49. Felter (2006).

50. See also Waller (2006).

51. Gunaratna (2002, 25).

52. We have excluded responses that seem impractical or whose success can only be expected in the long term, such as (1) changing the hearts and minds of terrorists or the regimes that support them through diplomatic activity, which can only be expected to succeed in the long term; and (2) working through nongovernmental organizations (NGOs) to improve economic, education and community conditions that may make it easier for individuals to join terrorist groups or to be recruited by terrorist groups. While naturally we are in favor of helping individuals and groups in poor circumstances around the world, we exclude these responses because their links to the operations of terrorist groups are tenuous and indirect. In any case, social and economic justice should be promoted as an end in itself, not as a response to terrorism, and certainly not in a manner that could be perceived as rewarding terrorism with investment.

53. Gunaratna (2002).

54. Sageman (2004).

55. See Ferracuti and Bruno (1984); Meade (1990).

Chapter 7

1. Jenkins (1985a). See also Hoffman (1998); Lesser (1999).

2. The 17 November terrorists in Greece, for example, carefully orchestrated their attacks so that they could easily be recognized as their own work, choosing targets of considerable difficulty that challenged their tactical skill (Kassimeris 2001). They also used the same "signature" weapon over several years (see Chapter 8).

3. However, there are ways in which we can protect large classes of targets, as occurred after the Tylenol case described in Chapter 15.

4. Drake (1998, 171). Jenkins (1974, 11) has made a persuasive argument for this view of terrorist thinking.

5. For example, the Angry Brigade in Britain lasted for only one year from mid-1970 (Drake 1998, 37).

6. English (2003).

7. We should recognize, however, that infrastructure is often a collateral target. For example, attacks against transportation systems may be directed simply at killing many people who are riding in a bus or airplane, not the infrastructure itself (such as various railway lines that are essential for trains to run). Thus, there are many different components of infrastructure, each of which will require a different analysis to determine the level of protection that is needed.

8. "The federal government has poured billions into airline security, while badly shortchanging railroads, buses and subways ... Now it is clear that aviation is not the only, and perhaps not even the primary, form of transportation threatened by terrorists. Congress should sharply increase the funds for rail, bus and subway security" (*New York Times* 2005, A22). Two days later it followed up this article by presenting data on terrorist attacks worldwide against ground transportation, in which the number of attacks against North America was far fewer than any other world region (Marsh 2005).

9. "The 9/11 commission recommended that antiterrorism funds be allocated solely based on risk, but some members of Congress have been trying to set aside much of the money for low risk areas. That is irresponsible. Congress should base as much of its financing plan as possible—ideally, 100 percent—on risk" (*New York Times* 2005, A22).

10. Understanding this important concept of risk also indicates that in cases in which a target itself if highly vulnerable and very difficult to protect, taking measures to reduce the damage resulting from an attack, such as having in place redundant systems or constructing a building of materials that will cause less injury in an explosion, works to reduce the effects of the terrorist act, and thus reduce the rewards for the terrorist (see Chapter 15).

11. Clarke (1999).

12. Clarke and Newman (2005).

13. Clarke (2002).

14. Installing more self-checkout facilities in drugstores would help to reduce these thefts

15. Clarke and Harris (1992).

16. In this respect, single attacks differ from a series of attacks carried out by the same group over many months or years, such as the IRA attacks in Northern Ireland. While the government has ultimate political responsibility for these attacks, the direct responsibility for dealing with them falls on local authorities, the police or the military.

17. Our approach bears some similarity to that used in other scenario-based methodologies developed in engineering and military operations that assess the inherent vulnerabilities in physical structures, networks space systems, power systems and grids and even waste management. See, for an engineering example of prioritizing infrastructures for protection, Apostolakis and Lemon (2005).

18. English (2003).

19. Operatives of both the IRA and the Red Brigade are on record expressing regret at having killed innocent civilians when they were subjected to harsh public outcry (Drake 1998, 76). More recently, during the wave of suicide bombings in Iraq in April and May 2005, after the new government was formed, Abu Musab al-Zarqawi found it necessary to justify having killed innocent Muslims in the series of attacks on civilians in Iraq and after the bombing of the hotel in Jordan in November 2005, which caused considerable outcry even from his own tribe in Jordan.

20. Some terrorist groups write and say very little, such as the French *Action Directe*. Many are prolific, such as the Belgian Communist Combatant Cells and the Italian Red Brigades, perhaps the most prolific after the IRA. For an incisive analysis of the writings of terrorist groups, what they say, what they think they are doing and the justifications for their violence, see Cordes (2001). Public opinion of the local population where the terrorist operations are based is extremely important to the terrorists, and clearly influences their decisions. See Bloom (2005); Pape (2005).

21. Kassimeris (2001). These became standard fare in all major media, focusing entirely on attempts to explain their violent acts to a public that seemed largely unimpressed by their stated goals. Greece gradually moved toward democracy regardless of the 17 November attempts to derail it, although it was highly impressed by the spectacle of the terrorist acts, which seemed confined to just that—a form of media entertainment, rather than a political movement. Over its 35 years of activity, it failed to garner popular support and remained a very small group.

22. This thinking dominated the PIRA strategies during the fortification of Derry in the 1970s, which became *the* challenge for terrorists to overcome: "Once the security forces decided to put security barriers around the town our strategy was then to break through them. It was—how many bombs can you get inside their net? Every bomb was . . . a victory for us" (Drake 1998). It was behind the thinking of the PIRA attacks on London's square mile in the 1990s (English 2003). And it was no doubt behind the planning of the bombing of the U.S. military mess hall, presumed to be a secure sanctuary for U.S. servicemen in Northern Iraq in December 2004. The 17 November terrorists prided themselves in attacking only very hard targets so that they could demonstrate their great superiority over the government, military and police (Kassimeris 2001).

23. In the following discussion, it is important to recognize the distinction between assessing the risk involved from attacks on targets compared with their vulnerability. As noted earlier, risk includes not only the vulnerability of targets to attack, but the expected loss, damage and long-term effects that will follow should a target be hit. EVIL DONE assesses only the vulnerability of targets and this vulnerability is derived from viewing the target from the terrorist's perspective. The widely used

acronym CARVER merges both vulnerability and risk assessments: **C**riticality, **A**ccessibility, **R**ecuperability, **V**ulnerability, **E**ffect and **R**ecognizability. It assesses targets from the point of view of the target or victim. This risk assessment tool has been applied widely throughout the security field, and elaborate checklists for detailed risk assessments for a wide variety of targets, from food to buildings, have been constructed. See, for example, McNamara (2005). EVIL DONE has been combined with CARVER and other rating scales in Clarke and Newman (2007).

24. See, for example, Clarke and Newman (2005); Clarke and Newman (2007).

25. Jacobs (1998, 151) lists 13 sources that "constitute a brief list of individuals who share this perspective."

26. As noted in Chapter 14, the targeting of government and military personnel in Iraq was about equal to the targeting of Iraqi citizens, although more targeting of civilians has been evident during 2005 and 2006.

27. In the United States, before 9/11, constant tension between the federal government and the private sector prevailed for many years concerning the regulation of safety and security of many infrastructures, particularly transportation of all kinds (rail, highways, sea ports, air). This regulation has been traditionally concerned with the transport of hazardous materials, trespass, smuggling and protection of passengers from accidents. See Johnston and Amala (2004). Only the airline industry was subject to specific regulation concerning passenger protection from terrorist attacks, the result of hijackings in the 1970s (Seidenstat 2004). See also Chapter 4. After 9/11, the federal government depended on the private sector, through its various trade associations, to upgrade its security levels to respond to the terrorist threat. Only in the airline industry was security completely taken over by the federal government because of the real or perceived mismanagement of security by the private security industry.

28. For a sense of the challenge facing a national government in protecting infrastructure, see Haynes (2004).

29. Statistics available for Israel reported in Table 5.2 show zero infrastructure attacks, although there were many attacks against Israeli buses.

30. Chan (2005a).

31. It is often difficult to distinguish between the infrastructure itself as a target and the infrastructure as a collateral target, or whether the infrastructure itself has been targeted rather than a specific building or facility contained within the infrastructure. Data were classified as follows: physical structures including hotels, checkpoints, churches, restaurants, buildings, cafes and so on; infrastructure including utilities (electricity grids, oil/fuel pipelines, telecommunications towers, antennas and so on). Iraq was excluded in this analysis

32. In failed or weak states, attacking infrastructure has devastating consequences, as was clear during the early phases of the insurgency in Iraq after the U.S. occupation. See Chapter 12.

33. It follows from this that less developed countries are far more vulnerable to terrorist attack than are developed countries. This is one reason why Al Qaeda, for example, has managed in its short history to take over at least two countries (Somalia and Afghanistan) where basic infrastructure was weak and poorly developed. There were, of course, other factors involved in the takeover of these countries. It is also worth noting that in regions that do not depend on national infrastructures for their survival, such as the isolated mountainous regions of Pakistan and Afghanistan border areas, these are less vulnerable to infrastructure attack and thus more difficult to take over. Takeover of failed states is also affected by organized crime (see Chapter 10).

34. Chan (2005b).

35. We are indebted to Nick Ross for this example.

Chapter 8

1. Graduate Institute of International Studies (2003). Ninety-eight countries produce small arms, but production is confined to just over 1,000 companies. Production is concentrated in North America, but the Asia Pacific region is a significant contributor.

2. Taylor in Alexander (2002).

3. Schmid (2000).

4. U.S. Federal Bureau of Investigation (2004).

5. Hanley (2006)

6. Wilkinson and Jenkins (1998).

7. Boettcher and Arnesen (2002).

8. Although the bulk of the gun is made of polymer, the barrel and other parts are metallic and therefore in principle are detectable by metal detection machines.

9. Marighella (1971).

10. English (2003, 213).

11. While the overall rate of fatalities for both bombings and shootings by PIRA from 1970 through 1993 declined, it was far more precipitous for shootings. There were 192 persons shot to death from 1970 through 1981, compared with 69 killed by bombings. However, from 1982 through 1993, only 27 people were gunned down, compared with 27 killed by bombings. In fact, for the final period of 1990–93, the number of people killed by bombings (12) exceeded those killed by guns (9). Data taken from Drake (1998).

12. In the United States, National Guard armories are an obvious target. There is at least one instance of an attempted burglary by a homegrown U.S. terrorist militia, headed by Donald Beauregard in 1997 that was thwarted by the FBI. There are scattered reports of burglaries, but no compilation of the extent of the targeting of armories throughout the United States.

13. Reported in Johnson (2003).

14. Graham (2005).

15. Drake (1998, 89).

16. The attempt to bring down an El Al airliner by the Black September movement missed and brought down a Yugoslav airlines plane instead, because of improper use of the RPG-7 grenade launcher. There are other examples. See Clutterbuck (1994, 45); Jackson (2002).

17. Milhollin (2004).

18. Dunnigan (2004).

19. Drake (1998, 82).

20. Dunnigan (2004).

21. Merari (2004a, 2004b, 2004c).

22. Jackson (2002, 236).

23. Beam (1992). See also Chapter 6 concerning terrorist group structure.

24. Terrorist groups with staying power may also manufacture their own weapons or explosives. The IRA, during a period when it lacked financial support, set up a small manufacturing plant to make rifles, and it has used its homemade mortar since 1972 (Drake 1998, 91).

Chapter 9

1. If there are any doubts that these tools are essential for successful terrorist attacks, consider the practice in Iraq on voting days for both the new constitution and the new parliament, where all traffic was banned for the entire day. Few terrorist attacks occurred on either day; in fact, the media reported only rare attempts and no suicide bombings. One study counted 48 different types of public and personal records that terrorists had used in the course of their activities (Haggerty and Gazso 2005).

2. Natarajan, Clarke and Belanger (1997).

3. Technology constantly increases the efficiency in the way we work, especially in how people work together. See Malone (2004).

4. For a review of many of the techniques and security issues concerned with ecommerce crime, see Newman and Clarke (2003). Identity theft in various forms is a major cottage industry among Al Qaeda. See Mcgrory (2001).

5. Taylor (2002, 202). This number may seem high, but it should be seen in the context of more than 35,000 shootings and more than 15,000 bombings for the same period, according to the Royal Ulster Constabulary statistics.

6. See Chapter 7 on products "CRAVED" by thieves.

7. Napoleoni (2005)

8. The Economist (2005a).

9. HFG (2005). See also Chapter 8.

10. For example, Hawalas and other informal transfer systems. See Alexander (2004); Economic and Social Council, Transnational Communities Programme (2001); Napoleoni (2005); Pieth (2002).

11. Clarke and Newman (2005).

12. Newman (2004).

13. It may also have the added benefit of reducing corruption. Palestinian Authority police rioted when the European Union required Arafat no longer to pay their salaries in cash, in an attempt to force a money trail on Arafat to eliminate the siphoning off of money for his own or for terrorist purposes. See the Debka File (2004); The Economist (2004). It is widely believed that some of the EU money was used to fund Al Aqsa suicide terrorism.

14. The U.K. plans to introduce biometric universal ID cards, although some question has been raised as to their cost. See The Economist (2005b). At the time of writing, the U.K. plan for a universal ID card is in the process of implementation. See http://www.identitycards.gov.uk/.

Chapter 10

1. Richards (1999).

2. In his detailed study of Informal Value Transfer Systems (IVTS), Passos (2005) has also recommended that, because some of these systems offer legitimate means of transfer where no other alternative is available, some effort should be made to make IVTS available within the formal banking systems so that alternatives are available. This is an excellent study based on interviews with users and dealers in Hawalas and other forms of IVTS.

3. Because the categories of ESEER are not mutually exclusive, the classification would not pass the scientific test of parsimony. However, we have not developed it as a scientific tool, but rather to assist policy analysts in thinking about how to reduce the threat of any particular variety of crime or terrorism. Making a list of facilitating conditions is the first step to thinking about how they might be addressed and our classification should help to ensure that the list is complete.

4. Steinhausler (2003).

5. Potter, Ferguson and Spector (2004).

6. Jacobs (1998, 151) lists 13 sources that "constitute a brief list of individuals who share this perspective."

7. According to Stone (2001), "Russia's nuclear arsenal of about 20,000 strategic and nuclear warheads poses some risks, but the warheads are not the main problem, experts say: they are relatively well secured and their fissile material is hard to remove. The real threat comes from the world's largest stockpile of highly enriched uranium and plutonium—about 600 metric tons—that's not already incorporated into warheads. This nuclear legacy is stored at weapons labs, civilian research centers and naval shipyards. Much of the material is vulnerable to inside jobs, because many Cold War–era safeguards still in place—guards, guns and gates—'were designed with spies in mind.'"

8. Theodore Taylor, the distinguished nuclear engineer, said in testimony before a Senate committee that "it is highly credible that a small group of people could design and build fission explosives, using information and non-nuclear materials that are accessible to the public worldwide. Under some circumstances, it is quite conceivable that this could be done by one person working alone" (quoted in Beres 1979, 23).

9. Steinhausler (2004).

10. Taylor and Horgan (2000).

11. According to Allison (2004), the completion date for the Department of Energy's Off-Site Source Recovery Project to secure 18,000 unwanted, privately held radioactive sources is not until 2010.

12. Under the provisions of the waste shipping plan for spent nuclear materials, "The materials required for the construction of a radioactive dispersal weapon will be readily available to terrorists in the United States beginning in approximately 2010. These materials will be transported in lightly guarded shipments traveling over known highway routes or transported as general cargo on railroads" (Dilger and Halstead 2003, 796).

13. These costs are estimated to be between $30 and $50 billion (Allison 2004, 213).

14. A particularly egregious example, noted in the Bulletin of the Atomic Scientists (Brian, Eisenman and Stockton 2002) concerns the Rocky Flats nuclear weapons manufacturing facility in Colorado. This was flagged as being particularly vulnerable to attack by a truck bomb, because the vehicle barrier cable had been placed on the outside fence rather than the inside one. Terrorists could cut the cable on the unalarmed outside fence and ram a large truck through both fences up against the vault containing plutonium before any defense could be mounted. This problem remained 16 years after the Beirut marine barracks bombing, 4 years after the president's directive on terrorism and 2.5 years after Rocky Flats was first ordered to fix it.

15. Lee (2003).

16. See Jacob (1998) for a summary of these arguments.

17. Norton and Greenberg (1979, 3) have shown that the problem of nuclear terrorism has been recognized since the beginning of the nuclear age: "For example, the Jefferies Report written at the Metallurgy Lab of the University of Chicago in 1944 discusses the possibility of a political group's unleashing a nuclear blitzkrieg by smuggling its weapons in commercial aircraft and secreting them in anticipation of the attack."

18. Skogan and Frydl (2002, 40) have concluded: "The basic technical information needed to construct a workable nuclear device is readily available in the open literature."

19. "Preventing any extremist group from achieving their goals of large-scale nuclear violence can best be done by denying them access to highly enriched uranium or plutonium, the essential ingredients of any nuclear device" (Maerli, Schaper and Barnaby 2003, 727).

20. According to Jacobs (1998), Potter (1995) lists "seven major diversions and seizures of nuclear materials that are known to have taken place between 1992 and 1994"; Lee (2003) reports that The International Atomic Energy Agency recorded 18 seizures of highly enriched uranium and plutonium in 1993–2001.

21. Weights provided in Allison (2004, 211).

22. Guerette and Clarke (2005).

23. Allison (2004).

24. Eck, Clarke and Guerette (in press).

Chapter 11

1. Crelinsten (2001).

2. Rossmo (2000). Typically, offenders commit their crimes within one or two miles of their homes. An analysis of more than one-quarter of a million crimes made by offenders arrested over a two-year period by the West Midlands Police (see Clarke and Eck 2005), one of the largest police forces in Britain, found that: (1) Distance traveled varied with the offense. For example, shoplifters tended to travel further than many other kinds of offenders. (2) Individual offenders varied considerably in crime trips. Some usually committed crimes in their local neighborhoods. Others traveled further particularly when working with co-offenders.

3. Drake (1998, 173).

4. Kitchen (2001).

5. Coaffee (2003).

6. Alexander (2002, 201) claims 3,636 people killed up to 2000; McKitrick et al. (2004) reports 1,781 deaths up to 2005; the Sutton CAIN database at University of Ulster (http://cain.ulst.ac.uk/cgi-bin/tab2.pl, accessed May 29, 2006) reports a total of 3,523 deaths from 1969 through 2001. These statistics are widely contested on various Web sites.

7. Alexander (2002, 169–78).

8. Alexander (2002, 172–73).

9. National Commission on Terrorism Attacks upon the United States (2004, 177–78). Ressam flew from France to Montreal using a photo-substituted French passport under a false name. He also supported himself by selling stolen documents to a friend

who was a document broker for Islamist terrorists. Eventually, he obtained a genuine Canadian passport through a document vendor who stole a blank baptismal certificate from a Catholic church. With this document he was able to obtain a Canadian passport.

10. Thomas and Znaniecki (1919).

11. Clarke and Brown (2003).

12. Eck and Gersh (2000).

13. Newman (2006).

14. Levi and Naylor (2000).

15. See the U.S. State Department Web site. Data extracted from the official U.S. State Department listing of terrorist groups, most recently available, 2000–01.

16. Other students of terrorism have noted the importance of ethnic communities for terrorism from afar. See, for example, Rapoport (2001b, 51).

17. The median longevity of those groups receiving financial support was 28 years compared to 17.5 years for those not receiving support (U.S. Department of State 2005). When longevity is assessed for a more complete list of terrorist groups, far fewer last beyond two years. See Figure 6.1.

18. Clan Na Gael has been the principle money raiser in the United States. See, for example, Benton (1999, A8).

19. For a comprehensive account of the complex ways by which terrorist groups obtain financial support from international sources, see Napoleoni (2005).

20. This statistic does not include those attacks that occurred against U.S. facilities or citizens abroad.

21. It might be argued that the reverse is true: that groups move their base of operations to be close to their targets. Examination of the details of the events suggests that this is unlikely within the United States; however, as we have noted previously, this is what does occur with foreign-based terrorist groups.

22. The independent "cell" type of decentralized terrorist organization has been widely adopted by many terrorist groups for decades. See Crenshaw (1995).

23. Of these single-issue terrorist groups, antiabortionists are the only groups to have killed in recent years, with the obvious exception of Timothy McVeigh. Since 1998, there have been four terrorist incidents in the United States directed at abortion-related targets. According to the Rand database, only one incident, conducted in Birmingham, Alabama, by the Army of God on January 29, 1998, resulted in a fatality.

24. The extent to which one would call the "organization" or group from which McVeigh received inspiration is a matter for disagreement. See Hamm (2001).

25. The size of the explosion and the enormous damage and casualties that followed are cause to wonder whether, in fact, it was purely the result of a single-issue terrorist group. It gives the impression of a single attack rather than a bombing that would typically be carried out by a homegrown terrorist group that was settling into a routine. Richard Clarke, counterterrorism czar for the White House, has refused to rule out the possibility of an Al Qaeda link for three reasons: (1) before the bombing, none of Terry Nichol's (McVeigh's confederate) attempts to make a bomb were successful; (2) before the bombing, Nichols was in Cebu City in the Philippines with his Philippine wife on the same days as were Al Qaeda operatives Ramzi Yousef and Khalid Sheik Muhammad; and (3) Nichols continued to make calls to Cebu long after his wife returned to the United States. Thus, some speculate that Nichols may have learned how to successfully make a large bomb, one that, in retrospect, was rather

similar to that used in the first attack on the World Trade Center. If true, this attack is better classified as a hybrid of terrorism from afar combined with homegrown single-issue terrorism. However, while the patterning of the attack fits a single attack from afar, the lack of links to a supportive immigrant community close to the target does not. Nonetheless these questions have fueled the ever-popular American conspiracy theories. See Davis (2004).

26. It is difficult to prove conclusively that terrorist groups (and other types of offenders for that matter) copy what they see or hear on the media. At a minimum, it is reasonable to conclude that the media plays some role in the sporadic nature of terrorist acts. For a general review of the evidence, see Coleman (2004). For a specific study of 168 terrorist attacks against migrants, see Bjorgo (1993).

27. Hoffman and Chalk (2002).

28. Of course, earlier U.S. history is full of periods of terrorism that may reasonably be termed routine: the marauding bands just before and after the civil war, the Ku Klux Klan, the U.S. War of Independence. An analysis of the conditions that facilitated these periods of routine terrorism would obviously take us far beyond the scope of this book.

29. Several of the FALN were imprisoned in the 1980s. President Clinton pardoned 16 of these terrorists in 2000, causing a political uproar.

30. See Chapter 6 for a discussion of the internal conflicts inherent in terrorist groups.

31. Without more information, it is difficult to assess the reliability of this conclusion. This is because it is possible that the "other" attacks may have been carried out by various former factions of the FALN that had broken from the main terrorist group. Certainly, it is possible that some of the groups may have been composed of disaffected individuals who were members of former groups that, in 1970, merged into the FALN (Sater 1981). Sater focuses on attacks made by the FALN on various electrical installations. However, by far, the major targets by these Puerto Rican independence terrorist groups were government buildings and personnel of the United States in Puerto Rico, as well as Puerto Rican government and business establishments, especially banks, in the United States and Puerto Rico.

32. The Mara Salvatrucha (MS) is one such gang with foreign ties, which also split into two competing branches. See The Economist (2005c, 29).

33. There remains the interesting question why the Black Panthers movement did not reach the same level of routine terrorism as the Puerto Rican terrorists, particularly because it could be argued that they had the advantage of attacking on home turf. An historic analysis of the turbulent events during that period would be needed to answer this puzzle.

34. The Economist (2005c, 19–21; 2006, 23–26).

35. Napoleoni (2005). A bloody raid on a drug cartel compound by Colombian police on March 10, 1984, which netted 13.8 tons of cocaine, also revealed that FARC was providing military protection for the organized drug trade in return for a tax of 10 percent on all coca growers in the cartel area. FARC, in its communiqués, claims to reject drug running, but it seems to imply that, because the illegal drug problem is one created by the United States, their exploitation of it is therefore justified. See http://www.farcep.org/pagina_ingles/.

36. The Economist (2005c, 19–21; 2006, 23–26).

37. Gang warfare is common in Los Angeles and other inner cities that are havens to gangs. See, for example, Scott (1993). Scott depicts gang wars as

insurgency. There is some similarity of such warfare to routine terrorism, when one considers that terrorist groups that have operated for many years, such as the IRA in Northern Ireland or Hamas in Palestine, typically fight among themselves. During the "ceasefire" period in Northern Ireland in the 1980s, the IRA took to violently policing and punishing various other terrorist or splinter groups (English 2003). From 1969–93, more than 5 percent of the killings were reprisals by Northern Ireland Loyalists against their own splinter groups and almost 3 percent of the killings by the IRA against its splinter groups (Drake 1998, 32).

Chapter 12

1. It is also unlikely that routine terrorism motivated by Islamic extremism could take hold in the United States. We have read in Chapter 11, for example, that the attempts at routine terrorism by the Puerto Rican Independence movements in the United States have been largely short lived and on a small scale, although there are considerable conditions within the United States that are favorable for its growth. Designing another single attack in the United States will be much more difficult for Al Qaeda, but if its leadership remains intact, it remains a possibility.

2. Attacks against civilians as against government-related personnel will depend on the tactics in play. The terrorist attacks in Iraq have clearly changed emphasis from almost solely being made against U.S. military and government personnel to attacks on international organizations, then after the provisional government was formed, attacks focused mainly on Iraqi civilians and government personnel.

3. We include this incident as an attack from afar, although it occurred in Lebanon and was carried out by what was probably a local terrorist group, Hezbollah, because this group was just beginning to establish roots in Lebanon in the Palestinian refugee camps. In subsequent years, this group was able to conduct routine terrorism in Israel as well as in Lebanon, both countries close to their base in the Palestinian camps. In this case, it made sense for President Reagan to remove the U.S. presence from Lebanon, for it surely would have created an attractive target to the growing routine terrorist capabilities of Hezbollah.

4. Enders and Sandler (1993).

5. Frey (2004). However, econometric studies tend to study terrorism in general, rather than examine specific types of terrorist events. We know, for example, that trying to measure whether increasing punishments for crime in general reduces crime is a hopeless project. However, measuring the specific effects of a deterrent intervention for a specific crime (e.g., random breath tests for drunk drivers) does, in fact, reduce this crime. There is reason to think, therefore, that a specific intervention for a specific type of terrorist event may have a reductive effect, and there is ample evidence for this. See Clarke (1997) and many studies reported in the 20 volumes of Crime Prevention Studies (NY: Criminal Justice Press).

6. Inman (1985).

7. U.S. Department of State (1999). This report produced findings similar to those found by the Inman Report some 10 years earlier. A major effort was spearheaded by Richard Clarke, Clinton terrorism czar, after these two bombings, which resulted in

considerable improvement in U.S. embassy protection, but this was nevertheless resisted by the U.S. Department of State.

8. Grams (2000).

9. U.S. Department of State (1999, 10).

10. "... [State] has not developed a comprehensive strategy that clearly identifies safety and security requirements and resources needed to protect U.S. officials and their families abroad from terrorist threats outside the embassy." U.S. Government Accountability Office (2005, 3).

11. We also doubt the efficacy of the use of any measure of "crime" cross-nationally to be a reliable or valid indicator of threat because of the many methodological difficulties in measuring and defining crime using official statistics cross-nationally. However, some of the difficulties may be overcome by using victimization surveys, but these are not available for all countries. See Newman and United Nations Centre for International Crime Prevention (1999) for a review of these problems.

12. U.S. General Accounting Office (2002). It is very likely that the list is driven by "real time threat analysis"—by tactical assessments of threat based on intelligence concerning the supposed activities of various terrorist organizations (i.e., who is talking to whom). It is for this reason, we suspect, that the list is classified.

13. Pape (2005).

14. See Pape (2005) and Chapter 12 for a summary of the rationale for this foreign policy.

15. Pape (2005).

16. Protection of U.S. citizens abroad is probably the most difficult challenge. When we consider that the most lethal attack on U.S. citizens abroad was the blowing up of Pan Am 103, the U.S. State Department is probably not the agency responsible for such protection. Similarly, attacks on private education or recreation facilities frequented by Americans seem to lie outside the responsibility of any government department. Clearly, nothing can be done without a concerted effort on the part of the government to work closely with the private sectors—from the highest level of airline security to the lowest level of establishing guidelines for securing recreation and education facilities abroad. See Chapter 17.

17. The U.S. Department of Defense is an excellent starting point. The standards are developed on an assessment of target attractiveness and weapons capability (U.S. Department of Defense 2003).

Chapter 13

1. There are many accounts of the origins of the "ring of steel" in Belfast. The basic facts as presented here are undisputed. Our account draws heavily on Coaffee (2003).

2. See the London congestion charge Web site that includes an extensive explanation as to why this charge was needed: http://www.cfit.gov.uk/congestioncharging/factsheets/london/

3. The confluence of these historic conditions and events is ripe for various conspiracy theories about police, city authorities and businesses conspiring to produce a "fortress society."

4. Coaffee (2003, 117).

5. Coaffee (2003, 113).

6. The bombings on London's subway system and one bus were immediately hailed as "homegrown" terrorism. However, it soon became apparent, with the failed second attempt, that these were bombings inspired by Al Qaeda from abroad and that they could not be sustained as routine terrorism.

7. This account of the Manchester bombing and its aftermath is based on Kitchen (2001).

8. See "Shopping in and around greater Manchester," available at http://www.manchester2002-uk.com/shopping.html.

9. We do not wish to take our criticism of the London response to the repeated terrorist attacks too far, though. After all, London is the symbolic and actual core of the United Kingdom and some argue that cities are natural targets simply because there are more people in them. However, most historians observe that cities originated from the security needs of people who found that they were sitting ducks isolated on the farm out in the open. Walled cities were an efficient defense against marauders from outside. Walls can still be extremely useful means of defense—as we saw in Belfast's ring of steel. The ring of steel was certainly needed in Belfast, but it was not needed in the single attack in Manchester and, in fact, it probably would have been counterproductive. As technology changes, defenses once effective become less so. See Glaeser and Shapiro (2002).

Chapter 14

1. Hoffman and Chalk (2002).

2. U.S. Department of Defense (2003).

3. U.S. Department of Defense (2003, 19).

4. Clarke, Richard (2004, 104). The GAO completed a survey in 1998 that displayed similar concerns. See Ungar (1998).

5. Presumably also cognizant of the Black September attack on the Munich Olympic Games in 1972.

6. As we have noted in EVIL DONE, the attributes of targets constrain terrorist choices. With the exception of attacks on funerals and places of worship in the Middle East, it is our impression that there have been very few terrorist attacks on entertainment, sport or even political events attended by masses of people, and this observation would hold for the period well before the enormous security measures now routinely applied to such events. The difficulties in planning and implementation are the obvious explanations for this rarity. However, the rarity is only an impression and requires more research to support or refute it. The exception to this observation may be the attack on the Munich Olympic Games, but even here the type of attack was focused on a specific group of Israeli athletes, not against the massive number of people attending a stadium event. Thus, studying that event may not be of relevance to protecting the whole of an Olympic Games venues as was done in Atlanta. We repeat here, and elsewhere, that it is extremely difficult and probably dangerous to extrapolate from one terrorist event to another in a different place.

7. Clarke, Richard (2004, 127).

8. Clarke (2004, 127).

9. All U.S. states are receiving these trailers. As one of many examples, see Associated Press Newswires (2003).

10. Diamond and Kelley (2002).

Chapter 15

1. See Newman and Clarke (2003) on e-commerce crime, Newman and McNally (2005) on identity theft, Clarke and Brown (2003) on international auto theft, and Wortley and Smallbone (2006) on child sexual abuse.

2. See Jotcham (2005).

3. However, there may be times when it is strategically advisable to give minor concessions to terrorists. Pape (2005, 248–50) argues that the higher the level of protection implemented by a country, the easier it is to grant concessions to terrorists.

4. One study of suicide bombers in Israel, however, did find that the targeted killing of terror suspects resulted in an increase in terrorist recruitment. See Kaplan et al. (2005).

5. There is an extensive literature in criminology concerning the "techniques of neutralization" that offenders use to justify, excuse, or rationalize their acts either before or after the fact. Al-Khattar (2003) applies this theory to understand religious terrorism, arguing, among other things, that terrorists are no different from ordinary criminals and use the same neutralizing techniques.

6. Kaplan et al. (2005).

7. As we read in previous chapters, conditions of routine terrorism did exist in Northern Ireland, and the IRA unsuccessfully attempted to establish such conditions also in London during its series of London bombings in the 1990s.

8. Chan (2005a); New York Times (2005, A22).

9. The widespread deployment of CCTV in London was apparently not useful in identifying suspect bombers at entry points to mass transit, but it was useful in identifying them after the attack. The utility of CCTV as a prevention device would therefore seem to promote the false idea that catching the terrorists (identified by CCTV) will prevent terrorist attacks, which it obviously did not in the London bombings. And it probably does not in Israel either, although without collection of the appropriate data, the effectiveness of this approach cannot be determined. Recent research on whether offenders are deterred by the presence of a CCTV supports this observation. The majority of those interviewed said that they were not deterred by cameras from carrying out their burglaries or thefts. Painter and Tilley (1999).

10. Haddon (1999); Haddon, Suchman and Klein (1964).

11. Mashaw and Harfst (1990); Nader (1966).

12. This was not an easily implemented solution because it required cooperation between government regulatory agencies and cost-obsessed automobile manufacturers (Newman 2004). The process took many years, but the resulting reduction in trauma from road deaths has been dramatic. See Centers for Disease Control (1999).

13. Yet, a recent report concluded that barriers did not reduce vulnerability to attack against U.S. facilities overseas. Apart from the poor quality of the data used in the studies reviewed, none of those studies took into account that protection is an ongoing process, as we note below. See Lum, Kennedy and Sherley (2006, 26–27). Of course, scientific research has already established the setback distances for buildings to reduce damage from various explosive devices, as we noted in Chapter 14.

14. Termed by some in crime prevention as an "arms race" (Ekblom 2001/2002). See also Ekblom and Tilley (2000).

15. For a detailed review of such criticisms and our responses to them, see Newman and Clarke (2003, chapter 8). Schneir (2003) has also examined this problem in considerable depth.

16. There are many other examples, not to mention the earliest loss of anonymity when governments began to collect information concerning where people lived, streets were named and house numbers assigned. While this information allowed governments to more easily collect taxes and locate specific individuals when they wanted, it also made the conveyancing of property and communication via postal services much more efficient. Some may regret this loss, yet the romantic notion of the small village where everyone knows each others' business surely intrudes into individuals' privacy much more. Market economies introduced a measure of freedom for individuals to conduct their business, but at the same time required that individuals give up a measure of their anonymity in return for the convenience and efficiency of the marketplace

17. See The Economist (2005d).

18. The U.S. total information awareness program that conducts surveillance of individuals' private records and computers was ordered shut down by the U.S. Congress, although it is purported to still continue. See Sullivan (2004). Even the government's attempt to establish a combined database of criminal history data—presumably a somewhat more focused database than collecting information of all individuals' transactions using credit cards—was, in the end, able to enlist the support of only two states. See Greenemeier (2005).

19. See, for example, Eck and Gersh (2000); Harocopos and Hough (2005).

20. See The Economist (2005d).

21. Obviously, CCTV did not prevent the London Underground bombings, although they were useful in tracking down suspects after the attack. See also note 6 above.

22. Newman (2004).

23. Ekblom (1997).

24. Clarke (1999); Clarke and Newman (2005).

25. It is worth noting, though, that concrete barriers are constructed for the specific purpose of guiding vehicles in particular directions and withstanding impact from vehicles. They are not built to withstand explosive devices, so there is the possibility that shards of concrete could cause extensive injury during an explosion. See McDevitt (2000).

26. Clarke and Newman (2005). In respect to automobiles, see Barthe (2004) in Maxfield and Clarke (2004).

Chapter 16

1. Attributed to Brian Jenkins by Nacos (1994, 75).

2. We would not want to underrate the effectiveness of this kind of publicity, especially in the light of work on scale-free networks (Watts 2003) and small-world communication (Milgram 1967). In this respect, the use of informants by the government may be an especially effective mode of publicity, as we note later in this chapter.

3. Social scientists have long recognized that violence is a form of communication. See Schmid and de Graaf (1982). The debate concerning violence as a means of communication in terrorism is mainly a debate about what is being communicated. See Crelinsten (2002); Tuman (2003).

4. See, for example, Wilkinson (1997).

5. Huddy et al. (2003); Keinan, Sadeh and Rosen (2003); Nacos (1994); Slone (2000).

6. Sufficient evidence shows that particular acts of terrorism, especially those that are innovative, such as the notorious skyjacking by D.B. Cooper, may be emulated by others, who may or may not share the "cause" of the terrorists. See Court TV's Crime Library (2005). It also appears that terrorist acts can occur in "rashes" (see Chapter 11) that are disconnected, for reasons that are not well understood. See Weimann and Winn (1994). However, the so-called contagion of terrorism via publicity remains controversial (Picard 1991).

7. Wieviorka (1994) argues that there are terrorist groups who are indifferent to the media. However, if violence is a form of communication that will invariably be reported by mass media (and even by word of mouth, as observed earlier), simply by choosing violence as their mode of operation makes it inevitable that terrorists cannot be indifferent to the media. See Crelisten (2002) for a critique.

8. Viera (1991). This common reaction to terrorist violence may explain in part why democracies have been the major targets of suicide bombing over the past 50 years, as argued by Pape (2005).

9. Anderson (1993).

10. Alexander and Latter (1990).

11. Norris, Kern and Just (2003) clearly demonstrate the incredible complexity in how terrorist events become framed by often-competing media outlets and processes. It is difficult to see how any government could have any lasting influence on how the media portray terrorist events. Attempts to shape the "meaning" of any terrorist event are therefore fruitless, because governments have no control over the staging of such events. However, it is also clear that government, using experts in the media, can use it to send messages to the terrorist groups, using approaches similar to advertising or marketing (i.e. by staging their own events).

12. For the typical argument that governments control the media theater of terrorism see Gerbner (1991). It is of course true that nondemocratic governments such as North Korea and Myanmar can control the media much more effectively than democracies.

13. Gerbner (1991).

14. Nacos (1994, 2002).

15. Of course, in countries that are not democratic, one of the first priorities is to establish state ownership of the media.

16. Schmid (1992).

17. It is true that the IRA, for example, adopted a dual policy of "guns and ballot box," but this was at great cost in terms of internal conflict. (See, for example, O'Brien 1999). Furthermore, even after some electoral success, the IRA was unable completely to denounce violence, and its refusal to disarm remained a hindrance to final peace negotiations. The same problem now faces Hamas after its electoral success in Palestine in 2006.

18. See also Chapters 6 and 7.

19. Thus, governments that imprison terrorists and keep them isolated from the public provide an opportunity for terrorists to charge their captors with inhumane and cruel treatment. The IRA used this tactic effectively, with its policy of noncooperation

and hunger strikes in prisons that dominated the media for many months, if not years, in the latter half of the twentieth century.

20. Without this understanding, responses are inevitably focused on pressuring the media to say or do particular things. See, for example, Perl (1997). We must understand that corporate mass media is effectively out of the control of any policymakers as far as terrorism is concerned, especially in regard to the visual media, which is driven by violence, spectacle and the generation of crises. To this extent, terrorists have an "advantage" in that they can be ensured that violence will be reported. They cannot ensure, however, how it will be reported or how it will be interpreted by the media and, in the long run, by the public. Furthermore, we recognize that politicians, in particular, often must respond quickly to media questions regarding terrorist events. But this is a good reason to have a clear understanding of what to say to and about the terrorists via the media, regardless of the particular event. For an excellent review of the detailed and difficult situations in which politicians must deal with the media on terrorism, see Crelinsten (1997).

21. Of course, this assumes that we know what terrorist group conducted the attack. In the field of crime prevention, we may not know who the offenders are, although we may know where they operate and generally the people with whom they hang out. It is likely that we would have similar information concerning terrorist groups, especially those that have developed to the stage of routine terrorism. The reduction in juvenile gang shootings was achieved by a publicity campaign coupled with targeted police patrols in high–gun crime, juvenile gang areas. See Box 16.1 (Kennedy, Braga and Piehl (2001).

22. Adapted from Bowers and Johnson (2005).

23. Barthe (2004).

24. Some publicity directed primarily toward the public about vigilance and bomb recognition does indirectly affect the terrorist's perception of the risks and difficulty of their task.

25. Cornish and Clarke (2003).

26. Barthe (2004).

27. Clarke and Weisburd (1994).

28. We saw in Chapter 6, for example, that offering rewards such as reduced sentences to terrorists who inform or give themselves up to the authorities may help undermine group membership. This technique was used with some success against the Red Brigades in Italy, although its success most likely depends on the developmental stage of the terrorist group and would possibly work best to hasten group disintegration that is already ongoing.

29. Marongiu and Newman (1987, 1995).

30. Dialog does not mean giving in to terrorist demands, particularly in hostage situations. In such cases, decisions on what to say publicly to terrorists are much more complex and are best left to the experts who are dealing with the immediate hostage situation.

Chapter 17

1. Cohen and Felson (1979).

2. For example, in 1995, 72 percent of 18-year-old women in the United Sates had licenses to drive compared with only 20 percent before 1941 (Felson 1998).

3. Under the laws of economics, which decreased the value of the additional labor women provided, women quite quickly found that they had to work to afford not just the new luxuries but also the ordinary necessities of life.

4. Wilson and Kelling (1982); also see Kelling and Coles (1996). For COMP-STAT information, see http://www.nyc.gov/html/nypd/html/chfdept/compstat.html.

5. Brooks (2005, 12).

6. Felson (2002); Garland (2000, 2001).

7. These now greatly outnumber sworn police in the United States and are beginning to do the same in some other countries. See Cunningham, Stauchs and Van Meter (1990); Grabosky (1996). It is generally agreed that private security personnel outnumber public police by a factor of 3:1 with some international variability. The ratio in South Africa is 4:1; in the United Kingdom, Canada and Australia 2:1; and the United States 3:1. See de Waard (1999); Gaines and Miller (2004); Schönteich (1999). Unfortunately, most of these guards, like their counterparts in the police, have little training in situational crime prevention.

8. Businesses and industry have tended to take their effectiveness for granted and, as long as they could continue to market them, have had little incentive to prove their value. Criminologists have neglected to evaluate them because of their general lack of interest in situational solutions to crime. Security administration specialists in the universities have lacked the necessary evaluation skills and, in any case, have been preoccupied with management issues concerning the place of security within the business and corporate culture. Finally, because of the private sector involvement, governments have generally regarded improved security as being outside the province of crime control policy. Furthermore, government officials have had the uncomfortable feeling that funding research on security services and devices could bring them into conflict with powerful business interests when evaluations were unfavorable and, when positive, with antibusiness constituencies.

9. Martha Smith enumerated 130 situational crime prevention projects. See Smith, Clarke and Pease (2002).

10. www.popcenter.org.

11. For example, it is not mentioned in Crime Drop in America (Blumstein and Wallman 2000), an authoritative book on the topic sponsored by the National Consortium on Violence Research and the Harry Frank Guggenheim Foundation.

12. Huntington's controversial thesis (Huntington 1996) that the "clash of civilizations" has produced many motivated Islamic fundamentalists is but one of the many theories arguing over the cause or causes for the rise of terrorism. Globalization along with the break up of the Soviet Union have also added to the rise in nationalistic causes. The 9/11 report indicated globalization as a significant contributor to terrorism. Many publications have linked terrorism to globalization and to nationalism. See, for example, Aydinli and Rosenau (2004); Cutter, Richardson and Wilbanks (2003). Other recent theses argue that the major motivation is one of resentment of foreign occupying forces, namely the United States, in the Middle East. See Bloom (2005) and Pape (2005). See also Chapters 6 and 10 that consider the role of globalization in facilitating terror and financial networks, respectively.

13. Some of these requirements would hold for any target-hardening program, whether or not informed by situational prevention and, indeed, governments may already be doing some of what we recommend. To review what they are doing would

divert us too far from the purpose of this discussion and, given the speed of the developments, would result in an incomplete and possibly misleading picture.

14. The Department of Homeland Security has recently established the Homeland Infrastructure Threat and Risk Analysis Center (HITRAC), which presumably could be the repository of such expertise.

15. Christine E. Wormuth of the Center for Strategic and International Studies made the case for establishing a "National Homeland Security Risk Assessment" in her testimony before the House Subcommittee on Intelligence, Information Sharing and Terrorism Risk Assessment on November 17, 2005.

16. Clarke and Eck (2005).

17. Local police should be tasked with reviewing the security plans of the most vulnerable businesses and corporations within their jurisdictions, such as port or airport operators, utility companies and mass transit providers. To perform this role adequately, they would need to be trained in security and situational prevention techniques. Improved relations with local businesses would also assist police in their increasingly recognized role of combating homegrown terrorism by obtaining information from the community about potentially dangerous activities or individuals. Sir Ian Blair, commissioner of the Metropolitan Police in the United Kingdom, has argued that closer relationships between police and the home communities of the suicide bombers might have helped forestall the London Underground attacks of July 2005.

18. The privatization of infrastructure, while at its peak in the United States, is now spreading throughout many countries of the world, and in many instances, government and the private sector share ownership of communications, transportation and other essential services. This was highlighted in March 2006 with the revelation that the majority of U.S. ports were owned or operated by foreign companies (Kaplan 2006).

19. Nalla and Newman (1990).

20. Even in this regard, there are some notable contradictions in the business. A good example is that of credit card fraud in retail stores. Retailers rarely ask local police to deal with such offences. On the one hand, they often consider that the police can't do anything, so why call them. On the other hand, they blame the police for not being able to "solve" such crimes. Yet the solution to the problem lies far beyond the capabilities of local police. It requires major changes in the ways that credit cards are produced, marketed, issued and verified, involving national and international banks and the credit card issuers. Furthermore, businesses often view losses from crime as a "cost of doing business" based on their assessment that it would cost more to prevent the losses than to simply absorb them. For all these reasons it is clear that fundamental changes of attitude and values are needed if corporate resistance to taking a more active role in prevention of crime and terrorism is to be overcome.

21. Different corporate sectors will need to develop or acquire specific kinds of prevention expertise depending on whether the focus is weapons (guns or explosives and their utility to terrorists and availability for theft), targets (train stations, coffee shops and malls), tools (high-tech visas, smartcards and so on) or facilitators (effective authentication procedures at banks.

22. Goldstein (1990); Scott and Goldstein (2005).

23. Clarke and Newman (2005a, 2005b).

24. For example, in the case of the Tylenol incident noted previously, Johnson & Johnson stood to lose an enormous amount of their market share of pain relievers if

they did not act swiftly to ensure their customers that tampering with their products could never happen again. They quickly worked out a scheme with the government (the Federal Trade Commission) and consumer advocates to introduce tamper-evident packaging. Thus, a revolution in the packaging of an enormous variety of consumer goods was begun.

25. The points in this paragraph are discussed more fully in Susman (2003), a valuable report issued by The Business Roundtable, which we found at a late stage in the production of this book.

26. Our point about government support for measures that have the dual benefit of preventing crime and terrorism applies also to measures that lie outside the corporate sphere. For example, improved border controls and immigration procedures (including stronger controls on visa and passports) not only might help to keep out terrorists, but also illegal immigrants and criminals.

Chapter 18

1. "Recommendation: The Department of Homeland Security and its oversight committees should regularly assess the types of threats the country faces to determine (a) the adequacy of the government's plans—and the progress against those plans—to protect America's critical infrastructure and (b) the readiness of government to respond to the threats that the United States might face" (National Commission on Terrorism Attacks upon the United States, 2004, 428).

2. National Commission on Terrorism Attacks upon the United States (2005). An "unsatisfactory" rating was awarded to only 2 other of the 14 recommendations.

3. For example, it issued the National Strategy for the Physical Protection of Critical Infrastructure and Key Assets in February 2003. However, this was primarily a catalog of infrastructures and key assets with a list of objectives for securing them, rather than any sort of detailed plan for meeting these objectives.

4. We recognize that a great deal of valuable work to improve security is being done worldwide by airlines, transportation companies, port authorities, energy providers, telecommunications companies, malls and hotels, campuses, hospitals and even police (Finnegan 2005).

5. In fact, the question of the proper balance between taking out terrorists and reducing vulnerabilities to attack has less relevance for research priorities simply because the costs of research are but a tiny fraction of the costs of protection. In the case of the United States, given the vast budget of the Department of Homeland Security, the government can certainly afford to mount a program of research dedicated to finding ways to reduce vulnerabilities to attack, which would complement the research already being funded. If the program succeeded in establishing priorities for protection and in identifying efficient forms of protection, it would repay its costs many times over. Finally, because many of the security improvements would also help protect businesses, facilities and government property from criminal attack, it meets the "dual benefit" criterion for justifying additional expenditures on protection from terrorism.

6. As mentioned in Chapter 1, the cost to the government of doing nothing is further complicated by the Terrorism Risk Insurance Act that requires the government to cover up to 90 percent of insured losses after a deductible is met. On October 27, 2005, a jury found the New York Port Authority 68 percent liable for the first World

Trade Center bombing. The primary reason given for the judgment was that the owners of the Twin Towers had failed to heed security experts' advice to block off public access to the parking garage beneath the Twin Towers. See Hartocollis and McGeehan (2005).

7. EVIL DONE may be used most effectively in conjunction with other rating scales of risk and vulnerability such as CARVER. See Clarke and Newman (forthcoming, 2007).

8. National Research Council (2004).

9. This belief in the inevitability of displacement is not confined to police alone. In the course of undertaking some work for the London Underground one of us (Clarke) discovered that officials believed that their success in modifying new ticket machines to eliminate 50 pence slugs had simply displaced the problem to pound slugs, which began to appear as soon as the 50 pence ones were eliminated. However, analysis showed that (1) the scale of the pound slug problem (less than 3,500 per month) never approached that of the 50 pence slugs (95,000 per month at their height); (2) the pound slugs were found in stations not previously affected by 50 pence slugs; (3) any boy or girl could make a 50 pence slug by wrapping a 10 pence coin in silver foil, but only people with the right equipment could make the pound slugs by filling copper pipes with solder and then slicing them carefully. These facts suggested that the 50 pence and pound slugs were probably separate problems and that the latter did not arise as consequence of displacement (Clarke, Cody and Natarajan 1994).

10. The parallel motto from the rapid appraisal field is "it is better to be vaguely right than precisely wrong" (Carruthers and Chambers 1981, 418).

11. "Rapid appraisal is an approach for developing a preliminary, qualitative understanding of a situation. This paper identifies three basic concepts—(1) a system perspective, (2) triangulation of data collection, and (3) iterative data collection and analysis—and suggests that they provide a conceptual foundation for rapid appraisal and a rationale for the selection of specific research techniques. The basic concepts and their related research techniques provide a flexible but rigorous approach for data collection and analysis by a team of two or more individuals, usually with different academic discipline backgrounds" (from the abstract to Beebe 1995).

References

Alali, A. Odasuo, and Kenoye Kelvin Eke, eds. 1991. *Media Coverage of Terrorism: Methods of Diffusion*. Newbury Park, CA: Sage.

Alexander, Dean C. 2004. *Business Confronts Terrorism: Risks and Responses*. Madison: University of Wisconsin Press.

Alexander, Yonah, ed. 2002. *Combating Terrorism: Strategies of Ten Countries*. Ann Arbor: University of Michigan Press.

Alexander, Yonah, and Richard Latter. 1990. *Terrorism and the Media: Dilemmas for Government, Journal Lists and the Public*. Washington, DC: Brassey's.

Al-Khattar, Aref M. 2003. *Religion and Terrorism: An Interfaith Perspective*. Westport, CT: Praeger.

Allison, Graham. 2004. *Nuclear Terrorism: The Ultimate Preventable Catastrophe*. New York: Times Books.

Anderson, Terry. 1993. "Terrorism and Censorship: The Media in Chains." *Journal of International Affairs* 47(1):127–36.

Andrabi, Tahir, Jishnu Das, Asim Ijaz Kaja, and Tristan Zajonc. 2005. *Religious School Enrollment in Pakistan: A Look at the Data*. Cambridge, MA: Harvard University, John F. Kennedy School of Government.

Andreas, Peter. 2001. "The Transformation of Migrant Smuggling Across the U.S.-Mexico Border," In *Global Human Smuggling: Comparative Perspectives*, ed. David Kyle and Rey Koslowski, 108–25. Baltimore, MD: Johns Hopkins University Press.

Apostolakis, George E., and Douglas M. Lemon. 2005. "A Screening Methodology for the Identification and Ranking of Infrastructure Vulnerabilities Due to Terrorism." *Risk Analysis* 25(2):361–76.

Argo, Nichole. 2004. "Understanding and Defusing Human Bombs: The Palestinian Case and the Pursuit of a Martyrdom Complex." Paper presented at the International Studies Association Annual Convention, Montreal, Quebec, March 20.

Arquilla, John, and David Ronfeldt, eds. 2001. *Networks and Netwars: The Future of Terror, Crime, and Militancy.* Santa Monica, CA: Rand, MR-1382-OSD.

Associated Press Newswires. 2003. "State Gets Decontamination Trailers." Greenwich, CT: Associated Press, February 16.

Atran, Scott. 2003. "Genesis of Suicide Terrorism." *Science* 299(5612):1534–39.

Atran, Scott. 2004. "Mishandling Suicide Terrorism." *Washington Quarterly* 27(3):67–90.

Aydinli, Ersel, and James N. Rosenau, eds. 2004. *Globalization, Security, and the Nation State: Paradigms in Transition.* Albany, NY: State University of New York Press.

Bajpai, Chailendra, and J.P. Gupta. 2005. "Site Security for Chemical Process Industries." *Journal of Loss Prevention in the Process Industries* 18(4–6):301–9.

Barthe, Emmanuel. 2004. "Publicity and Car Crime Prevention." In *Understanding and Preventing Car Theft,* ed. Michael G. Maxfield and Ronald V. Clarke, 193–216. Crime Prevention Studies, vol. 17. Monsey, NY: Criminal Justice Press.

BBC News. 2000. "Paracetamol Overdoses 'Falling'." June 9.

Beam, Louis. 1992. "Leaderless Resistance." *The Seditionist.* Available at http://www.louisbeam.com/leaderless.htm (accessed on May 30, 2006).

Bean, Frank D., Jennifer Lee, Jeanne Batalova, and Mark Leach. 2000. "Immigration and Fading Color Lines in America." Washington, DC: Rand Population Reference Bureau. Available at http://www.prb.org (accessed on May 30, 2006).

Beebe, James. 1995. "Basic Concepts and Techniques of Rapid Appraisal." *Human Organization* 54(1):42–51.

Benton, Joshua. 1999. "Irish-Americans Provide Money, Moral Support." *Blade,* p. A8, November 28.

Beres, Louis R. 1979. *Terrorism and Global Security: The Nuclear Threat.* Boulder, CO: Westview Press.

Berman, Eli, and David D. Laitin. In press. "Rational Martyrs vs. Hard Targets: Evidence on the Tactical Use of Suicide Attacks." In *Suicide Bombing from an Interdisciplinary Perspective,* ed. E. Meyersson Milgrom. Princeton, NJ: Princeton University Press.

Beyler, Clara. 2004, March 7. "Female Suicide Bombers: An Update." Available at http://www.ict.org.il/articles/articledet.cfm?articleid=508 (accessed on May 27, 2006).

Bjorgo, Tore. 1993. "Role of the Media in Racist Violence." In *Racist Violence in Europe,* ed. Tore Bjorgo and Rob Witte, 96–112. London: Macmillan.

Bjorgo, Tore, ed. 2005. *The Root Causes of Terrorism.* London: Routledge.

Bloom, Mia. 2005. *Dying to Kill: The Allure of Suicide Terror.* New York: Columbia University Press.

Blumstein, Alfred E., and Joel Wallman. eds. 2000. *The Crime Drop in America.* New York: Cambridge University Press.

Boettcher, Mike, and Ingrid Arnesen. 2002. "Al Qaeda Documents Outline Serious Weapons Program: Terrorist Group Placed Heavy Emphasis on Developing Nuclear Device." Available at http://cnn.allpolitics.printthis.clickability.com/pt/cpt?action=cpt&title=CNN.com+-+Al+Q (accessed on March 14, 2006).

Bolkom, Christopher, Andrew Feikert, and Bartholomew Elias. 2005. Homeland Security: Protecting Airliners from Terrorist Missiles. Congressional Report for Congress. Congressional Research Service. Washington, DC: The Library of Congress. Received through the CRS Web, updated February 15, 2005.)

Bowers, Kate, and Shane Johnson. 2005. "Using Publicity for Preventive Purposes." In *Handbook of Crime Prevention and Community Safety,* ed. Nick Tilley, 329–54. Cullompton, UK: Willan.

Brian, Danielle, Lynn Eisenman, and Peter D.H. Stockton. 2002. "The Weapons Complex: Who's Guarding the Store?" *Bulletin of the Atomic Scientists* 58(1):48–55.

Brooks, David. 2005. "The Virtues of Virtue." *New York Times*, August 7, p. 12.

Brown, Rick, and Ronald V. Clarke. 2004. "Police Intelligence and Theft of Vehicles for Export: Recent UK Experience." In *Understanding and Preventing Car Theft*, ed. M. Maxfield and R.V. Clarke. Crime Prevention Studies, vol. 17. Monsey, NY: Criminal Justice Press.

Cairns, E. 2002. "The Object of Sectarianism: The Material Reality of Sectarianism in Ulster Loyalism." *Journal of the Royal Anthropological Institute* 6(3):437–52.

Carroll, Stephen J., Tom LaTourrette, Brian G. Chow, Gregory S. Jones, and Craig Martin. 2005. *Distribution of Losses from Large Terrorist Attacks Under the Terrorism Risk Insurance Act*. Santa Monica, CA: Rand Center for Terrorism Risk Management Policy. Available at http://www.rand.org/pubs/monographs/2005/RAND_MG427.pdf (accessed on May 27, 2006).

Carruthers, Ian, and Robert Chambers. 1981. "Rapid Appraisal for Rural Development." *Agricultural Administration* 8(6):407–22.

Cauley, Joe, and Eric Iksoon Im. 1988. "Intervention Policy Analysis of Skyjackings and Other Terrorist Incidents." *American Economic Review* 78(2):27–31.

Centers for Disease Control. 1999. "Achievements in Public Health, 1990–1999: Motor-Vehicle Safety: A 20th Century Public Health Achievement." *MMWR Weekly* (May 14) 48(18):369–74.

Chan, Sewell. 2005a. "Easing Anxiety on Mass Transit." *New York Times*, July 17, p. 4.

Chan, Sewell. 2005b. "Terrorism Expert Advised City on Searches." *New York Times*, November 7, p. B3.

Chauncey, Robert. 1975. "Deterrence: Certainty, Severity, and Skyjacking." *Criminology* 12(4):447–73.

Choi, Jin-Tai. 1994. *Aviation Terrorism: Historical Survey, Perspectives and Responses*. New York: St. Martin's Press.

Chow, Peter, James Chiesa, Paul Dreyer, Mel Eisman, Theodore W. Karasik, Joel Kvitky, Sherrill Lingel, David Ochmanek, and Chad Shirley. 2005. *Protecting Commercial Aviation Against the Shoulder-fired Missile Threat*. Santa Monica, CA: Rand.

Clarke, Richard V. 2004. *Against All Enemies: America's War on Terror*. New York: Free Press.

Clarke, Ronald V. 1980. "Situational Crime Prevention: Theory and Practice." *British Journal of Criminology* 20(2):136–47.

Clarke, Ronald V., ed. 1992. *Situational Crime Prevention: Successful Case Studies*. 1st ed. New York: Harrow and Heston.

Clarke, Ronald V. 1995. "Situational Crime Prevention." In *Building a Safer Society: Strategic Approaches to Crime Prevention,* ed. Michael Tonry and David Farrington, 92–150. Crime and Justice: A Review of Research, vol. 19. Chicago: University of Chicago Press.

Clarke, Ronald V., ed. 1997. *Situational Crime Prevention: Successful Case Studies*. 2nd ed. Monsey, NY: Criminal Justice Press.

Clarke, Ronald V. 1999. *Hot Products: Understanding, Anticipating and Reducing Demand for Stolen Goods*. Police Research Series, Paper 112. London: Home Office. Available at http://www.homeoffice.gov.uk/prgpubs.htm (accessed on May 30, 2006).

Clarke, Ronald V. 2002. *Shoplifting*. Problem-Oriented Guides for Police, No. 11. Washington, DC: U.S. Department of Justice, Office of Community-Oriented Policing Services. Available at http://popcenter.org (accessed on May 30, 2006).

Clarke, Ronald V. 2005. "Seven Misconceptions of Situational Crime Prevention." In *Handbook of Crime Prevention and Community Safety,* ed. Nick Tilley, chap. 3. Cullompton, UK: Willan.

Clarke, Ronald V., and Rick Brown. 2003. "International Trafficking in Stolen Vehicles." In *Crime and Justice: A Review of Research,* ed. Michael Tonry, vol. 30, 197–227. Chicago: University of Chicago Press.

Clarke, Ronald V., Ronald P. Cody, and Mangai Natarajan. 1994. "Subway Slugs: Tracking Displacement on the London Underground." *British Journal of Criminology* 34(2):122–38.

Clarke, Ronald V., and Derek B. Cornish. 1985. "Modeling Offenders' Decisions: A Framework for Research and Policy." In *Crime and Justice: A Review of Research*, ed. Michael Tonry and Norval Morris, vol. 6, 147–85. Chicago: University of Chicago Press.

Clarke, Ronald V., and Derek B. Cornish. 2001. "Rational Choice." In *Explaining Criminals and Crime: Essays in Contemporary Criminological Theory,* ed. Raymond Paternoster and Ronet Bachman, 23–42. Los Angeles: Roxbury.

Clarke, Ronald V., and John E. Eck. 2005. *Crime Analysis for Problem Solvers In 60 Small Steps*. Washington, DC: U.S. Department of Justice, Office of Community-Oriented Policing Services.

Clarke, Ronald V., and Patricia Harris. 1992. "Auto Theft and Its Prevention." In *Crime and Justice: A Review of Research*, ed. Michael Tonry, vol. 16, 1–54. Chicago: University of Chicago Press.

Clarke, Ronald V., and David Lester. 1989. *Suicide: Closing the Exits*. New York: Springer-Verlag.

Clarke, Ronald V., Rick Kemper, and Laura Wyckoff. 2001. "Controlling Cell Phone Fraud in the US: Lessons for the UK 'Foresight' Prevention Initiative." *Security Journal* 14(1):7–22.

Clarke, Ronald V., and Pat Mayhew. 1988. "The British Gas Suicide Story and Its Criminological Implications." In *Crime and Justice: A Review of Research*, ed. Michael Tonry and Norval Morris, vol. 10, 79–116. Chicago: University of Chicago Press.

Clarke, Ronald V., and Graeme R. Newman, eds. 2005a. *Designing Out Crime from Products and Systems*. Crime Prevention Studies, vol. 18. Monsey, NY: Criminal Justice Press.

Clarke, Ronald V., and Graeme R. Newman. 2005b. "Modifying Criminogenic Products: What Role for Government?" In *Designing Out Crime from Products and Systems,* ed. Ronald V. Clarke and Graeme R. Newman, 7–83. Crime Prevention Studies, vol. 18. Monsey, NY: Criminal Justice Press.

Clarke, Ronald V., and Graeme R. Newman. 2005c. "Security Coding of Electronic Products." In *Designing Out Crime from Products and Systems,* ed. Ronald V. Clarke and Graeme R. Newman, 231–65. Crime Prevention Studies, vol. 18. Monsey, NY: Criminal Justice Press.

Clarke, Ronald V., and Graeme R. Newman. Forthcoming, 2007. *Countering the Terrorist Threat*. Washington, DC: U.S. Department of Justice, Office of Community-Oriented Policing Services.

Clarke, Ronald V., and David Weisburd. 1994. "Diffusion of Crime Control Benefits: Observations on the Reverse of Displacement." In *Crime Prevention Studies*, ed. Ronald V. Clarke, vol. 2, 165–83. Monsey, NY: Criminal Justice Press.

Clutterbuck, Richard. 1994. *Terrorism in an Unstable World*. London and New York: Routledge.

CNN.com. "Timothy McVeigh Timeline." Available at http://www.cnn.com/CNN/Programs/people/shows/mcveigh/timeline.html (accessed on June 1, 2006).

Coaffee, Jon. 2003. *Terrorism, Risk and the City: The Making of a Contemporary Urban Landscape*. Aldershot, UK, and Burlington, VT: Ashgate.

Cohen, Lawrence E., and Marcus Felson. 1979. "Social Change and Crime Rate Trends: A Routine Activities Approach." *American Sociological Review* 44(4):588–608.

Coleman, Loren. 2004. *The Copycat Effect: How the Media and Popular Culture Trigger the Mayhem in Tomorrow's Headlines*. New York: Paraview Pocket Books.

Communique from Direct Action. 1984. *Ligne Rouge*, July 13.

Cordes, Bonnie. 2001. "When Terrorists Do the Talking: Reflections on Terrorist Literature." In *Inside Terrorist Organizations,* ed. David Rapoport, 150–71. London and Portland, OR: Frank Cass.

Cornish, Derek B. 1994. "The Procedural Analysis of Offending and Its Relevance for Situational Crime Prevention." In *Crime Prevention Studies*, ed. Ronald V. Clarke, vol. 3, 151–96. Monsey, NY: Criminal Justice Press.

Cornish, Derek B., and Ronald V. Clarke, eds. 1986. *The Reasoning Criminal: Rational Choice Perspectives on Offending*. New York: Springer-Verlag.

Cornish, Derek B., and Ronald V. Clarke. 2003. "Opportunities, Precipitators and Criminal Decisions: A Reply to Wortley's Critique of Situational Crime Prevention." In *Theory for Practice in Situational Crime Prevention,* ed. Martha J. Smith and Derek B. Cornish, 41–96. Crime Prevention Studies, vol. 16. Monsey, NY: Criminal Justice Press.

Court TV's Crime Library. 2005. "The Copycats." Available at http://www. crimelibrary.com/criminal_mind/scams/DB_Cooper/9.html?sect=27 (accessed on July 12, 2005).

Crelinsten, Ronald D. 1997. "Television and Terrorism: Implications for Crisis Management and Policy-Making." *Terrorism and Political Violence* 9(4):8–32.

Crelinsten, Ronald D. 2001. "The Internal Dynamics of the FLQ During the October Crisis of 1970." In *Inside Terrorist Organizations,* ed. David Rapoport, 59–89. London and Portland, OR: Frank Cass.

Crelinsten, Ronald D. 2002. "Analysing Terrorism and Counter-Terrorism: A Communication Model." *Terrorism and Political Violence* 14(2):77–122.

Crenshaw, Martha. 1995. "An Organizational Approach to the Analysis of Political Terrorism." *Orbis* 29(3):465–89.

Crenshaw, Martha. 2001. "Theories of Terrorism: Instrumental and Organizational Approaches." In *Inside Terrorist Organizations,* ed. David Rapoport, 13–31. London and Portland, OR: Frank Cass.

Cunningham, William C., John J. Strauchs, and Clifford W. Van Meter. 1990. *Private Security Trends, 1970–2000: The Hallcrest Report II.* Boston: Butterworth-Heinemann.

Cutter, Ana. 1998. "Tamil Tigresses." *Slant: The Magazine of Columbia University's School of International and Public Affairs,* Spring. Available at http://www.columbia. edu/cu/sipa/PUBS/PLANT/SPRING98/article5.html (accessed on July 10, 2005).

Cutter, Susan L., Douglas B. Richardson, and Thomas J. Wilbanks, eds. 2003. *The Geographical Dimensions of Terrorism.* New York and London: Routledge.

Damphousse, Kelly R., and Brent L. Smith. 2004. "Terrorism and Empirical Testing: Using Indictment Data to Assess Changes in Terrorist Conduct." In *Terrorism and Counter-terrorism: Criminological Perspectives,* ed. Mathieu Deflem, 75–89. New York: Elsevier.

Davies, Heather J., and Gerard R. Murphy. 2004. *Working With Diverse Communities.* Protecting Your Community From Terrorism: The Strategies for Local Law Enforcement Series, vol. 2. Washington, DC: U.S. Department of Justice, Office of Community-Oriented Policing and Police Executive Research Forum.

Davies, Heather J., and Martha R. Plotkin. 2005. *Partnerships to Promote Homeland Security.* Protecting Your Community From Terrorism: The Strategies for Local Law Enforcement Series, vol. 5. Washington, DC: U.S. Department of Justice, Office of Community-Oriented Policing and Police Executive Research Forum.

Davis, Jayna. 2004. *The Third Terrorist: The Middle East Connection to the Oklahoma City Bombing.* Nashville, TN: WND Books.

de Waard, Jaap. 1999. "The Private Security Industry in International Perspective." *European Journal on Criminal Policy and Research* 7(2):143–74.

Debka File. 2004. "Arafat: They're After Me and My Money." February 18, 2004, 5:09 p.m. (GMT+02:00).

Deflem, Mathieu, ed. 2004. *Terrorism and Counter-terrorism: Criminological Perspectives.* Amsterdam and Boston: Elsevier.

Dehai News. 2003. "A Guide to al Qaeda Groups Across the World." August 20.

Diamond, John, and Jack Kelley. 2002. "Suicide Bombs Expected in USA: FBI Chief Calls Such Attacks 'Inevitable.'" *USA Today*, May 21, p. A1.

Dilger, Fred, and Robert Halstead. 2003. "The Next Species of Trouble: Spent Nuclear Fuel Transportation in the United States, 2010–2048." *American Behavioral Scientist* 46(6):796–811.

Dingley, James. 2004. "The Human Body as a Terrorist Weapon: Hunger Strikers and Suicide Bombers." Manuscript under review. Belfast: University of Ulster.

Dobson, Christopher, and Ronald Payne. 1982. *Counterattack: The West's Battle Against the Terrorists.* New York: Facts on File, page viii (quoted by St. John, 1991, p. 40).

Drake, C.J.S. 1998. *Terrorists' Target Selection.* New York: St. Martin's Press.

Dugan, Laura, Gary LaFree, and Alex Piquero. 2005. "Testing a Rational Choice Model of Airline Hijackings." *Criminology* 43(4):1031–66.

Dunnigan, James. 2004. "Tracking al Qaeda Bomb Makers." *The Strategy Page*, February 26. Available at http://strategypage.com/dls/articles/2004226.asp (accessed on May 27, 2006).

Eck, John E., Ronald V. Clarke, and Rob T. Guerette. In press. "Risky Facilities: Crime Concentration in Homogeneous Sets of Establishments and Facilities." In *Imagination for Crime Prevention: Essay in Honor of Ken Pease,* ed. Graham Farrell, Kate Bowers, Shane Johnson, and Michael Townsley. Monsey, NY: Criminal Justice Press.

Eck, John E., and Jeffrey S. Gersh. 2000. "Drug Trafficking as a Cottage Industry." In *Illegal Drug Markets: From Research to Prevention Policy,* ed. Mangai Natarajan and Mike Hough, 241–71. Crime Prevention Studies, vol. 11. Monsey, NY: Criminal Justice Press.

Economic and Social Council, Transnational Communities Programme. 2001. "U.S.-Led Clamp Down on Informal Banking Network Allegedly Financing Terrorism Threatens Migrants' Remittances." *Traces*, no. 15, July–September. Available at http://www.transcomm.ox.ac.uk/traces/issue15pg1.htm (accessed on May 27, 2006).

Economist. 2004. "Mess of Fact and Fiction: Arafat and the Cash." 373(8402):50, November 20.

Economist. 2005a. "A New Offensive: How America Can Help Prise the IRA Away from Its Guns." 374(8416):11–12, March 3.

Economist. 2005b. "The Card is Coming: Identity Cards." 376(8433):50, July 2.

Economist. 2005c. "Going Global: Why Street Thugs are Getting Nastier." 374(8415):29, February 26.

Economist. 2005d. "Looking in the Wrong Places: Financing Terrorism." 377(8449):73–75, October 22.

Economist. 2005e. "New Team, Old Terrors: As Its Temporary Government at Last Takes Office, Iraq Looks as Fragile as Ever." 375(8425):19–21, May 7.

Economist. 2006. "Out of the Underworld." 378(8459):23–26, January 7.

Ekblom, Paul. 1997. "Gearing Up Against Crime: A Dynamic Framework to Help Designers Keep Up With the Adaptive Criminal in a Changing World." *International Journal of Risk, Security and Crime Prevention* 2(4):249–65.

Ekblom, Paul. 2001/2002. "Future Imperfect: Preparing for the Crimes to Come." *Criminal Justice Matters* 46(Winter):38–40.

Ekblom, Paul, and Nick Tilley. 2000. "Going Equipped: Criminology, Situational Crime Prevention and the Resourceful Offender." *British Journal of Criminology* 40(3):376–98.

Emsley, Clive. 1994. "The History of Crime and Crime Control Institutions, c. 1770–c. 1945." In *The Oxford Handbook of Criminology,* ed. Mike Maguire, Rod Morgan, and Robert Reiner, 149–82. Oxford: Clarendon Press.

Enders, Walter, and Todd Sandler. 1993. "The Effectiveness of Antiterrorism Policies: A Vector-Autoregression-Intervention Analysis." *American Political Science Review* 87(4):829–44.

Enders, Walter, and Todd Sandler. 2000. "Is Transnational Terrorism Becoming More Threatening?" *Journal of Conflict Resolution* 44(3):307–32.

Enders, Walter, and Todd Sandler. 2006. *The Political Economy of Terrorism.* Cambridge: Cambridge University Press.

Enders, Walter, Todd Sandler, and Joe Cauley. 1990. UN Conventions, Technology and Retaliation in the Fight Against Terrorism: An Econometric Evaluation." *Terrorism and Political Violence* 2(1):83–105.

English, Richard. 2003. *Armed Struggle: The History of the IRA.* New York: Oxford University Press.

Falkenrath, Richard S., Robert D. Newman, and Bradley A. Thayer. 1999. *America's Achilles' Heel: Nuclear, Biological, and Chemical Terrorism and Covert Attack.* Cambridge, MA: MIT Press.

Felson, Marcus. 1998. *Crime and Everyday Life.* 2nd ed. Thousand Oaks, CA: Pine Forge.

Felson, Marcus. 2002. *Crime and Everyday Life.* 3rd ed. Thousand Oaks, CA: Pine Force.

Felson, Marcus, Mathieu E. Belanger, Gisela M. Bichler, Chris D. Bruzinski, Glenna S. Campbell, Cheryl L. Fried, Kathleen C. Grofik, Irene S. Mazur, Amy B. O'Regan, Patricia J. Sweeney, Andrew L. Ullman, and LaQuanda M. Williams. 1996. "Redesigning Hell: Preventing Crime and Disorder at the Port Authority Bus Terminal." In *Preventing Mass Transit Crime,* ed. Ronald V. Clarke, 5–92. Crime Prevention Studies, vol. 6. Monsey, NY: Criminal Justice Press.

Felter, Joseph. 2006. "Recruitment for Rebellion and Terrorism in the Philippines." In *The Making of a Terrorist: Recruitment, Training, and Root Causes*, ed. James F. Forest, vol. 1, 84–104. Westport, CT: Praeger Security International.

Ferracuti, Franco. 1982. "A Sociopsychiatric Interpretation of Terrorism." *Annals of the Academy of Political and Social Sciences* 463:129–40.

Ferracuti, Franco, and Francesco Bruno. 1984. "Psychiatric Aspects of Terrorism in Italy." In *The Mad, the Bad and the Different,* ed. Israel Barak-Glantz and C.R. Huff, 199–213. Lexington, MA: Lexington Books.

Finckenauer, James O. 2001. "Russian Transnational Organized Crime and Human Trafficking," In *Global Human Smuggling: Comparative Perspectives,* ed. David Kyle and Rey Koslowski, 166–86. Baltimore, MD: Johns Hopkins University Press.

Finnegan, William. 2005. "The Terrorism Beat: How is the NYPD Defending the City?" *New Yorker* 81(21):58–71.

Forest, James F., ed. 2006. *The Making of a Terrorist: Recruitment, Training, and Root Causes.* 3 vols. Westport, CT: Praeger Security International.

Frey, Bruno S. 2004. *Dealing with Terrorism: Stick or Carrot?* Cheltenham, UK: Edward Elgar.

Gaines, Larry, and Roger LeRoy Miller. 2004. *Criminal Justice in Action with Infotrac: The Core.* Belmont, CA: Thomson Wadsworth.

Gambetta, Diego, ed. 2005. *Making Sense of Suicide Missions.* Oxford: Oxford University Press.

Ganor, Boaz, ed. 2001. *Countering Suicide Terrorism: An International Conference.* Herzliya, Israel: International Policy Institute for Counter-Terrorism, 97–104.

Ganor, Boaz. 2002. "Suicide Attacks in Israel." In *Countering Suicide Terrorism: An International Conference,* ed. Boaz Ganor, 140–252. Herzilya, Israel: The International Policy Institute for Counter-Terrorism.

Ganor, Boaz. 2003. "Suicide Attacks: An Overview/Analysis." *Ma'ariv.* Available at http://www.ict.org/il/articles/articledet.cfm?articleid=128 (accessed on May 27, 2006).

Garland, David. 2000. "The New Criminologies of Everyday Life: Routine Activity Theory in Historical and Social Context." In *Ethical and Social Issues in Situational Crime Prevention,* ed. Andrew von Hirsch, David Garland, and Alison Wakefield, 215–24. Oxford and Portland, OR: Hart.

Garland, David. 2001. *The Culture of Control: Crime and Social Order in Contemporary Society.* Chicago: University of Chicago Press.

Gerbner, George. 1991. "Symbolic Functions of Violence and Terror." In *In the Camera's Eye: News Coverage of Terrorist Events,* ed. Yonah Alexander and Robert Picard, 3–9. Washington, DC: Brassey's.

Gibson, Campbell. 1998. *Population of the 100 Largest Cities and Other Urban Places in the United States: 1790 to 1990.* Population Division Working Paper, No. 27. Washington, DC: Population Division, U.S. Bureau of the Census.

Glaeser, Edward L., and Jesse M. Shapiro. 2002. "Cities and Warfare: The Impact of Terrorism on Urban Form." *Journal of Urban Economics* 51(2):205–24.

Goldstein, Herman. 1990. *Problem-Oriented Policing.* New York: McGraw-Hill; Philadelphia: Temple University Press.

Gotkine, Elliott. 2004. "The Day the Maoists Went to Court." *BBC News,* Lima, November 6. Available at http://news.bbc.co.uk/2/hi/americas/3987741.stm (accessed on May 27, 2006).

Grabosky, Peter N. 1996. *The Future of Crime Control*. Trends and Issues in Crime and Criminal Justice, No. 63. Canberra: Australian Institute of Criminology.

Graduate Institute of International Studies. 2003. *Small Arms Survey 2003: Development Denied*. Oxford: Oxford University Press

Graham, Bradley. 2005. "Calls for Shift in Iraq Strategy Growing: Lawmakers, Experts Urge Military to Focus More on Protecting Population Centers." *Washington Post*, November 11, p. A16.

Graham, John. 1989. *Auto Safety: Assessing America's Performance*. Dover, MA: Auburn House Publishing Company.

Grams, Rod. 2000. "Vulnerable Embassies? Don't Blame Congress. Conventional Wisdom at State Blames Lagging Construction on Low Appropriations. That's Not True." Available at http://www.afsa.org/fsj/jun00/grams.cfm (accessed on May 27, 2006).

Greenemeier, Larry. 2005. "Matrix Retrenched." *Government Enterprise*, June 2. Available at http://www.governmententerprise.com/showArticle.jhtml?articleID=163700613 (accessed on May 27, 2006).

Gruen, Madelaine. 2006. "Innovative Recruitment and Indoctrination Tactics by Extremists: Video Games, Hip-Hop, and the World Wide Web." In *The Making of a Terrorist: Recruitment, Training, and Root Causes*, ed. James F. Forest, vol. 1, 11–22. Westport, CT: Praeger Security International.

Guerette, Rob T., and Ronald V. Clarke. 2005. "Border Enforcement, Organized Crime and Deaths of Smuggled Migrants on the United States–Mexico Border." *European Journal on Criminal Policy and Research* 11(2):159–74.

Gunaratna, Rohan. 2001. "Suicide Terrorism in Sri Lanka and India." In *Countering Suicide Terrorism: An International Conference*, ed. Boaz Ganor. Israel: Interdisciplinary Center Herzliya Projects Limited.

Gunaratna, Rohan. 2002. *Inside Al Qaeda: Global Network of Terror*. New York: Columbia University Press.

Gurr, Ted Robert, Peter N. Grabosky, and Richard C. Hula. 1977. *The Politics of Crime and Conflict: A Comparative History of Four Cities*. Beverly Hills, CA: Sage.

Haddon, William, Jr. 1999. "The Changing Approach to the Epidemiology, Prevention, and Amelioration of Trauma: The Transition to Approaches Etiologically Rather Than Descriptively Based." *Injury Prevention* 5:231–36.

Haddon, William, Jr., Edward A. Suchman, and David Klein. 1964. *Accident Research: Methods and Approaches*. New York: Harper & Row.

Haggerty, Kevin D., and Amber Gazso. 2005. "Seeing Beyond the Ruins: Surveillance as a Response to Terrorist Threats." *Canadian Journal of Sociology/Cahiers canadiens de sociologie* 30(2):169–87.

Hamm, Mark S. 2001. *In Bad Company: America's Terrorist Underground*. Boston: Northeastern University Press.

Hanley, Charles J. 2006. "Mini-Manhattan Project Spending Billions to 'Defeat' Iraqi IEDs: Bombers Stay a Step Ahead." Associated Press. Available at http://articles.news.aol.com/news/article.adp?id=20060313161309990013 (accessed on March 13, 2006).

Harocopos, Alex, and Mike Hough. 2005. *Drug Dealing in Open-Air Markets.* Problem-Oriented Guides for Police: Problem-Specific Guides Series, No. 31. Washington, DC: U.S. Department of Justice, Office of Community-Oriented Policing Services.

Harrison, Mark. 2004. *An Economist Looks at Suicide Terrorism.* Warwick, UK: Department of Economics, University of Warwick. First draft October 3, 2001. This draft January 20, 2004. Available at http://www2.warwick.ac.uk/fac/soc/economics/staff/faculty/Harrison/papers/terrorism.pdf (accessed on May 27, 2006).

Hartocollis, Anemona, and Patrick McGeehan. 2005. "Port Authority Fears Costs From Verdict." *New York Times,* Friday Late Edition—Final, October 28, p. B1.

Hassan, Nasra. 2001. "An Arsenal of Believers: Talking to the Human Bombs." *New Yorker* 77(36):36–41.

Hassan, Nasra. 2004. "Al-Qaeda's Understudy." *Atlantic Monthly* 293(5):42–43.

Haynes, Wendy. 2004. "Seeing Around Corners: Crafting the New Department of Homeland Security." *Review of Policy Research* 21(3):369–95.

Hesseling, Rene B.P. 1994. "Displacement: A Review of the Empirical Literature." In *Crime Prevention Studies,* ed. Ronald V. Clarke, vol. 3, 197–230. Monsey, NY: Criminal Justice Press.

HFG. 2005. *Review Small Arms and Light Weapons: A Call for Research.* Spring. New York: Harry Frank Guggenheim Foundation.

Hill, Peter. 2005. "Kamikaze, 1943–1945." In *Making Sense of Suicide Missions,* ed. Diego Gambetta, 1–42. Oxford: Oxford University Press.

Hirschman, Albert O. 1970. *Exit, Voice and Loyalty: Responses to Decline in Firms, organizations and States.* Cambridge, MA: Harvard University Press.

Hoffman, Bruce. 1998. *Inside Terrorism.* New York: Columbia University Press.

Hoffman, Bruce, and Peter Chalk. 2002. *Security in the Nation's Capital and the Closure of Pennsylvania Avenue: An Assessment.* Santa Monica, CA: Rand.

Hogg, Ian V., and John Weeks. 1977. *Military Small Arms of the 20th Century.* London: Arms & Armour Press.

Hopgood, Stephen. 2005. "Tamil Tigers, 1987–2002." In *Making Sense of Suicide Missions,* ed. Diego Gambetta, 43–76. Oxford: Oxford University Press.

Howard, Lawrence, ed. 1992. *Terrorism: Roots, Impact, Responses.* New York: Praeger.

Huddy, Leonie, Stanley Feldman, Gallya Lahav, and Charles Taber. 2003. "Fear and Terrorism: Psychological Reactions to 9/11." In *Framing Terrorism: The News Media, the Government and the Public,* ed. Pippa Norris, Montague Kern, and Marion Just, 255–78. New York: Routledge.

Huntington, Samuel P. 1996. *The Clash of Civilizations: Remaking of World Order.* New York: Touchstone.

Inman, Bobby Ray. 1985. *Report of the Secretary of State's Advisory Panel on Overseas Security (The Inman Report).* Washington, DC: U.S. Department of State.

Israel Defense Forces. 2006. "Successful vs. Unsuccessful (Thwarted) Terrorist Attacks." Available at http://www1.idf.il/SIP_STORAGE/DOVER/files/6/31646.doc (accessed on May 30, 2006).

Jackson, Brian A. 2002. "Technology Acquisition by Terrorist Groups." In *America Confronts Terrorism,* ed. John Prados, 216–43. Chicago: Ivan R. Dee.

Jackson, Brian A., with John C. Baker, Kim Cragin, John Parachini, Hoacio R. Trujillo, and Peter Chalk. 2005. *Aptitude for Destruction.* Vol. 1, *Organizational Learning in Terrorist Groups and Its Implications for Combating Terrorism.* Santa Monica, CA: Rand.

Jacobs, Stanley S. 1998. "The Nuclear Threat as a Terrorist Option." *Terrorism and Political Violence* 10(4):149–63.

Jenkins, Brian M. 1974. *International Terrorism: A New Kind of Warfare.* Santa Monica, CA: Rand.

Jenkins, Brian M. 1975. *High Technology Terrorism and Surrogate War: The Impact of New Technology on Low-Level Violence.* Santa Monica, CA: Rand.

Jenkins, Brian M. 1985a. *International Terrorism: The Other World War.* Santa Monica, CA: Rand.

Jenkins, Brian M. 1985b. *The Likelihood of Nuclear Terrorism.* Santa Monica, CA: Rand.

Jenkins, Brian M. 1998. "Aviation Security in the United States." *Terrorism and Political Violence* 10(3):101–11.

Johnson, Graham. 2003. "We Buy Bag of Semtex From Terrorists." *Sunday Mirror,* December 10.

Johnston, Van R., and Amala Nath, eds. 2004. "Terrorism and Transportation Security." *Review of Policy Research* 21(3):253–403.

Jotcham, Richard B. 2005. "Authentication, Antitamper, and Track-and-Trace Technology Options to Protect Foods." *Journal of Food Protection* 68(6):1314–17.

Kaplan, Eben. 2006. "Q&A: The UAE Purchase of American Port Facilities." *New York Times.com,* February 23.

Kaplan, Edward H., Alex Mintz, Mishal Shaul, and Claudio Samban. 2005. "What Happened to Suicide Bombings in Israel? Insights from a Terror Stock Model." *Studies in Conflict and Terrorism* 28(3):225–35.

Kassimeris, George. 2001. *Europe's Last Red Terrorists: The Revolutionary Organization 17 November.* New York: New York University Press.

Keinan, Giora, Avi Sadeh, and Sefi Rosen. 2003. "Attitudes and Reactions to Media Coverage of Terrorist Acts." *Journal of Community Psychology* 31(2):149–65.

Kelling, George L., and Catherine M. Coles. 1996. *Fixing Broken Windows: Restoring Order and Reducing Crime in Our Communities.* New York: Free Press.

Kennedy, David M., Anthony Braga, and Anne M. Piehl. 2001. *Reducing Gun Violence: The Boston Gun Project's Operation Ceasefire.* National Institute of Justice Research Report. Washington, DC: U.S. Department of Justice, National Institute of Justice.

Kimhi, Shaul, and Shemeul Even. 2004. Paper presented at the Twenty-Seventh Annual Meeting of the International Society for Political Psychology, Lund, Sweden, July 15.

Kirby, Maurice W. 2003. *Operational Research in War and Peace: The British Experience from the 1930s to 1970.* London: Imperial College Press.

Kitchen, Ted. 2001. "Planning in Response to Terrorism: The Case of Manchester, England." *Journal of Architectural and Planning Research* 18(4):325–40.

Krebs, Valdis E. 2002. "Mapping Networks of Terrorist Cell." *Connections* 24(3): 43–52.

Kushner, Harvey W., ed. 1998. *The Future of Terrorism: Violence in the New Millennium.* Thousand Oaks, CA: Sage.

Lacoste, Julie, and Pierre Tremblay. 2003. "Crime and Innovation: A Script Analysis of Patterns in Check Forgery." In *Theory for Practice in Situational Crime Prevention,* ed. Martha J. Smith and Derek B. Cornish, 169–96. Crime Prevention Studies, vol. 16. Monsey, NY: Criminal Justice Press.

LaFree, Gary, and Laura Dugan. 2004. "How Does Studying Terrorism Compare to Studying Crime." In *Terrorism and Counter-Terrorism: Criminological Perspectives,* ed. Mathieu Deflem, 54–56. New York: Elsevier.

Langan, Patrick A., and David P. Farrington. 1998. *Crime and Justice in the United States and in England and Wales, 1981–1996.* Washington, DC: U.S. Department of Justice, Office of Justice Programs, Bureau of Justice Statistics.

Laycock, Gloria, and Barry Webb. 2005. "Designing Out Crime from the U.K. Vehicle Licensing System." In *Designing Out Crime from Products and Systems,* ed. Ronald V. Clarke and Graeme R. Newman, 203–30. Crime Prevention Studies, vol. 18. Monsey, NY: Criminal Justice Press.

Lee, Rensselaer. 2003. "Nuclear Smuggling: Patterns and Response." *Parameters* (Spring):95–111.

Lesser, Ian O. 1999. *Countering the New Terrorism.* Santa Monica, CA: Rand.

Levi, Michael, and R. Thomas Naylor. 2000. "Organized Crime: The Organization of Crime, and the Organization of Business." Research Paper, CD Annex, in *Turning the Corner: Crime 2020.* Foresight Panel. London: DTI.

Loyka, Stephan A., Donald A. Faggiani, and Clifford Karchmer. 2005. *The Production and Sharing of Intelligence.* Protecting Your Community From Terrorism: The Strategies for Local Law Enforcement Series, vol. 4. Washington, DC: U.S. Department of Justice, Office of Community-Oriented Policing Services and Police Executive Research Forum.

Lum, Cynthia, Leslie W. Kennedy, and Alison J. Sherley. 2006. *The Effectiveness of Counter-terrorism Strategies: A Campbell Systematic Review.* Available at http://www.campbellcollaboration.org/CCJG/reviews/CampbellSystematicReview OnTerrorism02062006FINAL_REVISED.pdf (accessed at May 27, 2006).

Maerli, Morton Bremer, Annette Schaper, and Frank Barnaby. 2003. "The Characteristics of Nuclear Terrorist Weapons." *American Behavioral Scientist* 46(6): 727–44.

Malone, Thomas W. 2004. *The Future of Work: How the New Order of Business Will Shape Your Organization, Your Management Style, and Your Life.* Cambridge MA: Harvard Business School Press.

Manchester, City of. n.d. "Shopping In and Around Greater Manchester." Available at http://www.manchester2002-uk.com/shopping.html (accessed on May 26, 2006).

Mannes, Aaron. 2004. *Profiles in Terror: A Guide to Middle East Terror Organizations*. Lanham, MD: Rowman & Littlefield.

March, James G., and Herbert A. Simon. 1958. *Organizations*. 1st ed. New York: John Wiley.

Marighella, Carlos. 1971. *Minimanual of the Urban Guerilla*. Harmondsworth, UK: Penguin.

Marongiu, Pietro, and Graeme R. Newman. 1987. *Vengeance: The Fight Against Injustice*. Totowa, NJ: Rowman & Littlefield.

Marongiu, Pietro, and Graeme R. Newman. 1995. *Vendetta*. Milano: Giuffre.

Marsh, Bill. 2005. "The Half-Life of Anxiety." *New York Times*, July 10, 4.

Martin, Gus, ed. 2004. *The New Era of Terrorism*. Thousand Oaks, CA: Sage.

Mashaw, Jerry L., and David L. Harfst. 1990. *The Struggle for Auto Safety*. Cambridge, MA: Harvard University Press.

McCormick, Gordon H. 2001. "The Shining Path and Peruvian Terrorism." In *Inside Terrorist Organizations,* ed. David Rapoport, 109–26. London and Portland, OR: Frank Cass.

McDevitt, Charles F. 2000. "Basics of Concrete Barriers." *Public Roads* 63(5):10–14. Available at http://www.tfhrc.gov/pubrds/marapr00/concrete.htm (accessed on May 27, 2006).

McGrory, Daniel. 2001. "Terrorists' Trade in Stolen Identities." *Times* (London), September 22.

McKitrick, David, Seamus Kelters, Brian Feeney, Chris Thornton, and David McVea, eds. 2004. *Lost Lives*. Edinborough: Mainstream Publishing.

McNamara, Ann Marie. 2005. "Food Defense: Auditing and Interpretation." Paper presented at the Meat Industry Research Conference AMI World Wide Food Expo, Chicago, October 26.

Meade, Robert C. 1990. *Red Brigades: The Story of Italian Terrorism*. New York: St. Martin's Press.

Merari, Ariel. 1998. "Attacks on Civil Aviation: Trends and Lessons." *Terrorism and Political Violence* 10(3):9–26.

Merari, Ariel. 2004a. "Political, Organizational, and Psychological Factors in Suicide Terrorism." Paper presented at the NATO Advanced Research Workshop on Suicide Terrorism—Strategic Importance and Counterstrategies, Lisbon, Portugal, June 10–14.

Merari, Ariel. 2004b. "Suicidal Terrorism." In *Assessment, Treatment and Prevention of Suicidal Behavior,* ed. Robert I. Yufit and David Lester. New York: Wiley.

Merari, Ariel. 2004c. "Suicide Terrorism in the Context of the Israeli-Palestinian Conflict." Paper presented at the Suicide Terrorism Conference, National Institute of Justice, Washington, DC, Office of Justice Programs Building, October 25–26. Available at http://www.nijpcs.org/terror (accessed on May 27, 2006).

Milbank, David L. 1978. "International and Transnational Terrorism: Diagnosis and Prognosis." In *Contemporary Terrorism: Selected Readings,* ed. John D. Elliott and Leslie K. Gibson. Gaithersburg, MD: International Association of Chiefs of Police.

Milgram, Stanley. 1967. "The Small World Problem." *Psychology Today* 1(May): 61–67.

Milhollin, Gary. 2004. "Can Terrorists Get the Bomb?" In *The New Era of Terrorism,* ed. Gus Martin, 188–93. Thousand Oaks, CA: Sage.

Murphy, Gerard R., and Martha R. Plotkin. 2003. *Improving Local-Federal Partnerships.* Protecting Your Community From Terrorism: The Strategies for Local Law Enforcement Series, vol. 1. Washington, DC: U.S. Department of Justice, Office of Community-Oriented Policing Services and Police Executive Research Forum.

Nacos, Brigitte L. 1994. *Terrorism and the Media: From the Iran Hostage Crisis to the Oklahoma City Bombing.* New York: Columbia University Press.

Nacos, Brigitte L. 2002. *Mass-Mediated Terrorism: The Central Role of the Media in Terrorism and Counterterrorism.* Lanham, MD: Rowman & Littlefield.

Nader, Ralph. 1966. *Unsafe at Any Speed: The Designed-In Dangers of the American Automobile.* New York: Pocket Books.

Nalla, Mahesh, and Graeme R. Newman. 1990. *A Primer in Private Security.* New York: Harrow and Heston.

Napoleoni, Loretta. 2005. *Terror Incorporated: Tracing the Dollars Behind the Terror Networks.* New York: Seven Stories Press.

Natarajan, Mangai, and Ronald V. Clarke. 2004. "Understanding and Controlling Organised Crime: The Feasibility of a Situational Approach." Paper presented at the 12th International Seminar on Environmental Criminology and Crime Analysis, Wellington, New Zealand, July 2–4.

Natarajan, Mangai, Ronald V. Clarke, and Mathieu Belanger. 1997. "Drug Dealing and Pay Phones: The Scope for Intervention." *Security Journal* 7(4):245–51.

National Commission on Terrorism Attacks upon the United States. 2004. *The 9/11 Commission Report: Final Report of the National Commission on Terrorism Attacks upon the United States.* New York: Norton.

National Commission on Terrorism Attacks upon the United States. 2005. Report on the Status of 9/11 Commission Recommendations, Part I: Homeland Security, Emergency Preparedness and Response. September 14.

National Research Council, Committee on Science and Technology for Countering Terrorism. 2002. *Making the Nation Safer: The Role of Science and Technology in Countering Terrorism.* Washington, DC: National Academies Press.

New York Times. 2005. "Protections for the United States." July 8, p. A22.

Newman, Graeme R. 2004. "Car Safety and Car Security: An Historical Comparison." In *Understanding and Preventing Car Theft,* ed. Michael G. Maxfield and Ronald V. Clarke, 217–48. Crime Prevention Studies, vol. 17. Monsey, NY: Criminal Justice Press.

Newman, Graeme R. 2006. *Exploitation of Trafficked Women.* Problem Oriented Guides for Policing. Washington, DC: U.S. Department of Justice, Office of Community-Oriented Policing.

Newman, Graeme R., and Ronald V. Clarke. 2003. *Superhighway Robbery: Preventing E-Commerce Crime.* Cullompton, UK: Willan.

Newman, Graeme R., and Megan McNally. 2005. *Identity Theft Literature Review.* Washington, DC: U.S. Department of Justice, National Institute of Justice.

Newman, Graeme, Shlomo G. Shoham, and Ronald V. Clarke, eds. 1997. *Rational Choice and Situational Crime Prevention: Theoretical Foundations.* Farnsborough, UK: Dartmouth.

Newman, Graeme R., ed., and United Nations Centre for International Crime Prevention. 1999. *Global Report on Crime and Justice.* New York: Oxford University Press.

Norris, Pippa, Montague Kern, and Marion Just, eds. 2003. *Framing Terrorism: The New Media, the Government and the Public.* New York: Routledge.

Norton, Augustus R., and Martin H. Greenberg, eds. 1979. *Studies in Nuclear Terrorism.* Boston: G.K. Hall.

O'Brien, Brendan. 1999. *The Long War: The IRA & Sinn Féin.* Dublin: O'Brien Press.

Orbach, Israel. 2004. "Terror Suicide: How Is It Possible?" *Archives of Suicide Research* 8:115–30.

Painter, Kate, and Nick Tilley, eds. 1999. *Surveillance of Public Space: CCTV, Street Lighting and Crime Prevention.* Crime Prevention Studies, vol. 10. Monsey, NY: Criminal Justice Press.

Patil, Prasad, trans. 2003. *The Al Qaeda Manual.* Parts I and II. Available at http://www.hvk.org/articles/0303/15.html (accessed on May 27, 2006).

Pape, Robert A. 2003. "The Strategic Logic of Suicide Terrorism." *American Political Science Review* 97(3):343–61.

Pape, Robert A. 2005. *Dying to Win: The Strategic Logic of Suicide Terrorism.* Chicago: University of Chicago Press.

Passos, Nikos. 2005. *Informal Value Transfer Systems, Terrorism and Money Laundering.* Washington, DC: U.S. Department of Justice: NCJRS. Award No. 2002-IJ-CX-0001.

PBS Frontline. "McVeigh Chronology." Available at http://www.pbs.org/wgbh/pages/frontline/documents/mcveigh (accessed on June 1, 2006).

Pedhazur, Ami. 2005. *Suicide Terrorism.* London: Polity Press.

Perl, Raphael F. 1997. "Terrorism, the Media and the Government: Perspectives, Trends, and Options for Policymakers." *CRS Issue Brief,* October 22. Washington, DC: Congressional Research Service, Library of Congress. Available at http://www.fas.org/irp/crs/crs-terror.htm (accessed on May 27, 2006).

Picard, Robert G. 1991. "News Coverage as the Contagion of Terrorism: Dangerous Charges Backed Up by Dubious Science." In *Media Coverage of Terrorism: Methods of Diffusion,* ed. A. Odasuo Alali and Kenoye Kelvin Ede, 49–62. Newbury Park, CA: Sage.

Pieth, Mark, ed. 2002. *Financing Terrorism.* Dordrecht, Netherlands, and Boston: Kluwer Academic.

Post, Jerrold M., Ehud Sprinzak, and Laurita M. Denny. 2003. "The Terrorists in Their Own Words: Interview with 35 Incarcerated Middle Eastern Terrorists." *Terrorism and Political Violence* 15(1):171–84.

Potter, William C. 1995. "Before the Deluge? Assessing the Threat of Nuclear Leakage from the Post-Soviet States." *Arms Control Today* 25(October):9–16.

Potter, William C., Charles D. Ferguson, and Leonard S. Spector. 2004. "The Four Faces of Nuclear Terror." *Foreign Affairs* 83(3):130–32.

Poyner, Barry. 2005. *Crime-free Housing in the 21st Century*. London: Jill Dando Institute of Crime Science, University College London.

Poyner, Barry, and Barry Webb. 1991. *Crime-Free Housing*. Oxford: Butterworth-Architecture.

Price, Willard. 2004. "Reducing the Risk of Terror Events at Seaports." *Review of Policy Research* 21(3):329–49.

Radzinowicz, Sir Leon, and Joan King. 1977. *The Growth of Crime: The International Experience*. New York: Basic Books.

Rand–National Memorial Institute for the Prevention of Terrorism. n.d. Terrorism Incident Database. Available at http://www.tkb.org (accessed on June 1, 2006).

Rapoport, David C., ed. 2001a. *Inside Terrorist Organizations*. London and Portland, OR: Frank Cass.

Rapoport, David C. 2001b. "The International World as Some Terrorists Have Seen It: A Look at a Century of Memoirs." In *Inside Terrorist Organizations,* ed. David Rapoport, 32–58. London and Portland, OR: Frank Cass.

Raymond, Janice G., and Donna M. Hughes. 2001. *Sex Trafficking of Women in the United States: International and Domestic Trends*. North Amherst, MA: Coalition Against Trafficking in Women. Available at http://www.ojp.usdoj.gov/nij/international/programs/sex_traff_us.pdf (accessed on May 27, 2006).

Rechnitzer, George. 2000. "Risk Control Systems in Road Safety: Relevant Applications for the Prevention of Occupational Trauma." *Safety Science Monitor* 4:1–2. Available at http://www.monash.edu.au/muarc/ipso/vol4/2rechnit.pdf (accessed on May 27, 2006).

Reich, Walter, ed. 1998. *Origins of Terrorism: Psychologies, Ideologies, Theologies, States of Mind*. 2nd ed. Washington DC: Woodrow Wilson Center and Johns Hopkins University Press, 192–207.

Reuland, Melissa, and Heather J. Davies. 2004. *Preparing For and Responding to Bioterrorism*. Protecting Your Community From Terrorism: The Strategies for Local Law Enforcement Series, vol. 3. Washington, DC: U.S. Department of Justice, Office of Community-Oriented Policing and Police Executive Research Forum.

Richards, James R. 1999. *Transnational Criminal Organizations, Cybercrime, and Money Laundering: A Handbook for Law Enforcement Officers, Auditors, and Financial Investigators*. Boca Raton, FL: CRC Press.

Ricolfi, Luca. 2005. "Palestinians, 1981–2003." In *Making Sense of Suicide Missions,* ed. Diego Gambetta, 77–130. Oxford: Oxford University Press.

Ronfeldt, David. 2005. "Al Qaeda and Its Affiliates: A Global Tribe Waging Segmental Warfare?" *First Monday*. Available at http://www.firstmonday.dk/issues/issue10_3/ronfeldt/index.html (accessed on May 30, 2006).

Rossmo, D. Kim. 2000. *Geographic Profiling*. Boca Raton, FL: CRC Press.

Ryf, Kara C. 2002. "The First Modern Anti-Slavery Law: the Trafficking Victims Protection Act of 2000." *Case Western Research Journal of International Law* 34(1):45–71.

The Safer Cities Programme: The Role of the City in Crime Prevention. 2004. World Urban Forum, September 14.

Sageman, Marc. 2004. *Understanding Terror Networks.* Philadelphia: University of Pennsylvania Press.

Salt, John. 2000. "Trafficking and Human Smuggling: A European Perspective." *International Migration* 38(3):31–56.

Sater, William. 1981. *Puerto Rican Terrorists: A Possible Threat to U.S. Energy Installations.* Santa Monica, CA: Rand.

Schmid, Alex P. 1992. "Terrorism and the Media: Freedom of Information vs. Freedom of Intimidation." In *Terrorism: Roots, Impact, Responses,* ed. Lawrence Howard, 95–117. New York: Praeger.

Schmid, Alex P. 2000. "Terrorism and The Use of Weapons of Mass Destruction: From Where The Risk?" In *The Future of Terrorism,* ed. Max Taylor and John Horgan, 106–32. London and Portland, OR: Frank Cass.

Schmid, Alex P. 2004. "Statistics on Terrorism: the Challenge of Measuring Trends in Global Terrorism." *Forum on Crime and Society* 4(1–2):49–69.

Schmid, Alex P. 2006. Personal communication, March 14.

Schmid, Alex P., and Janny de Graaf. 1982. *Violence as Communication: Insurgent Terrorism and the Western News Media.* Beverly Hills, CA: Sage.

Schneir, Bruce. 2003. *Beyond Fear: Thinking Sensibly About Security in an Uncertain World.* New York: Copernicus Books/Springer-Verlag.

Schönteich, Martin. 1999. "Fighting Crime With Private Muscle: The Security Industry in International Perspective." *African Security Review* 8(5):65–75.

Scott, Kody. 1993. *Monster: the Autobiography of an L.A. Gang Member.* New York: Atlantic Monthly Press.

Scott, Michael S., and Herman Goldstein. 2005. *Shifting and Sharing Responsibility for Public Safety Problems.* Problem-Oriented Guides for Police: Response Guide Series, No. 3. Washington, DC: U.S. Department of Justice, Office of Community-Oriented Policing.

Seidenstat, Paul. 2004. "Terrorism, Airport Security, and the Private Sector." *Review of Policy Research* 21(3):275–91.

Shiqaqi, Khalil. 2002. "The Views of Palestinian Society on Suicide Terrorism." In *Countering Suicide Terrorism: An International Conference,* ed. Boaz Ganor, 155–64. Herzilya, Israel: International Policy Institute for Counter-Terrorism.

Shover, Neal. 1991. "Burglary." In *Crime and Justice: A Review of Research,* ed. Michael Tonry, vol. 14, 73–113. Chicago: University of Chicago Press.

Simon, Steven, and Jeff Martini. 2004–5. "Terrorism: Denying Al Qaeda its Popular Support." *Washington Quarterly* 28(1):131–45.

Skogan, Wesley G., and Kathleen Frydl, eds. 2004. *Fairness and Effectiveness in Policing: The Evidence.* Washington, DC: National Academies Press.

Slone, Michelle. 2000. "Responses to Media Coverage of Terrorism." *Journal of Conflict Resolution* 44(4):508–22.

Smith, Brent L., and Kelly R. Damphousse. 2002. American Terrorism Study: Patterns of Behavior, Investigation and Prosecution of American Terrorists, Final Report. National Institute of Justice.

Smith, Martha J., Ronald V. Clarke, and Ken Pease. 2002. "Anticipatory Benefits in Crime Prevention." In *Analysis for Crime Prevention,* ed. Nick Tilley, 71–88. Crime Prevention Studies, vol. 13. Monsey, NY: Criminal Justice Press.

Spener, David. 2001. "Smuggling Migrants Through South Texas: Challenges Posed by Operation Rio Grande," In *Global Human Smuggling: Comparative Perspectives,* ed. David Kyle and Rey Koslowski, 115–37. Baltimore, MD: Johns Hopkins University Press.

Sprinzak, Ehud. 2001. "From Messianic Pioneering to Vigilante Terrorism: The Case of the Gush Emunim Underground." In *Inside Terrorist Organizations,* ed. David Rapoport, 194–216. London and Portland, OR: Frank Cass.

St. John, Peter. 1991. *Air Piracy, Airport Security, and International Terrorism.* New York: Quorum Books.

St. John, Peter. 1998. "The Politics of Aviation Terrorism." *Terrorism and Political Violence* 10(3):27–49.

Steinhausler, Friedrich. 2003. "What It Takes to Become a Nuclear Terrorist." *American Behavioral Scientist* 46(6):782–95.

Steinhausler, Friedrich. 2004. "Exotic Terrorism." In *The New Era of Terrorism,* ed. Gus Martin, 124–34. Thousand Oaks, CA: Sage.

Stern, Jessica. 2003. *Terror in the Name of God: Why Religious Militants Kill.* New York: Harper Collins.

Stone, Richard. 2001. "Nuclear Trafficking: 'A Real and Dangerous Threat.'" *Science* 292(5522):1632–36.

Stork, Joe. 2002. *Erased In A Moment: Suicide Bombing Attacks Against Israeli Civilians.* New York: Human Rights Watch.

Sullivan, Andy. 2004. "U.S. Government Still Data Mining, GAO Says: Computer Surveillance Rings Alarm Bells for Privacy Experts." *MSNBC.* Available at http://msnbc.msn.com/id/5077342 (accessed on May 30, 2006).

Susman, Thomas M. 2003. *Terrorism: Real Threats, Real Costs, Joint Solutions.* Washington, DC: Business Roundtable. Available at http://www.businessroundtable.org/pdf/984.pdf (accessed on June 15, 2006).

Sweet, Kathleen M. 2002. *Terrorism and Airport Security.* Lewiston, NY: Edwin Mellen Press.

Taylor, Max, and John Horgan, eds. 2000. *The Future of Terrorism.* London and Portland, OR: Frank Cass.

Taylor, Terence. 2002. "United Kingdom." In *Combating Terrorism: Strategies of Ten Countries,* ed. Yonah Alexander, 187–223. Ann Arbor: University of Michigan Press.

Thomas, William I., and Florian Znaniecki. 1919. *The Polish Peasant in Europe and America.* Chicago: University of Chicago Press.

Tuman, Joseph S. 2003. *Communicating Terror: The Rhetorical Dimensions of Terrorism.* Thousand Oaks, CA: Sage.

Ungar, Bernard L. 1998. "General Services Administration: Many Building Security Upgrades Made But Problems Have Hindered Program Implementation," Statement of Bernard L. Ungar, Director, Government Business Operations Issues, General Government Division, before the Subcommittee on Public Buildings and Economic Development, Committee on Transportation and Infrastructure, House of Representatives. Washington, DC: U.S. General Accounting Office.

U.S. Department of Defense. 2003. *Unified Facilities Criteria (UFC): DoD Minimum Antiterrorism Standards for Buildings.* UFB 4-010-01 8. Washington, DC: U.S. Department of Defense.

U.S. Department of State. 1999. *Report of the Accountability Review Boards on the Embassy Bombings in Nairobi and Dar es Salaam on August 7, 1998* (Chairman: Admiral Crowe.) Washington, DC: U.S. Department of State.

U.S. Department of State. 2001. *Patterns of Global Terrorism, 2000.* Washington, DC: U.S. Department of State.

U.S. Department of State. 2005. *Patterns of Global Terrorism, 2000–2003.* Washington, DC: U.S. Department of State

U.S. Department of State, Bureau of Diplomatic Security. 1987–2002. *Political Violence Against Americans* (formerly: *Significant Incidents of Political Violence Against Americans.* Available at http://state.gov/m/ds/rls/rpt/19691.htm (accessed on May 30, 2006).

U.S. Federal Aviation Administration. 1994–96. Annual Report to Congress on Civil Aviation Security. Washington, DC: U.S. Department of Transportation.

U.S. Federal Aviation Administration. 1996–99. Criminal Acts Against Civil Aviation. Washington, DC: U.S. Department of Transportation, Federal Aviation Administration, Office of Civil Aviation Security.

U.S. Federal Bureau of Investigation. 2004. *Terrorism, 2000–2001.* Washington, DC: U.S. Federal Bureau of Investigation.

U.S. General Accounting Office. 2002. *Building Security: Security Responsibilities for Federally Owned and Leased Facilities.* Report to Congressional Requesters. Washington, DC: U.S. General Accounting Office.

U.S. Government Accountability Office. 2005. *Overseas Security: State Department Has Not Fully Implemented Key Measures to Protect U.S. Officials from Terrorist Attacks Outside of Embassies.* Report to the Chairman, Subcommittee on National Security, Emerging Threats, and International Relations, Committee on Government Reform, House of Representatives. Washington, DC: U.S. Government Accountability Office.

U.S. President's Commission on Aviation and Terrorism. 1990. *Report to the President.* Washington, DC: U.S. President's Commission on Aviation and Terrorism.

Viera, John David. 1991. "Terrorism at the BBC: The IRA on British Television." In *Media Coverage of Terrorism: Methods of Diffusion,* ed. A. Odasuo Alali and Kenoye Kelvin Ede, 73–85. Newbury Park, CA: Sage.

Wall Street Journal. 2006. "Open the Iraq Files." March 3, p. A10.

Waller, Michael J. 2006. Prisons as Terrorist Breeding Grounds." In *The Making of a Terrorist: Recruitment, Training, and Root Causes,* ed. James F. Forest, vol. 1, 23–40. Westport, CT: Praeger Security International.

Walsh, Dermot. 1986. "Victim Selection Procedures Among Economic Criminals: The Rational Choice Perspective." In *The Reasoning Criminal: Rational Choice Perspectives on Offending,* ed. Derek B. Cornish and Ronald V. Clarke, 39–52. New York: Springer-Verlag.

Watts, Duncan J. 2003. *Six Degrees: The Science of a Connected Age.* New York: Norton.

Weimann, Gabriel. 2006. Terrorist Dot Com: Using the Internet for Terrorist Recruitment and Mobilization. In *The Making of a Terrorist: Recruitment, Training, and Root Causes,* ed. James F. Forest, vol. 1, 53–65. Westport, CT: Praeger Security International.

Weimann, Gabriel, and Conrad Winn. 1994. *The Theater of Terror: Mass Media and International Terror.* New York: Longman.

Wieviorka, Michel (translated by David Gordon White). 1994. *The Making of Terrorism.* Chicago: University of Chicago Press.

Wilkinson, Paul. 1997. "The Media and Terrorism: A Reassessment." *Terrorism and Political Violence* 4(2):5–64.

Wilkinson, Paul. 1998. "Enhancing Global Aviation Security?" *Terrorism and Political Violence* 10(3):147–66.

Wilkinson, Paul, and Brian M. Jenkins, eds. 1998. *Aviation Terrorism and Security.* London and Portland, OR: Frank Cass.

Willis, Henry H., Andrew R. Morral, Terrence K. Kelly, and Jamison Jo Medby. 2005. *Estimating Terrorism Risk.* Santa Monica, CA: Rand Center for Terrorism Risk Management Policy. Available at http://www.rand.org/pubs/monographs/2005/RAND_MG388.pdf (accessed on May 27, 2006).

Wilson, James Q. 1973. *Political Organizations.* New York: Basic Books.

Wilson, James Q., and George L. Kelling. 1982. "Broken Windows: The Police and Neighborhood Safety." *Atlantic Monthly* 249(3):29–38.

Winer, John M. 2002. "Globalization, Terrorist Finance, and Global Conflict: Time for a White List?" In *Financing Terrorism,* ed. Mark Pieth, 5–40. Dordrecht, Netherlands, and Boston: Kluwer Academic.

Wolf, John B. 1989. *Antiterrorist Initiatives.* New York: Plenum Press.

Wortley, Richard, and Stephen Smallbone, eds. 2006. *Situational Prevention of Child Sexual Abuse.* Crime Prevention Studies, vol. 19. Monsey, NY: Criminal Justice Press.

Yost, Pete. 2002. "Mueller Says Walk-In Suicide Bombers 'Inevitable' in United States," Associated Press, Monday, May 20.

Index

About the Authors

RONALD V. CLARKE is Professor of Crisminal Justice at Rutgers University. He is the coauthor of *Superhighway Robbery: Preventing E-commerce Crime* and *Suicide: Closing the Exits,* among other titles. He is the editor of *Designing Out Crime from Products and Systems, Understanding and Preventing Car Theft* and several other titles. He is Associate Director at the Center for Problem-Oriented Policing (www.popcenter.org).

GRAEME R. NEWMAN is Distinguished Teaching Professor of Criminal Justice at the State University of New York (SUNY) at Albany. He has written several books for the U.S. Department of Justice and is the coauthor of *Superhighway Robbery: Preventing E-commerce Crime, Designing Out Crime from Products and Systems* and other titles. He is Vice President of the Center for Problem-Oriented Policing (www.popcenter.org).